Lecture Notes in Computer Science

Commenced Publication in 1973
Founding and Former Series Editors:
Gerhard Goos, Juris Hartmanis, and Jan van Leeuwen

Torsten Braun   Georg Carle
Sonia Fahmy   Yevgeni Koucheryavy (Eds.)

Wired/Wireless Internet Communications

4th International Conference, WWIC 2006
Bern, Switzerland, May 10-12, 2006
Proceedings

 Springer

Volume Editors

Torsten Braun
University of Bern
Institute of Computer Science and Applied Mathematics
Neubrückstrasse 10, 3012 Bern, Switzerland
E-mail: braun@iam.unibe.ch

Georg Carle
University of Tübingen
Wilhelm-Schickard-Institute for Computer Science
Department of Computer Networks and Internet
Auf der Morgenstelle 10 C, 72076 Tübingen, Germany
E-mail: carle@uni-tuebingen.de

Sonia Fahmy
Purdue University
Department of Computer Science
250 N. University Street, West Lafayette, IN 47907-2066, USA
E-mail: fahmy@cs.purdue.edu

Yevgeni Koucheryavy
Tampere University of Technology
Department of Information Technology
Korkeakoulunkatu 1, 33720 Tampere, Finland
E-mail: yk@cs.tut.fi

Library of Congress Control Number: 2006925106

CR Subject Classification (1998): C.2, D.4.4, D.2, H.3.5, H.4, K.6.4
LNCS Sublibrary: SL 5 – Computer Communication Networks and Telecommunications

ISSN   0302-9743
ISBN-10   3-540-34023-8 Springer Berlin Heidelberg New York
ISBN-13   978-3-540-34023-2 Springer Berlin Heidelberg New York

Springer is a part of Springer Science+Business Media

springer.com

© Springer-Verlag Berlin Heidelberg 2006
Printed in Germany

Typesetting: Camera-ready by author, data conversion by Scientific Publishing Services, Chennai, India
Printed on acid-free paper   SPIN: 11750390   06/3142   5 4 3 2 1 0

Preface

Welcome to the proceedings of the 4th International Conference on Wired/ Wireless Internet Communications held at the University of Bern from May 10–12, 2006. As in 2005, WWIC was selected as the official conference by COST Action 290, and Springer accepted to publish the conference proceedings in the LNCS series. These facts have helped to again attract a large number of high-quality paper submissions. We received 142 submissions out of which 29 papers were selected by the International Program Committee for presentation at the conference. This resulted in a low acceptance rate of 21%. To limit the load on individual Program Committee members, we increased the Technical Program Committee size to 63 members. An additional 60 reviewers supported the review process. We would like to thank all TPC members and reviewers for their careful reviews, Microsoft Research for providing the online conference management toolkit, and TNO Delft for hosting the physical TPC meeting.

The selected papers are organized into eight sessions on the following topics:

- Wireless Networks
- UMTS and OFDM
- Mobile Ad-Hoc Networks
- Power Saving and Sensor Networks
- Voice and Video Over Wireless Networks
- Mobility
- TCP
- Signalling, Charging, and Security

The selected presentations and invited talks from distinguished international speakers formed an extremely exciting program. We hope that all attendees enjoyed both the scientific and social program as well as the city and the surroundings of Bern, the capital of Switzerland. We look forward to welcoming you at WWIC 2007, to be held in Coimbra, Portugal.

May 2006

Torsten Braun
Georg Carle
Sonia Fahmy
Yevgeni Koucheryavy

Organization

Steering Committee

Torsten Braun	University of Bern, Switzerland
Georg Carle	University of Tübingen, Germany
Giovanni Giambene	University of Siena, Italy
Yevgeni Koucheryavy	Tampere University of Technology, Finland
Peter Langendörfer	IHP Microelectronics, Germany
Ibrahim Matta	Boston University, USA
Vassilis Tsaoussidis	Demokritos University, Greece
Nitin Vaidya	University of Illinois, USA

Executive Committee

General Chairs:	Torsten Braun (University of Bern, Switzerland)
	Yevgeni Koucheryavy (Tampere University of Technology, Finland)
TPC Co-chairs:	Georg Carle (University of Tübingen, Germany)
	Sonia Fahmy (Purdue University, USA)

Technical Program Committee

Bengt Ahlgren	SICS, Sweden
Ozgur B. Akan	Middle East Technical University, Turkey
Khalid Al-Begain	University of Glamorgan, UK
Manuel Alvarez-Campana	Universidad Politecnica de Madrid, Spain
Farooq Anjum	Telcordia Technologies, USA
Chadi Barakat	INRIA, France
Bharat Bhargava	Purdue University, USA
Chris Blondia	University of Antwerp, Belgium
Fernando Boavida	University of Coimbra, Portugal
Torsten Braun	University of Bern, Switzerland
Wojciech Burakowski	Warsaw University of Technology, Poland
Georg Carle	University of Tübingen, Germany
Xiuzhen Cheng	George Washington University, USA
Hermann de Meer	University of Passau, Germany
Ruy de Oliveira	CEFET-MT, Brazil

Miki Yamamoto	Kansai University, Japan
Ossama Younis	University of Arizona, USA
Chi Zhang	Florida International University, USA
Martina Zitterbart	University of Karlsruhe, Germany
Michele Zorzi	University of Padova, Italy

Organizing Committee

Thomas Bernoulli	University of Bern, Switzerland
Ruth Bestgen	University of Bern, Switzerland
Marc Brogle	University of Bern, Switzerland

Additional Reviewers

Slim Abdellatif	Patrick Goering	Tanguy Perennou
Olivier Alphand	Alberto Hernandez	Saul Pomares
Sebastien Ardon	Richard Holzer	Ioannis Psaras
Ana Belen Garcia	Amine Houyou	Jean-Louis Rougier
Andreas Berl	Guy Juanole	Puri Saiz
Thomas Bohnert	Georgios Karagiannis	Alfonso Sanchez
Nafeesa Bohra	Jerome Lacan	Julian Satran
Yannick Brehon	Oscar Lazaro	Matthias Scheidegger
Guido Bruck	Fei Liu	Rute Sofia
Roberto Canonico	Jorge Lopez de Vergara	Herve Thalmensy
Edurado Cerqueira	German Madinabeitia	Ljiljana Trajkovic
Claude Chaudet	Lefteris Mamatas	Ageliki Tsioliaridou
Marilia Curado	Paulo Mendes	Francesco Vacirca
Laurent Dairaine	Michael Menth	Enrique Vazquez
Luca Decicco	Dragan Milic	Markus Wälchli
Ivan Dedinski	Dmitri Moltchanov	Jean-Frédéric Wagen
Roman Dunaytsev	Edmundo Monteiro	Omar Walid
Silvia Farraposo	John Murphy	Attila Weyland
David Fernandez	Roald Otnes	Patrick Wuechner
Andres Ferragut	P. Papadimitriou	Jian Xhang

Table of Contents

Session 4: Signalling, Charging, and Security

Session 5: UMTS and OFDM

Session 6: Voice and Video over Wireless Networks

Session 7: Wireless Networks

Session 8: Power Saving and Sensor Networks

Simulating Mobile Ad-Hoc Networks in City Scenarios

Illya Stepanov and Kurt Rothermel

Institute of Parallel and Distributed Systems (IPVS), Universität Stuttgart,
Universitätsstr. 38, 70569 Stuttgart, Germany
{stepanov, rothermel}@informatik.uni-stuttgart.de

Abstract. Simulation tools are frequently used for performance evaluations of mobile ad-hoc networks. Currently the tools poorly support urban scenarios, since they do not take a spatial environment into account. In this paper, we describe a platform for the modeling of city scenarios. We extend ns-2 with corresponding mobility and wireless transmission models. By using its emulation facility, we integrate unmodified applications and real implementations of network protocols. We demonstrate the usefulness of the platform for performance evaluations by modeling a mobile application in a simulated environment of Stuttgart downtown. We show that it helps identifying application problems before deployment.

1 Introduction

Mobile ad-hoc networks (MANETs) are formed by wireless peers without relying on a fixed infrastructure. The devices communicate directly with each other while they are in transmission range. A typical communication technology in MANETs is IEEE 802.11 [28].

Many usage scenarios have been proposed for MANETs in city areas, e.g., Useneton-the-Fly [2], CarTALK 2000 [6], and Ad- Hoc City [18]. Network simulation tools [4], [12], [23] are frequently used for performance analysis. They have three common shortages.

First, they typically offer only simple user mobility models. For example, the widely used random waypoint mobility model [5] simulates the straight movement between randomly chosen points of the area. The model does not consider spatial constraints of the area like roads. It also neglects user travel decisions and realistic movement dynamics.

Secondly, the tools rely on rather simple wireless transmission models. Such models (e.g., Friis free space model [8] or the two-ray ground model [11]) assume an obstacle-free area and a line-of-sight between all communicating partners. As a consequence, the communication range is modeled by a circle around a mobile device. It is assumed that other devices residing within this circle receive the transmitted frames without errors. Communication with the devices beyond the circle is not possible. This model poorly reflects radio wave propagation in typical outdoor environments such as cities, in which buildings significantly affect the communication between mobile devices. The usage of more realistic radio propagation models changes simulation results considerably [24].

T. Braun et al. (Eds.): WWIC 2006, LNCS 3970, pp. 1 – 12, 2006.

Thirdly, the network simulation tools use own (simplified) implementations of the network protocol stack. They differ from modules of real operating systems. Simulators do not execute real applications either. The applications need to be reprogrammed in order to fit a simulator's API. As we show in this paper, this hides many factors that influence the performance of applications in realistic situations.

In this paper, we extend ns-2 [4] for the modeling of city scenarios. We choose ns-2, since it is a major if not the most frequently used MANET simulator in our community. We integrate more realistic mobility and wireless transmission models. They consider a road network and radio propagation obstacles taken from a digital map of the area. We also use a fine-grained model of transmission errors, which is based on measurements of an IEEE 802.11 card manufacturer [17]. Ns-2 also provides an emulation facility for injecting traffic from real networks. We use it for integrating unmodified mobile applications and real implementations of network protocols running in separate virtual machines. We demonstrate the usefulness of the platform for performance evaluations by modeling a MANET application in a simulated environment of Stuttgart downtown. We show that it helps identifying application problems before deployment. Our implementations are publicly available[1].

The remainder of this paper is structured as follows. In Section 2, we briefly describe our approach to model user mobility in city areas. Section 3 describes a more realistic wireless transmission model. Section 4 demonstrates the integration of real applications and protocols into ns-2. In Section 5, we describe a MANET application, which we use for our evaluations. Section 6 describes our simulation scenario. We analyze simulation results in Section 7. Section 8 gives an overview of related work. Finally, Section 9 concludes the paper.

2   Modeling User Mobility

Our approach to model mobility of users in city areas (Fig. 1) is described in [25]. It reflects the following key factors that impact user movements:

- City environment with points of interest and movement constraints (spatial model)
- User travel decisions (user trip model)
- User movement dynamics (movement dynamics model)

The spatial model contains elements of a city environment. Some of them, such as streets and roads, constrain movements of users. Another group consists of the so-called "points of interest" (e.g., supermarkets or museums) that serve as destination points of movement. For each element, its properties (e.g., shop opening time, road speed limitation) and geometry are stored. The latter is used for constructing a street network graph. The spatial model can be initialized from digital maps in various formats, e.g., GDF [9] or GML [10].

Obviously, people do not move completely random in the target area. According to the activity-based travel demand approach [21], people move to perform an action in

---

[1] http://www.ipvs.uni-stuttgart.de?id=illya.stepanov&lang=en

certain places, for example, shopping in particular shops or visiting predefined sights. A sequence of such actions (trip sequence) describes user movements in the area. The user trip model contains all the trip sequences that users perform during the simulation. It also performs movement path selection, e.g., using approaches from discrete choice theory [3].

In addition, mobile clients exhibit different movement dynamics. For example, pedestrians tend to move at lower speeds with frequent interruptions, while vehicles move at higher

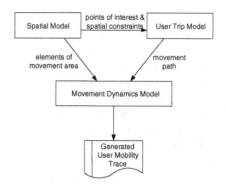

Fig. 1. Design of the mobility model

speeds and influence dynamics of neighboring vehicles. The movement dynamics model uses approaches from transport planning, physics, and vehicular dynamics [13], [27] to obtain user position changes along his/her movement paths. The position changes constitute a mobility trace, which is used as an input for MANET simulation tools, such as ns-2.

3 Modeling Wireless Transmission

The modeling of wireless transmission in MANETs includes the following steps: determination of signal receive power, computation of noise and interference, and packet reception [26].

Each time a mobile node transmits a frame, a simulator uses a radio propagation model to compute the signal receive power for every potential receiver. The result depends on attenuation that the signal experiences during propagation, e.g., due to environment. The noise and interference is the sum of powers of other signals and the receiver thermal noise. The signal to interference and noise ratio (SNIR) is the ratio of the signal receive power computed to the noise and interference. It has a correlation with bit-error rate of the received frame. The latter is used together with the frame length to estimate a probability of successful frame reception.

To model radio propagation in city areas, we rely on "intelligent ray tracing" model [29]. It considers a geographic map of the simulation area. In order to accelerate the performance of ray tracing, the model preprocesses the digital map and computes visibility relations between walls. Thereby it is about 1000 times faster than the classical ray tracing approach. The accuracy of the model is proven by measurements in European cities. For Stuttgart downtown, the mean error is 0.3 dB and the standard deviation is 5.8 dB [15].

The full details of integrating the model into ns-2 are given in [24]. We use a commercial implementation of the intelligent ray tracing model (WinPROP by AWE Communications [1]). For any given sender position (and other constant parameters like sender height, transmission power, wavelength etc.), WinPROP computes a map of receive power values for a grid, representing possible positions of a receiver. In our simulations, we use a 5 m × 5 m grid, which is the smallest grid size we could handle (smaller grid sizes would require much longer computation time and more disk space). We performed a separate investigation to assure that the chosen grid size has minor impact on simulation results.

For optimal performance, we precalculated the receive power values for each possible sender-receiver pair and stored them in a database. Each time ns-2 needs a receive power value, our radio propagation module reads the appropriate value from the dataset. To reduce the data access overhead, our module uses a caching strategy. As a result, the overall ns-2 simulation time with our module is comparable to the simulation time with a simpler model, such as two-ray ground.

Ns-2 decides on successful packet reception by only checking if a frame's receive power is above or below the receive threshold of the network equipment. In order to perform more realistic simulations, we also use a fine-grained model of wireless transmission errors.

The model is based on measurements of a card manufacturer [17]. They correlate frame's bit-error rate with the signal-to-noise ratio and the modulation scheme at the given transmission speed. We use the implementation from [30]. It models errors upon transmissions of control and data frames. The implementation determines target bit-error rate from a table using the transmission speed and the computed signal-to-noise ratio as indexes.

4   Integrating Real Mobile Applications

Next, we integrate MANET applications into ns-2 (Fig. 2). The simulator has an emulation facility (nse) allowing real network traffic to pass through it. We start mobile applications on separate computers corresponding to individual network users. In order to simulate more users than the number of physical hosts that we have, we use User-mode Linux (UML) [7] virtual machines. They run as user processes on top of operating system of physical hosts. A virtual machine appears as a single computer with own network interface for an application being executed inside of it.

Layer 3 traffic of virtual machines is injected into ns-2. On physical hosts, the traffic is received by switching daemons, which is a standard way of providing the UML hosts with an access to outer network. We modify switching daemons to tunnel the traffic to "network" and "tap" objects of ns-2. The "tap" objects inject the traffic into simulated mobile devices. Ns-2 models the physical layer and the data link layer of Wireless LAN, as well as the mobility of network users. The packets received by the simulated devices are tunneled to the corresponding virtual hosts in a similar fashion.

This described approach to traffic capturing allows the integration of unmodified MANET applications and real protocol implementations into ns-2. In future, it should be possible to replace UML with emulators of mobile devices (e.g., mobile phones, PDAs) to support other mobile platforms.

Virtual hosts and ns-2 perform in real time. We are confident that running several virtual hosts on one physical host and the centralized emulation of ns-2 do have impact on obtained simulation results. To assure that we stay below system load limit, we monitor packet drops at the ends of tunnel and CPU load of

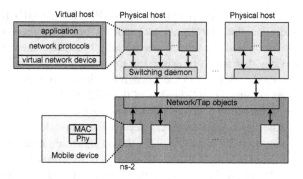

Fig. 2. Integrating real mobile applications into ns-2

physical hosts. To improve the accuracy of ns-2 real-time scheduler, we use the extensions from [20]. They also provide those "network" and "tap" objects that serve as a basis for our implementation.

5 Sample MANET Application: Usenet-on-the-Fly

We use the described platform for simulating MANET applications in city scenarios. Here we describe relevant aspects of Usenet-on-the-Fly [2], which we use in this paper.

Usenet-on-the-Fly is an implementation of the well-known Usenet system for ad-hoc networks [16]. The corresponding client application (Fig. 3) is implemented in Java. Hence, it runs on various hardware platforms, in particular, on PDAs. The graphical user interface (GUI) allows subscribing/unsubscribing to newsgroups (channels) and posting (publishing) of new messages. If a user posts a message to a specific channel, all subscribed users will receive it. Each message is distinguished by a unique ID.

We assume that mobile users carry PDAs. The devices are equipped with an IEEE 802.11 Wireless LAN card. Every device is identified with a unique IP address. Unlike in wired networks, MANET devices must cope with limited connectivity and frequent topology changes. Hence, the messages are disseminated through diffusion. This involves periodical exchange between the devices that are in transmission range.

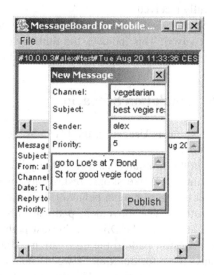

Fig. 3. Usenet-on-the-Fly screenshot

The application is multithreaded. Besides the GUI thread, the application uses 3 additional threads: "broadcast sender", "broadcast receiver", and "SOAP engine".

The "broadcast sender" periodically broadcasts the device's IP address. The mobile devices that are in transmission range receive the packet. Thereby the devices learn about other devices in their proximity. It is important to note that broadcast transmissions are unacknowledged as of the IEEE 802.11 standard. Hence, in the case of collisions there are no retransmissions performed.

The "broadcast receiver" receives the broadcasted IP addresses from neighbors. Upon receiving an address, the thread algorithm issues a Simple Object Access Protocol (SOAP) call "Get All Message IDs" addressed to the neighbor. The call returns the IDs of all the messages that are stored at the neighbor. Then they are compared with the receiver's own messages. If the neighbor has any new messages, the "broadcast receiver" issues a SOAP call "Get Message Bodies". The IDs of the required messages are passed as parameters. The received messages are added to the local database. In the current implementation, the database stores all the messages. The GUI performs the necessary filtering to display only the messages from the subscribed channels.

The "SOAP engine" thread processes sequentially incoming SOAP requests, such as "Get All Message IDs" and "Get Message Bodies".

The application has the following parameters:

- *BroadcastInterval*: time interval between two successive broadcasts of a device's IP address,
- *ServerSocketTimeout*: TCP timeout that the SOAP engine waits for a client to establish a connection,
- *ClientSocketTimeout*: TCP timeout that the SOAP engine waits for a request to be fully received,
- *SOAPTimeout*: TCP timeout that the "broadcast receiver" waits for a response to be received. This includes the time for connection establishment, message delays for transmitting request and response, and message processing on the remote side.

6   Simulation Scenario

We simulate Usenet-on-the-Fly in Stuttgart downtown. We use a digital map 1.5 km × 1.5 km.

In the simulated snapshot of city life, pedestrians move between different "points of interest", like shops, restaurants, or museums. Since we currently do not have access to real human behavior data, we randomly generate user trips between these locations. The movement paths are obtained from the linked topological graph of the area using the Dijkstra shortest-path algorithm (we assume the users move along the shortest path to the destination). Upon arriving to a "point of interest", the user stays there for duration between 10 and 15 minutes. Then the movement to the next trip point is initiated. The movement speeds are between 0.56 and 1.74 m/s [14].

They follow Gaussian distribution with mean 1.34 m/s and standard deviation 0.26 m/s [27]. The chosen speeds are kept constant during the movement between two points.

The simulated users carry mobile devices running Linux (the same operating system is started on our virtual hosts). The devices are equipped with wireless LAN cards. We use the parameters of Compaq© iPAQ 3660 PocketPCs and ORiNOCO© 802.11b WLAN cards in our simulations (Table 1). Since ns-2 does not support automatic switching between transmission speeds, we use the fixed speed of 1 Mbps.

The simulated message postings resemble 2-hour traffic from a real newsgroup (free-time activities). It consists of 18 postings. We assume that all the users are subscribed to this channel (newsgroup). The total simulation time is set to 8100 s, so the messages posted at the end have a chance to get spread in the network.

We create 5 virtual hosts on each physical host. The number was chosen in accordance with the number of mobile users and the number of physical hosts available. In spite of 5 parallel running virtual machines, CPU load of virtual hosts was low (nearly 0%), since the Usenet-on-the-Fly application performs little computational activity.

In simulations with more than 100 users, we noticed significant packet drops at the simulation front-end running ns-2. This makes communication between mobile hosts impossible even if they are in transmission range. The reasons for this are: 1) high network traffic load from virtual hosts, and 2) absence of flow control, since we used UDP for the tunnel between the switching daemons and ns-2. We will improve it in the future. Currently we support up to 100 of mobile users.

Table 1. Simulation parameters

Simulation time	8100 s
Number of mobile users	30, 50, 75, and 100
iPAQ battery capacity	3.7 V * 1350 mAh
Transmission power	15 dBm
Radio frequency	2.442 GHz
Transmission speed	1 Mbps
WLAN power consumption	idle mode: 0.045 W, receive mode: 0.925 W, transmit mode: 1.425 W
Broadcast interval	1, 2, 5, 10, and 20 minutes
Server socket timeout	10 s
Client socket timeout	20 s
SOAP timeout	30 s

7 Simulation Results

In our simulations, we are mostly interested in analyzing message spreading with time. We define the spreading as a ratio of mobile users who received the posting. Fig. 4 and Fig. 5 present the results for different numbers of network users and broadcast intervals. The charts present the average for 18 postings.

The curves differ from common considerations, e.g., [2], which imply that a message spreads faster between more network users. Our results show the opposite. Moreover, the fact that a message spreads faster with less broadcasts seems to be irrational.

Precise investigation of application logs pointed out the problem. The operating system buffers the received broadcasts. The "broadcast receiver" processes them one after another. The "SOAP Timeout" parameter controls how long the thread waits for a SOAP response (performing necessary retransmissions, since SOAP relies on TCP). The default value is 30 seconds. However, according to Fig. 6, in more than 60% of cases two users spend less than 30 s in each other's transmission range. Consequently, if a SOAP request fails (e.g., because of mobility), the likelihood is high that the next broadcast read from the socket is from the user, who already left the transmission range. The chains of failed requests add significant delays to the message exchange. This problem occurs more often as the number of broadcasts increases, e.g., more users or a shorter broadcast interval. Such an effect of "SOAP timeout" could not be determined in [2], since the application was reimplemented for a simulation environment. The reimplented version neither used a real SOAP library nor considered socket timeouts.

Instead of simply adjusting the timeout value, we solve the problem in a different way. We modify the "broadcast receiver", so it does not issue SOAP calls any more. It processes the received broadcasts immediately and stacks the extracted addresses ("last in, first out" paradigm). An extra thread called "synchronization scheduler" processes the stacked items and issues SOAP calls. Hence, the more

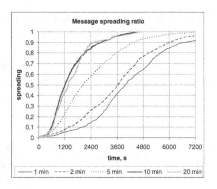

Fig. 4. Message spreading ratio between 100 mobile users for different broadcast intervals

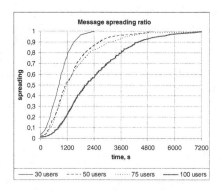

Fig. 5. Message spreading ratio for different numbers of mobile users. Broadcast interval is 5 minutes

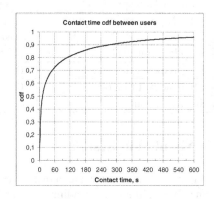

Fig. 6. Cumulative distribution function of contact time between 100 mobile users

recently received broadcasts are processed before others. It also performs item aging, so the addresses received more than "SOAP timeout" seconds ago are removed without processing. This reduces the lock probability. The modified implementation performs as expected (Fig. 7-Fig. 10).

Fig. 7 shows the message spreading time for different broadcast intervals. Clearly, more frequent broadcasts lead to faster neighbor discovery, and hence, to faster message exchange.

Obviously, the configured broadcast interval impacts device energy consumption (Fig. 8). We used ns-2 to estimate the energy spent for communication (without consideration of other energy-consuming components, such as CPU, display, etc.). The results are presented both in Joules and in percent of the capacity of an iPAQ battery.

The most essential conclusion from the results is that a message reaches 90% of users even with 20 min broadcast interval. However, an interval of 1 min requires more than 6% of device energy spent only on communication in 2 hours, while 20 min interval requires about 2.5%. Clearly, the interval duration must be configured taking the desired message spreading delay and energy consumption into account.

The message spreading time is variable in scenarios with different numbers of mobile users (Fig. 9). As the number of users increases from 30 to 75, we get faster message spreading, as expected. Increasing the number of users further leads to a slower spreading. According to application logs, the number of failed SOAP requests grows due to collisions in a denser network. This also makes a device spend more energy on retransmissions (Fig. 10).

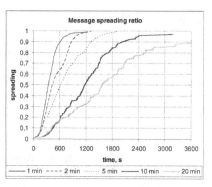

Fig. 7. Message spreading ratio between 100 mobile users for different broadcast intervals. Modified application

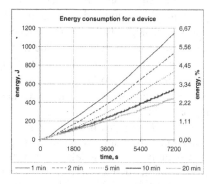

Fig. 8. Average energy consumption for a mobile device. Modified application, 100 mobile users, different broadcast intervals

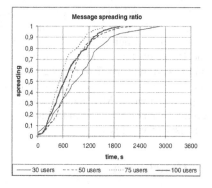

Fig. 9. Message spreading ratio for different numbers of mobile users. Modified application, broadcast interval is 5 minutes

8 Related Work

To the best of our knowledge, we are the first to simulate a real MANET application with such a detailed platform in a city scenario. Most of MANET evaluations use either synthetic traffic such as constant-bit rate, or reimplement applications for a specific simulation environment. As we showed in this paper, this may hide some implementation-specific aspects of an application.

As for mobility modeling, most of MANET papers use the random waypoint mobility model described in [5].

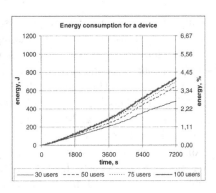

Fig. 10. Average energy consumption for a mobile device. Modified application, 5 minutes broadcast interval, different number of mobile users

The model neglects user trip sequences and movement area constraints. Hence, it is unrealistic for city scenarios. The MANET simulation tools [4], [12], [23] commonly use this model primarily due to its simplicity. In [18], the authors simulate mobility according to real-world traces. However, they use a simple radio propagation model, which assumes an obstacle-free area and a free line-of-sight between all communicating partners.

Detailed statistics in [19] about publications at premium conferences in the field proves that the papers with such simple radio propagation models outnumber others significantly. These models poorly reflect radio wave propagation in a typical outdoor environment, such as city, in which buildings significantly affect the communication between mobile devices. The mentioned MANET simulation tools offer only the simple models. It is has been shown that the usage of more realistic radio propagation models changes simulation results considerably [24].

Also transmission errors are reflected seldom in MANET simulations. Like this paper, [22] and [30] rely on measurements from [17]. However, they still use the simple propagation models, which poorly reflect city scenarios.

As for live network traffic capturing, the ns-2 offers only passive capturing using the Berkeley Packet Filter. The implementation from [20] supports traffic capturing and injection to and from UML virtual machines. However, all the processes must run on the local host. The code also requires root privileges. Our approach support traffic capturing from UML machines running on remote hosts. Since we use only UNIX domain sockets for communication with virtual hosts, our code does not require super-user privileges.

9 Conclusion

In this paper, we extended ns-2 for the modeling of MANET applications in city scenarios. We applied more realistic mobility and wireless transmission models. They consider movement area constraints and communication obstacles, which are taken from a digital map. We also integrated real MANET applications and implementations of network protocols.

We used the described platform for evaluating the performance of a real application (Usenet-on-the-Fly) in Stuttgart downtown. We prepared the corresponding simulation scenario. We showed that the described platform helps identifying application problems before deployment. For example, we noticed the negative effect of message buffering upon device discovery and improved the implementation. The presented simulation results give an impression of the performance of the application and energy consumption.

References

[1]   AWE Communications Home Page. Available at http://www.awe-communications.com
[2]   C. Becker, M. Bauer, and J. Hähner, "Usenet-on-the-fly: supporting locality of information in spontaneous networking environments," in *Proceedings of CSCW 2002 Workshop on Ad hoc Communications and Collaboration in Ubiquitous Computing Environments*, New Orleans, USA, 2002.
[3]   M. Ben-Akiva, M. Bierlaire, "Discrete choice methods and their applications to short-term travel decisions," in R. Hall (ed.), *Handbook of Transportation Science*, International Series in Operations Research and Management Science, Vol. 23, Kluwer, 1999.
[4]   L. Breslau, D. Estrin, K. Fall, S. Floyd, J. Heidemann, A. Helmy, P. Huang, S. McCanne, K. Varadhan, Y. Xu, and H. Yu, "Advances in Network Simulation," *IEEE Computer*, Vol. 33, No. 5, May 2000.
[5]   J. Broch, D. A. Maltz, D. B. Johnson, Y.-C. Hu, and J. Jetcheva, "A Performance Comparison of Multi-Hop Wireless Ad Hoc Network Routing Protocols," in *Proceedings of the 4th Annual ACM/IEEE International Conference on Mobile Computing and Networking*, Dallas, TX, October 1998.
[6]   CarTalk 2000 Project Home Page. Available at http://www.cartalk2000.net
[7]   J. Dike, "A user-mode port of the Linux kernel", in *Proceedings of the 4th Annual Linux Showcase & Conference*, Atlanta, USA, October 2000.
[8]   H. Friis, "A note on a simple transmission formula," in *Proceedings of IRE*, Vol. 41, 1946.
[9]   Geographic Data Files (GDF) Home Page. Available at http://www.ertico.com/en/links/links/gdf_-_geographic_data_files.htm
[10] Geometry Markup Language (GML) 2.0, OpenGIS® Implementation Specification, OGC Document Number: 01-029, 20 February 2001. Available at http://www.opengis.net/gml/01-029/GML2.html
[11] J. Gibson, *The Communications Handbook*, CRC Press, ISBN: 0849383498, 1997.
[12] GloMoSim: Global Mobile Information Systems Simulation Library. Available at http://pcl.cs.ucla.edu/projects/glomosim
[13] D. Helbing, A. Hennecke, V. Shvetsov, and M. Treiber, "Micro- and Macrosimulation of Freeway Traffic," *Mathematical and Computer Modelling*, Vol. 35, 2002.
[14] D. Helbing and P. Molnár, "Social force model for pedestrian dynamics," *Physical Review E* 51, 1995.
[15] R. Hoppe, G. Wölfle, and F. Landstorfer, "Fast 3D Ray Tracing for the Planning of Microcells by Intelligent Preprocessing of the Database," in *Proceedings of the 3rd European Personal and Mobile Communications Conference (EPMCC) 1999*, Paris, France, March 1999.
[16] M. Horton, "Standard for interchange of USENET messages," RFC 850, June 1983. Available at http://www.faqs.org/rfcs/rfc850.html
[17] *Intersil® HFA3861B Direct Sequence Spread Spectrum Baseband Processor Data Sheet.* File Number 4816, January 2000.

[18] J. Jetcheva, Y.-C. Hu, S. PalChaudhuri, A. Saha, and D. Johnson, "Design and Evaluation of a Metropolitan Area Multitier Wireless Ad Hoc Network Architecture," in *Proceedings of the 5th IEEE Workshop on Mobile Computing Systems & Applications*, Monterey, USA, October 2003.

[19] D. Kotz, C. Newport, R. Gray, J. Liu, Y. Yuan, and C. Elliott, "Experimental Evaluation of Wireless Simulation Assumptions", in *Proceedings of the ACM/IEEE International Symposium on Modeling, Analysis and Simulation of Wireless and Mobile Systems (MSWiM'04)*, Venice, Italy, October, 2004.

[20] D. Mahrenholz and S. Ivanov, "Adjusting the ns-2 Emulation Mode to a Live Network," in *Proceedings of Communication in Distributed Systems 2005 (KiVS'05)*, Kaiserslautern, Germany, March 2005.

[21] E. I. Pas, "Recent Advances in Activity-Based Travel Demand Modeling," in *Proceedings of Activity-Based Travel Forecasting Conference*, New Orleans, USA, June 1996.

[22] J. del Prado and S. Choi, "Link Adaptation Strategy for IEEE 802.11 WLAN via Received Signal Strength Measurement," in *Proceedings of the 38th annual IEEE International Conference on Communications (ICC)*, Anchorage, USA, May 2003.

[23] G. Riley, "The Georgia Tech Network Simulator," in *Proceedings of ACM SIGCOMM Workshop on Models, Methods and Tools for Reproducible Network Research (MoMe-Tools'03)*, Germany, August 2003.

[24] I. Stepanov, D. Herrscher, and K. Rothermel, "On the Impact of Radio Propagation Models on MANET Simulation Results," in the *Proceedings of 7th IFIP International Conference on Mobile and Wireless Communications Networks (MWCN 2005)*, Marrakech, Morocco, September 2005.

[25] I. Stepanov, P. Marron, and K. Rothermel, "Mobility Modeling of Outdoor Scenarios for MANETs," in *Proceedings of the 38th Annual Simulation Symposium (ANSS'38)*, San Diego, USA, April 2005.

[26] M. Takai, J. Martin, and R. Bagrodia, "Effects of wireless physical layer modeling in mobile ad hoc networks", in *Proceedings of the 2nd ACM International Symposium on Mobile Ad-Hoc Networking and Computing (MobiHoc'01)*, Long Beach, USA, October 2001.

[27] U. Weidmann, "Transporttechnik der Fussgaenger," *Schriftenreihe des Instituts für Verkehrsplanung, Transporttechnik, Strassen- und Eisenbahnbau*, Nr. 90, ETH, Zuerich, 1993.

[28] *Wireless LAN Medium Access Control (MAC) and Physical Layer (PHY) Specifications*, IEEE Standard 802.11b, 1999.

[29] G. Wölfle, R. Hoppe, and F. Landstorfer, "A Fast and Enhanced Ray Optical Propagation Model for Indoor and Urban Scenarios, Based on an Intelligent Preprocessing of the Database," in *Proceedings of the 10th IEEE International Symposium on Personal, Indoor and Mobile Radio Communications (PIMRC)*, Osaka, Japan, September 1999.

[30] X. Wu and A. Ananda, "Link Characteristics Estimation For IEEE 802.11 DCF Based WLAN," in *Proceedings of the 29th Annual IEEE Conference on Local Computer Networks (LCN 2004)*, Tampa, USA, November 2004.

Context Discovery Using Attenuated Bloom Filters in Ad-Hoc Networks

Fei Liu and Geert Heijenk

University of Twente, P.O. Box 217,
7500 AE Enschede, The Netherlands
{fei.liu, geert.heijenk}@utwente.nl

Abstract. A novel approach to performing context discovery in ad-hoc networks based on the use of attenuated Bloom filters is proposed in this paper. In order to investigate the performance of this approach, a model has been developed. This document describes the model and its validation. The model has been implemented in Matlab, and some results are also shown in this document. Attenuated Bloom filters appear to be a very promising approach for context discovery in ad hoc networks.

1 Introduction

Ad-hoc networks are non-infrastructure wireless networks in which most of the terminals are both mobile and power-consumption constrained. When one needs to obtain a service or context information from other devices, querying and fixing the location of the service or context information source might generate a lot of traffic. In a network with a high query rate, such traffic can be rather heavy. As a result, the terminals consume quite an amount of power and bandwidth for querying. An efficient context discovery mechanism needs to be developed for such situations.

This paper describes the development of a discovery mechanism for networks that are context aware. These networks utilize context information to improve their operation, or to enrich the services provided to users. We propose a novel approach to discover context information sources in an ad-hoc network based on the use of attenuated Bloom filters, which represents a decentralized space-efficient discovery method. Instead of broadcasting full information about the type and location of context information, nodes send attenuated Bloom filters which contain context type information for all the reachable nodes up to a certain number of hops away. Moreover, Bloom filters have a special feature of false positive probability, which leads to probabilistic querying. Queries are only forwarded in the directions which possibly contain the required information. Our analysis reveals that this type of probabilistic discovery method can substantially reduce the network load compared to discovery using traditional approaches.

This paper is structured as follows. Section 2 will introduce our novel approach for performing context discovery using attenuated Bloom filters. In Section 3 we will describe an approximate model for the transmission costs of our method. Further we compare it with context discovery without attenuated Bloom filters. In Section 4 we will provide numerical results. Finally in Section 5, we present our conclusions and proposed future work.

T. Braun et al. (Eds.): WWIC 2006, LNCS 3970, pp. 13–25, 2006.

2 Context Discovery Using Attenuated Bloom Filters

2.1 Related Work on Context Discovery

Context discovery has a lot of resemblance to service discovery. Service Discovery Protocols (SDPs) can be classified into centralized and decentralized architectures. In an Ad-hoc network environment, nodes are both mobile and mostly battery-powered. Those characteristics fit well with some features of decentralized architectures. The choice for a proactive or reactive SDP in decentralized architectures depends substantially on the network and service context and on the interaction with the underlying routing protocol [1].

Service descriptions are different for various SDPs. The most popular format is the attribute-value structure [2]. For instance, the Service Location Protocol (SLP) [3] uses service templates which predefine the attributes in a template document readable by humans and machines. Service agents (SAs) advertise the location of one or more services; directory agents (DAs) store service location information centrally. Whenever necessary, user agents will look for the required services at SAs and DAs. A client/server structure is used in the Bluetooth Service Discovery Protocol. Bluetooth SDP [4] defines a service record consisting of the entire list of attributes, which is then stored in the SDP server. Clients will send requests to the SDP server to obtain the required services.

Further, hierarchical attribute-value pairs, which mostly rely on eXtensible Markup language (XML), are also used in some protocols, such as Global Service Discovery Architecture (GloSev) [5] and Group-based Service Discovery protocol (GSD) [6]. GloSev is proposed for worldwide and local area network usage. Services are described and categorized hierarchically by using the Resource Description Framework (RDF) which is based on Uniform Resource Identifiers (URI) and XML. This hierarchical service architecture is similar to the DNS domain name architecture. GSD is a distributed service discovery protocol for Mobile Ad hoc NETworks (MANETs). Services are described based on DARPA Agent Markup Language (DAML+OIL). Advertisements are sent periodically to nodes within a maximum number of hops. Each node has peer-to-peer caching to keep a list of local and remote services that a node has received from advertisements. Services are also grouped to ease service discovery by selectively forwarding queries.

In some protocols, such as Jini [7], attributes are described as Java objects. Service objects are registered in service registries, which are also used to look up services. A client needs to download the service object and invoke it to access the service.

Among the protocols mentioned above, GloSev was developed for wide area networks. SLP and Jini were designed for local area networks. GSD and Bluetooth SDP were specifically for MANETs. Further, it is clear that whichever method is used to describe services, sending the complete service attributes causes heavy traffic. It is inefficient in a high-density mobile ad hoc network with many services to be advertised and\or queried. Due to the limited battery power of terminals, a simple, efficient context description and discovery mechanism is required. Clearly, a mobile ad hoc network is less suitable for a centralized structure due to the mobility of the nodes. Nodes should not depend on other specific nodes to reach the required context information. Context discovery using attenuated Bloom filters can solve this problem in ad hoc networks.

2.2 Brief Introduction of Attenuated Bloom Filters

A Bloom filter [8] is a data structure for representing a set in order to support membership queries. It can denote a set simply and efficiently, with a small probability of false positives. Bloom filters can be used in various network applications, such as distributed caching, P2P/overlay networks, resource routing, packet routing, and measurement infrastructure [9]. Bloom filters were also proposed to be used as an efficient approach for lossy aggregation and query routing for a Secure Service Discovery Service in [10]. Recently, researchers have explored the applications of Bloom filters to Ad hoc networks, such as speeding-up cache lookups [11], group management [12], and hotspot-based trace back [13].

A Bloom code can represent a set of context information types. Each context type will be coded by using b independent hash functions over the range $\{1...w\}$, where w is the width of the filter. The default value for each bit in the Bloom code is 0. The bits of positions associated with the hashes will be set to 1. Our approach uses attenuated Bloom filters, each of which consists of a few layers of basic Bloom filters. The first layer of the filter contains the context type information for the current node, while the second layer contains the information about the nodes one hop away, and so on. In other words, a node can find the context type information i hops away in the ith layer. When querying for a certain type of context information, the same hash functions are performed. If all positions in a Bloom filter indicated by one of the hashes contain a 1, the presence of the queried context type is likely (but not certain). Otherwise the context type is not present. The use of these attenuated Bloom filters introduces the possibility of having false positives, which will be resolved during a later stage of the context discovery process. By using attenuated Bloom filter consisting of multiple layers, context sources at more than one hop distance can be discovered, while avoiding saturation of the Bloom filter by attenuating (shifting out) bits set by sources further away.

For example, we assume a 6-bit Bloom filter with b equal to 2. If location information is hashed into $\{1, 3\}$ and temperature information is mapped into $\{2, 5\}$, we obtain the filter shown in Fig. 1.

The filter will give a positive answer to queries for location or temperature information. It definitely does not contain presence information which is hashed into $\{0, 3\}$. Nodes may also think humidity information $\{1, 5\}$ is contained in this filter, but actually it is not. This situation is termed false positive [9].

```
 0  1  2  3  4  5
 0  1  1  1  0  1
```

Fig. 1. A simple 6-bit Bloom filter

Context aggregation can be simply implemented by attenuated Bloom filters. When a node A receives incoming Bloom filters *filter$_B$* and *filter$_C$* from neighbors B and C respectively, it shifts all the contents of *filter$_B$* and *filter$_C$* one layer down and discards the last layer. The first layers will be filled with 0s. An OR operation will be done to those new filters, $filter_B$' and $filter_C$', and the first layer will filled by (first layer of) $filter_A$. Consequently, the Bloom filter of node A is updated such that the first layer represents the local information from node A; the second layer contains the information from neighbor B and C; the third layer covers the information two hops away which can be reached via B or C. Fig. 2 shows the process of context aggregation in a node.

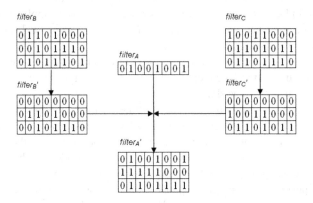

Fig. 2. Context aggregation

2.3   Context Discovery with Attenuated Bloom Filters

Context discovery by using attenuated Bloom filters is a method combining proactive and reactive discovery mechanisms. Nodes can obtain an overview of available context types and their distribution by exchanging Bloom filters. When a node enters a new environment, it first sends a Bloom filter with its own context information types to its neighbors. When neighbors receive this filter, they will merge it to their existing attenuated Bloom filters by shifting the incoming filter and doing an OR operation, as explained in Section 2.2, and rebroadcast the updated filter. The new node stores the incoming Bloom filters separately for each neighbor, and also generates a new filter aggregating all the reply filters with the local one. This new filter will be sent to the neighbors in the next advertisement. The Bloom filters will be exchanged periodically, or when they change.

When there is a query, the node will first check locally whether the required context information exists. If not, the query will be encoded into a Bloom code using the same hash functions and compared with the locally stored filters. If there is a match at any layer in any of the local filters, a query message containing the Bloom code will be sent to the neighbor from which the stored filter was received. The same action will be taken by a node receiving a query. When a node receives the same query again, it will drop the query. Further the path of the query message will be recorded by each node. If an exact match is finally found, a Context-Available (CAL) reply will be sent back along the same path. If no match is found, e.g., because of a false positive match in an earlier node, the query will be discarded. In this way, query messages will be filtered out as early as possible, depending on the stored attenuated Bloom filters. The originating node will set up a connection to the destination node based on the best CAL reply. Note that a hop counter is used to restrict the query range. Queries will only be sent a limited number of hops away, based on the depth of the Bloom filters. If no CAL is received by the originating node after a time out, it understands the required information is unavailable in the current range. It will make a choice to enlarge the discovery area or send the query again after a certain time.

Note that recording the path of the query message requires maintaining (soft) state routing information in the nodes. This can put a burden on these nodes. Alternatively, the return path for CAL replies can be stored in the query messages. This will result in increased transmission costs. The detailed network architecture is described in [14].

3   Performance Modeling

Queries due to false positives can potentially contribute significantly to the costs of context discovery. In order to reduce the number of unnecessary queries, we have to reduce the rate of false positives. However, the minimum false positive rate, which is by definition equal to 0, will result in large Bloom filters. We believe there is a balance to be struck between a reasonable false positive rate and the size of Bloom filters to achieve the optimal network cost. The size of Bloom filters is decided by their width, depth, the number of hash functions, and the cardinality of the represented set. The goal of the model is to find the optimum balance between those parameters to minimize the network cost. Further comparisons between context discovery with and without Bloom filters will be made.

3.1   Assumptions and Related Vital Parameters

Ideally, the two-dimensional radio coverage of a mobile terminal is a circle. Therefore, a circular structured network is assumed in our modeling. The communication range of nodes will be generalized as a set of concentric circles. Nodes located in the inner circle are the ones reachable within one hop from the center node. Nodes in one ring outside the inner circle are the ones reachable in two hops, and so on.

Each node in the network is supposed to have the same number of context (or service) information types, s. Further all context types are supposed to be unique, and taken out of an infinitely large set of possible context types. The same width, w, and depth, d, of attenuated Bloom filters, and the same b hash functions are used for the entire network. Queries are forwarded at most d hops, based on the depth of Bloom filters.

We assume that the communication range, r, of a node is 30 meters. The density of the network is n nodes/m^2 in average. Assuming 4 neighbors per node, we obtain $n \approx 0.0007$ [14].

General notation is listed in the Table 1.

Table 1. Notation

General		Bloom Filter	
Nota-tion	Description	Nota-tion	Description
s	number of services (context information types) per node	w	the width of the filter
μ	advertisement (update) rate	d	the depth of the filter
λ	query rate	b	number of hash functions
n	network density (nodes/m^2)		
r	communication range		

3.2 Model

There are two kinds of traffic in the network: advertisements and queries. Three types of advertisement messages can be identified: normal advertisement, updates, and maintenance. We assume that advertisements are broadcast periodically at a constant rate. Among queries, there are also two types based on the different answers: positive query and false positive query. Note that there is no false negative in Bloom filters. Therefore, the cost for a node is defined as the sum of the advertisement cost, positive cost and false positive cost. We determine the cost considering the transmission cost of a single node in the network. The cost is expressed in bits per second per node:

$$cost = adcost + pcost + fpcost \tag{1}$$

Since advertisements are broadcasted periodically, *adcost* can be derived by:

$$adcost = \mu \cdot adpack \tag{2}$$

where μ is the advertisement (update) rate; *adpack* is the advertisement packet size.

The positive cost is denoted as *pcost*. To simplify the problem, we assume that queried services are not available in the network, which indicates all queries will result in a negative answer, or a false positive, i.e. *pcost* = 0.

Then *fpcost* represents the false positive cost of a node. In order to be able to determine these costs, let us first determine the probability of generating a false positive as a result of a query. We define $P_{fp,j}$ as the probability of a false positive for layer j $(1 \le j \le d)$ of an attenuated Bloom filter, where x_j represents the number of services available in layer j. In this paper, we assume that the hash functions we choose are perfectly random. The probability that a specific bit is 0 is equal to:

$$\left(1 - \frac{1}{w}\right)^{bx_j} \approx e^{-bx_j/w} \tag{3}$$

So we have:

$$P_{fp,j} = \left(1 - \left(1 - \frac{1}{w}\right)^{bx_j}\right)^b \approx \left(1 - e^{-bx_j/w}\right)^b \tag{4}$$

Formula (4) shows that the false positive probability depends on the width (w) and number hash functions (b) of the Bloom filters, and the number of services contained inside the filter. We define the number of services in j^{th} hop as:

$$x_j = s \cdot n\pi(j \cdot r)^2 \tag{5}$$

The assumption is that all services that are reachable in j or fewer hops are represented at the jth layer. A service that is represented at a certain layer is also assumed to be represented at all layers below, because of likely alternative paths with more hops to the node containing that service, which will impact the broadcast attenuated Bloom filters.

We have to consider all transmission costs for false positive queries incurred by a query initiated in the node under consideration. Transmission of such query messages can take place on all links up to d hops away from the node under consideration. Thus, we can denote the false positive cost as:

$$fpcost = \lambda \cdot \sum_{i=1}^{d} cost_{fp,i} \tag{6}$$

We assume queries are performed with a certain rate λ, i.e., λ queries will be initiated per second per node. $cost_{fp,i}$ denotes the total cost of all false positive queries transmitted to nodes i hops away from the node under consideration.

In order to obtain this false positive query cost to the ith hop, we have to count the possible number of query transmissions sent by nodes i-1 hops away to their neighbors, $numofTransmission_{fp,i}$. Such a transmission is indeed done, with a packet size $qpack$, if the attenuated Bloom filter received from the intended receiver of the query gives a false positive in any of the layers 1 to d-i+1. A false positive in a layer beyond d-i+1 does not result in a query message being transmitted, because that would lead to a query being transmitted more than d hops from the originating node. Note that false positives at multiple layers of the Bloom filter will result in multiple transmissions being counted for the relevant link. We are still investigating if this can be avoided in our system, but also assume that the false positive probability is so small, that we can neglect this effect. The resulting false positive query cost to the ith hop can be given as:

$$cost_{fp,i} = \sum_{j=1}^{d-i+1} P_{fp,j} \cdot numofTransmission_{fp,i} \cdot qpack \tag{7}$$

For determining $numofTransmission_{fp,i}$, let us suppose that each node can reach all the nodes within communication range, which are $(n\pi r^2 - 1)$ nodes excluding the querying node itself. When a node forwards a query to the next hop, there are potentially $(n\pi r^2 - 1)$ neighbors to transmit the query to. These transmissions to the ith hop will potentially be done by all nodes that can be reached within i-1 hops from the node under consideration, excluding those that can also be reached within i-2 hops. Therefore, there will be $(n\pi(i-1)^2 r^2 - n\pi(i-2)^2 r^2) = (2i-3)n\pi r^2 \ (i>1)$ nodes involved in transmission. These results in the following potential number of transmission sent in the ith hop. Note that this also includes transmissions to nodes that have already received the query before. These duplicates will be discarded upon reception.

$$numofTransmission_{fp,i} = (2i-3)n\pi r^2 \cdot (n\pi r^2 - 1) \quad 2 \leq i \leq d \tag{8}$$

For the first hop, the original querying node will send the query to all the nodes in range, so that the number of transmissions sent in 1st hop equals:

$$numofTransmission_{fp,1} = n\pi r^2 - 1 \tag{9}$$

So the false positive query cost at hop i is:

$$cost_{fp,i} = \begin{cases} \sum_{j=1}^{d}(1-e^{-bx_j/w})^b \cdot (n\pi r^2 - 1) \cdot qpack & i=1 \\ \sum_{j=1}^{d-i+1}(1-e^{-bx_j/w})^b \cdot (2i-3)n\pi r^2 \cdot (n\pi r^2 - 1) \cdot qpack & 2 \leq i \leq d \end{cases} \tag{10}$$

For the sizes of the advertisement and query packets, we assume that the context discovery protocol using Bloom filters is running on top of UDP. For both advertisements and queries, besides the header of Bloom Filters protocol, the headers of UDP, IP, and MAC layer will be attached. The advertisements and queries packet size are defined as follows:

$$adpack = header_{MAC} + header_{IP} + header_{UDP} + header_{AD} + w \times d \tag{11}$$

$$qpack = header_{MAC} + header_{IP} + header_{UDP} + header_{Q} + w \tag{12}$$

3.3 Two Extreme Cases

To evaluate the performance of context discovery using attenuated Bloom filters, we have compared it with two alternative discovery solutions: complete advertisement and non advertisement.

Complete advertisement floods all network nodes within d hops with complete descriptions of all context information types. Nodes had the complete map of the network, which indicates how nodes can send queries directly to the destination. It is a proactive protocol. The advertisement cost is the main concern in this situation. We assume that each context information type can be presented in c bits, so we have:

$$cost = \mu \times numofTrans \times (header_{MAC} + header_{IP} + header_{UDP} + header_{AD} + s \times c) \tag{13}$$

where $numofTrans$ denotes the number of transmissions for the entire advertisement within d hops. We suppose each node up to d-1 hops away to broadcast the advertisement, so that we have:

$$numofTrans = (1 + n\pi((d-1) \cdot r)^2) \tag{14}$$

In the non-advertisement case, nodes do not advertise context information types. When a query comes, nodes forward it to all the neighbors. It is a reactive protocol.

Nodes do not have any idea about the network. The queries are spreading around the whole network, up to d hops from the originator. There is no way to stop forwarding queries, even though the query node has already received an answer. The cost for querying is counted as the cost for sending queries to the network, which is:

$$cost = \lambda(header_{MAC} + header_{IP} + header_{UDP} + header_Q + c)\left(1 + n\pi(d \cdot r)^2\right) \qquad (15)$$

4 Experimental Results

The model described above has been implemented in Matlab 6.5. Using the model, four sets of experiments are done. The following tables and figures show the results of the experiments. In all the experiments below, we assume the update frequency $\mu = 0.1$ and each context information type can be represented in 32 bits, i.e., $c = 32$ bits. The sizes of headers are assumed as follows [15]: $header_{MAC} = 160$ bits; $header_{IPv6} = 320$ bits; $header_{UDP} = 64$ bits; $header_{AD} = 32$ bits [14]; $header_Q = 192$ bits [14].

There are 4 sets of experiments done in this section. Experiment 1 is used to achieve the optimal cost by choosing the proper width, w, of the Bloom filter and the number of hash functions, b, with given depth, d, of the filter, query rate, λ, and number of services, s, per node. Experiment 2 shows the influence of the query rate, λ, on the network cost for given d and s. The influence of the query range, d, is evaluated in Experiment 3. In the final experiment, we show the impact of density of services, s, in the network.

4.1 Experiment 1

In this experiment, we assume query rate $\lambda = 0.1$, $s = 1$. For each given value of depth of filter, the experiment result shows there exists a certain value of w and b which leads to the minimum network cost. The result is shown in Table 2. It is also compared with the complete and non advertisement under similar situations.

As we see from Table 2, for each depth of the filter, the proper width and number of hash functions leads to a minimum network cost which is much lower than for the cases of a complete advertisement and a non-advertisement. The difference becomes larger as query range d increases. The final column shows the maximum number of services that are covered by one Bloom filter based on the related size of Bloom filter.

Table 2. Optimal BF cost for certain depth d compared with complete and non advertisment

d	w (bit)	b	BF cost (bit/s)	Complete Advertisement (bit/s)	Non Advertisement (bit/s)	Maximum number of services in BF
3	128	5	114	547	1459	18
5	512	8	328	2006	3917	49
7	1024	8	809	4438	7603	97
10	2048	8	2231	9910	15437	198

4.2 Experiment 2

Using Bloom filters, we can reduce the packet size by using simple and efficient coding. However, false positives also create redundant traffic. We expect that there exists a point at which the traffic generated due to false positives is much more than the benefit of using Bloom filters. In contrast, if there are only few queries in the network, it does not pay to broadcast the context information to the entire network. A non-advertisement protocol can perform better in this case. This experiment is going to discuss the suitable range of using Bloom filters for context discovery to achieve the minimum network cost.

We set μ as a reference, and change the value of λ. Here we talk about λ/μ. The experiments show that the suitable range of λ/μ decreases when the depth of the filter, d, increases. When each node has only one service ($s = 1$), the Bloom filter context discovery algorithm performs better than the non-advertisement algorithm when λ is at least 0.1 times μ. When $d = 3$, the Bloom filter algorithm performs better than the complete advertisement algorithm even if λ is 10^8 times μ. When $d = 10$, this decreases to 10^4 times. Fig. 3a shows the situation when $d = 5$.

When each node has 4 services ($s = 4$), the network requires larger Bloom filters to contain more information. The results show that for $d = 3$, the proper range of λ/μ is (0. 1, 100); for $d = 10$, the proper range of λ/μ is (0.8, 1.6). Fig. 3b shows the result when $d = 5$.

We found that in practical situations the Bloom filter algorithm has a better performance. Therefore, it is a promising algorithm for mobile ad hoc networks. Note that the axes in Fig. 3 are represented in log scale.

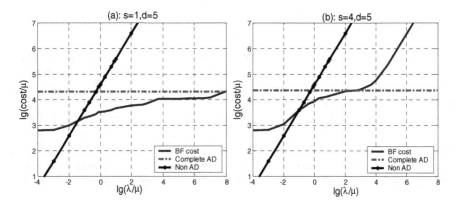

Fig. 3. Performance results for λ/μ when $s = 1$ (a) and $s = 4$ (b)

4.3 Experiment 3

With a larger search range (larger d), there are more context information types available within the range. On the other hand, a larger d also leads to larger Bloom filter. In this set of experiments, we would like to see the impact of d.

We set the depth of the Bloom filter, d, from 3 to 10, and compare the performance with different values of s and λ (fixed $\mu = 0.1$). The results show that, in general, the

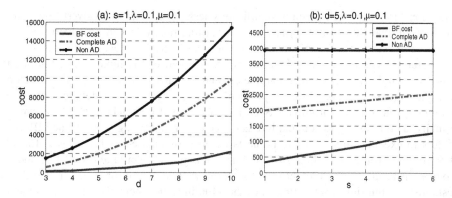

Fig. 4. when $\lambda = 0.1$: (a) impact from change of d ($s = 1$); (b) impact from change of s ($d = 5$)

Bloom filter algorithm has better performance than complete and non-advertisement algorithms. There is a limit to the number of services and the query rate for which the algorithm has the best performance. When exceeding that limit, the performance of Bloom filter becomes worse. When the number of services within the range (this depends on both d and s) and the query rate is quite high, the cost of using the Bloom filter algorithm increases significantly. For instance, this happens when $s = 4$, $\lambda = 1$, and $d > 7$. Fig. 4a shows the curve when $s = 1$, $\lambda = 0.1$.

4.4 Experiment 4

From the experiment above, we find that the number of services per node also has some influence on the network cost. In this set of experiments, we would like to investigate it in detail. We do this for fixed d and λ. The results show that s has some influence from s, but not much. When s increases from 1 to 6, i.e., the number of context sources increases from 0.0007 to 0.0042 per m^2, a Bloom filter still gives the best result among three alternative algorithms. The network cost of using a Bloom filter increases only a little bit faster for than the complete advertisement algorithm. We can expect the Bloom filter algorithm to perform worse when s is really large, which will seldom happen in reality (for given d and λ). Fig. 4b shows the curve for three alternative algorithms when $d = 5$, $\lambda = 0.1$.

5 Conclusions and Further Work

The use of attenuated Bloom filters for advertising available context types in ad-hoc networks is very promising. Results obtained from the model presented in this paper reveal the combined cost of advertising and doing unsuccessful queries due to false positives. There exists a proper size of Bloom filters to achieve optimal network cost. The performance of Bloom filters also highly depends on the ratio of query and advertisement rates, and query range of nodes. Density of network context information sources also has some influences. For a fully distributed ad hoc network in practical situations, this approach requires significantly less traffic load than advertising a full map of all available context types, or broadcasting queries when no advertisements are used. As such, it is a very promising compromise between these two extremes.

Future research should include further refinement of the model, e.g., finding a more thorough investigation of parameters and scenarios. A next step is to develop the idea further, by specifying a protocol, and testing this in a detailed, discrete event simulator and/or prototype. Security issues are also subject to future research. Finally, an interesting idea to explore is to use the broadcasting of attenuated Bloom filters to execute directed route requests (instead of undirected broadcasts) for ad hoc routing protocols such as AODV. Such an approach would allow ad-hoc nodes to establish routes only to other nodes with relevant context information, rather than establishing multiple routes first, and then finding out where the relevant context information is.

Acknowledgements

This work is part of the Freeband AWARENESS project (http:// awareness.freeband.nl). Freeband is sponsored by the Dutch government under contract BSIK 03025. We would also like to thank Patrick Goering for his helpful comments.

References

1. Jeroen Hoebeke, Ingrid Moerman, Bart Dhoedt, Piet Demeester, "Anaylsis of Decentralized Resource and Service Discovery Mechanisms in Wireless Multi-hop Networks", *Third International Conference, Wired/Wireless Internet Communications 2005 Xanthi*, Greece, May 2005, Proceedings.
2. R. Marin-Perianu, P. H. Hartel, J. Scholten, "A Classification of Service Discovery Protocols", *Centre for Telematics and Information Technology, Univ. of Twente, The Netherlands*, Technical report nr. TR-CTIT-05-25, June 2005.
3. E.Guttman, C. Perkins, J. Veizades, M. Day, "Service Location Protocol version 2", *IETF, RFC 2608*, June 1999.
4. Bluetooth Consortium, "Specification of Bluetooth System Core Version 1.0b: Part e, Service Discovery Protocol (SDP)", November 1999.
5. Knarig Arabshian, Henning Schulzrinne, "GloServ: Global Service Discovery Architecture", *MobiQuitous*, pages 319-325, IEEE Computer Society, June 2004.
6. Diapanjan Chakraborty, Anupam Joshi, Tim Finin, Yelena Yesha, "GSD: a Novel Group-based Service Discovery Protocol for MANETs", *4th IEEE Conference on Mobile and Wireless Communication Networks (MWCN)*, September 2002.
7. Sun Microsystems, "Jini Architecture Specification Version 2.1", Nov 2005.
8. Burton H. Bloom, "Space/Time Trade-offs in Hash Coding with Allowable Errors", *Communications of the ACM 13(7)*: 422-426.
9. Andrei Broder, Michael Mitzenmacher, "Network Applications of Bloom Filters: A Survey", *Internet Math 1(2003)*, no.4, 485-509.
10. S. E. Czerwinski, B. Y. Zhao, T. D. Hodes, A. D. Joseph, R. H. Katz, "An Architecture for a Secure Service Discovery Service", In *Proc. Of MobiCom-99*, pages 24-35, N. Y., August 1999.

11. E. Papapetrou, E. Pitoura, and K. Lillis, "Speeding –up Cache Lookups in Wireless Ad-Hoc Routing Using Bloom Filters", *the 16th Annual International Symposium on Personal Indoor and Mobile Radio Communications (PIMRC 2005)*, Sept 11-13, 2005, Berlin, Germany, 2005.

12. J. Liu, F. Sailhan, D. Sacchetti, V. Issarny. "Group Management for Mobile Ad hoc Networks: Design, Implementation and Experiment", in *Proceedings of the 6th IEEE International Conference on Mobile Data Management (MDM'2005)*, May 2005.

13. Yi-an Huang, Wenke Lee, "Hotspot-Based Traceback for Mobile Ad Hoc Networks"., in *Proceedings of the ACM Workshop on Wireless Security (WiSe'05)*, September 2005.

14. Fei Liu, Geert Heijenk, "Context Discovery Using Attenuated Bloom Codes: Model Description and Validation", Technical Report University of Twente, TR-CTIT-06-09, ISSN 1381-3625, March 2006.

15. James F. Kurose, Keith W. Ross, "Computer Networking: A Top-Down Approach Featuring the Internet*", Addison Wesley Longman, Inc.* ISBN 0 2-1 47711 4, 2001.

A Cluster-Label-Based Mechanism for Backbones on Mobile Ad Hoc Networks

Vitaly Li[1], Hong Seong Park[2], and Hoon Oh[3]

[1,2] Department of Electrical and Computer Engineering, Kangwon National University
192-1 Hyoja 2 Dong, Chuncheon, 200-701, Korea
vitaly@control.kangwon.ac.kr, hspark@kangwon.ac.kr
[3] Deptartment of Electrical and Computer Engineering, University of Ulsan, Korea
hoonoh@ulsan.ac.kr

Abstract: This paper presents the Cluster-label-based mechanism for Backbones (CLaB) used in mobile ad hoc networks. The proposed mechanism provides a distributed topology control and consists of three parts: the part creating a backbone, the routing part, and the maintenance part on the backbone. The first part creates a clustered topology using a unique ID called a cluster label and establishes connections between neighboring clusters to create a backbone. The second part adapts existing routing protocols on the backbone. The third part maintains links on the backbone to minimize the influence of node movements, and needs no rerouting mechanism. The mechanism especially concentrates on maintenance by introducing constantly connected backbone elements based on cluster labels. A comparison with other backbone-based mechanisms is presented featuring different node densities and mobility levels. The results validate the effectiveness of the proposed mechanism.

1 Introduction

Multi-hop wireless ad hoc networks consisting of mobile hosts are receiving significant attention from both researchers and application developers. Hosts forming an ad hoc network take equal responsibility in maintaining networking functions. Every host provides a routing service to deliver messages to remote destinations. Because wireless ad hoc networks do not rely on fixed infrastructure and centralized administration, they have broad applications in volatile environments such as battlefields and disaster relief situations.

In ad hoc networks, a channel is usually shared by many hosts. This sharing introduces some problems such as increased complexity of route discovery and reduction of network performance. To cope with these problems, topology control is used in ad hoc networks, where it consists of three parts: formation, maintenance, and routing, to be explained later. Note that topology control optimizes network topology and reduces routing cost by restricting the links among pairs of hosts. If an ad hoc network were to be represented as a graph G = (V, E), in which V is the host set and E is the set of links between hosts, the initial graph would be heavily connected [1]. Topology control removes unnecessary links from the initial graph and then builds a connected

T. Braun et al. (Eds.): WWIC 2006, LNCS 3970, pp. 26–36, 2006.

subgraph with fewer links, which enables efficient routing. The subgraph is called a backbone. The node that is not included in the backbone has, in its neighboring nodes, at least one node that is in the backbone. That is, all the nodes in the network are connected through the backbone.

It is desirable to form a small backbone to save more energy, which is one of the important factors considered in ad hoc networks. The problem of constructing a backbone with a minimum number of nodes is equivalent to finding the Minimum Connected Dominating Set of a graph. This problem has been proven to be NP-complete even when the complete network topology is available [1]. In ad hoc networks, node movement and the high cost of transferring information across the whole network make it impractical to use a centralized algorithm for backbone construction. Thus, many distributed algorithms have been proposed [2-6].

A kind of distributed algorithm forms a backbone through network-wide negotiations among all nodes in an ad hoc network, where nodes decide to join or quit a backbone mostly based on their observation of the nearby topology change [2-4]. In SPAN [4], a node joins the backbone if it has two neighbors that are not connected either directly or through a third node. A similar idea was also explored and proven correct in [2]. GAF [3] constructs the backbone based on the geographic location of the nodes. Algorithms based on network-wide negotiations require extensive exchange of control messages, however, to obtain information on the existing backbone. Considering that the process of backbone formation has to be executed periodically, network performance decreases drastically for high-mobility networks.

Another type of algorithm builds a backbone based on connections of clusterheads [5-6], which are selected according to local conditions such as the node ID, the node degree, received-signal strength variations, the power level, and the speed at which the nodes are moving. The clusterheads then choose their neighbors as gateways to connect with other clusterheads. The backbone is built using clusterheads and gateways. The drawback of this type of algorithm is that a cluster is highly dependent on the positions of the clusterheads. The movement of a clusterhead breaks the backbone due to the invalidation of the cluster.

Most studies on distributed topology control mechanisms deal mainly with the creation of a backbone but hardly with its maintenance, which has many effects on network performance. In previous studies, the creation of a backbone takes a significant amount of time compared with the typical time required for backbone maintenance.

This paper proposes a distributed mechanism called CLaB (Cluster-Label-based mechanism for Backbones) on mobile ad hoc networks. It uses the clustering approach in the generation and maintenance of a backbone. A unique and virtual ID is assigned to each cluster, which is called a cluster label in this paper, upon the cluster's creation to distinguish it from other clusters. The backbone maintenance mechanism is proposed to keep connections between neighboring clusters without changing cluster labels. The routes are constructed on the basis of cluster labels rather than node IDs. Therefore, a route is valid for as long as the connections between the clusters involved in the route are valid.

The rest of this paper is organized as follows. Section 2 presents an overview of CLaB. Section 3 describes the mechanism in detail. Section 4 presents the CLaB performance measures. The concluding remarks are given in Section 5.

2 Overview of Cluster-Label-Based Backbone

For each node in a network, the following are supposed to hold: every node has the same transmission range, and therefore, the links are bidirectional; the nodes are not aware of location, and the distribution of the nodes is uniform.

In CLaB, the backbone is formed in a manner similar to the one introduced by CBRP [5]. A coordinator, called a clusterhead, is selected, according to local conditions, in the lowest ID among the one-hop neighbors at the first creation of the cluster. CBRP has a serious problem, though: the movement of a clusterhead breaks the backbone and then invalidates the cluster itself. To cope with this problem, CLaB uses the unique identifier of the cluster called the cluster label, which consists of the lowest ID used at the first creation of the cluster and the counter number. The counter provides uniqueness to the cluster label in case one node creates a new cluster several times, and prevents duplication of the cluster label used. Note that the counter is incremented by one whenever the same node becomes a clusterhead upon the creation of a cluster. Once a cluster label is generated, it is not changed for as long as at least one member exists in the cluster, even though the clusterhead has moved out. In this last case, a new clusterhead is selected without changing the cluster label. The selection of a new clusterhead is made based on the preservation of the connections with neighboring clusters. This situation is illustrated in Fig. 1.

In Fig. 1(a), 20 nodes are grouped into three clusters (1.1, 2.1 and 3.1) with nodes 1, 2 and 3 as the clusterheads, respectively. Cluster 1.1 has connections with clusters 2.1 and 3.1 through gateway nodes 4 and 12, respectively. Cluster 2.1 and cluster 3.1 have connections with clusters 1.1 and 3.1 through gateway nodes 4 and 8, and with clusters 1.1 and 2.1 through gateway nodes 8 and 12, respectively. Consider the following situation: assume that node 1 (the clusterhead of cluster 1.1) moves and loses its connections with 2.1 and/or 3.1 [Fig. 1(b)]. In other words, node 1 is no longer operating as the clusterhead. In this case, a new clusterhead for cluster 1.1 should be selected. The clustering algorithm should select a node that would be able to support connections with clusters 2.1 and 3.1. From this viewpoint, node 15 becomes the new clusterhead of cluster 1.1, preserving the cluster label and keeping connections with clusters 2.1 and 3.1. Next, assume that nodes 1 and 18 moved and at some point detected that no clusterheads are in the transmission range. Since all nodes should be members of a cluster, nodes 1 and 18 will start clustering. Node 1, being the node with the lowest ID, becomes the clusterhead of the new cluster and should generate and propagate the cluster label. As previously mentioned, since node 1 already generated a cluster once (cluster 1.1), it increases the counter by one and generates a new cluster label, 1.2 [Fig. 1(c)]. Node 18 associates itself with cluster label 1.2 as a member of the cluster. Similarly, nodes 3, 4 and 5 now have direct links with the clusterheads of more than one cluster and play the roles of gateways.

The crux of this approach lies in that cluster label slowly changes against node mobility. Thus, if cluster labels are used instead of node IDs for routing information, the advantage is obvious since the routes are much less dependent on node movement.

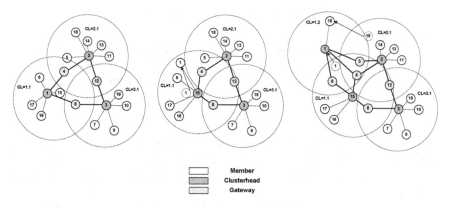

Fig. 1. Illustration of CLaB

3 Cluster-Label-Based Mechanism for Backbone

The Cluster-label-based mechanism for Backbones (CLaB) consists of the formation part, the routing part, and the maintenance part. The formation part is executed when a backbone is initially constructed and orphan nodes want to join the backbone constructed. The routing part utilizes the existing routing protocols such as DSR [7] and DSDV [8]. Note that the routing part provides paths between clusters rather than from one node to another. The maintenance part reconstructs and/or repairs both the backbone and the cluster itself.

Considering the node's role from the viewpoint of the backbone, every node has one of three states: Orp, ChB, or CMB, which means Orphan, Clusterhead-constructing Backbone, and Cluster Member included in ChB, respectively. Fig. 2 shows the state diagram of a node. The initial state of each node is Orp. Periodically, nodes exchange "Hello" messages to collect local information such as the neighbor list and the list of connections with other clusters. Note that the neighbor list contains the IDs and states of the neighboring nodes. The node with the lowest ID among the neighbor Orphan nodes becomes the clusterhead and enters the ChB state. In other words, the clusterhead is first selected. Then it transmits a "Hello" message to its neighboring nodes. Upon receiving the "Hello" message from the clusterhead, each of the orphan nodes joins the clusterhead to form a new cluster, and enters the CMB state. In cases in which a node in the CMB state does not receive a "Hello" message from a clusterhead within a given interval, the node's state should transit to Orp. CLaB defines a special control message, called "UpdateState," for maintenance purposes. The "UpdateState" message is sent only to the node that is the clusterhead or that is going to replace the clusterhead. Whenever a node in the ChB state receives an "UpdateState" message from a node in the CMB state, it should enter into the CMB state. Note that when a node in the CMB state sends an "UpdateState" message, it should enter into the ChB state to become a clusterhead. Therefore, one clusterhead exists at any time in any given cluster. It is assumed that the network is configured

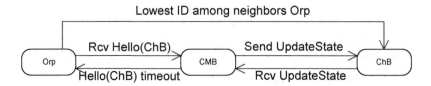

Fig. 2. CLaB state diagram of node

properly so that the time duration of the clusterhead replacement will not exceed the time the clusterhead will take to leave the cluster. This means that there should be no direct transition from the ChB state to the Orp state. This assumption is thought to be general.

The detailed operations are shown in Figs. 3-4, which are written in SDL (System Description Language) [10]. Fig. 3 shows an algorithm for the formation part, which is operating in Orp. In general, backbone formation can take a significant amount of time. In CLaB, however, the formation algorithm is executed only once during the initial construction of the backbone. Therefore, the time required for this part is very short compared to the total time the backbone is maintained. The formation part is based on exchanges of "Hello" messages. After obtaining local information on neighboring nodes, the node with the lowest ID among the neighbors and that does not belong to any cluster becomes a clusterhead (ChB). The formation algorithm does not require acknowledgments from members of the cluster. Therefore, the algorithm ends as soon as the last clusterhead is selected.

Fig. 4 shows the processes that take place in the maintenance part from the point of view of a clusterhead (ChB) and a cluster member (CMB), respectively. Whenever a ChB recognizes that any connection with neighboring ChBs is lost, it tries to give up its ChB role by sending an "UpdateState" message with both the list of previous connections and the list of current connections. The ChB waits for the "UpdateState" message from the CMBs to confirm the replacement. If such message is received, the ChB changes its status to CMB. Otherwise, the ChB keeps its status. The process is shown in Fig. 4(a).

To make clusterhead replacement possible, every node must collect information on connections with neighboring clusters. Such information consists of the list of nodes that are within the transmission range of the node and that simultaneously belong to another cluster. By comparing the list of connections from incoming messages with the list of potential connections, the node decides whether or not it will replace the ChB. If it decides to do so, it enters the ChB state and sends an "UpdateState" message. This process is shown in Fig. 4(b).

From the formation part, the cluster label is generated, spreads among the cluster members, and is not changed since. In the case of clusterhead replacement, the new clusterhead should keep the cluster label, which provides stability to the constructed backbone. It should be noticed; that since clusterheads are replaced without needs for reclustering, the initial choice of clusterheads does not affect the power consumption and the performance of the network.

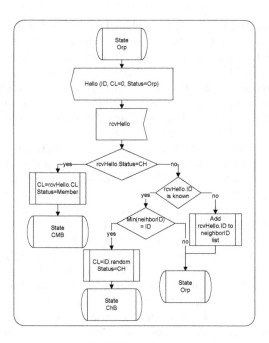

Fig. 3. Formation

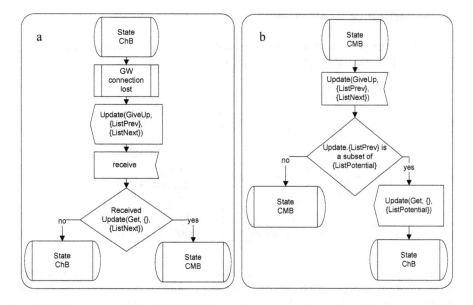

Fig. 4. Maintenance

The routing part can use one of two approaches: the CLaB with reactive routing (CLaB-RR) and CLaB with global view (CLaB-GV). The CLaB-RR is based on the

DSR [7] algorithm and the CLaB-GV is based on DSDV [8] algorithm. Initial route establishment is the same for both approaches. Whenever a route to a remote node is needed, the RREQ, with the source node's ID and the destination node's ID, is sent to source's clusterhead. The clusterhead then discovers the route by forwarding the RREQ to clusterheads of neighbor clusters. The process is repeated, until the cluster of the destination node is found. Upon receiving the RREQ, the destination node sends RREP back to source node using reversed route in the following form: {sourceID, sourceCL, CL1, CL2, ..., destCL, destID}, in which sourceID and destID are IDs of source and destination nodes, respectively; sourceCL and destCL are the cluster labels of source and destination clusters, respectively; and CL1, CL2, ... are cluster labels of intermediate clusters. Since the impact of the nodes' movement on the connections between the clusters is reduced by the maintenance part of CLaB, route repair mechanism is applied only on the source and the destination nodes. As soon as the destination node changed its cluster and cluster label, it should have notified the clusterhead of the previous cluster. The clusterhead of the previous cluster would send notification to the source node using the reverse route, and the source node would decide whether to use the updated route or discover a new one. If a new route is discovered for CLaB-RR, the DSR algorithm is used to discover the route from source cluster to destination cluster, issuing the clusterRREQ by source clusterhead. In CLaB-GV, clusterheads periodically exchanges their lists of current connections. Therefore, having knowledge of entire cluster network by any clusterhead, the route to new destination cluster would be obtained immediately.

4   Performance Evaluation

To evaluate the performance of the proposed mechanism, simulations were made in ns2-2.26 [9]. Table 1 shows the general parameters for simulations.

Table 1. Simulation parameters

Space	1000x1000 m^2
Simulation time	600s
Traffic	CBR, 10pkt/s
Packet size	512bytes
Mobility	Random Waypoint
Transmission range	250m
Bandwidth	11mbit/s
Number of sources	60% of nodes

Fig. 5 shows the relationship between delivery ratio and pause time for a maximum node speed of 20 m/s. Both CLaB based routing protocols show about 15% more delivery ratio compared with CBRP, in case of the constant mobility, which is equivalent to pause time of zero. As the pause time increases, the performance gap is slightly reduced. However, even in case of near-static network that corresponds to the pause time of 600s equal to simulation time, it shows that the CLaB-based routing outperforms the CBRP by almost 10%.

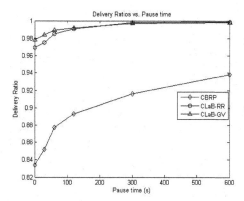

Fig. 5. Delivery ratios vs. Pause time

Figure 6 shows the delivery ratios vs. the density of the network for a high speed rate of 20 m/s. Similarly, the CLaB based routing protocols shows up to 30% improvement in delivery ratio over CBRP. As the number of nodes increases, the CLaB-GV that uses a proactive approach achieves higher performance than CLaB-RR and CBRP.

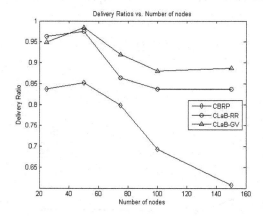

Fig. 6. Delivery ratios vs. Network density

Fig. 7 shows the average lifetime of particularly traced routes according to the change of node speed. The route's lifetime is measured as the interval between route requests for observed pair of nodes. For node speed of 5m/s, the lifetime of routes in CLaB based routing protocols is about 330 seconds while that in CBRP is about 90 seconds. Both protocols show linear dependency on node speed equally; however, the performance gap gets bigger with the increase of node mobility. This result supports the good scalability and stability of the CLaB based protocol.

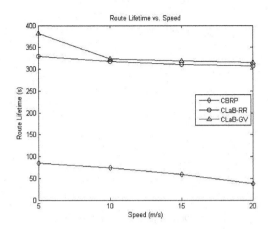

Fig. 7. Average route's lifetime vs. Node speed

Fig. 8 shows the normalized routing overhead vs. the number of nodes in the network for a high speed rate of 20 m/s. With an increasing number of nodes, the overhead in the CLaB-based routing algorithms is changes slower than in CBRP routing algorithms. Since CLaB-based routing shows a long lifetime of routes, the routing overhead remains almost the same and does not depend on the density of the network.

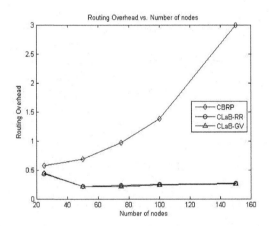

Fig. 8. Routing Overhead vs. Number of nodes

Fig. 9 shows the normalized routing overhead vs. the speed of the nodes for a 50-node network. In this case, the normalized routing overhead increases with the speed in all protocols. Since CLaB-based routing is less dependent on the location of the node the normalized overhead increases slightly. The difference between CBRP and CLaB-based routing algorithms increases with speed.

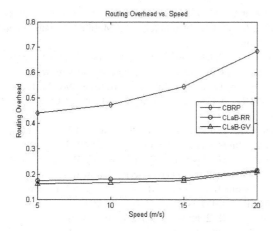

Fig. 9. Routing Overhead vs. Speed

Figs. 5-9 show that CLaB-GV provides slightly better performance than CLaB-RR.

5 Conclusions

In this paper, the Cluster Label based mechanism for Backbone (CLaB) and the related routing protocols has been proposed for mobile ad hoc networks. The proposed mechanism provides a distributed topology control and consists of three key functions: the function creating a backbone, the routing function, and the maintenance function on the backbone. The creation of the clustered topology includes assigning a unique cluster label to each cluster. The CLaB minimizes affects of clusterhead movement by preserving cluster labels among all cluster members. This is the important characteristic of the CLaB. Various types of existing routing algorithms can be easily applied to the constructed backbone. The fact that the cluster label is not changed with time makes routes more stable and reliable, where the routes are based on cluster labels. The simulations show that CLaB provides better delivery ratio and lifetime for long-term connections than CBRP even in cases of the network with high mobility and/or dense network. It is worth nothing that the proactive CLaB-GV protocol provides better performance than the other reactive protocols, even in case of high node mobility and high node density.

References

1. Liu, H., and Gupta, R. Selective backbone construction for topology control. In 1st IEEE International Conference on Mobile Ad-hoc and Sensor Systems (MASS) (2004).
2. J. Wu and H. Li, "On calculating connected dominating set for efficient routing in ad hoc wireless networks," Workshop on Discrete Algorithms and Methods for MOBILE Computing and Communications, pages 7-14, 1999.

3. Y. Xu, J. S. Heidemann, and D. Estrin, "Geography-informed energy conservation for Ad Hoc routing," ACM International Conference on Mobile Computing and Networks (Mobi-Com), pages 70-84, July 2001.

4. B. Chen, K. Jamieson, H. Balakrishnan, and R. Morris, "Span: an energy-efficient coordination algorithm for topology maintenance in ad hoc wireless networks," ACM Intl. Conf. on Mobile Computing and Networking (MobiCom), pages 85-96, 2001.

5. Jiang Mingliang, CBRP: A Cluster Based Routing Protocol for Mobile Ad Hoc Networks, Globecom, 1999

6. Chiang C.-C., Wu H.-K., Liu W., Gerla M., "Routing in Clustered Multihop, Mobile Wireless Networks with Fading Channel", SICON'97, April 1997.

7. Johnson, Maltz and Hu. The Dynamic Source Routing Protocol for Mobile Ad Hoc Networks (DSR). draft-ietf-manet-dsr-09.txt, Internet Draft, IETF, April 2003. 8. C.E. Perkins, "Highly Dynamic Destination-Sequenced Distance-Vector Routing (DSDV) for Mobile Computers", ACM SIGCOMM'94, pages 234-244, 1994

8. The network simulator – NS-2, http://www.isi.edu/nsnam/ns.

9. Andreas Mitschele-Thiel, "System Engineering with SDL", John Wiley & Sons LTD., 2000.

Comprehensive Analytical Models to Evaluate the TCP Performance in 802.11 WLANs

Boris Bellalta[1], Michela Meo[2], and Miquel Oliver[1]

[1] Universitat Pompeu Fabra, Spain
boris.bellalta@upf.edu, miquel.oliver@upf.edu
[2] Politecnico di Torino, Italy
michela.meo@polito.it

Abstract. The interaction between TCP flows and the IEEE 802.11 MAC protocol is analyzed in this paper. The goal is to provide comprehensive models capable of predicting the TCP performance (throughput) in WLAN Hot-Spot networks with persistent elastic flows. A model of the IEEE 802.11 MAC protocol is first introduced and validated through simulations. Using the MAC model as a basis, we then analyze several modeling strategies to catch the main interactions between TCP and MAC protocols. Results obtained from the models are compared among themselves and against simulations, and show the accuracy and the superior simplicity of the proposed models with respect to previously published work.

1 Introduction

WLAN cells (or hot-spots) based on the IEEE 802.11 technology [1] are deployed massively in business or public areas. Na et al. [2] analyze the traffic composition of several hot-spots. The authors report that more than 90% of the total traffic is TCP-based, mainly due to HTTP transactions; however, it is remarkable the presence of peer-to-peer (P2P) traffic, which reaches values higher than those obtained by the email or FTP services. Another interesting observation is the asymmetry of the traffic flows, where 85% of the total go from the fixed network to mobile nodes (downlink) and the remaining 15%, which is a significant value, from mobile nodes to the fixed network (uplink).

Currently, some papers address the issue of analytically modeling TCP in WLAN networks. Basically, for the downlink direction, Bruno et al. [3], Miorandi et al. [4] and Lebeugle et al. [5] present several models to compute the WLAN throughput but with similar theoretical basis. In the uplink direction, a model is presented by Leith et al. [6] with also similar applicability. For what concerns TCP flows simultaneously active in both directions, Pilosof et al. [7] explain the major observed phenomena but, to the best of our knowledge, the only work which treats it analytically is presented by Bruno et al. [8] under the assumption that the TCP advertisement window is equal to one.

This paper propose simple MAC/TCP models and shows how they accurately predict TCP performance over WLANs (results are validated against simulation

T. Braun et al. (Eds.): WWIC 2006, LNCS 3970, pp. 37–48, 2006.
© Springer-Verlag Berlin Heidelberg 2006

and real data). The models have been developed to provide fast estimation of the TCP throughput when solving resource scheduling problems in WLANs. However, the model can be also used by hot-spot operators to estimate the TCP achievable bandwidth for different MAC parameters configurations of their Access Points (APs) or Mobile Nodes (MNs).

2   A Hot-Spot Wireless Scenario

The considered scenario is a WLAN cell with a single AP providing access to a fixed network to n MNs. The MNs and the AP use the DCF (Distributed Coordination function) of the IEEE 802.11 MAC and the DSSS PHY specifications in the 2.4 GHz band [1]. The system parameters are reported in Table 1. We assume ideal channel conditions, i.e., no packet is lost due to channel errors or the hidden terminal phenomenon. The fixed network is modeled by a simple 100 $Mbps$ full duplex link with a propagation delay of $\delta = 2\ ms$ in each direction. This link is used to interconnect a fixed node (server) where one end-point of the traffic flows resides. The other end-points are in the MNs, which are linked to the server through the access point.

Table 1. System Parameters of IEEE 802.11b (DSSS) specification [1]

Parameter	Value	Parameter	Value
R_{data}	11 $Mbps$	R_{basic}	2 $Mbps$
DIFS	50 μs	CW_{min}	32
SIFS	10 μs	CW_{max}	1024
SLOT (σ)	20 μs	m	5
EIFS	212 μs	ACK	112 $bits$ @ R_{basic}
RTS	160 $bits$ @ R_{basic}	CTS	112 $bits$ @ R_{basic}
MAC header	240 $bits$ @ R_{data}	MAC FCS	32 $bits$ @ R_{data}
PLCP preamble	144 $bits$ @ R_{basic}	PLCP header	48 $bits$ @ R_{basic}
Retry Limit (R)	7	Q (Queue length)	50 $packets$

3   A Model of the IEEE 802.11 MAC Layer

Bianchi [9] provides a model of the DCF under saturation conditions, i.e., all stations compete always and continuously to transmit a packet to the channel. In this situation, the assumption of independence among MNs and of equal and constant collision probability for all stations, simplifies the mathematical complexity and provides an impressive good accuracy. The main limitations of the Bianchi's model are the lack of applicability in real scenarios (which normally work under non-saturation conditions), the difficulties to provide user-level metrics and the complexity to parameterize the model when the MNs are not exactly equal (different frame lengths, heterogeneous transmission rates, etc.). To cope with these limitations, we propose a simple user-centric model where each MN is modeled by a finite length queue with network-dependent service time. When the MN i is active, it carries a traffic flow with bandwidth B_i bps and an average packet length of L_i bits which gives an arrival rate of λ_i packets, assuming that the packet arrival process is Poisson and the service time is exponentially distributed. This last assumption is clearly non realistic but allows us to model each node by a simple $M/M/1/Q_i$ queue, obtaining simple expressions to measure the quality of service observed by a node in terms of blocking probability, average queue length and average transmission delay (including the service time),

$$P_{b,i} = \frac{\nu_i^{Q_i}}{\sum_{j=0}^{Q_i} \nu_i^j} \qquad EQ_i = \frac{\sum_{j=0}^{Q_i} j\nu_i^j}{\sum_{j=0}^{Q_i} \nu_i^j} \qquad ED_i = \frac{EQ_i}{\lambda_i(1 - P_{b,i})} \qquad (1)$$

where ν_i is the offered traffic load and $P_{b,i}$ the packet blocking probability. Another important question to be addressed is the distribution of the number of MNs that have a packet ready to be transmitted, thus competing to access the channel. Under the assumption of independence among nodes and Poisson packet arrival process, the distribution of the number of instantaneous backlogged nodes can be modeled by a binomial probability distribution with parameter ρ_i (steady state probability that the queue contains at least a packet). A MN attempts to transmit in a given slot with steady state probability

$$\tau_i = \frac{E[Pr(Q_i(t) > 0)]}{EB_i + 1} = \frac{\rho_i}{EB_i + 1} \qquad (2)$$

where EB_i is the average number of slots selected by node i at each transmission attempt. For the computation of EB_i we have also assumed that at each attempt, the MN sees a constant conditional collision probability p_i. Obviously, this is a simple approximation, since we do not model the existent correlation among the instantaneous queue occupation of each node, the instantaneous backoff stage and collision probability. In order to address these issues refer to [10]. The service time, i.e., the time interval from the instant in which a packet enters in service until it is completely transmitted or discarded, is given by,

$$X_i = (M - 1)\left(EB_i\alpha_i + ET_{c,i}^{ba||rts}\right) + EB_i\alpha_i + T_{s,i} \qquad (3)$$

where M is the average number of transmissions, α_i is the average slot duration and $ET_{c,i}$ is the average duration of a collision of node i where we neglect the fact that more than two packets collide simultaneously. Note that if the RTS/CTS access scheme is used, $ET_{c,i}^{rts}$ is constant and equal for all nodes. The average number of transmissions that a packet undergoes is computed under the decoupling or independence assumption as,

$$M = \frac{1 - p_i^{R_i+1}}{1 - p_i} \qquad (4)$$

A node frozes its backoff counter every time the channel is sensed busy and releases it after the channel is sensed free for a $DIFS$ period. Therefore, the time between two backoff counter decrements is a random variable which depends on the behavior of the other nodes. By letting α_i be the average time between two backoff counter decrements, or equivalently, the average slot duration, we have

$$\alpha_i = p_{e,i}\sigma + p_{s,i}(ET_{s,i}^{ba||rts,*} + \sigma) + p_{c,i}(ET_{c,i}^{ba||rts,*} + \sigma) \qquad (5)$$

where $ET_{s,i}^{ba||rts,*}$ and $ET_{c,i}^{ba||rts,*}$ are the average durations of an observed successful transmission or a collision for node i when it is performing a backoff instance. The probabilities $p_{e,i}$, $p_{s,i}$ and $p_{c,i}$ are related to the channel status in a given slot when a node is in backoff: $p_{e,i}$ is the probability that a slot is observed empty, $p_{s,i}$ the probability that in a slot a successful transmission occurs and $p_{c,i}$ is the probability that a collision occurs. Note that at the end of a successful transmission or a collision we add the duration of an empty slot, since the backoff counter is only decreased after the channel is sensed empty for the full duration of a slot. These channel probabilities can be computed as

$$p_{e,i} = \prod_{j \neq i}(1 - \tau_j) \quad p_{s,i} = \sum_{z \neq i}\tau_z \prod_{j \neq z \neq i}(1 - \tau_j) \quad p_{c,i} = 1 - p_{e,i} - p_{s,i} \qquad (6)$$

A more detailed explanation of this model, including the computation of the different frame durations, can be found in [11].

3.1 Model Validation

In order to validate the model and analyze the performance of the IEEE 802.11 MAC protocol, we consider a single-hop ad hoc scenario with three different types of flows whose characteristics are summarized in Table 2. The network comprises n nodes where each one uses the BA access scheme and carries a single traffic flow. We refer to streaming (non-saturated) type 1 and streaming (non-saturated) type 2 flows with $S1$ and $S2$, respectively; and we use $E1$ to refer to elastic (saturated) flows. In this example, the values of $R_{data} = 2$ Mbps and $R_{basic} = 1$ Mbps are considered.

Table 2. Traffic Profiles

Traffic Flow	Bandwidth	Frame Length	Retry Limit
elastic (E1)	max.available	1540 Bytes	7
streaming type 1 (S1)	100 Kbps	400 Bytes	7
streaming type 2 (S2)	250 Kbps	700 Bytes	7

Analytical results are compared against simulations performed using the ns-2 package [12] and a simulator of the IEEE 802.11 MAC protocol which has been developed using the COST (Component Oriented Simulation Toolkit) simulation package [13]. Our simulator provides equivalent results to ns-2 but allowing a higher flexibility to monitor the dynamics and values of the MAC parameters.

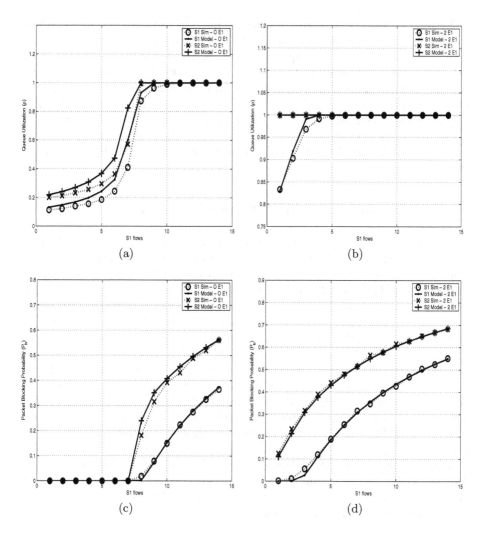

Fig. 1. (a) and (b) Queue utilization, (c) and (d) Blocking Probability

Figure 1 reports the MAC transmission queue utilization and blocking probability for the two streaming traffic classes, showing almost the same behavior and values between simulation and analytical results. Two scenarios are analyzed, with and without elastic (E1) flows. In the first one (sub-figures (a) and (c)) we increase the number of $S1$ flows when in the system there are 2 active $S2$ flows. In the second scenario (sub-figures (b) and (d)) we include also 2 E1 flows. From the plots, we would like to underline that: i) the presence of elastic traffic (TCP-based) in the system causes a clear degradation of the $S1$ and $S2$ performance (their queues saturate earlier) and ii) in both the scenarios, the model captures the point where $S1$ and $S2$ flows fail to achieve their bandwidth requirements.

Notice that, despite the independence assumption and the use of expectations rather than distributions of the involved variables, the model is remarkably accurate. This means that the impact of these approximations on the steady state behavior of the system is limited. The reason for this limited impact may reside in the joint effect of the randomness introduced in the nodes behavior by the access protocol, the backoff mechanism in particular, and the multiplexing of different sources sharing the same radio resources. While an analytical prove of this limited impact is unfeasible, we believe that the comparison of analytical results against results obtained through detailed simulators validates the model.

4   TCP Performance in Hot-Spot WLANs

To evaluate the TCP performance in a Hot-Spot scenario, we use the ns-2 simulator and a real test-bed based on a *Linksys WRT54GS* AP with the *DD-WRT*[1] firmware. The ns-2 simulator is configured to use persistent new-RENO TCP connections and a TCP MSS of 1460 Bytes. As a test-bed, we use the *iperf*[2] tool which allows us to obtain the maximum achievable bandwidth for TCP flows. We compare these results with those obtained by using the model presented in previous section. Both simulation, real and analytical results are derived considering the use of the *RTS/CTS* mechanism. Model and simulation results are evaluated in terms of MAC layer throughput which includes the upper layers overhead, however, test-bed results provide directly the TCP throughput. To clarify the notation, we refer to every parameter related with the AP with the subscript d (downlink) and with the subscript u (uplink) we refer to the parameters of the MNs. The number of elastic flows in the downlink (uplink) will be denoted by $n_{e,d}$ ($n_{e,u}$).

We first consider only $S_{e,d}^{tcp}$ downlink and $S_{e,u}^{tcp}$ uplink TCP flows is shown in Tables 3 and 4. The maximum TCP window size has been fixed to $W = 1$ and $W = 42$ (as it is commonly used in the operative TCP versions [7]).

Two basic system throughput tendencies can be underlined:

- The increment of the number of downlink TCP flows does not reduce the aggregated throughput since TCP reduces the channel contention [3] (the average number of backlogged nodes with feedback traffic is lower than the number of TCP flows).
- As we increase the number of TCP flows in the uplink, the aggregate throughput increases since the TCP window of MNs reaches its maximum value (for $W > 1$) despite packet losses and the starvation of the downlink ACK flow [6].

Some pieces of work previously mentioned show that some unfairness exists among TCP flows in both uplink and downlink directions. We have observed similar results with significant throughput differences among nodes. However,

---

[1] http://www.dd-wrt.org/
[2] http://dast.nlanr.net/Projects/Iperf/

Table 3. ns2 - Aggregate throughput for persistent TCP flows (Mbps)

	W=1				W=42			
	Downlink	Uplink	Bid.		Downlink	Uplink	Bid.	
Flows	$S_{e,d}^{tcp}$	$S_{e,u}^{tcp}$	$S_{e,d}^{tcp}$	$S_{e,u}^{tcp}$	$S_{e,d}^{tcp}$	$S_{e,u}^{tcp}$	$S_{e,d}^{tcp}$	$S_{e,u}^{tcp}$
1	1.690	1.689	1.679	1.680	4.184	4.183	0.762	3.447
2	3.353	3.362	2.060	2.092	4.191	4.789	0.000	4.772
3	3.888	4.022	2.074	2.084	4.191	5.156	0.000	5.201
4	4.121	4.158	2.076	2.083	4.169	5.201	0.000	5.168
6	4.182	4.181	2.081	2.091	4.172	5.195	0.000	5.206
8	4.169	4.170	2.028	2.029	4.191	5.298	0.000	5.155
10	4.179	4.140	1.948	1.779	4.114	5.180	0.000	5.253

Table 4. TestBed - Aggregate throughput for persistent TCP flows (Mbps)

	W=42			
	Downlink	Uplink	Bid.	
Flows	$S_{e,d}^{tcp}$	$S_{e,u}^{tcp}$	$S_{e,d}^{tcp}$	$S_{e,u}^{tcp}$
1	4.20	4.16	0.88	3.38
2	4.11	4.26	0.65	3.65
3	4.10	4.37	–	–

for the sake of simplicity, we assume that all flows share fairly the aggregate throughput, then each flow receives $S_{e,z}^{tcp}/n_{e,z}$ bps, with $z = \{d, u\}$.

4.1 Downlink TCP Flows

In the downlink, TCP flows compete, through the AP, with their own feed-back traffic sent by the MNs. With $W = 1$ and a single TCP flow, there is no competition to access the channel between the AP and the MN because the two nodes never simultaneously have a packet ready to be transmitted at the MAC queue. From Table 3, as the number of simultaneous TCP flows increases, despite keeping $W = 1$, the AP queue tends to have always a packet ready to transmit, which justifies the assumption to model the access point as a saturated queue [3–5], which is obviously confirmed for values of $W > 1$. For each received packet, a MN sends the correspondent ACK (we have not considered the delayed ACKs technique as in [4]). Therefore, the number of ACK packets sent by a MN will be $1/n_{e,d}$ per packet emitted by the AP. To analyze this situation, several approximations can be used.

All sources are saturated (Model A_d). In this model, both the AP and the MNs are considered as saturated with data and ACK packets, respectively. This approximation provides pessimistic results because the level of contention suffered by data packets is very high as the AP has to compete with all the MNs.

A time-scale decomposition (Model B_d) [3–5]. Introduced by [3] and used also by [4, 5], this model computes the distribution of backlogged nodes (the

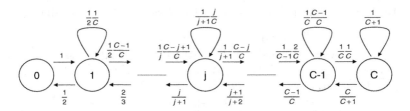

Fig. 2. Discrete Markov Chain describing the evolution of the number of backlogged nodes

probability that $n_{e,d}^b$ of the $n_{e,d}$ MNs are backlogged) and the system throughput is computed averaging the throughput obtained with $n_{e,d}^b$ saturated nodes for $n_{e,d}^b = 0 \ldots n_{e,d}$. We suggest a novel variant of this model, where transitions between states are done after any successful transmission in the channel and not only after a successful transmission of the AP as in [3]. In Figure 2 we show the DTMC (Discrete-Time Markov Chain) which governs the average number of backlogged nodes as a function of the number of TCP flows, C. Note that the DTMC changes its state after any successful transmission over the channel, independently on that it has been done by the AP or a MN. The probability to move from state $j-1$ to state j depends on the probability that the AP transmits $(1/j)$ and the probability that the packet was sent to a non-backlogged MN $((C-j+1)/C)$. The probability to remain in the same state j is the probability that the AP transmits $(1/(j+1))$ a packet, which is sent to a backlogged node (j/C). Finally, the probability to move from state j to state $j-1$ is the probability that a backlogged MN transmits $(j/(j+1))$. Note that only one ACK is stored in each MN queue.

Un-correlated ACKs (Model C_d). Finally, the ACK arrival process at the MNs is assumed to be Poisson with rate $\lambda_{ack,u} = \lambda_{e,d}/n_{e,d}$, where $\lambda_{e,d}$ is the maximum packet arrival rate at the AP under saturation assuming that the TCP packets are being distributed uniformly among destination nodes. This model does not consider the inherent correlation among the reception of TCP packets and the generation of ACKs; however, it provides very good results. This is motivated by the randomization caused by the backoff algorithm which mitigates this inherent correlation. It is worth noting that we can model the delayed ACK technique by simply dividing the value of $\lambda_{ack,u}$ by the delayed ACK factor γ, $\lambda_{ack,u} = \lambda_{e,d}/(\gamma \cdot n_{e,d})$.

In Figure 3.(a) the downlink throughput obtained by simulation is compared with the outcomes of the three models previously described. Note how model A_d clearly overestimates the negative effects of the feedback traffic and thus, the throughput obtained is lower than in simulation. Model B_d provides a very good approximation. Finally, model C_d also shows very accurate results, despite the assumption of Poisson arrivals for the ACK packets, that corresponds to assuming that there is no correlation with the reception of TCP data packets. These results allow us to validate our model in this new scenario.

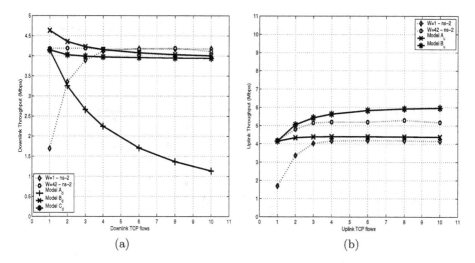

Fig. 3. TCP throughput (Mbps) (a) Downlink (b) Uplink

4.2   Uplink TCP Flows

Several applications need to transmit data from the MN (typically the client) to a node in the fixed network (the server); e.g., files sharing in P2P networks. In this case, TCP flows in the uplink compete among themselves and with the feedback traffic from the AP ACKs.

Leith et al. [6] show the existing unfairness among competing uplink TCP flows and, in order to evaluate their performance, propose an analytical model for the uplink TCP throughput. They address an ACK prioritization scheme at the AP using the EDCA to reduce the inherent asymmetry of the WLAN, which is given by the different access opportunities to transmit TCP data packets. Their model assumes that the MNs are saturated and compute the transmission probability of the AP as the probability that the AP observes a successful transmission in the channel, i.e, $\tau_d = p_{s,d}$, with $p_{s,d}$ computed as in (6). This first model is called Model A_u.

In Figure 3.(b) we compare the results obtained by simulation for $W = 1$ and $W = 42$ with the results obtained by previous Model A_u and an additional model which simply assumes that the AP is also saturated (Model B_u). Both models provide good accuracy.

4.3   Simultaneous Downlink and Uplink TCP Flows

When the AP carries simultaneous downlink / uplink flows, the performance of downlink flows is severely affected, showing values of downlink throughput near 0 when the TCP congestion window is larger than $W = 1$ (Figure 4.(a)). This is caused by the starvation of TCP downlink packets in the AP queue. The AP queue is shared by both ACKs and data packets while the MNs only send either TCP data packets or ACKs (in the system there are $n_{e,u}$ MNs sending TCP

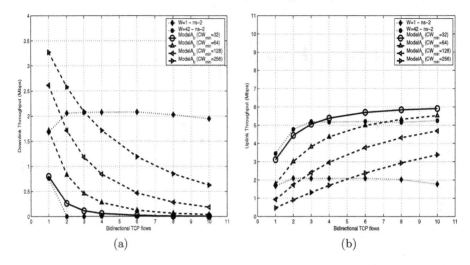

Fig. 4. Throughput comparison with simultaneous TCP downlink/uplink flows (Mbps)

data packets and $n_{e,d}$ sending ACKs). The results confirm those in [7] about the different behavior of the TCP window for the uplink and downlink flows. Pilosof et al. argue that the TCP window for uplink senders reaches the maximum value, even with high ACK losses at the AP buffer, while downlink flows struggle with low window values ($0-2$ packets) caused by frequent timeouts due to data packet drops. Moreover, for $W = 1$, uplink and downlink throughput is the same. This result was also appointed in [8], where it is also showed that by setting $W = 1$ fair access to the channel can be provided to the TCP flows.

Modeling the presence of simultaneous bidirectional flows is very complex due to the interaction in the AP queue of the two types of packets: ACK and TCP downlink data packets. We suggest a simple approximation (Model A_b) which captures the main tendencies observed in the simulations:

- The downlink queue is always saturated. The average packet length transmitted by the AP is computed from $EL_d = \phi_d L_{tcp} + \phi_u L_{ack}$ where ϕ_d and ϕ_u are the probability that a packet sent by the AP is a data or an ACK packet.
- These probabilities are computed from: $\phi_d = 1 - \phi_u$ and $\phi_u = E\tau_{e,u} \cdot n_{e,u}/(E\tau_{e,u}n_{e,u} + \tau_{e,d})$. The $E\tau_{e,u}$ parameter is the MN expected uplink slot transmission probability (considering only the nodes with uplink TCP data packets) and $\tau_{e,d}$ is the AP slot transmission probability.
- MNs with uplink TCP data packets are always saturated.
- Nodes with uplink ACKs have $\lambda_{ack,u} = \lambda_{e,d}/n_{e,d}$, where $\lambda_{e,d} = \phi_d/X_d(EL_d)$.

At the AP queue ACKs controlled by the transmission opportunities of MNs compete with data packets of downlink flows. As the number of uplink flows increases, since MNs have more transmission opportunities than the AP, the number of ACKs in the AP increases. Thus, the downlink flows suffer for both contending for buffer space in the AP, and for contending on the access to the channel, which causes that downlink TCP flows tend to starve. To solve this limitation, a properly MAC parameter tuning can be done, for example increasing the CW_{min} parameter of uplink TCP flows, which reduces their slot transmission probability $\tau_{e,u}$. Results for different values of CW_{min} are also plotted in Figure 4. These results suggest that a cross-layer solution between transport and MAC layer could improve the overall performance.

5 Conclusions

In this paper, we have presented an accurate and flexible model of the IEEE 802.11 MAC protocol. Through the model we can capture and study the TCP protocol behavior in WLAN networks and the interactions between TCP and MAC protocols. The proposed model can be instrumental to the performance evaluation of admission control schemes, and the radio resource dimensioning and management strategies for WLAN hot-spots.

Acknowledgments

This work was partially supported by Catalonian Government under the i2CAT project, Spanish Government under project TIC2003-09279- C02-01, and by the European Commission under NEWCOM NoE. The authors also acknowledge the valuable comments of the anonymous reviewers.

References

1. IEEE Std 802.11; Wireless LAN Medium Access Control (MAC) and Physical Layer (PHY) specifications, IEEE Std 802.11-1999 (Revised 2003).
2. C. Na, J. K. Chen, T. S. Rappaport; Hotspot Traffic Statistics and Throughput Models for Several Applications, IEEE Globecom 2004, Dallas, Texas, USA, November 2004.
3. R. Bruno, M. Conti, E. Gregori; Analytical Modeling of TCP Clients in Wi-Fi Hot Spot Networks, Networking 2004, LNCS 3042, pp. 626-637, 2004.
4. D. Miorandi, A. A. Kherani, E. Altman; A Queuing Model for HTTP Traffic over IEEE 802.11 WLANs, ITC Specialist Seminar on Performance Evaluation of Wireless and Mobile Systems, Antwerp, September 2004.
5. F. Lebeugle, A. Proutire; User-level performance in WLAN hotspots, ITC Specialist Seminar on Performance Challenges for Efficient Next Generation Networks, China, September 2005.
6. D.J. Leith, P.Clifford; Using the 802.11e EDCF to Achieve TCP Upload Fairness over WLAN links, Modeling and Optimization in Mobile, Ad Hoc, and Wireless Networks (WiOpt), Trentino, Italy, 205.
7. S. Pilosof, R. Ramjee, D. Raz, Y. Shavitt, and P. Sinha; Understanding TCP fairness over Wireless LAN, IEEE Infocom, San Francisco, USA, March - April 2003.

8. R. Bruno, M. Conti, E. Gregori; Stochastic Models of TCP Flows over 802.11 WLANs, Technical Report IIT TR-11/2005, CNR-IIT, 2005.
9. G. Bianchi; Performance Analysis of the IEEE 802.11 Distributed Coordination Function, IEEE Journal on Selected Areas in Communications, Vol. **18**, No. 3, March 2000.
10. M. Garetto, C-F. Chiasserini; Performance Analysis of 802.11 WLANs under Sporadic Traffic, Networking 2005, Waterloo-Ontario, Canada, May 2005.
11. B. Bellalta, M. Meo, M. Oliver; Admission Control in IEEE 802.11e EDCA-based WLANs, Technical Document TD(06)12. 5th COST 290 MCM Meeting. Delft, The Netherlands, February 2005.
12. Ns2 Network Simulator, http://www.isi.edu/nsnam/ns/
13. Gilbert (Gang) Chen; Component Oriented Simulation Toolkit, http://www.cs.rpi.edu/~ cheng3/

A Blind Method Towards Performance Improvement of High Performance TCP with Random Losses

Qiang Fu and Grenville Armitage

Centre for Advanced Internet Architectures,
Swinburne University of Technology, Melbourne, VIC 3122, Australia
{qfu, garmitage}@swin.edu.au

Abstract. The deployment of high performance networks and the emergence of broadband wireless access technologies challenge the performance of standard TCP. Recent years have seen a few high performance and aggressive TCP variants being proposed. These TCP variants still suffer significant performance degradation from random/transient packet losses. In this paper, we introduce and evaluate a new method to improve high performance TCP in the presence of random packet losses. It is 'blind' in that our method does not attempt to differentiate between random and congestion-induced losses. Our method combines both TCP parallelisation and modification to the aggressiveness of studied AIMD algorithms. We show that our proposed method is no more aggressive than the studied TCP variants in the presence of congestion but more effectively utilises bandwidth in the presence of random packet losses.

1 Introduction

The future Internet is likely to be dominated by long-distance high-bandwidth links and increased diversity in lossy wireless network access technologies. Standard TCP struggles to achieve optimal utilisation of end-to-end paths that concurrently exhibit high bandwidth-delay product (BDP) and random/transient packet losses.

More recent work has resulted in TCP variants such as Scalable TCP [5], HSTCP [6], HTCP [7], BIC [8], CUBIC [9], etc. These variants increase their congestion window more aggressively in a round-trip time (RTT), release a smaller portion of bandwidth in response to loss events and thus improve overall bandwidth utilisation. For instance, in [1] Barman, etc. show that with a buffer size equal to 20% of the BDP the bandwidth utilisation of HSTCP can be up to 98% (standard TCP requires a larger buffer size for similar utilisation). However, their reliance on loss-driven congestion detection means such TCP variants still suffer from random/transient packet losses.

In this paper, we focus on improving the tolerance of high performance TCP to random packet losses without challenging their underlying loss-driven congestion detection and congestion control mechanisms. We combine TCP parallelisation with modifications to the aggressiveness of high performance TCP's AIMD algorithms. Our approach is 'blind' in that it does not attempt to differentiate between random and congestion-induced losses.

The current author's previous work [10] has demonstrated that TCP parallelisation with multiple TCP connections can improve performance when experiencing various

T. Braun et al. (Eds.): WWIC 2006, LNCS 3970, pp. 49–61, 2006.

packet losses. Use of multiple TCP connections, in conjunction with small amounts of FEC, has been indicated as a useful technique to maximise bandwidth utilisation over wireless links by Barakat, etc. [2]. In [3] and [4], Zhang and Tsaoussidis explored the interrelation of TCP smoothness and responsiveness and studied how TCP behaves by manipulating its AIMD increase and decrease parameters.

To demonstrate our idea we have specifically chosen to evaluate the performance improvement seen by HSTCP, HTCP and BIC when dual connections are established along with modified AIMD aggressiveness. We tune their AIMD parameters such that two parallel connections yield the same level of aggressiveness as a single unmodified high performance TCP connection. Our proposed method is no more aggressive in the presence of congestion but more effectively utilises bandwidth in the presence of random packet losses.

The paper is organised as follows. Section 2 briefly reviews the studied TCP variants. Section 3 outlines our proposed aggressiveness modifications in conjunction with TCP parallelisation. Section 4 introduces the simulation environment. Section 5 presents performance evaluation, and the paper concludes in Section 6.

2   An Overview of High Performance TCP Variants

First we briefly review HSTCP, HTCP and BIC. Although these variants continue to undergo development we believe our review captures the essence of these protocols. We use the term "AIMD" (additive increase multiplicative decrease) in a generic sense - AI to denote AIMD increase parameter (window increment in response to a single ACK) and MD to denote AIMD decrease parameter (window decrement in response to a loss event).

2.1   HSTCP

HSTCP [6] uses the standard AIMD algorithm to probe network capacity when *cwnd* is small, less than a window threshold – *low_window*. However, when *cwnd* is larger than *low_window* HSTCP uses the current *cwnd* as an indication of the path's bandwidth-delay product - AI and MD are modified as a function of the current *cwnd* and observed packet loss rate. For a single ACK, HSTCP's congestion window increases by AI=$a(cwnd)/cwnd$. For a congestion event, the window decreases by MD=$b(cwnd)cwnd$. AI increases with *cwnd* while MD decreases with *cwnd*. Consequently HSTCP releases substantially less network bandwidth than *1/2cwnd* on packet loss, and recovers more aggressively than standard TCP.

2.2   HTCP

HTCP [7] uses the elapsed time (*DT*) between loss events to indicate path bandwidth-delay product. When *DT* is less than a threshold, *D*, HTCP increases its window size like standard TCP. When *DT* is larger than *D*, AI varies as a function of *DT*. To yield a response function similar to that of HSTCP, for a single ACK AI=$[1+10(DT-D)+(DT-D)^2/4]/cwnd$. AI is also scaled by path RTT to limit unfairness between competing flows with different round-trip times. HTCP has two versions of MD - simply set MD to 0.2*cwnd*, or use adaptive backoff adjusted based on an estimate of the queue provisioning on a path. For a congestion event the congestion window is decreased by MD=$(1-RTT_{min}/RTT_{max})cwnd$ (where if $RTT_{min}/RTT_{max}>0.8$ then MD is set to $0.2cwnd$). If the throughput change is more than 20% from one congestion epoch to another, MD is set to $cwnd/2$ to enable fast throughput convergence.

2.3 BIC

BIC [8] has a unique window growth function. For a loss event, BIC reduces its window by MD=$0.2cwnd$. Window size prior to reduction is set to the maximum W_{max} and window size after reduction is set to the minimum W_{min}. If the distance between the "midpoint" $((W_{max}+W_{min})/2)$ and the current minimum W_{min} is larger than predefined constant S_{max}, BIC increases the current window size by AI=$S_{max}/cwnd$. Otherwise, BIC performs a binary search by increasing its window size to the "middle point", AI=$(W_{max}-W_{min})/2cwnd$. The updated window size becomes the new minimum. This continues until the window increment is less than a small constant S_{min} (at which point the window is set to the current maximum). After a window reduction the window growth function is linear (additive increase) then logarithmic (binary search) approaching the maximum W_{max}. If a loss event occurs before reaching W_{max} with the current window (W) the new minimum is set to the window size just after the window reduction. However, the new maximum is set to $(W+W_{min})/2$ for fast convergence.

If the window grows past the maximum, BIC enters a "max probing" phase. Initially the window grows slowly to find a new nearby maximum. If it cannot find the new maximum (no packet losses for a period of slow growth), it switches to a faster additive increase where the window size is increased by a large fixed increment. When a loss event is detected, the new maximum and minimum are set to the window size just before and after the window reduction, respectively.

3   Integrated Aggressiveness Modification and TCP Parallelisation

The author's previous research has shown that TCP parallelisation can improve TCP performance and simply going from one to two connections provides the most substantial improvement in performance relative to minimising additional complexity [10] [11]. Therefore, the proposed 'blind' method uses two parallel sub-connections for data transfer. This approach is referred to as Dual-Connection (DC) while the standard single connection based approach is called Single-Connection (SC) in this paper. For the 'blind' method, we propose to make DC as aggressive as SC by modifying one or both of the AI or MD parameters for the sub-connections within DC. When competing with SC, DC aims to achieve a similar throughput to SC if both of its sub-connections are turned on and half of SC's throughput if only one sub-connection is turned on. Our proposed modifications for DC are shown in Table 1.

With experimental verification, simplicity and synchronised loss model drove our particular choice of aggressiveness modifications shown in Table 1. For simplicity, we only modify AI if we do not have to modify MD because AI governs window growth (HSTCP/HTCP). Based on synchronised loss model and with constant decrease factor in MD (HTCP/BIC), AI is expected to be divided by a factor of 2. For BIC, we do not modify its binary search and thus we have to increase the decrease factor in its MD. For HSTCP, the decrease factor in MD, $b(cwnd)$, decreases linearly with $log(cwnd)$. As a result, its AI is expected to be divided by a factor less than 2. The synchronised loss model has been used in related work in [8] and [12] and observed by some early work [13] and unpublished sources [14]. The model may be particularly valid in this paper as the proposed 'blind' method and comparison are of source synchronisation and uniform RTT by nature. No claim is made that these modifications are particularly optimal, and other specific modifications could certainly be proposed. The performance of different modifications may vary in different network contexts (as evidenced by the work of Zhang and Tsaoussidis in [3] and [4], which investigated the performance of the general AIMD).

Table 1. Modification of AIMD parameters for DC

	HSTCP	HTCP	BIC
AI	$a(cwnd)$/**1.39**$cwnd$	$[1+10(DT-D)+(DT-D)^2/4]$/**2**$cwnd$	S_{max}/**2**$cwnd$
MD	$b(cwnd)cwnd$	$0.2cwnd$	**0.32**$cwnd$

HSTCP's AI is divided by a factor of 1.39 while MD remains the same. Note that the decrease factor in MD, $b(cwnd)$, decreases with $cwnd$. Although MD is unchanged the new, less aggressive AI yields a smaller $cwnd$ and thus a larger $b(cwnd)$. For HTCP, we choose the simple back-off strategy of MD=$0.2cwnd$ and MD remains the same for DC. In contrast to HSTCP, the decrease factor in MD is fixed at 0.2 rather than increases with a less aggressive AI and recall that HTCP yields a response function similar to that of HSTCP. As a result, HTCP's AI must be divided by a larger factor of 2. BIC's window growth function has two stages - additive increase (which is divided by an additional factor of 2) and binary search (which remains unchanged). The decrease factor in MD is increased from 0.2 to 0.32.

Table 2. Throughput ratio between DC and SC

| Throughput / | HSTCP | | HTCP | | BIC | |
Throughput Ratio	1sub	2sub	1sub	2sub	1sub	2sub
SC(Mbps)	30.76	23.02	31.47	23.66	32.03/32.76	23.22/23.67
DC(Mbps)	15.52	23.11	15.79	23.67	15.30/14.53	24.03/23.53
Ratio(DC/SC)	0.50	1.00	0.50	1.00	0.48/0.44	1.03/0.99

We verify these modifications using the simulation environment described in Section 4 to create a "head-to-head" competition between a single SC flow and a single DC flow which has two sub-connections. Buffer overflow is the only source of packet losses. Table 2 shows the results in two columns under each of the three TCP variants ("1sub" means that when competing with the single SC flow the DC flow only opens one of its two sub-connections, while "2sub" means that both of its sub-connections are turned on). We see that with "1sub" the throughput ratio between DC and SC is 50% while with "2sub" the ratio is 100%. Note that for BIC we have two sets of results with MD decrease factor set to 0.30 and 0.32 on the left and the right, respectively (0.32 is used later in Section 5). Because of the unmodified binary search phase and the increased decrease factor, we see that for "1sub" the throughput ratio is substantially lower than the expected 50% while for "2sub" the ratio is close to 100%.

In the following two sections we present simulation results supporting our contention that modified AIMD aggressiveness in conjunction with dual-connection parallelisation results in greater resilience in the face of transient and random packet losses.

4 Simulation Environment

We performed all our simulations in NS-2 using the topology shown in Fig. 1, with the simulation system parameters shown in Table 3. The network topology is the typical single bottleneck "dumbbell" with a symmetric channel. The SC flow is established between sending host *S1* and receiving host *R1*. The competing DC flow is created between sending host *S2* and receiving host *R2*. A limited buffer is used on the bottleneck link between the two routers. The buffer size is set to 20% of the bandwidth-delay product (BDP) (based on work in [1] and [12] showing 20% of BDP is sufficient for the studied TCP variants to achieve almost their best performance). Packet losses occur due to buffer overflow and random (uniform and bursty) events on the forward path of the bottleneck link. Random packet loss rate varies from 10^{-7} to 10^{-1}. The reverse path is loss-free.

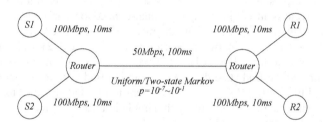

Fig. 1. Simulation topology

Table 3. Simulation parameters

TCP Schemes	HSTCP/HTCP/BIC
Local Link Capacity	100Mbps
Bottleneck Link Capacity	50Mbps
Link Delay	120ms (10+100+10)
Packet Size (MSS)	1,000bytes
Buffer Size	20% BDP(300pkts)
Error (*p*)	Uniform/Two-state Markov
Time Unit (Bad/Good State)	2ms
Simulation Time	2,000s

For bursty losses we use a discrete-time Markov chain with two states (Bad and Good) to model the loss characteristics [2]. A packet is lost if transmitted while the link is in the Bad state, and otherwise the packet is correctly received. Suppose that the link is currently in the Bad state for a given time unit. The burstiness is represented by the probability that the link still stays in the Bad state for the next time unit (note that the time unit can be replaced by a packet). Let Q denote the possibility, that is, the burstiness. If E is the average probability for a time unit that the link is in the Bad state, then we can get the probability (P) that the link passes from the Good state to the Bad state for a time unit: $P=(1-Q)E/(1-E)$. If for a time unit (2ms) the link is in the Bad state, it can destroy up to 13 back-to-back packets.

We set the simulation run-time to 2000 seconds because the studied TCP variants may need a long convergence time to enter the steady state [12]. The three TCP variants are extended with SACK option, which also uses Time-Stamp option to reduce timeouts by recovering the retransmitted packets. Recall that there are no packet losses on the reverse path, and thus one SACK block in the SACK option is already sufficient for the sender to construct a precise replica of the receiver's queue although there are 3 SACK blocks by default. As a result, timeouts rarely occur in the simulations (note that with timeouts our proposed method would have an even better performance as the impact of a timeout is limited within a specific sub-connection).

5   Performance Evaluation

In this section we present simulation results supporting our contention that modified AIMD aggressiveness in conjunction with dual-connection parallelisation results in greater resilience in the face of transient and random packet losses.

The simulations are run in two scenarios (scenario 1 and 2) with uniform and bursty packet loss rate from 10^{-7} to 10^{-1}. For bursty losses, the burstiness is set to 0.3 (after a time unit in the Bad state the link stays in the Bad state for the next time unit with a probability of 30%). For a time unit (2ms) in the Bad state, up to 13 back-to-back packets can be destroyed. In each simulation run we measure throughput performance and retransmission rates.

Scenario 1 measures SC's and DC's performances separately. A single SC or DC flow is run in the simulations, with no background or competing traffic present. In Scenario 2 an SC flow and a DC flow are mixed together and thus compete with each other. In each of the figures, legend items without a prefix represent performance measurements obtained from Scenario 1. The prefix "m" (m for "mixed") means that the performance measurement is obtained from Scenario 2. Suffixes "s" and "d" mean the measurement is for SC and DC, respectively. For instance, "hstcp-d" denotes the throughput performance of the DC flow with no background or competing traffic and "d/s" denotes the throughput ratio between the throughputs of the DC and the SC flows, which are obtained separately. For another example, "m:hstcp-s" denotes the throughput performance of the SC flow when competing with the DC flow; "m:(s+d)" represents the sum of the throughputs of the SC and DC flows; "m:rtxrate-d" denotes the retransmission rate of the DC flow; and "m:d/s" is for the throughput ratio between the DC and the SC flows.

5.1 HSTCP

To remove the impact of HSTCP's low window function, its *low_window* is set to 1 rather than 38 used in RFC 3649 (HSTCP's response function starts when *cwnd* is 1). Fig. 2 and 3 show the performance with uniform and bursty packet losses, respectively. In scenario 1, Fig. 2 shows that both the SC and the DC flows achieve the similar throughput when the random loss rate is low. As the random loss rate increases, the DC flow has a better throughput performance. Both approaches have the similar retransmission rate (not presented in the figure) except at the loss rate of 10^{-4} where the retransmission rate is 0.018% for the DC flow and 0.011% for the SC flow. Since 0.011% is very close to the random packet loss rate 10^{-4}, it suggests the SC flow cannot cause congestion-triggered packet losses while the DC flow can still trigger buffer-overflow packet losses. For random loss rates higher than 10^{-4} both approaches have a retransmission rate close to the random loss rate.

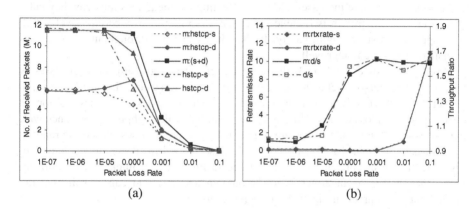

(a)   (b)

Fig. 2. Performance comparison between SC and DC-HSTCP-uniform

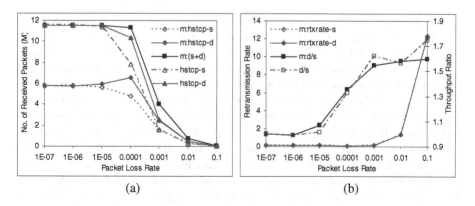

(a)   (b)

Fig. 3. Performance comparison between SC and DC-HSTCP-bursty

In scenario 2, with low random loss rates where congestion-triggered (buffer overflow) packet losses dominate it shows that the DC and the SC flows share the bandwidth fairly (Fig. 2 (a)). As the random loss rate increases from 10^{-7} to 10^{-4}, the throughput difference between the DC and the SC flows grows - SC's throughput decreases consistently while in contrast DC's throughput grows. In the meantime, both approaches have a similar retransmission rate (Fig. 2 (b)); however, a sharp reduction of retransmission rate is observed from loss rate 10^{-5} to 10^{-4}. For the SC flow the rate is reduced from 0.14% to 0.08% and for the DC flow the rate is down to 0.07% from 0.15%. This indicates a mixture of significant buffer overflow and random losses (a transition point from buffer overflow loss domain to random loss domain) and that the DC flow responds well to this situation. As the random loss rate increases further from 10^{-3} to 10^{-1}, both approaches suffer consistently (Fig. 2 (a)) and the retransmission rate for both approaches is close to the random loss rate (Fig. 2 (b)). In terms of throughput ratio in Fig. 2 (b), the DC flow does not steal bandwidth from the SC flow when the random loss rate is low but can significantly outperform it as the random loss rate increases. However, the improvement does not grow beyond a certain level – the growth is flattened after the loss rate passes a certain level where both approaches suffer significantly. It also shows that the throughput ratio in both scenarios match each other well.

With bursty losses in Fig. 3, the similar performance as with uniform losses is observed. The bursty packet losses are relatively clustered and thus with the same packet loss rate bursty losses (compared to uniform losses) may have a longer distance between loss events. This would result in better throughput performance with bursty losses when packet losses are dominated by random losses. When the random loss rate is higher than 10^{-4} it is observed that in scenario 1 the throughput achieved in Fig. 3 (a) is consistently higher than the one in Fig. 2 (a). Compared with uniform losses this may have an effect of lower random loss rate and can explain that the throughput ratio curves in Fig. 3 (b) grow more slowly.

5.2 HTCP

As HTCP has an AIMD response function similar to that of HSTCP, they both have the similar window growth pattern. Although the window increment is governed by different measures (elapsed time between loss events for HTCP and current window size for HSTCP), the performance is similar for these two TCP variants in terms of the comparison between SC and DC in both scenario 1 and 2 (Fig. 4 and 5). In scenario 1, with low random loss rate both the SC and the DC flows have the similar throughput. With high random loss rate, the DC flow has a better throughput performance. Both approaches have the similar retransmission rate except at the loss rate of 10^{-4} where the retransmission rate is significantly higher for the DC flow. This is because that the DC flow can create more buffer overflow losses due to its insensitiveness to random losses. In scenario 2, when competing with the SC flow the DC flow does not appear to be more aggressive in the presence of congestion but is more effective to utilise bandwidth when random losses become to dominate. The performance with bursty losses in Fig. 5 is similar to the one in Fig. 4.

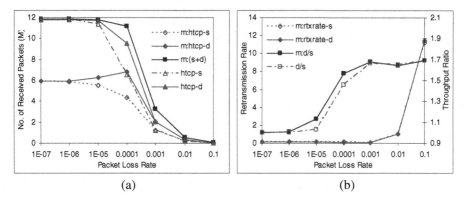

Fig. 4. Performance comparison between SC and DC-HTCP-uniform

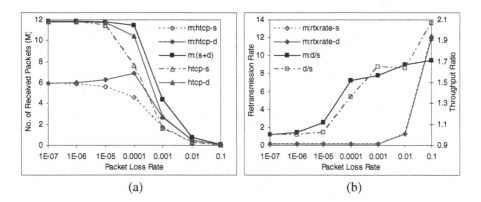

Fig. 5. Performance comparison between SC and DC-HTCP-bursty

5.3 BIC-TCP

A distinctive feature of BIC is that it sets a target window which is expected close to the available BDP. After fast growth when its *cwnd* is close to the target, it slows down approaching to the target. This is an appealing feature when the target is reasonably accurate. However, in a heterogenous environment (for instance, where random/transient losses prevail) this feature may suffer poor bandwidth utilisation.

In scenario 1, Fig. 6 shows that both approaches have the similar throughput and retransmission rate when buffer overflow losses dominate. After random loss rate increases more than 10^{-5}, both approaches suffer dramatically. However, the DC flow still starts to outperform the SC flow consistently. Both approaches have the similar retransmission rate close to the random loss rate, even at loss rate 10^{-4} (in contrast to HSTCP and HTCP) indicating that both approaches cannot create buffer overflow losses. In scenario 2, similar to the case with HSTCP and HTCP both approaches have a fair throughput share in the presence of congestion and the DC

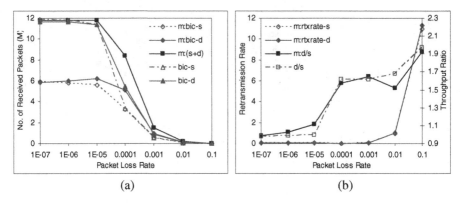

Fig. 6. Performance comparison between SC and DC-BIC-uniform

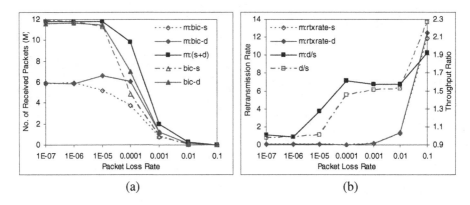

Fig. 7. Performance comparison between SC and DC-BIC-bursty

flow consistently outperforms the SC flow with increased random losses. However, the DC flow is losing its robustness to cope with random losses at lower random loss rate. This is due to the negative impact of the undervalued target window. The performance with bursty losses in Fig. 7 is similar to the one in Fig. 6.

5.4 Comparison Between Protocols

With uniform losses, Fig. 8 and 9 compare the three TCP variants with each other based on scenario 1 and 2, respectively. In the figures, "h", "hs" and "bic" stand for HTCP, HSTCP and BIC, respectively. Therefore, in Fig 8 (b) "s:hs/h" means the comparison between HSTCP and HTCP for the SC flow while "d:hs/h" denotes the comparison for the DC flow and the corresponding comparison in Fig. 9 (b) is "sm:hs/h" and "dm:hs/h". Fig. 8 (a) and 9 (a) show that for both approaches (SC and DC) HSTCP and HTCP have the similar throughput performance, which is due to their similar AIMD response function. It is also shown that BIC is outperformed by HTCP and HSTCP when random losses prevail; however, when buffer overflow losses dominate BIC has a better performance with significantly lower retransmission rate (not presented in the figures). This is due to BIC's gentle (less responsive) binary search. As a result in Fig. 8 (b) and 9 (b), for both approaches the throughput ratio between HTCP and HSTCP is close to 1. Note that we do not modify HTCP's low window function and thus at low window HTCP is less aggressive than HSTCP. This is why the throughput ratio is increased to 1.23 with random loss rate at 10^{-1}. The throughput ratio between BIC and HTCP/HSTP grows with the increase of random loss rate until the random loss rate reaches 10^{-1} where with serious packet losses and low window HTCP/HSTCP are not very aggressive/responsive and thus the throughput ratio is significantly reduced.

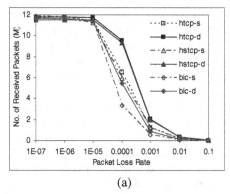
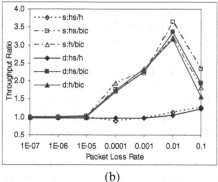

(a)   (b)

Fig. 8. Performance comparison in scenario 1

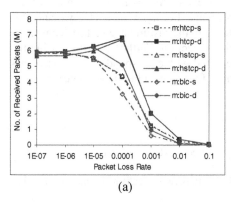
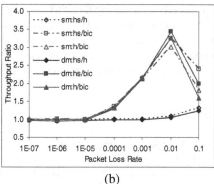

(a)   (b)

Fig. 9. Performance comparison in scenario 2

6   Discussion and Conclusions

We have presented and analysed a 'blind' method of improving the throughput of aggressive TCP variants such as HSTCP, HTCP and BIC in the presence of transient and random packet losses. We use dual-connection TCP parallelisation in conjunction with modified aggressiveness of each TCP variant's AIMD algorithm. Each TCP variant's AIMD algorithm is modified such that the dual-connection (DC) achieves a similar throughput to the unmodified single-connection (SC) if both of DC's sub-connections are turned on and half of SC's throughput if only one sub-connection is turned on. Our approach is 'blind' in that it does not need to differentiate between congestion-induced and random losses. It is no more aggressive than studied TCP variants in the presence of congestion but more effectively utilises bandwidth in the presence of random packet losses.

The aggressiveness of high-performance TCP variants is likely to create large and synchronised packet losses between competing flows in the presence of congestion. (The work in [8] and [12] are based on the synchronised model. Early research in [13] and some unpublished results from SLAC [14] and other researchers also show signs of loss synchronisation.) This is an area of ongoing research. Since our 'blind' method opens identical parallel sub-connections (for the DC flow) with uniform RTT and source synchronisation, the parallel sub-connections are likely to suffer synchronised losses in the presence of significant congestion. As the proposed aggressiveness modification is tuned based on the synchronised model, the 'blind' method (the DC flow) does not steal bandwidth in such a situation.

However, the 'blind' method increases the robustness in the face of transient and random losses. For the DC flow, it is more likely that one of its two sub-connections suffers a loss event at a time while the other one stays free from the disturbance. Thus the DC flow outperforms the equivalent SC flow when random losses dominate. Moreover, the 'blind' method is capable of adaptive backoff in response to different congestion levels. Heavy congestion tends to cause synchronised packet losses across sub-connections and thus heavy backoff; light/transient congestion has a better chance to cause losses within a specific sub-connection and thus light backoff. In addition, window reduction is not the only cost of a loss event. An SC flow does not increase the reduced *cwnd* during the RTT for fast recovery. For aggressive TCP variants this can be a significant cost. However, for a DC flow the disturbance of fast recovery is limited within the involved (packet loss) sub-connection. Furthermore, increasing the number of sub-connections beyond two, integrated with corresponding aggressiveness modifications, will achieve greater performance for some additional complexity.

References

1. D. Barman, G. Smaragdakis and I. Matta "The Effect of Router Buffer Size on HighSpeed TCP Performance", *Globecom* 2004, Dallas, USA
2. C. Barakat and E. Altman, "Bandwidth Tradeoff between TCP and Link-Level FEC", *Computer Networks*, 39(2), June 2002.
3. C. Zhang and V. Tsaoussidis, "The Interrelation of TCP Responsiveness and Smoothness in Heterogeneous Networks", *ISCC* 2002, Washington, USA
4. V. Tsaoussidis and C. Zhang, "The Dynamics of Responsiveness and Smoothness in Heterogeneous Networks", *IEEE J. on Selected Areas in Comm.*, 23(6), June 2005.
5. Tom Kelly, "Scalable TCP: Improving performance in highspeed wide area networks", *Computer Communication Review* 32(2), April 2003.
6. Sally Floyd, "HighSpeed TCP for Large Congestion Windows", *RFC 3649*, Dec. 2003.

7. R. Shorten and D. Leith, "H-TCP: TCP for high-speed and long-distance networks", *PFLDnet* 2004, Argonne, USA

8. L. Xu, K. Harfoush and I. Rhee, "Binary Increase Congestion Control for Fast Long-Distance Networks", *INFOCOM* 2004, Hong Kong, China

9. I. Rhee and L. Xu, "CUBIC: A New TCP-Friendly High-Speed TCP Variant", *PFLDnet* 2005, Lyon, France

10. Q. Fu and J. Indulska, "Examining TCP Parallelisation Related Methods for Various Packet Losses", *WWIC* 2005, Xanthi, Greece

11. Q. Fu and J. Indulska, "The Impact of Fast Recovery on Parallel TCP connections", *HET-NETs* 2004, Ilkley, UK.

12. Y. Li, D. Leith and R. Shorten, "Experimental Evaluation of TCP Protocols for High-Speed Networks", June 2005. URL: http://www.hamilton.ie/net/eval/results_HI2005.pdf

13. S. Shenker, L. Zhang, and D. Clark, "Some observations on the dynamics of a congestion control algorithm," *SIGCOMM* 1990

14. http://www.slac.stanford.edu/grp/scs/net/talk/fast-i2-apr03.ppt

Evaluating TCP Mechanisms for Real-Time Streaming over Satellite Links

Panagiotis Papadimitriou and Vassilis Tsaoussidis

Demokritos University, Electrical & Computer Engineering Department,
Xanthi, 67100, Greece
{ppapadim, vtsaousi}@ee.duth.gr

Abstract. Real-time streaming over satellite IP networks is challenging, since satellite links commonly exhibit long propagation delays and increased error rates, which impair TCP performance. In this context, we quantify the effects of satellite links on TCP efficiency and streaming video delivery. We investigate a solution-framework composed by TCP implementations which are expected to perform adequately in such environments. Furthermore, we study the supportive role of Selective Acknowledgments (SACK). Along with protocol performance, we also evaluate the impact of delayed acknowledgments. Our simulation results illustrate that most existing end-to-end solutions do not comply with the stringent QoS provisions of time-sensitive applications, resulting in inefficient bandwidth utilization and increased delays in data delivery. Finally, with the absence of a satellite-optimized TCP implementation for real-time streaming, we identify TCP Real as the most prominent solution, since it manages to alleviate most of the impairments induced by satellite links, sustaining a relatively smooth transmission rate.

1 Introduction

Satellite systems evolve towards the delivery of broadband IP services and are candidates to integrate the wireless data networks, due to their wide coverage and broadcast capabilities. Geostationary (*GEO*) and low-altitude earth orbit (*LEO*) satellites enable the delivery of time-sensitive data, such as audio and video content, over large coverage areas. Unfortunately, satellite networks demonstrate several drawbacks. Firstly, in order to provide services at a reasonable cost, satellite links exhibit bandwidth asymmetry, since they comprise a high-capacity forward space link and a low-bandwidth reverse (space or terrestrial) path. Some satellite networks are inherently bandwidth asymmetric, such as those based on a direct broadcast satellite (*DBS*) downlink and a return via a dial-up modem line. For purely GEO or LEO systems, many proposed systems offer the capability to download at tens of Mb/s, but they do not provide uplinks at rates faster than several hundred Kb/s or a few Mb/s, due to uplink carrier sizing. Furthermore, satellite networks demonstrate relatively increased propagation delays which dramatically affect the bandwidth-delay product (*BDP*). Long transmission distances result in fading channels and eventually in bit error rates (*BER*) which remain higher (10^{-6} or worse) than in terrestrial networks. Reception of corrupted data may trigger requests for retransmission resulting in possible congestion and increasing end-to-end delays.

T. Braun et al. (Eds.): WWIC 2006, LNCS 3970, pp. 62–74, 2006.
© Springer-Verlag Berlin Heidelberg 2006

Most Internet transport protocols exhibit limited efficiency under these awkward conditions. *Transmission Control Protocol (TCP)*, based on the principles of congestion management [9], *Slow-Start* [16], and *Additive Increase Multiplicative Decrease (AIMD)* [4], was designed to provide a reliable data delivery service for wired IP networks. As a result, it demonstrates inadequate performance in heterogeneous wired/wireless environments, such as satellite networks. Authors in [18] outline three major shortfalls of TCP: (i) ineffective bandwidth utilization, (ii) unnecessary congestion-oriented responses to wireless link errors (e.g. fading channels) and operations (e.g. handoffs), and (iii) wasteful window adjustments over asymmetric, low-bandwidth reverse paths. More precisely, TCP commonly sets the initial slow-start threshold (*ssthress*) to an arbitrary value independently of BDP. If *ssthress* is adjusted too high relatively to the network BDP, the exponential increase of congestion window (*cwnd*) may cause multiple packet drops and coarse timeouts. Inversely, in the situation of a relatively low value of ssthress the slow-start phase is concluded prematurely resulting in poor startup utilization. Furthermore, standard TCP is not able to detect the nature of the errors that cause packet drops and consequently determine the appropriate error-recovery strategy. Hence, TCP invokes congestion-oriented responses to all wireless errors, which are common in satellite links, resulting in unnecessary throughput degradation. Bandwidth asymmetry also impacts TCP performance [2]. Despite the small size of acknowledgment (*ACK*) packets, the reverse channel is often unable to carry the high rate of ACKs. The congestion in the reverse path inevitably increases *Round Trip Time (RTT)* diminishing the protocol efficiency.

Apart from the particular characteristics of satellite links, TCP should comply with the stringent requirements and constraints of time-sensitive traffic. Real-time applications are comparatively intolerant to delay and variations of throughput and delay. Furthermore, reliability parameters, such as packet drops and bit errors, usually compose an impairment factor, since they cause a perceptible degradation in media quality. Standard TCP usually induces oscillations in the achievable transmission rate and occasionally introduces arbitrary delays, since it enforces reliability and in-order delivery. In this context, several TCP protocol extensions [5, 22] have emerged to overcome the standard TCP limitations providing more efficient bandwidth utilization in order to achieve a smooth transmission and playback rate.

Along these lines, the constraints of transmission over satellite links, as well as streaming media requirements call for effective and robust transport protocol services. Although numerous research proposals have emerged towards improving transport services over wireless/satellite links, the converged domain of time-sensitive data delivery over satellite IP networks has not attracted the required attention from the research community. Realizing the issues and parameters that affect TCP performance over satellite links, our objective is to exploit TCP's potential for efficient streaming media delivery over such environments. In this context, we investigate a solution-framework based on the most prominent end-to-end solutions. Furthermore, we assess the impact of delayed ACKs and link asymmetry on TCP performance, as well as the associated impact of diverse link error rates. In this study, we do not include *User Datagram Protocol (UDP)* in our evaluation experiments; the protocol lacks all basic mechanisms for error recovery and flow/congestion control, and thus provides a different type of service. In [14] we have shown that UDP may perform worse than TCP in several occasions. In addition, the absence of congestion control poses a threat to network stability.

The rest of the paper is organized as follows. Section 2 summarizes related work, while in Section 3 we formulate a transmission gap model for asymmetric satellite links. Section 4 includes our evaluation methodology followed by Section 5, where we analyze the results of the experiments we performed. Finally, in Section 6 we highlight our conclusions and refer to future work.

2 Related Work

TCP's efficiency for streaming media delivery over satellite links has not been studied in depth. Proposed mechanisms range from minor tweaks, such as issuing delayed ACKs in order to reduce the network load in the reverse path, to sophisticated solutions, such as *TCP Spoofing* and split-connection protocols [3]. With the absence of a dedicated and efficient end-to-end solution, most research approaches commonly choose to tune an existing protocol in order to achieve the desired performance. Most related research efforts focus on bulk-data transmission over satellite IP networks and study the associated TCP performance [8, 15, 21, 2]. *TCP-Peach* [1] is a proposed congestion control scheme that explicitly addresses satellite IP networks. TCP-Peach incorporates two new algorithms, namely *Sudden Start* and *Rapid Recovery*, instead of the typical Slow-Start and Fast Recovery. Inline with the *Probing mechanism* and *Immediate Recovery* proposed in [17], these algorithms are based on the concept of using *dummy segments* to probe the availability of network resources without carrying any new information to the sender. The protocol achieves improved throughput performance; however, it does not account for the *Quality of Service* (*QoS*) provisions required by time-sensitive traffic.

TCP selective acknowledgments (*SACK*) options [11] were proposed in order to alleviate TCP's inefficiency in handling multiple drops in a single window. TCP SACK enables the receiver to inform the sender about segments that were received out of order. Hence, the sender avoids retransmitting segments whose successful delivery at the other end is not evident from the duplicate ACKs received. TCP SACK yields improved performance for a relatively large sending window. Furthermore, by reducing the rate of ACKs, remarkable gains can be attained in asymmetric links.

Several TCP protocol extensions have emerged to overcome the standard TCP limitations providing more efficient bandwidth utilization and sophisticated mechanisms for congestion control, which preserve the fundamental QoS guarantees for time-sensitive traffic. Authors in [5, 22] proposed a family of TCP compatible protocols, called *TCP-friendly*. TCP-friendly protocols achieve smooth window adjustments, while they manage to compete fairly with TCP flows. *TCP-friendly Rate Control* (*TFRC*) [5] is a representative TCP-friendly protocol, where its transmission rate is adjusted in response to the level of congestion, as indicated by the loss rate. Multiple packet losses in the same RTT are considered as a single loss event by TFRC and hence, the protocol follows a more gentle congestion control strategy. The protocol eventually achieves the smoothing of the transmission gaps and therefore, is suitable for applications requiring a smooth sending rate, such as streaming media. However, this smoothness has a negative impact, as the protocol becomes less responsive to bandwidth availability [20].

TCP Westwood [10] is a TCP-friendly protocol that emerged as a sender-side-only modification of TCP Reno congestion control. TCP Westwood exploits end-to-end bandwidth estimation in order to adjust the values of ssthresh and cwnd after a congestion episode. The protocol incorporates a recovery mechanism which avoids the blind halving of the sending rate of TCP Reno after packet drops and enables TCP Westwood to achieve a high link-utilization in the presence of wireless errors. However, in [13] we showed that TCP Westwood tends to overestimate the available bandwidth, due to ACKs clustering. *TCP Westwood+* is a recent extension of TCP Westwood, based on the *Additive Increase/Adaptive Decrease (AIAD)* mechanism. TCP Westwood+ obtains more accurate estimates of the available bandwidth [7].

TCP Real is a high-throughput transport protocol that incorporates congestion avoidance mechanism in order to minimize transmission-rate gaps. As a result, this protocol is suited for real-time applications, since it enables better performance and reasonable playback timers. *TCP Real* [19] employs a receiver-oriented and measurement-based congestion control mechanism that significantly improves TCP performance over heterogeneous networks and asymmetric paths. The protocol approximates a receiver-oriented approach beyond the balancing trade of the parameters of additive increase and multiplicative decrease. In this context, TCP Real introduces another parameter, namely γ, which determines the window adjustments during congestion avoidance. More precisely, the receiver measures the data-receiving rate and attaches the result to its *ACKs*, directing the transmission rate of the sender. When new data is acknowledged and the congestion window is adjusted, the current data-receiving rate is compared against the previous one. If there is no receiving rate decrease, the congestion window is increased by 1 *Maximum Segment Size (MSS)* every RTT ($\alpha = 1$). If the magnitude of the decrease is small, the congestion window remains temporarily unaffected; otherwise, the sender reduces the congestion window multiplicatively by γ. In [19] a default value of $\gamma = 1/8$ is suggested. However, this parameter can be adaptive to the detected conditions. Generally, TCP Real can be viewed as a TCP (α, β, γ) protocol, where γ captures the protocol's behavior prior to congestion, when congestion boosts up.

Besides transport layer modifications, there are several techniques operating on the link layer, which attempt to ameliorate the impact of wireless errors [3]. *Forward Error Correction (FEC)* introduces added overhead to data bits in order to cope with data corruption. Corrupted packets may be directly corrected, without retransmission, which is critical for lossy links exhibiting long delays. *Automatic Repeat Request (ARQ)* mechanisms are invoked when packets containing bit errors can not be corrected. In this case, the erroneous packets are discarded and a retransmission is directly triggered within TCP's timeout.

3 Transmission Gap Analysis of Asymmetric Satellite Links

In this section, we formulate a model for transmission gaps that explicitly addresses asymmetric satellite links. The proposed model applies to bi-directional satellite systems which exhibit bandwidth asymmetry; hence, both forward and reverse path have the same propagation delay P. Based on [12], we define the transmission period $t(n)$, as the period between two consecutive transmissions (with individual window sizes). In this context, we model t(n) as a function of transmission number n. We also define $W(n)$ as the number of data packets sent at the nth transmission. We assume that $W(0) = 1$ and $W(n)$ inflates up to the maximum window size advertised by the receiver. The transmission time $T(n)$ required for sending $W(n)$ data packets is:

$$T(n) = \frac{S \cdot W(n)}{BW_{Dn}}$$ (1)

where S and BW_{Dn} denote the fixed packet size (including TCP and IP headers) and the bandwidth of the downlink, respectively. After n^{th} transmission, $W(n)$ ACK packets are expected to reach the sender. Hence, the transmission time $T'(n)$ required for sending $W(n)$ ACKs is denoted by:

$$T'(n) = \frac{S' \cdot W(n)}{BW_{Up}}$$ (2)

where S' and BW_{Up} are the ACK packet size and the bandwidth of the uplink, respectively. ACKs transmission time is not negligible despite their small packet size S', since BW_{Up} is constrained. Ignoring any processing and queuing delays and with respect to equations (1) and (2), we can approximate RTT from the 1st transmission period where $W(0) = 1$:

$$RTT_{init} = 2 \cdot P + T(0) + T'(0)$$ (3)

$$RTT_{init} = 2 \cdot P + \frac{S}{BW_{Dn}} + \frac{S'}{BW_{Up}}$$ (4)

Equation (4) reveals that in a GEO satellite system with a propagation delay P typically exceeding 200ms, retransmitting a lost video packet is unfruitful either by TCP or link layer mechanisms, such as ARQ.

Transmission period t(n) is eventually determined by the maximum value of RTT_{init}, transmission rate T(n) and ACK transmission rate T'(n):

$$t(n) = \max(RTT_{init}, \; T(n), \; T'(n))$$ (5)

In the case of a relatively small window size $W(n)$, the system throughput does not reach the bandwidth of the downlink BW_{Dn} and hence, t(n) is determined by the value of RTT_{init}. As a result, only minimal variations may be induced in the transmission periods, since RTT_{init} is basically defined by the link propagation delay P. In this case, transmission gaps are minimized achieving a smooth sending and playback rate. On the other hand, whenever throughput instantly approximates BW_{Dn}, transmission time T(n) is maximized and eventually designates the transmission period t(n). Let a transmission number k, where all the available network resources are allocated, and consequently packet drops occur. According to standard TCP, the window of the next transmission $W(k+1)$[1] will be halved and the associated transmission time T(k+1) is expressed as:

$$T(k+1) = \frac{S \cdot \dfrac{W(k)}{2}}{BW_{Dn}} \qquad (6)$$

A similar outcome is reached in the situation of a link error, since TCP commonly invokes congestion-oriented responses and reduces its window. Under these conditions, apart from the impairments due to lost packets, the significant variations in the transmission periods induce gaps which further degrade media quality.

We additionally consider the implication where the sender does not receive a number of ACK packets, due to a constrained uplink bandwidth BW_{Up} or heavy back traffic. In this case, ACK transmission time T'(n) exceeds both T(n) and RTT_{init}, and consequently defines the value of t(n). Similarly, transmission delay variations in the reverse path impact the associated transmission periods and diminish real-time application performance. However, although TCP manages to relinquish the resources allocated, when it detects congestion according to (6), it is not able to relieve the congestion in the reverse path. Along these lines, reaching BW_{Up} capacity poses the highest threat on asymmetric links.

If we adopt the approach of delaying ACKs by a certain period d, we derive from (4) a modified RTT_{init} formula:

$$RTT'_{init} = 2 \cdot P + \frac{S}{BW_{Dn}} + \frac{S'}{BW_{Up}} + d \qquad (7)$$

Furthermore, let the receiver send L delayed ACK packets which correspond to the transmission of W(n) data packets. Consequently, ACK transmission time is now expressed as:

$$T''(n) = \frac{S' \cdot L}{BW_{Up}} \qquad (8)$$

A considerable ACK delay d is translated to a minimal number of L ACK packets, which may render ACK transmission time T''(n) negligible. From equations (7), (8), it is obvious that by issuing delayed ACKs, we effectively reduce back traffic in the expense of increasing RTT. With respect to (5), we reach the conclusion that delayed ACKs may degrade TCP performance in the case where t(n) = RTT'_{init}. That is, no

---

[1] We ignore the retransmission window. Consequently, after loss detection the TCP sender halves the congestion window at transmission number (k+1).

data/ACK congestion has occurred in the forward/reverse path. Inversely, gains are expected from delayed ACKs in the situation of congestion in the downlink channel $(t(n) = T(n))$, and especially during heavy back traffic, where $t(n) = T''(n) < T'(n)$.

4 Evaluation Methodology

The evaluation plan was implemented on the *NS-2* network simulator. LEO systems with RTTs in the range of 40-200ms cause slight degradation in TCP performance, despite the large RTT variations [8]. However, due to large RTTs (approximately 530ms), maintaining efficient TCP performance over GEO latencies is challenging. Along these lines, we focus on quantifying the effects of GEO systems on TCP efficiency and streaming video delivery. We simulated the system in Fig. 1, where *N* senders transmit an MPEG-4 video stream to *N* receivers through a bi-directional GEO satellite link with 5 Mbps downlink and 256 Kbps uplink channel. We consider the modeled satellite system, as a retransmitter of data traffic (received from a terrestrial gateway) to ground gateways and user terminals. The transmitted video streams are multiplexed in Station 1, before traversing the satellite link. In accordance with the lossy nature of satellite links, we simulated an error model for both forward and reverse satellite channels with configurable bit error rate (*BER*). BER is adjusted at 10^{-4}, unless otherwise explicitly stated.

We assume a window scale option which overcomes the limitation of the maximum window size (i.e. 64 KB) allowed by standard TCP. Hence, we adjusted the maximum window size at 240 KB. Segment size is set to 1000 bytes and consequently, a window may accommodate at the most 240 segments approximately. Since the simulated network exhibits an average RTT of 550ms, simulation running time was fixed to 200 seconds, an appropriate time-period for all the protocols to demonstrate their potential. We performed the experiments over standard TCP Reno, the modified TCP Reno variant [6], known as NewReno, augmented with the SACK [11] option, and the protocols TCP Westwood+ and TCP-Real. Concerning the relaxed packet loss requirements of time-sensitive applications, as well as the implications that may be induced by FEC/ARQ [3] in order to maximize reliability, we chose not to include such mechanisms in our experiments.

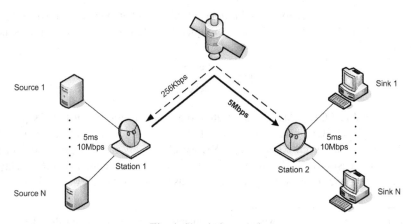

Fig. 1. Simulation topology

In order to simulate real-time traffic, we developed an *MPEG-4 Traffic Generator*. The traffic generated closely matches the statistical characteristics of an original video trace. We used three separate *Transform Expand Sample (TES)* models for modeling I, P and B frames, respectively. The resulting MPEG-4 stream is generated by interleaving data obtained by the three models. The MPEG traffic generator was integrated into NS-2 and provides the adjustment of the data rate of the MPEG stream, as well as useful statistical data (e.g. average bit-rate, bit-rate variance).

We hereby refer to the performance metrics supported by our simulation model. System goodput is used to measure the overall system efficiency in bandwidth utilization. In [14] we proposed a new metric for the performance evaluation of time-sensitive traffic, called *Real-Time Performance*. The metric monitors packet inter-arrival times and distinguishes the packets that can be effectively used by the client application from delayed packets (according to a configurable inter-arrival threshold). The proportion of the delayed packets is reflected in *Delayed Packets Rate*. Hence, *Real-Time Performance* index is defined as the ratio of the number of *timely received packets* over the total number of packets sent by the application:

$$\text{Real} - \text{Time Performance Index} = \frac{\#\text{timely received packets}}{\#\text{sent packets}} \leq 1$$

In accordance with video streaming requirements, we adjusted the inter-arrival threshold at 200ms. Since MPEG traffic is sensitive to packet drops, we additionally define *Packet Drop Rate*, as the ratio of the number of lost packets over the number of packets sent by the application. Most of our experiments were performed on several flows, so we present the average of the real-time performance of each MPEG flow.

5 Results and Discussion

In the sequel, we demonstrate and comment on the most prominent results from the experiments we performed based on three distinct scenarios. The basic parameters of each simulation scenario are as described in the previous section.

5.1 TCP Performance

Initially we performed a series of experiments in order to evaluate the video performance delivered by the selected TCP variants. We simulated a wide range of MPEG flows (1-50) adjusting the contention accordingly. We measured *goodput* and *real-time performance*, and we additionally selected statistics from delayed and lost packets, since both are influencing factors which impact video quality. We hereby demonstrate the associated results of TCP Reno, TCP NewReno with SACK, TCP Westwood+ and TCP Real (Figs. 2-5).

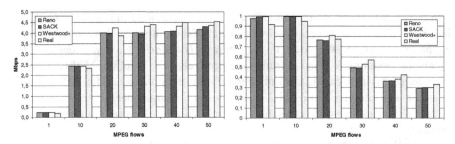

Fig. 2. System goodput   **Fig. 3.** Average Real-Time Performance

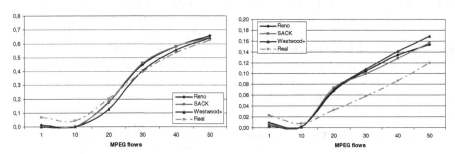

Fig. 4. Packet Drop Rate   **Fig. 5.** Delayed Packets Rate

With the exception of TCP Real (and in part of Westwood+), the protocols are unable to sustain goodput rates close to the bottleneck link rate (Fig. 2), despite the relatively large window (i.e. 240 KB). Therefore, the available bandwidth is not fully exploited, mainly due to link asymmetry and long latency. Inline with our analysis in Section 3, heavy ACK traffic across the constrained uplink channel extends the transmission periods $(t(n) = T'(n))$ and inevitably induces variable transmission gaps, which impair the performance of video delivery (Fig. 3).

A comparison between standard TCP Reno and TCP NewReno (with SACK) reveals that SACK alone is not sufficient to enable high performance (Figs. 2, 3). However, slight gains (especially for high contention) are eventually attained, since NewReno prevents coarse timeouts and multiple window reductions, while SACK accelerates the loss recovery phase. Both TCP Reno and TCP NewReno are based on "blind" increase/decrease window mechanisms that dynamically exploit bandwidth availability, without relying on precise measurements of current conditions. Furthermore, they invoke unnecessary congestion-oriented responses to the increased bit errors along the satellite link. Along these lines, they exhibit limited efficiency in the context of real-time application performance (Fig. 3), primarily due to the significant delays in video-data delivery. Fig. 5 illustrates that a notable proportion of packets reach the recipient exceeding the delay requirements of streaming video both for Reno and NewReno.

On the other hand, TCP Westwood+ and TCP Real rely on bandwidth estimation schemes and are intended to sustain a smooth sending rate minimizing the transmission gaps. TCP Westwood+, in contradiction to the initial version of

Westwood, computes one sample of available bandwidth every RTT using all data acked in the specific RTT, therefore obtaining more accurate estimates (Fig. 2). However, from the perspective of real-time delivery, Westwood+ efficiency is not so profound (Fig. 3), since it delivers a considerable amount of delayed packets (Fig. 4). Inline with our analysis, reaching the downlink capacity (i.e. flows 30-50) maximizes transmission time T(n) and generates variable transmission periods which impact video delivery.

Unlike Westwood, TCP Real yields satisfactory performance on video delivery for a wider range of flows (Fig. 3), which is the combined result of high goodput rates (Fig. 2) and a gentle proportion of delayed packets (Fig. 5). TCP Real effectively manages to amortize the low throughput of the initial window built across a longer period of high throughput. Furthermore, the protocol exploits the integrated error detection mechanism, as well as the additional parameter γ. In this context, the desired smoothness is counterbalanced with responsiveness, which is critical during congestion episodes.

5.2 TCP Performance vs. Error Rates

In this scenario, we performed our experiments using diverse bit error rate adjustments (BER: 10^{-6} - 10^{-3}). In satellite networks, BER scarcely exceeds 10^{-4}. However, we simulated a satellite link with BER as high as 10^{-3} in order to study protocol efficiency under error-prone connections. We hereby demonstrate results from 20 MPEG flows in order to investigate the associated impact on the performance of video delivery (Figs. 6-9).

TCP Westwood+ is the less sensitive protocol to the diverse bit error rates (Fig. 8), although it does not incorporate an inherent mechanism for error detection. Furthermore, it maintains an acceptable delayed packets rate for intensely error-prone satellite links (Fig. 9). On the contrary, TCP-Real demonstrates limited efficiency at high bit error rates, despite the incorporated error classification mechanism. Apparently, the mechanism operates inadequately for increased link errors. SACK's supportive role results in perceptible performance gains, since the loss recovery phase is accelerated and the packet drop rate is sustained to slightly lower levels (Fig. 8). However, inline with Reno, NewReno with SACK is still inefficient for excessively lossy links.

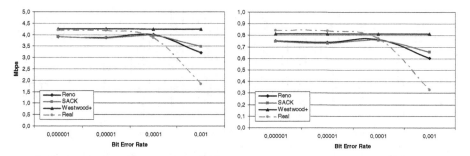

Fig. 6. System Goodput (20 flows)   **Fig. 7.** Average Real-Time Performance (20 flows)

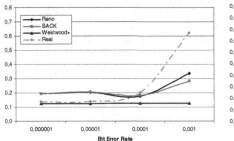

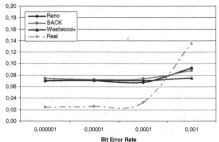

Fig. 8. Packet Drop Rate (20 flows)   **Fig. 9.** Delayed Packets Rate (20 flows)

5.3 Impact of Delayed ACKs

We conclude our evaluation scenarios by studying the impact of delayed ACKs on protocol efficiency in satellite environments. We also investigate whether reducing back traffic induces implications which affect the performance of video delivery. We performed our experiments issuing ACKs with no delay and with delays of 100ms, 200ms and 500ms, successively. In the sequel, we discuss the behavior of TCP NewReno with SACK which produced the most conclusive results (Figs. 10-13).

Although delayed ACKs tend to slow down the initial slow-start phase (due to the decreased number of ACKs sent by a delayed-ACK receiver), our results illustrate noticeable performance gains both for TCP efficiency (Fig. 10) and video quality (Fig. 11). The reported gains are attained in the situation where goodput reaches the capacity of downlink channel (Fig. 10: flows 20-50), and video transmission time is maximized according to our analysis. The delayed ACKs effectively reduce the traffic in the reverse path, which is a critical factor in asymmetric links. The beneficial role of delayed ACKs is illustrated in Fig. 13, where the number of delayed packets is slightly decreased (100ms and 500ms delack). However, we observe that issuing ACKs with delays more than 100ms does not result in perceptible performance gains (Figs. 10, 11), since the increased RTTs (as derived from equation (7)) counterbalance the benefits from the reduced ACK transmission time $T''(n)$ (equation (8)).

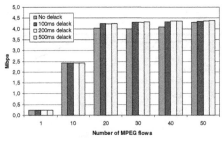

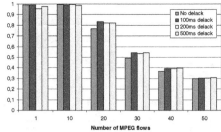

Fig. 10. System Goodput   **Fig. 11.** Average Real-Time Performance
(NewReno-SACK)   (NewReno-SACK)

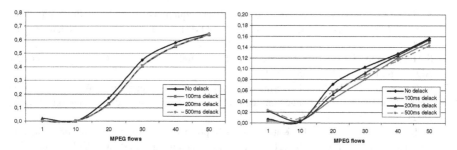

Fig. 12. Packet Drop Rate
(NewReno-SACK)

Fig. 13. Delayed Packets Rate
(NewReno-SACK)

6   Conclusions and Future Work

We demonstrated the challenges and limitations of TCP from the perspective of real-time performance over asymmetric satellite links. We identified that protocol efficiency over such environments is strictly related with effective bandwidth utilization and minimized transmission gaps. Focusing on the study of GEO systems where RTTs exhibit insignificant variations, transmission gaps are primarily induced by reaching downlink capacity, and especially by congested back traffic across a constrained reverse path. We also showed that issuing delayed ACKs occasionally results in performance gains.

The algorithms of TCP Westwood+ and TCP-Real do not always obtain accurate estimates, occasionally failing to achieve full utilization of asymmetric link capacities. However, they are more effective than "blind" increase/decrease window mechanisms (e.g. TCP Reno), which rely on specific events triggered by violated thresholds. TCP-Real, in particular, yields satisfactory performance regardless of link multiplexing; only link errors with BER in excess of 10^{-4} degrade its performance and the perceived video quality. However, error rates of this magnitude are uncommon in modern satellite systems. The investigation of additional protocols efficiency (e.g. SCTP), as well as alternative satellite systems, such as *Demand Assigned Multiple Access (DAMA)* satellite services, is under way.

References

1. I. F. Akyildiz, G. Morabito and S. Palazzo, TCP-Peach: A New Congestion Control Scheme for Satellite IP Networks, IEEE Transactions on Networking, 9(3), pp. 307-321, June 2001
2. H. Balakrishnan, V. Padmanabhan, G. Fairhurst and M. Sooriyabandara, TCP Performance Implications of Network Path Asymmetry, RFC 3449, December 2002
3. H. Balakrishnan, V. Padmanabhan, S. Seshan, and R. Katz, A Comparison of Mechanisms for Improving TCP Performance over Wireless Links, ACM/IEEE Transactions on Networking, 5(6), pp. 756-769, 1997
4. D. Chiu and R. Jain, Analysis of the increase/decrease algorithms for congestion avoidance in computer networks, Journal of Computer Networks, 17(1), pp. 1-14, 1989

5. S. Floyd, M. Handley, J. Padhye, and J. Widmer, Equation-Based Congestion Control for Unicast Applications, In Proc. of ACM SIGCOMM 2000, Stockholm, Sweden, August 2000

6. S. Floyd and T. Henderson, The NewReno Modification to TCP's Fast Recovery Algorithm, Internet RFC 2582, 1999

7. L. Grieco and S. Mascolo, Performance evaluation and comparison of Westwood+, New Reno, and Vegas TCP congestion control, ACM Computer Communication Review, 34(2), pp. 25-38, April 2004

8. T. R. Henderson and R. H. Katz, Transport protocols for Internet-compatible satellite networks, IEEE Journal of Selected Areas in Communications (JSAC), Vol. 17, pp. 326-344, Feb. 1999

9. V. Jacobson, Congestion avoidance and control, In Proc. of ACM SIGCOMM '88, Stanford, USA, August 1988

10. S. Mascolo, C. Casetti, M. Gerla, M. Sanadidi, and R. Wang, TCP Westwood: Bandwidth Estimation for Enhanced Transport over Wireless Links, In Proc. of MobiCom '01, Rome, Italy, July 2001

11. M. Mathis, J. Mahdavi, S. Floyd and A. Romanow, TCP Selective Acknowledgment Options, RFC 2018, October 1996

12. H. Obata, K. Ishida, J. Funasaka and K. Amano, TCP Performance Analysis on Asymmetric Networks Composed of Satellite and Terrestrial Links, In Proc. of 8th Int/nal Conference on Network Protocols (ICNP), Osaka, Japan, November 2000

13. P. Papadimitriou and V. Tsaoussidis, Assessment of Internet Voice Transport with TCP, To appear in Int/nal Journal of Communication Systems (IJCS), Wiley Academics

14. P. Papadimitriou and V. Tsaoussidis, On Transport Layer Mechanisms for Real-Time QoS, Journal of Mobile Multimedia (JMM), 1(4), pp. 342-363, January 2006

15. C. Partridge and T. J. Shepard, TCP/IP Performance over Satellite Links, IEEE Network, 11(5), pp. 44-49, September-October 1997

16. W. Stevens, "TCP Slow Start, Congestion Avoidance, Fast Retransmit, and Fast Recovery Algorithms, RFC 2001, January 1997

17. V. Tsaoussidis, H. Badr, TCP-Probing: Towards an Error Control Schema with Energy and Throughput Performance Gains, In Proc. of 8th Int/nal Conference on Network Protocols (ICNP), Osaka, Japan, November 2000

18. V. Tsaoussidis and I. Matta, Open issues on TCP for Mobile Computing, Journal of Wireless Communications and Mobile Computing, 2(1), pp. 3-20, February 2002

19. V. Tsaoussidis and C. Zhang, TCP Real: Receiver-oriented congestion control, Computer Networks, 40(4), pp. 477-497, November 2002

20. V. Tsaoussidis and C. Zhang, The dynamics of responsiveness and smoothness in heterogeneous networks, IEEE Journal on Selected Areas in Communications, 23(6), pp. 1178-1189, June 2005

21. L. Wood, G. Pavlou and B. Evans, Effects on TCP of Routing Strategies in Satellite Constellations, IEEE Communications Magazine, 39(3), pp. 172-181, March 2001

22. Y. R. Yang and S. S. Lam, General AIMD Congestion Control, In Proc. of 8th Int/nal Conference on Network Protocols (ICNP), Osaka, Japan, November 2000

New TCP Congestion Control Algorithm Based on Bandwidth Measurement for Seamless Vertical Handoffs in Heterogeneous Mobile Networks

An Kyu Hwang, Jae Yong Lee, Hyun Duk Kim,
Whoi Jin Jung, and Byung Chul Kim

Department of Information Communications Engineering,
Chungnam National University, 220, Gung Dong,
Yusung Gu, Daejeon 305-764, Korea
{akhwang, jyl, hdkim, wjjung, byckim}@cnu.ac.kr

Abstract. With the widespread use of wireless Internet and wireless LANs, different wireless technologies, such as 3G cellular networks and WLAN, will cooperate to support more users and applications with higher data rates over wider areas. When a mobile node moves between hybrid networks, a need arises for seamless vertical handoffs between different wireless networks in order to provide high performance data transmission. When an application with a TCP connection in a mobile node performs a vertical handoff, TCP performance is degraded due to packet loss even while the previous TCP state information is maintained during handoff, as 3G and WLAN have different available bandwidths. In this paper, a new congestion control algorithm is proposed for a vertical handoff that improves TCP performance by measuring the rough end-to-end available bandwidth and calculating the slow-start threshold. By ns-2 simulation it is shown that, compared to previous algorithms, the proposed algorithm enhances TCP performance during vertical handoffs.

1 Introduction

Recently, in addition to the sharp increase in the overall amount of mobile terminals, various kinds of mobile services, such as voice, video, multimedia, e-mail and file transfer services demand a high bandwidth and a large coverage area. There have been many wireless technologies developed for wireless Internet. Among these, 3G cellular networks and wireless LANs (WLANs) are the most widely used technologies. 3G cellular networks have high mobility and a large coverage area with a low bandwidth but a high cost. WLAN [1] supports a high data rate with a low cost, and it is appropriate for small hot-spot areas such as airports, hotels and large buildings. Thus, there is on-going research for a cooperation technology through which a mobile terminal can utilize 3G networks with their low speed and high cost in the absence of WLAN, but that can also immediately change its network attachment to WLAN with its low cost and high speed whenever it gradually moves to a WLAN service area. When this happens, the mobile terminal should have both physical interfaces (3G and WLAN) and the ability to perform vertical handoffs when moving between two network boundaries. In terms of vertical handoffs over horizontal

T. Braun et al. (Eds.): WWIC 2006, LNCS 3970, pp. 75–83, 2006.
© Springer-Verlag Berlin Heidelberg 2006

handoffs within the same network, many more aspects must be taken into consideration, as two different networks can have many different characteristics, such as the available amount of bandwidth and the wireless access delay.

The TCP protocol is the most widely used transport protocol for current Internet applications. It is estimated that more than 90% of Internet traffic is carried by TCP [2]. TCP continuously attempts to determine the optimal available bandwidth using a slow-start and the AIMD (additive increase and multiplicative decrease) congestion control mechanism. It maintains and updates the congestion window (*cwnd*) and the window threshold (ssthresh) to send data in relation to the current estimated bandwidth between the source and destination. However, since TCP is designed and tuned for the wired Internet, there are several problems with it in relation to mobile and wireless networks. TCP uses packet loss as a congestion indication, and to reduce its congestion window. It also recognizes random losses (not by congestion but by mobility and bit error) in the wireless networks as congestion and performs congestion control by reducing its congestion window. This is one of the main reasons for TCP throughput degradation in wireless networks. There have been many studies that address this problem in the literature [3] – [5].

In this paper, the focus is on TCP performance improvement for vertical handoffs between heterogeneous mobile networks. When an application with a TCP connection in a mobile station performs a vertical handoff, TCP performance is degraded due to the different available bandwidth between the 3G and WLAN networks, even while the previous TCP state information is maintained during the handoff. When the handoff is from WLAN to 3G, much packet loss can occur due to the lower available amount of bandwidth inherent with 3G compared to WLAN. In contrast, when the handoff is from 3G to WLAN, the older TCP state cannot adapt quickly to the larger available bandwidth of WLAN, thus TCP performance is degraded. In this paper, a new congestion control algorithm for TCP with vertical handoffs is proposed. For a handoff from WLAN to 3G, the algorithm performs a slow-start with "*cwnd* = 1" to determine the available bandwidth. For a handoff from 3G to WLAN, it also performs a slow-start using the previous congestion window before the handoff in 3G to quickly determine the available bandwidth in WLAN. In order to prevent substantial packet loss caused by overshoot during the slow-start, an approximate measurement of the available bandwidth after the handoff is taken and the congestion window threshold is set up (ssthresh) properly. According to ns-2 simulation, it is shown that the proposed algorithm enhances TCP performance during vertical handoffs compared to previous algorithms.

This paper is organized as follows. In Section 2, the concept of a vertical handoff and existing research in this area are presented. In Section 3, the design of the new TCP congestion control algorithm for vertical handoffs is proposed, and its detailed operation is explained. The performance of the proposed algorithms is shown by ns-2 simulation in Section 4. A conclusion and further study areas are given in Section 5.

2   Related Works

In this section, the kinds of handoffs in mobile networks are classified, and the requirements for mobile stations for cooperation between 3G and WLAN networks are presented. In addition the existing algorithms for TCP performance improvement in vertical handoff are reviewed.

2.1 Vertical Handoff and Dual-Mode Mobile Station

It is possible to classify the handoffs in mobile networks into horizontal handoffs and vertical handoffs [6]. A horizontal handoff is a handoff between base stations (BS) using the same wireless interface. A vertical handoff represents handoffs between two or more different wireless network interfaces. Additionally, it is possible to classify vertical handoffs into upward and downward types in a hierarchical mobile network structure [6]. The upward vertical handoff type denotes a handoff from small-coverage high-rate networks to large-coverage low-rate networks, for instance from WLAN to 3G networks. The downward vertical handoff signifies a handoff from large-coverage low-rate networks to small-coverage high-rate networks, such as from 3G to WLAN networks.

The mobile station used in a hybrid of 3G and WLAN networks should have dual-mode wireless interfaces and protocol stacks for both 3G and WLAN. It has to have the RF and antenna components for the corresponding frequency ranges of both network types. In addition, it needs a type of mobility protocol. When a mobile station moves within wireless networks, it should be able to provide continuous service to its applications without disconnection. The mobile IP (MIP) protocol [7] is an important mobility protocols that provide connection continuity in the session layer during physical layer handoffs in wireless networks. However, although a mobile station may have a mobility protocol such as MIP and can provide a continuous connection in the session level, the TCP protocol suffers performance degradation due to problems such as packet loss, packet reordering, timeout, as it was designed for wired network environments. There have been many studies concerning TCP performance improvement in wireless mobile networks. In the next subsection, a number of these are reviewed, in terms of their relation to the present study.

2.2 TCP Enhancement for Wireless Networks

The Freeze-TCP [3] protocol was proposed to avoid the degradation of TCP performance during handoffs in mobile networks. The mobile station can predict the impending handoff and disconnection by monitoring the signal strength using its wireless antenna. In this case, the TCP receiver in the mobile station advertises a zero receiver window size, and the TCP sender enters the ZWP (zero window probes) mode and keeps all TCP variables, including the congestion window, in a frozen state. After a handoff or reconnection, the receiver informs the sender of the possible receiver window size using a duplicate ACK. Through this mechanism, the TCP sender can maintain timer values, and can maintain the congestion window without the need for a reduction. It also prevents a spurious timeout during handoffs. However, although the Freeze-TCP protocol can improve the TCP performance during horizontal handoffs by maintaining the TCP states, it can cause some problems during vertical handoffs due to the different available bandwidths for the two different wireless technologies. In the downward vertical handoff, the congestion window and threshold used in low-rate networks may prevent the rapid usage of a large amount of available bandwidth in WLAN networks. In contrast, in the upward vertical handoff, the frozen TCP states with a large congestion window can lead to heavy packet losses and a congestion control procedure that severely degrades TCP performance.

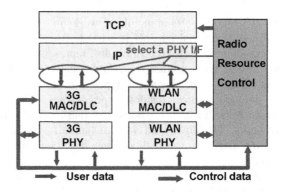

Fig. 1. Protocol stack of mobile station in SS-TCP

Kim and Copeland [8] proposed an algorithm to improve TCP performance during vertical handoffs using the physical layer information. This algorithm is termed "SS-TCP" in this paper. The protocol stack of a mobile station proposed with the SS-TCP algorithm is shown in Fig. 1. The mobile station has two network interfaces, one each for 3G and for WLAN. It also has a RRC (radio resource control) module that measures the received signal strength and informs TCP of impending handoff events. The TCP receiver in the mobile terminal advertises a zero receiver window and freezes the TCP sender states immediately before the handoff to prevent packet loss and timeouts. After the handoff, the receiver informs the sender regarding the vertical or horizontal handoff information using two option bits in the TCP header, as it sends a duplicate ACK to resolve the frozen states of the sender. In the case of a horizontal handoff, the sender operates in the same way as the Freeze-TCP protocol. For a vertical handoff, it discards all the TCP state information and resumes the slow-start with a congestion window of 1. Although the SS-TCP algorithm tries to adapt to the new network environment in the vertical handoff using the slow-start, it cannot use the existing TCP states in the case of the downward vertical handoff where the available bandwidth has increased, and may cause a large amount of packet loss during the slow-start after vertical handoffs.

3 A TCP Performance Enhancement Algorithm for Vertical Handoffs

In this section, a new congestion control algorithm for TCP performance improvements on vertical handoffs is proposed. It also uses an RRC module, as with SS-TCP, to detect impending handoffs. The mobile station distinguishes between upward and downward handoffs for vertical handoffs, and applies different window controls. For downward vertical handoffs, the TCP sender reuses the frozen variables and slow-starts from the previous congestion window. To prevent large packet losses during the slow-start, it takes a rough measurement of the available bandwidth in the new path and sets up an appropriate slow-start threshold (ssthresh) value. For upward vertical handoffs, it also performs a slow-start with a congestion window of 1. In these cases, it also measures the available bandwidth in order to properly set up the ssthresh value in order to prevent overshoot. This algorithm can quickly approach the available bandwidth of the new path after the handoff, while it preventing the overshoot that causes a great amount of packet loss during the slow-start, and allows the TCP to enter the congestion avoidance mode properly. In this paper, this algorithm is termed the "Measurement-based slow-start TCP (MSS-TCP)".

3.1 Measurement of the Available Bandwidth

The bandwidth measurement method proposed in [9] that uses the ACKs received at the sender is utilized, as shown in Fig. 2. If $BW_{E,k-1}$ is the estimated bandwidth at the arrival instant of the $(k-1)^{th}$ ACK, it is then possible to calculate the bandwidth $BW_{E,new}$ at the arrival instant of the kth ACK, as shown in (1), where T_k is the interarrival time between the $(k-1)^{th}$ and the kth ACKs, and the $Total\_packet\_size_k$

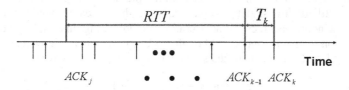

Fig. 2. The bandwidth measurement in MSS-TCP

represents the total packet size acknowledged between the two ACKs.

$$BW_{E,new} = \frac{BW_{E,k-1} \times RTT + Total\_packet\_size_k}{RTT + T_k} \tag{1}$$

The bandwidth at the kth ACK time, $BW_{E,k}$, is obtained by the EWMA (exponentially weighted moving average) method, as shown in (2), in which the parameter α is adjusted for smoothing.

$$BW_{E,k} = \alpha \cdot BW_{E,k-1} + (1-\alpha)BW_{E,new} \tag{2}$$

3.2 The MSS-TCP Algorithm

The MSS-TCP uses four options, with two option bits in the TCP header; whereas the SS-TCP uses three options. In Table 1, the processing rules for each option in the SS-TCP and the MSS-TCP are shown. The operation of the MSS-TCP is identical to that of the SS-TCP for horizontal handoffs. However, it is different for upward and downward types of vertical handoffs.

First, for downward vertical handoffs, the sender measures the available bandwidth immediately after the handoff in order to obtain the ssthresh, while maintaining the previous TCP state variables as in the Freeze-TCP. The ssthresh is calculated as follows:

$$ssthresh = \frac{BW_{E,k} \times RTT}{AveragePacketSize} \tag{3}$$

Table 1. Processing rules for each option

SS-TCP		MSS-TCP	
Option field	CWND	Option field	CWND
00 (No HO)	Same to TCP Reno	00 (No HO)	Same to TCP Reno
01		01(3G → WLAN)	Modified Freeze TCP
10 (Horizontal)	Freeze TCP	10 (WLAN → 3G)	Modified Slow-Start
11 (Vertical)	Slow-Start	11 (Horizontal)	Freeze TCP

If the measured bandwidth is higher than the previously used bandwidth, the TCP begins a modified slow-start to become equal to the increased bandwidth, until the congestion window becomes the new ssthresh. Following this, the TCP enters into the congestion avoidance mode. Although the congestion window increases by 1 for each received ACK, in the modified slow-start it increases as follows:

$$cwnd+ = \frac{cwnd - old\_cwnd + 1}{cwnd} \tag{4}$$

where *old_cwnd* denotes the congestion window value at the point of the slow-start after the bandwidth measurement. In other words, the effect of the old_cwnd is not included in the exponential increase of the congestion window in the present modified slow-start.

Secondly, for upward vertical handoffs, the sender performs the slow-start with a congestion window of 1, as in the normal TCP. However, by measuring the bandwidth and setting up the ssthresh, it prevents overshoot and packet loss after the handoff, which improves TCP performance.

4   Simulation Results

In this section, the simulation results for the vertical handoff performance of the normal TCP, the SS-TCP and the MSS-TCP using ns-2 simulator [10] are presented. The bandwidth is set to 0.144 Mbps, and the RTT to 300 m sec for 3G networks; these readings are 5.5 Mbps and 100 m sec, respectively, for the WLAN. The packet size isset to 1000 bytes and the parameter α to 0.75 for the MSS-TCP. The TCP performance using a FTP application is compared for the hybrid network topology in a simulation, as shown in Fig. 3.

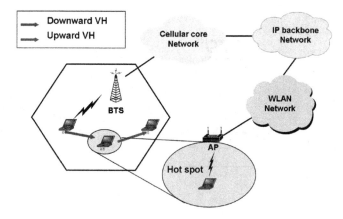

Fig. 3. Simulation topology

Fig. 4 shows the congestion window and amount of transmitted packets in the case of a downward vertical handoff. In Fig. 4 (a), the congestion window of the Freeze-TCP protocol increases slowly and linearly in the CA (congestion avoidance) mode, as in the previous network using identical TCP states, even after a handoff to a high-bandwidth network. The SS-TCP begins a slow-start after a handoff with $cwnd$ =1, which causes a sharp increase in the congestion window and results in very large amount of packet loss. The MSS-TCP proposed in this paper utilizes the previous congestion window as in the Freeze-TCP, but it performs the modified slow-starts to obtain the high available bandwidth quickly after the bandwidth measurement. There is no overshoot and packet loss, even in the slow-start period, due to the proper measurement-based setting of the ssthresh. Fig. 4 (b) shows that the MSS-TCP can transmit the largest number of packets among the three algorithms.

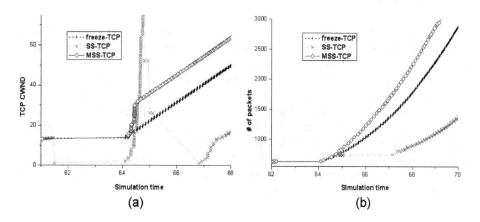

Fig. 4. Performance in a downward vertical handoff. (a) Congestion window (b) Number of packets transmitted after the handoff

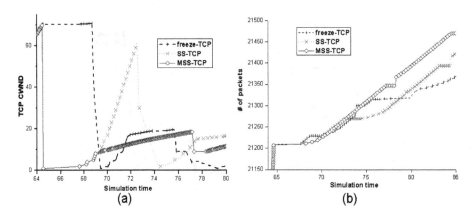

Fig. 5. Performance in an upward vertical handoff. (a) Congestion window (b) Number of packets transmitted after the handoff.

The congestion window and amount of transmitted packets in the case of a downward vertical handoff are shown in Fig. 5. In Fig. 5 (a), the congestion window of the Freeze-TCP decreases significantly, as it uses the frozen congestion window from the previous network even after the handoff to a low bandwidth network. The SS-TCP attempts to search for a proper congestion window using a slow-start from *cwnd* = 1; however, it experiences packet losses due to an inappropriate ssthresh. On the other hand, as the MSS-TCP can set the ssthresh to an appropriate value by measuring the available bandwidth, it does not suffer from a packet loss problem, and enters into the congestion avoidance mode smoothly. The MSS-TCP also shows the best performance in terms of the number of transmitted packets after the handoff.

5 Conclusion

In this paper, a seamless vertical handoff algorithm for TCP performance enhancement in hybrid wireless mobile networks is proposed. A TCP receiver in a mobile node informs of impending handoffs and handoff types using two bit option fields in a TCP ACK packet. The TCP sender manipulates the congestion window differently according to whether there will be a horizontal handoff, an upward vertical handoff or a downward vertical handoff. In case of a vertical handoff, the modified slow-start is adopted in order to quickly monitor the change in the available bandwidth while preventing overflow packet losses by the bandwidth measurement. By ns-2 simulation, it is shown that the MSS-TCP outperforms the existing TCPs. The MSS-TCP can be a promising transport protocol for a seamless vertical handoff for heterogeneous wireless mobile networks in the future.

Acknowledgements. This work was supported by the Korea Science & Engineering Foundation (KOSEF) under grant number R01-2003-000-10628-0.

References

1. LAN MAN Standards Committee of the IEEE Computer Society. : Wireless LAN Medium Access Control (MAC) and Physical Layer (PHY) Specifications. IEEE Standard 802.11., (1999)
2. Thomson, K., Miller, G. J., Wilder, R.: Wide-area Internet Traffic Patterns and Characteristics. IEEE Network, Volume 11., (1997) 10-23
3. Goff, T., Moronski, J., Phatak , DS., Gupta, V.: Freeze-TCP: A True End-To-End TCP Enhancement Mechanism for Mobile Environments. In: Proceedings of IEEE INFOCOM, Volume 3., (2003) 1537-1545
4. Balakrishnan, H., Seshan, S., Katz, R.H.: Improving Reliable Transport and Handoff Performance in Cellular Wireless Networks. ACM Wireless Networks, Volume 1., (1995) 469-481
5. Brown , K., Singh, S.: M-TCP : TCP for Mobile Cellular Networks. ACM SIGCOMM Computer Communication Review, Volume 27., (1997) 19-43
6. Stemm, M., Katz, R.H.: Vertical Handoffs in Wireless Overlay Networks. ACM Mobile Networking and Applications (MONET), Volume 3., (1998) 335-350
7. Perkins, C. Ed., : "IP Mobility Support for IPv4", IETF RFC 3220 (2002)
8. Kim, S., Copeland, J.: TCP for Seamless Vertical Handoff in Hybrid Mobile Data Networks. In: Proceedings of IEEE GLOBECOM, San Francisco, Volume 2., (2003) 661-665
9. Xu, K., Tian, Y., Ansari, N.: TCP-Jersey for Wireless IP Communications. IEEE J. Select. Areas Comulications, Volume 22., (2004) 747-756
10. The Network Simulator ns-2. Available: http://www.isi.edu/nsnam/ns

On the Potential of Heterogeneous Networks

Marc Danzeisen, Torsten Braun, Isabel Steiner, and Marc Heissenbüttel

University of Bern, Bern, Switzerland
{danzeis, braun, isteiner, heissen}@iam.unibe.ch

Abstract. Many research work is going on in the domain of pure ad-hoc networking and even more issues are raised due to the missing central infrastructure to properly manage resources, guarantee fairness, and provide security features. On the other hand lot of research effort is spent to increase the performance of infrastructure-based access networks to cope with the steadily increasing demand for broadband data. When making a step back, the most promising evolution of heterogeneous networking is the integration of both paradigms. Taking advantage of the well controlled cellular environment and the high capacity of ad-hoc and direct node-to-node communication. The resulting hybrid networks are incorporating the best of both worlds. The concept of *Cellular Assisted Heterogeneous Networking* (CAHN) provides a framework to offer convenient and secure management of heterogeneous end-to-end sessions between nodes. The introduced separation of the signaling and the data plane allows to switch on power demanding broadband interfaces like GPRS, UMTS, or even WLAN only, if actually required, i.e., data has to be sent or received. The proposed out-of-band signaling enables furthermore the integration of ad-hoc links to offer best performance whenever nodes are within vicinity. Extensive simulations show that both, the integration of ad-hoc links and the selective activation of high power broadband interfaces, can significantly increase the performance of heterogeneous networks.

1   Introduction

The layered structure of the ISO/OSI communication stack has enabled high flexibility by decoupling the underlying network technology from the applications to a certain extend. However, most of the applications are not independent of the communication characteristics provided by the underlying network. Applications often require a certain level of bandwidth, delay or security to work properly. Analyzing further these applications reveals that their requirements also depend on the user's situation. The level of mobility has an impact on the way applications (or services) are used. The capabilities of the devices used in the different situations is very much influencing the requirements on the service and therefore on the underlying network. A single network can not cope anymore with the different and often changing requirements. The development and deployment of the 3G cellular network clearly showed the complexity to build up one network, which fits all the requirements of nowadays and future mobile applications. To optimally meet the applications need, different communication technologies have to collaborate.

T. Braun et al. (Eds.): WWIC 2006, LNCS 3970, pp. 84–95, 2006.

The motivation for such a collaboration is further discussed in [1], where the vision of being *always best connected* is introduced, connecting mobile nodes with the most appropriate communication technology. Dynamically assigning the most appropriate networking resources to each node, depending on its actual needs and capabilities, may increase the customer satisfaction and the overall performance of the heterogeneous network at the same time. The middleware presented in [2] and [3] is able to gather context information of the application layer to optimize the handover decision. However, network environment information is also permanently influencing the proper selection of the most appropriate communication technology. Mobility poses an additional challenge by constantly changing the network environment, e.g., used networks become unavailable or new ones get detected.

The concept of MIRAI [4, 5, 6] addresses this problem by defining dynamically one channel to be used for signaling information and negotiation of handover decisions. The authors proposed an agent based platform that provides location-based information on available access networks through a so-called basic access signaling, which is assumed to have a larger coverage than all other access networks. This concept is very beneficial, especially if the basic access signaling channel is a low power channel. In [7] it has been shown that such a signaling channel does not have to provide high data rates. MIRAI focuses on infrastructure-based access networks only. But communicating nodes can come close enough to establish direct links based on short range and infrastructure-less communication technologies. These links have the potential to deliver data rates which are orders of magnitude higher than infrastructure-based links will ever do. Especially in scenarios, where nodes are moving in groups and the probability of being within the range of direct communication is high, the average data rates can be considerably increased. This is the case for public transportation, battlefield scenarios, but also in smaller campus networks.

Extending the vision of being always-on and best connected to infrastructure-less communication technologies introduces a major conflict between the interests of a network operator and the ones of the end users. Offering better performance in terms of bandwidth and costs, it might become the first choice to exchange large amounts of data between nodes. At first glance, there is no motivation in keeping infrastructure-based connections offered by the operator in that case. However, simulations presented later in this paper are showing that the benefit of using direct links is considerably increased if infrastructure-based networks can take over the session whenever the direct link is lost. The usage of infrastructure-less links might also become economically interesting for the network operator. If the price of broadband connectivity is further falling, the operators will be forced to reduce the costs of their infrastructure. Introducing an intelligent resource management for heterogeneous network resources could help to reduce the cost of a data session. The possibility to offer connectivity through infrastructure-less technologies, which are already built in nowadays devices, may offer an interesting option.

The integration of both network paradigm is also beneficial for infrastructure-less communication technologies. Due to the missing authentication infrastructure, the provisioning of security features in pure ad-hoc networks is still challenging. In hybrid networks combining infrastructure-based and ad-hoc elements some of the problems can be solved. Therefore, efficient and secured signaling over infrastructure-based networks will probably be a key value proposition, even if the actual data is transported using ad-hoc networks free of charge.

The next section is addressing the possibilities of such a broadband on-demand mode and the integration of ad-hoc links enabled by the concept of *Cellular Assisted Heterogeneous Networking* in further detail. Detailed evaluations on the improvement potential of an intelligent end-to-end session management for the end user experience and for the operator are presented in the simulation section. The last section concludes the paper.

2   Cellular Assisted Heterogeneous Networking

When considering the interconnection of any two nodes, the optimal data path might be very heterogeneous. Depending on the available networks, the optimal end-to-end data path between the nodes can consist of infrastructure-based and ad-hoc links. Fig. 1 illustrates a scenario where two communicating nodes are moving abroad connecting to UMTS and Wireless LAN (e.g., Public Hotspot). Initially, node 1 and node 2 are communicating using the cellular network (step 1). Then the node 1 changes its point of attachment to WLAN and sends an update message to the node 2 (step 2). If now the nodes move towards the same WLAN access point, the session path can be optimized (step 3). The traffic is not further sent trough the Internet. If both nodes come close enough to each other, the session is switched to direct node-to-node communication (step 4).

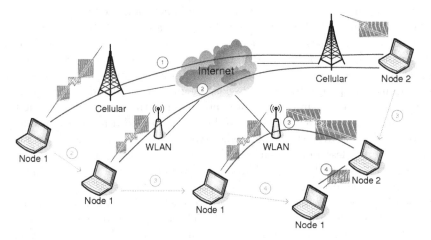

Fig. 1. Handover between Infrastructure-based and Infrastructure-less Communication

The integration of infrastructure-less connections between communicating nodes to enhance the performance is very challenging. The missing infrastructure to properly and automatically negotiate required parameters to establish a secured and optimized direct links is imposing some major hurdles that have to be taken before users can benefit from higher performance without compromising security.

To enable such heterogenous networking enabling an always best connected experience throughout all available communication technologies including direct peer-to-peer links, a novel architecture and protocol was implemented and presented in [8, 9]. The system architecture proposed allows the independent routing of signaling and data related information over different communication technologies. Unlike the inband signaling of IP, where the data channel has to be established before the first signaling messages can be exchanged, the ability to first exchange signaling information on a dedicated signaling channel is highly beneficial in heterogeneous environments. The separated treatment of signaling and data related information allows optimal resource management. During the data session establishment the nodes can learn about the networking capabilities and actual environment, such as the currently available networks at the peer's location. Although the system architecture can be used to dynamically route the signaling messages over any type of communication technology, we argue that the use of the existing cellular mobile network as the primary signaling plane has several advantages. The well established and power optimized location, paging, and mobility management services can implicitly be shared for other communication technologies and networks, which are lacking such functionality. Especially the low power characteristics of the cellular mobile network is beneficial when addressing the power management of heterogeneous communication. With the help of the concept and architecture proposed in [10, 11], such a general signaling service could be offered to handle any type of transport network. To further increase the efficiency of the signaling of heterogeneous end-to-end sessions, we propose to do only the bootstrapping through the valuable cellular network, if no other secured IP connectivity is available. Furthermore, the signaling messages are sent inband after successful data channel setup, whenever possible. The end-to-end session management, together with the separation of signaling and data related information facilitates the concept of being reachable without wasting valuable networking resources. The ability to reach any node through the low power cellular network allows switching power demanding broadband data channels to sleep mode if no actual data session is going on. Reachability is no longer coupled with power demanding broadband IP connectivity. Waking up data channel interfaces only on-demand can considerably increase the power efficiency of the mobile devices. This *on-demand mode* also has the potential to increase the efficiency of allocated networking resources because the nodes are only attached to the network when data has to be transferred.

Furthermore, the security relation between the cellular subscriber and the network operator together with the roaming relations between the operators offer a secured communication channel which can be used to securely exchange the protocol messages. Especially if the establishment of infrastructure-less communication channels is considered, the secure exchange of configuration and security related parameters is absolutely mandatory to securely bootstrap the connections. Having established a secured initial communication between the communicating entities, all other parameters required to establish further communication channels can securely be negotiated. The concept of Cellular Assisted Heterogenous Networking (CAHN) provides the missing part to securely extend the scope of heterogeneous networking also to ad-hoc links. The ability of CAHN to securely bootstrap infrastructure-less communication between nodes enables the system to consider also direct node-to-node links when evaluating the most appropriate connection. Throughout the rest of this paper this feature is also referred to as *ad-hoc mode*.

3 Simulations

3.1 The Heterogeneous Network Simulator

We implemented a dedicated network simulator that allows the modeling of heterogeneous networks at a simplified level. The simulator does not account for any physical propagation medium properties or MAC layer functionality and simulates sessions between peer mobile nodes at the application level, i.e., the simulations are flow based. There are several reason why we did not use existing network simulators (ns2, Qualnet, OpNet, etc.). Among others they do not provide appropriate support for the simulation of heterogeneous networks with dynamic vertical handovers during runtime, end-to-end communication between nodes using different wireless technologies simultaneously, and switching between infrastructure and ad-hoc mode of operation. Furthermore, these simulators either do not yet implement certain wireless technologies, e.g., GPRS in Qualnet, or implement different technologies for different incompatible versions, e.g., UMTS for ns-2.26 and GPRS for ns-2b7a. The necessary modifications to the network simulators to enable the simulations of the intended scenarios would require a tremendous implementation work and is out of scope of this paper.

The transmission ranges for different wireless technologies are modeled as circles with varying radiuses with respect to their characteristics, e.g., small radius for broadband technologies such as WLAN and larger radius for 2.5 and 3 G technologies with narrower bandwidth such as GPRS and UMTS. Even though the simulator does not take into account the lower layers of the protocol stack, it allows the estimation of the possible benefits of the two main features of CAHN in heterogeneous networking environments, namely the ad-hoc and on-demand mode.

The different access technologies can be defined with limited capacity and adaptive data rates delivered to each node depending on the actual load of the cell or access point as described below. To model the bandwidth assignment for a UMTS node, we considered the up- and downlink channel separately. The uplink bandwidth is statically set to $64\,kbit/s$ per node, independently of the assigned downlink bandwidth. The overall capacity m offered by the base station is assigned to the attached nodes n until there is no capacity left to assign.

$$\text{bandwidth}_{up} = \begin{cases} 64\,kbit/s, \; \frac{m}{n} \geq 64 \\ \\ 0\,kbit/s, \text{ otherwise} \end{cases}$$

The downlink bandwidth is equally distributed to the attached nodes. The UMTS provides different bandwidth rates, namely $384\,kbit/s$, $128\,kbit/s$, and $64\,kbit/s$. If n is the number of nodes and m is the maximum capacity offered by the base station, the assigned bandwidth is modeled as follows:

$$\text{bandwidth}_{down} = \begin{cases} 384\,kbit/s, \; \frac{m}{n} \geq 384 \\ \\ 128\,kbit/s, \; \frac{m}{n} \geq 128 \\ \\ 64\,kbit/s, \; \frac{m}{n} \geq 64 \\ \\ 0, \text{ otherwise} \end{cases}$$

GPRS is modeled based on TDMA slots. The coding scheme (CS) is statically set to CS4, which is providing $21.4\,kbit/s$ per slot. In the model we assume that CS4 can be used for up- and downlink independent of the distance between the node and the base station. We further assume class 10 devices, allowing 4 downlink and 2 uplink slots maximum. The number of assigned slots is depending on the availability of slots. The network tries to assign the maximum number of slots supported but dynamically adapts the assignment to guarantee uniform distribution of the available resources. For the uplink this results in the following slot assignment model, where n is again the number of nodes and m the maximum capacity offered by the base station.

$$\text{bandwidth}_{up} = \begin{cases} 42.8\,kbit/s, \; \frac{m}{n} \geq 42.8 \\ \\ 21.4\,kbit/s, \; \frac{m}{n} \geq 21.4 \\ \\ 0\,kbit/s, \text{ otherwise} \end{cases}$$

The downlink slot assignment is modeled similarly, but allowing up to 4 slot per node.

$$\text{bandwidth}_{down} = \begin{cases} 85.6\,kbit/s, \; \frac{m}{n} \geq 85.6 \\ \\ 42.8\,kbit/s, \; \frac{m}{n} \geq 42.8 \\ \\ 21.4\,kbit/s, \; \frac{m}{n} \geq 21.4 \\ \\ 0, \text{ otherwise} \end{cases}$$

The medium access mechanism of WLAN is aiming at the provisioning of equal bandwidth for all attached nodes. Unlike in GPRS or UMTS, the up- and downlink are not treated separately. Sending and receiving nodes are competing for the same medium. To simplify the modeling of WLAN we assume that no collisions occur and the maximum available capacity can equally be assigned to the nodes without loss because of collision recovery mechanisms (e.g. backoff). The model used for resource assignment for WLAN nodes is consequently as follows, where n is the number of nodes competing for the medium and m the overall capacity of the medium:

$$\text{bandwidth}_{up/down} = \frac{m}{n}, kbit/s$$

3.2 Simulation Scenarios

The simulation area is set to $2000\,m$ x $2000\,m$ where the nodes move according to the random waypoint mobility model with a speed in the interval $[1, 15]m/s$ and a pause time of $30\,s$. The simulation time was set to $4600\,s$ including a $1000\,s$ warm-up phase for the mobility model to reach a stable state. Random sessions are established between pairs of nodes, where the session arrival rate is Poisson distributed with a rate of two sessions per hour and source-destination pair. The amount of data transferred per session is Pareto distributed between $10\,KB$ - $100\,MB$.

Each node always uses the available wireless technology with the highest bandwidth, i.e., a vertical handover occurs whenever a nodes moves into the range of a technology with a higher bandwidth. Consequently, the effective session transfer rate is the minimum bandwidth of the technologies, currently used by the two communicating nodes.

Three different wireless infrastructure-based technologies, namely GPRS, UMTS, WLAN, are deployed over the simulation area. Furthermore, there is an infrastructure-less wireless technology that allows for peer-to-peer communication for which we also used WLAN. The overall capacity for GPRS nodes is set dynamically according to the number of nodes for each simulation. Assuming that network operators deploy enough bandwidth to serve all nodes, which equals n, with the minimal data rate of one TDMA slot for both, the up- and downlink, we define the overall capacity of GPRS as n up- and n downlink slots. These slots are uniformly distributed among the GPRS cells, resulting in blocked sessions if the nodes are not equally distributed among the cells. In all simulation scenarios GPRS covers the whole simulation area and the coverage of UMTS is set to 80 % and the WLAN coverage to 10 % of the overall simulation area. UMTS cells with coverage radius of $450\,m$ are supposed to offer a maximum capacity of $1024\,kbit/s$, which is uniformally distributed among the nodes according to the model previously defined. Analogously, the transmission range of WLAN is set to $150\,m$ and the maximum capacity (m) per access point was set to $11\,Mbit/s$ as provided by the 802.11b standard.

3.3 Simulation Results

We analyze the influence of CAHN on the overall network performance. The simulation results have been analyzed in terms of network load and efficiency, throughput, and session block and drop rates. The different terms are defined in the following sections. All simulation results are given with a 95 % confidence interval. We also conducted simulations with higher session arrival rate, lower coverage of UMTS and WLAN, and other mobility models. However due to lack of space, the results are not given in this paper.

Network Load. The overall network load is calculated based on the load of each technology. Each load is weighted according to the coverage provided by that specific technology. This reflects the fact that the overall network load is mainly dependant on the load of technologies serving a large area. The network load is evaluated for different numbers of nodes and sessions. Both CAHN features, the ad-hoc and on-demand modes, are enabled and disabled to analyze the impact on the overall network load. Figure 2 shows the four resulting network loads as a function of the number of nodes. The ability to liberate network resources by

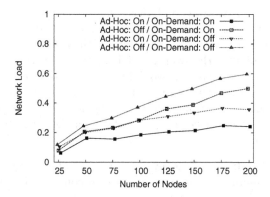

Fig. 2. Network Load

switching ongoing sessions to infrastructure-less technologies whenever possible reduces the network load by up to 24 %. Thus, the network is able to serve more nodes with the same capacity if the ad-hoc feature is enabled. The on-demand feature further increases the number of nodes that can be served. With the on-demand feature, inactive nodes do not occupy cellular network resources. The less sessions the nodes have, the higher the resource saving potential of this feature. With 2 sessions per hour about up to 12 % of the network resources can be liberated due to the on-demand feature and eventually assigned to other nodes.

Network Efficiency. To further measure the influence when the ad-hoc mode is enabled, we introduce a new metric called network efficiency. With regards to the ad-hoc feature, we define the network efficiency as the ratio between traffic sent using ad-hoc links and the overall traffic sent by the nodes. This indicates how much traffic the network can offload to the direct ad-hoc links. The bigger this ratio, the less operator resources are used to transfer the session data. We additionally run simulations with an arrival rate of eight sessions per

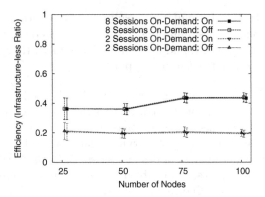

Fig. 3. Network Efficiency

hour as depicted in Fig. 3. We can observe that the efficiency is not dependant on the number of nodes and is approximately 20 % and 40 % for the lower and higher session arrival rate, respectively. Similarly, the influence of the on-demand feature is almost negligible. However, for higher number of sessions the efficiency increases by more than a factor of two. This is mainly due to the high network load, which decreases the availability of the infrastructure-based links and thus their average throughput per source-destination pair, and consequently increases the impact of the data transferred using the high data rates offered by the infrastructure-less connections.

Session Block Probability. Whenever a node is not able to start the session because of missing available network resources this is considered as a session block. The node continuously tries to start the data transmission until either another node releases resources in the congested cell or the node moves to another cell with available capacity. If the preferred technology is not available, the node connects to any other available networking technology, independent whether it is the most appropriate for that actual session. Thus, the network overrides the node's preference

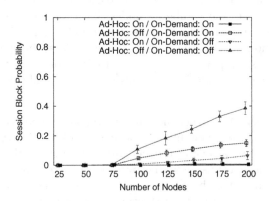

Fig. 4. Session Block Rate

if the overall network performance can be increased. The network is able to serve approximately 75 nodes without blocking any resource request as depicted in Fig. 4. The nodes are therefore distributed to all available networks. The network forces the nodes to switch to another technology if this increases the overall number of servable nodes. Depending on whether the ad-hoc and on-demand mode are enabled, the increase of the session block probability is steeper for a higher number of nodes. When both features are disabled, the probability for a block session is approximately 40 % for 200 nodes. The on-demand mode reduces that probability to less than the half. The ad-hoc mode has even a bigger impact on the session block probability. Together with the on-demand feature, the blocking probability can be kept close to 0 for up to 200 nodes.

Session Drop Rate. Whenever a communicating node comes into a congested cell, the ongoing session is dropped. The cell is congested if according to the resource assignment model, the remaining capacity of the base station is smaller than the minimum assignable bandwidth.

Figure 5 shows the number of drops that occur during a session. If more than 75 nodes are using the network, the sessions get continuously dropped, frequently more than once, i.e., sessions are interrupted several times before completing. If there are more than 125 nodes, the average number of drops per session reaches its maximum.

During the time when a node is not connected because it suffered from a dropped call, no further drops can occur, which results in a decreasing number of drops per session again because the simulation period is limited and unfinished session are stopped at the end of the simulation. If the network load is high enough, the sessions do not terminate during the simulation period and tend thus to have less drops. In this stage, the network is not able to serve additional sessions, which further decreases the average number of drops per session.

With the on-demand mode the drops can be avoided completely due to the released network resources between the sessions. The ad-hoc feature considerably reduces the drop rate but is not able to avoid all session drops.

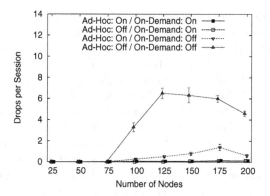

Fig. 5. Session Drop Rate

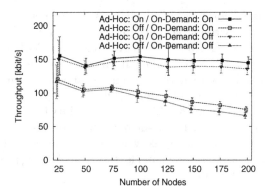

Fig. 6. Session Throughput

Session Throughput. The amount of data transmitted is simply derived from the time attached to a certain technology and its bandwidth. The average session throughput includes the delays and outages imposed by the session blocking and dropping, which may occur if nodes have to share the network capacity. These delays increase the duration of a session and, thus, decrease the average throughput of the session. Furthermore, the actual throughput is decreased whenever the network has to perform load balancing. If a node moves into a congested UMTS cell, the network assigns GPRS instead. The ad-hoc mode is much more beneficial for the the throughput than the on-demand mode is as shown in Figure 6 and can increase the data rate from approximately 100 kbit/s to more than 150 kbit/s. This is mainly due to the high data rates offered by the ad-hoc links which provide much higher bandwidth links. The on-demand mode only marginally increases the average session throughput by freeing network resources from inactive nodes which increases the probability for transmitting nodes to use an available technology with a higher bandwidth.

4   Conclusion

In this paper we addressed the potential impact of the proposed CAHN concept on the performance of heterogeneous networks. We first introduced the two main features offered by CAHN, namely the ability to use power demanding broadband communication technologies only on-demand and bootstrap ad-hoc connection between nodes, whenever they are within the range of direct communication. We then presented the Heterogeneous Network Simulator, which allows the simulation of data sessions beyond the boundaries of communication technologies. The simulation results shows that the two features of CAHN enable the efficient use of available network resources. In certain scenarios the network load can be decreased by about 50 %, which results in lower session drop and blocking rates. Furthermore, the throughput can almost be doubled, depending on the number of nodes. These results motivate the tight collaboration of various communication networks, including both, infrastructure-based and ad-hoc technologies.

References

1. Gustafsson, E., Jonsson, A.: Always Best Connected. IEEE Wireless Communications Magazine **10** (2003) 49–55
2. Calisti, M., Lozza, T., Greenwood, D.: An agent-based middleware for adaptive roaming in wireless networks, AAMAS workshop on agents for ubiquitous computing, new york (2004)
3. Bhargava, B., Wu, X., Lu, Y., Wang, W.: Integrating heterogeneous wireless technologies: a cellular aided mobile ad hoc network (CAMA). Mob. Netw. Appl. **9**(4) (2004) 393–408
4. Wu, G., Mizuno, M., Havinga, P.J.M.: MIRAI architecture for heterogeneous network. IEEE Communications Magazine **40**(2) (2002) 126–134
5. Inoue, M., Mahmud, K., Murakami, H., Hasegawa, M.: MIRAI: A solution to seamless access in heterogeneous wireless networks. In: Proceedings of the IEEE ICC. (2003) 1033–37
6. Inoue, M., Mahmud, K., Murakami, H., Hasegawa, M., Morikawa, H.: Novel out-of-band signaling for seamless interworking between heterogeneous networks. IEEE Wireless Communications Magazine **11**(2) (2004) 56–63
7. et al., K.M.: On the required features and system capacity of basic access network in the MIRAI. In: WPMC. (2001) 1199–1204
8. Danzeisen, M., Braun, T., Rodellar, D., Winiker, S.: Heterogeneous communication enabled by cellular operators. Vehicular Technology Society (2006)
9. Danzeisen, M., Braun, T., Rodellar, D., Winiker, S.: Implementation of a cellular framework for spontaneous network. In: Proceedings of IEEE WCNC. (2005)
10. Danzeisen, M., Braun, T., Rodellar, D., Winiker, S.: Heterogeneous networking establishment assisted by cellular operators. In: Proceedings of MWCN. (2003)
11. Danzeisen, M., Rodellar, D., Winiker, S., Braun, T.: (Heterogeneous networking facilitated by cellular networks)

Optimal Placement of Anchor Points Within Large Telecommunication Networks

Florian Liers, René Böringer, and Andreas Mitschele-Thiel

Faculty of Computer Science and Automation,
Technical University of Ilmenau, Germany
{Florian.Liers, Rene.Boeringer, Mitsch}@tu-ilmenau.de

Abstract. Classical micro-mobility solutions focus on accelerating local handovers and on minimizing signalling traffic. However, the micro-mobility components also slow down the service times in the user traffic domain. This is a critical drawback in terms of the hard delay requirements of future IP-based radio access networks. Network operators need algorithms to determine the optimal number and placement of anchor points within his network to balance both handover latency and user traffic delay.

This paper presents a very fast and exact mathematical method for selecting the optimal number and placement of nodes supporting micro-mobility functionality for telecommunication networks. The method is in particular applicable for large networks, which is demonstrated by means of an optimization of a real wireless access network with more than 150 nodes. In order to ensure the applicability in real network scenarios we additionally provide a solution to estimate the stability of the optimal configuration. The presented method allows the autonomous and optimal configuration of the network's micro-mobility functionality as described in concepts of zero-touch networks. Due to the optimization network operators can reduce the administration cost and maximize the quality of service as well.

1 Introduction

Due to the increasing number of mobile users, modern wireless access networks face growing traffic volume. Additionally, the traffic load shifts from the circuit switched domain to the packet switched domain. This causes that many mobile users are permanently connected to the network. Both the increasing traffic volume and the shift of the traffic load cause the demand for efficient mobility protocols in the packet switched domain. Micro-mobility protocols handling the local movement of the users are of great interest for the quality of service (QoS) offered by the access network. There are a number of different micro-mobility protocols discussed in various papers (e.g.[1]). A comparison of these algorithms can be found in [2,3]. However, the optimal application of these protocols and distribution of their functionality within the network has not yet been surveyed. This paper focuses on the optimal usage of existing, hierarchical micro-mobility

T. Braun et al. (Eds.): WWIC 2006, LNCS 3970, pp. 96–107, 2006.

protocols. Therefore the user traffic delay and the handover signalling latency are taken into account at the same time. The objective is the optimal placement of micro-mobility functionality within an existing IP-based wireless access network. A network operator has to weight the importance of fast handover supported by the mobility protocol in comparison to its higher user traffic delay. The stability of the optimal network configuration based on this weight is discussed in detail later on.

The term for a node providing mobility functionality differs, depending on the particular mobility protocol: Regional Foreign Agent in Hierarchical MIP v4 [4], I-MPLS-enabled Access Point (IAP) in I-MPLS [5] or Mobility Anchor Point in Hierarchical MIP v6 [6]. In this paper we use "anchor points" as a general term for these nodes.

1.1   Hierarchical Micro-mobility Protocols

Fig. 1 shows a wireless access network with three access points (K_1, K_2 and K_3), two anchor points (K_A and K_B) and one gateway (K_G). A mobile node (MN) registered with the network is sending and receiving data via a forwarding path between access point K_1 and the gateway K_G. In case it moves towards the access point K_2 this forwarding path has to be redirected by the network. The cross-over point of the old and the new forwarding path K_A is responsible for switching the path from access point K_1 to K_2. The handover process is now completed and the upper level of the hierarchy does not need to be notified. If the mobile node moves to access point K_3 the handover can not be handled by anchor point K_A, because it is not situated on the new path. The handover signalling has to inform the first cross-over node, which is the gateway in this example. Thus the gateway has to create a new forwarding path from K_3 via anchor point K_B to K_G. On one hand, this example shows the important role of the anchor points concerning the duration of a handover. On the other hand, it shows the limitations of this concept, if the topology does not match the user movements very well.

Additionally, an anchor point may influence the forwarding delay of the user traffic due to encapsulations, for example in IP tunnels (IP-in-IP) or MPLS Label Switched Path (LSP). Fig. 2 shows the principal differences between packet forwarding on a regular MPLS node (a) and an anchor point (b) within an MPLS access network using I-MPLS as micro-mobility protocol. I-MPLS is a micro-mobility approach, which is transparent for the macro-mobility protocol Mobile IP [5]. A regular node uses the fast MPLS packet forwarding, but an anchor point has to unpack the packets from one LSP and to put them into another tunnel. Because of the scalability it has to use the slower IP forwarding, which approximately doubles the processing time for a packet. This is a descriptive example, but other micro-mobility protocols shows similar drawbacks like larger address lookup tables and IP-in-IP encapsulation.

If a wireless access provider upgrades all inner nodes of his network to anchor points, he will accelerate the handover and reduce the packet loss in the downlink, but he has to pay for this benefit with slower user traffic. Thus the provider wants

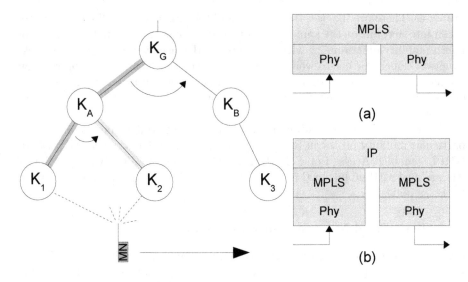

Fig. 1. Hierarchical Micro-mobility Management   **Fig. 2.** Basic Packet Forwarding in I-MPLS

to use as many anchor points as necessary but also as less as possible. The anchor point problem can be formulated to be the problem of finding an optimal set of nodes providing micro-mobility functionality.

1.2   Related Work

The published work on micro-mobility mainly describes extensions to protocols or compares different micro-mobility solutions. The example networks used for these comparisons are quite small. In case of a hierarchical protocol the gateway acts as anchor point for its whole subnet and no optimization is done concerning its placement. To our knowledge, there is no publication dealing with optimization of the placement of mobility functionality in a network.

Some optimization issues similar to the anchor point problem can be found in mathematical literature. The k-median-problem addresses the placement of k facilities in a graph, depending on the nodes' demand for the specific service [7]. In operation research various location-routing problems are known [8]. Because of the special rules for completing a handover and the strong dependency of the load on the placement itself, all standard methods for solving these problems are not applicable for the described placement problem of anchor points.

Therefore we have developed a new model, which is presented in the following.

2   Input Variables and the Optimization Objective

As mentioned above the most important input variables for mobile network optimization are the delay for the user traffic, the handover duration and the packet loss due to handoffs. This paper considers the first two of them. The third one depends on the wireless access technology and can be approximated by the duration of the handover. In case of a handoff in Wireless-LANs, the packet loss in the downlink is proportional to the time the access network needs to re-establish the routing information. In contrast, a handover in UMTS does not necessarily cause packet loss. However, in both cases a handover initiates signalling traffic, which requires bandwidth and processing time at the involved nodes. Therefore the delay and the signalling duration are the only factors being considered.

The sole optimization of a single input variable is trivial and does not suffice the needs of a network operator. In case the average handover duration is minimized in order to meet the QoS requirement for packet loss e.g. for VoIP, the network will contain many anchor points. This configuration will lead to huge delays for the user traffic and causes high administration and maintenance expenses. In case the average user packet delay is minimized, the network will not contain any anchor point, which implies quite long handover durations. Only the consideration of both parameters will lead to a useful and efficient network configuration providing fast handovers, low average delay of user traffic and the lowest possible administration costs.

In addition to the network topology, the following traffic data are necessary for the optimization:

- u_i - user traffic per access point K_i ,
- h_{ij} with $i \neq j$ - handover from access point K_i to access point K_j and
- h_{ii} - handover from external networks or (re-)registrations of new mobiles at access point K_i.

It is common practice to count the number of handovers between two access points and the user traffic transferred by an access point. The units of the traffic data will be discussed in detail later on. The traffic data defines a specific traffic scenario for the optimization. Thus the calculated optimal configuration of the network is only valid for this special scenario. This dependency will be discussed in detail in Sec. 6.

The goal of the optimization is the reduction of the mean handover duration and the reduction of the mean delay of the user traffic. This is achieved by selecting an optimal set of nodes, handling the mobility management functionality. In addition the optimization has to determine the routing information for the user traffic, if the network contains cycles. The objective function (1) sums up the costs for the signalling and the user traffic load of all nodes in the network.

$$\min_x c_G = \sum_{i \in I} w * c_u(u_i, x_i) + c_s(s_i, x_i) \tag{1}$$

The set I used in Equation 1 consists of all node indices of a network. The functions c_u and c_s transform the user traffic load u_i respectively the handover signalling load s_i to cost values for the objective function. This conversion has to be adapted to the specific characteristics of the micro-mobility protocol in use. The anchor point selection is described by zero-one-variables x_i. In general c_u and c_s are linear functions:

$$c_d(a, x) = a * t_d * (1 + z_d * x) \; ; \; d \in \{u, s\} \tag{2}$$

The (signalling and user traffic) load implies fixed costs of $a * t_d$ and an overhead depending on the type of the node. $z_d > 0$ stands for the extra costs for forwarding a user packet respectively handling a signalling message (e.g. $z_u = 0.2$ means 20% higher traffic costs for anchor points). The traffic data are scaled by a time factor t_d (e.g. t_u or t_s) which converts the traffic data into convenient units. If the user traffic is measured in packets per time, the factor t_u converts it into delay per time. From a mathematical point of view these two factors can be merged into the weight factor w, which balances the costs for the user traffic and the costs for the signalling. For this multi-criteria-problem the weight factor is a very important parameter and will be reviewed in the practical Sec. 6 again. Nevertheless t_u and t_s are helpful for the estimation of the weight factor.

Actually the conversion from load to costs is non-linear, which can be proved by queuing theory. Due to the discrete decision variable x, $c_d(a, x)$ is only valid for the two values of x. If the parameters of the linear function are chosen correctly, the non-linear conversation can be replaced by a linear $c_d(a, x)$. This simplification reduces the complexity of the problem and accelerates the numerical optimization algorithm.

The optimization does not modify the considered network structure. It neither adds nodes nor links nor does it shift the location of the gateway.

3   Modelling Networks

Based on the traffic parameters mentioned in the previous paragraph it is possible to calculate the traffic load of the inner nodes of the network. Up- and downlink traffic use the same forwarding path. From the model point of view only the uplink direction is considered. By inserting the sum of the traffic data for up- and downlink, the traffic on both directions influences the optimal placement.

Decision variables are needed in order to set up the equations. The placement of anchor points is described by zero-one-variables $x_i \in \{0, 1\}$ for all nodes in $I = \{1, \ldots, n\}$ in the network. If $x_i = 0$ the node i is a regular node without micro-mobility functionality. If $x_i = 1$ the node i is an anchor point. The vector $x = (x_1, \ldots, x_n)$ is referred to as the configuration of a network without cycles. For networks with cycles the configuration has to be extended by the routing information for the user traffic. Two zero-one-variables r_i^j and $r_j^i \in \{0, 1\}$ are introduced for each link (i, j) which is part of a cycle. If $r_i^j = 1$ the uplink traffic is forwarded from i to j and if $r_j^i = 1$ it will take the other direction. Certainly, both variables can not be equal to one, but both can be equal to zero if the link is not being used. Additionally, each node has to forward its traffic to exactly one other node. Both requirements can be expressed by means of linear constraints:

$$r_i^j + r_j^i \leq 1 \tag{3}$$

$$\sum_{i \in I} r_i^j = 1 \; \forall j \in I \tag{4}$$

For gateways these constraints can be simplified because they absorb the traffic from the model point of view.

The next passage deals with the modelling of networks without cycles. After these basic principals the necessary extensions for networks with cycles are discussed.

3.1 Modelling Tree Networks

In a tree-like wireless access network the user traffic is forwarded from the access point serving the mobile node to the gateway. Since there is only one path without cycles, no routing decision has to be made. The traffic is forwarded through all nodes located on this path from the access point to the gateway. This uplink-based view leads to a hierarchical system of equations, applicable for downlink traffic, too. An inner node K_i as depicted in Fig. 3 forwards all traffic from its subnets S_i it serves to its parent node. This parent node is the next node on the path to the gateway. Each subnet is represented by a root node. The indices of the direct children of node K_i are in set N_i. The user traffic load of an inner node K_i is equal to the sum of the load of all its children.

$$u_i = \sum_{j \in N_i} u_j \tag{5}$$

The calculation of the signalling load differs from the calculation of the traffic load, because it strongly depends on the placement of the anchor points. If the network topology allows the completion of a handover in the lower level of

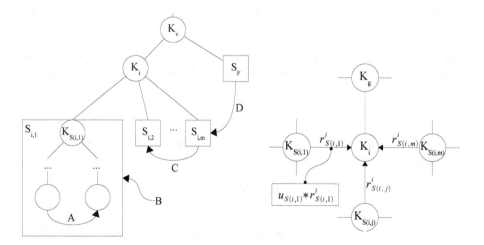

Fig. 3. Nodes and Subnetworks of node K_i

Fig. 4. Forwarding of User Traffic in Networks with Cycles

the hierarchy and an anchor point is situated accordingly, the handover can be completed before it reaches the gateway. This hierarchical model differs from the model of the user traffic, which is completed from the gateway only. Four principal handover situations are shown in Fig. 3. A handover within a subnet (A) can be completed by the root $K_{S(i,1)}$ of the subnet if the root is an anchor point. In case a new mobile node is logging on to the network (B) the signalling always reaches node K_i, and has to be forwarded to the gateway, in order to set up the complete path initially. If a mobile node moves between two different subnets of node K_i, the signalling of a handover always reaches K_i as well. In contrast to (B) node K_i gets the first chance to complete the handover. Handovers coming from nodes of the access network S_F, which do not belong to one of the subnets of K_i, into one of the subnets of node K_i (D) have to be forwarded to the parent node of K_i. In contrast to (B) the handovers may be completed before they reach the gateway in case there exist a cross-over node below the gateway.

Additional variables per node are introduced in order to describe these differences within the mathematical formulation: h_i^N and h_i^I. The variable h_i^N stands for the handovers between two nodes of two different subnetworks of node K_i (C). These handovers can be completed by node K_i for the first time.

$$h_i^N = \sum_{s \in N_i} \sum_{k \in L_s} \sum_{l \in L_i - L_s} h_{kl} \tag{6}$$

The set L_i consists of the indices of all access points within the subnet of node K_i. Equation 6 sums all handover between access points from one subnet L_s to access points within other subnets of node K_i ($L_i - L_s$).

The number of all handover which can be completed at node K_i is given by h_i^I (A +C). It adds the handovers which can be completed but have not been completed $(1 - x_s)$ from all subnets of node K_i to h_i^N:

$$h_i^I = h_i^N + \sum_{s \in N_i} h_s^I * (1 - x_s) \tag{7}$$

Handovers which are not completed at a node are forwarded to the parent node of the node. These uncompleted handovers of an inner node K_i are summed up in h_i:

$$h_i = \left(\sum_{k \in N_i} h_k \right) - h_i^N \tag{8}$$

For access points, h_i^I is always zero and the definition of h_i sums the incoming handovers for an access point:

$$h_i = \sum_{j \in I} h_{ji} \tag{9}$$

The outgoing handovers can be neglected, because their processing delay does not produce any cost from the user's point of view. From the providers point of view their processing is not time critical and can be done in the idle time of the network components.

The complete signalling load s_i of node K_i consists of the forwarded and completed handover:

$$s_i = h_i + h_i^I * x_i \tag{10}$$

3.2   Modelling Networks with Cycles

The presented definitions of the previous paragraph have to be extended by routing decision in case cycles are present in the network. The situation is illustrated in Fig. 4 for the inner node K_i. The user traffic reaching node $K_{S(i,1)}$ is forwarded to node K_i if and only if $r_{S(i,1)}^i = 1$. Therefore Equation 5 has to be modified to:

$$u_i = \sum_{j \in N_i} u_j * r_j^i \tag{11}$$

The other equations of Sec. 3.1 have to be extended by these routing variables, too.

In addition the model has to prevent cycles within the routing decision. As mentioned above there can be cycles between two adjacent nodes, which will be easily prevented by a single linear constraint per edge. In order to exclude larger loops between more than two nodes the model has to be extended by constraints. The number of constraints depends exponentially on the size of the problem [8]. These constraints will be added to the mathematical model during the optimization process, if they are necessary [8, 9].

4   Optimization

The equation constructed according to the presented rules and which is based on the topology of the network can be optimized for the numerical optimization algorithm. The symbolic simplification of the equations, their conversation to fast evaluable structures and the constraint reduction by inserting them directly in the objective function enable a significant reduction of the run time of the algorithms. The constraint reduction causes three versions of the model discussed in the following sections on studies of real world examples.

The optimization itself consists of three classical steps:

1. relaxation of the decision variables,
2. solving a continuous optimization problem and
3. calculating a discrete solution via branch and bound algorithms.

The relaxation transfers the discrete problem with sole zero-one variables into a continuous problem with variables defined for the domain $(0, 1)$. The relaxed decision variables for the anchor point selection x_i can be interpreted as probability for completing handovers, which can be completed. The well known method of branch and bound is used in order to transform the result of the relaxation back into discrete values. It divides a problem based on one non discrete x_i^* of the relaxed result. The algorithm solves the two subproblems recursively, one with $x_i = 0$ and the other one with $x_i = 1$. Then it chooses the

Table 1. Characteristics for the Scenario of Halle

version	1	2	3
number of variables	664	366	166
number of constraints	498	200	-
obj. function length	9303	6157	6954
constraint length	9645	5747	-
duration [s]	4442.3	872.3	9.5

solution with the smaller objective value. Mostly the anchor point problem for a tree network is "integer friendly". Thus the result from the relaxation is already suitable for the original problem with zero-one variables. However, for networks with cycles the routing variables tend to be real-valued. Therefore the branch and bound method divides the problem on the routing variables first.

The numerical optimization algorithm `fmincon` out of the "Optimization Toolbox" of Matlab was employed for the computation. It is a sequential quadratic programming algorithm, which is documented in [10]. The CPU processing time needed to solve an optimization problem was measured on a AMD Athlon64 with 1800 MHz. The parameters for the presented optimization are: $z_u = 0.1$, $z_s = 0.2$ and $t_u = t_s = w = 1$.

5   Optimizing a Wireless Access Network of the City of Halle

The UMTS radio access network (UTRAN) for the city of Halle upon river Saale (Germany) shown in Fig. 5 consists of 166 nodes. The picture shows the UTRAN elements, the links between them and the main traffic routes of the city. The traffic data mentioned in Sec. 2 were derived from these main traffic routes and information about the users and their behaviour on them. The anchor point optimization algorithm is controlled by the tool TRIAS of

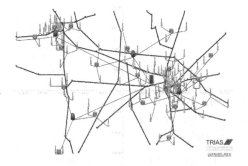

Fig. 5. Wireless Access Network of the City of Halle with Traffic Routes

the IDEO Laboratories GmbH. TRIAS provides the possibility to compute the traffic data and to pass their data directly to our optimization algorithm. Also the representation of results is done by TRIAS similar to Fig. 5.

Tabular 1 shows the characteristics of three different versions of the optimized model for the access network of Halle. The length of the constraints and of the objective function is given in characters after the symbolic reduction was applied. The first version adopts the definition from the model without modifications. It needs 664 variables where 2/3 of them are bound by constraints. The second version inserts all constant variables into the other equations especially those of the traffic data. Mainly the decision variables and some helper variables of the inner nodes remain as independent variables. The length of the objective function decreases after the insertion and due to the greater opportunity to simplify the function symbolically. The third version inserts all constraints into the objective function. Only the 166 decision variables for the anchor point selection remain in the unrestricted objective function, which than can be optimised within 9.5 seconds. The length of the objective function increases, compared to the second version. This is caused by the insertion of long constraints, which over compensate the savings of the symbolical simplification. The third version does not support cycle networks, because of the circular dependency of the variables among each other. Nevertheless the third version provides a basic model description, which can efficiently be optimised.

6 Stability of the Optimization Results

The optimal configuration strongly depends on the traffic data and on the parameters for the optimization itself. Theoretically, a new set of anchor points will be optimal for each traffic situation during a day. Especially for the autonomic configuration process of zero-touch networks the question of the stability of the optimal solution arises. The well known sensibility indicators like dual solutions or gradients are less useful, because they correspond to changes of the constant parts of the constraints or the changes of the variables, respectively. They are not sufficient to consider changes of factors within the equations like the traffic data or optimization parameters. The stability concerning these factors can be approximated locally by a profit and loss comparison. Equation 12 shows this comparison for a node K_i, assuming a constant number r_i of following non-anchor points on the path from the node to the gateway.

$$
\begin{aligned}
Profit &= Savings - Cost \\
&= (r_i + 1) * h_i^I - w * u_i * z_u \\
&\quad - (h_i^I + h_i^N) * z_s
\end{aligned}
\tag{12}
$$

In order to find nodes with small profit Equation 12 can be investigated concerning the traffic data h_i^I, h_i^N and u_i. The optimal configuration of these nodes may change quickly, if the traffic data are modified. During a sensitivity analysis this local stability approximations helps to estimate the quality of the configuration determined by the optimization algorithm. If the sensitivity analysis is done concerning the optimization parameters w, z_u and z_s Equation 13 can be derived from Equation 12:

$$
p_{=0}(z_s) = w * z_u = \frac{r_i * h_i^I}{u_i} - \frac{h_i^I + h_i^N}{u_i} * z_s
\tag{13}
$$

This function is shown in Fig. 6. The point $P = (w * z_u, z_s)$ represents the parameter used for an optimization run. If the parameters change, point P will

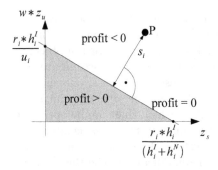

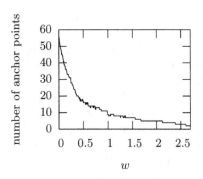

Fig. 6. Local Stability concerning the Optimization Parameter w, z_u and z_s

Fig. 7. Optimal Number of Anchor Points Depending on the Weight w

move. However, $p_{=0}$ will not change because of the constant configuration and because of the independency of the parameter of function $p_{=0}$. The minimal distance s_i between function $p_{=0}$ and point P is a measure for the sensitivity of the algebraic sign of the profit. A great distance enables changes of the parameters without the danger of having a change in the sign of the profit. In contrast a small distance is a warning that the sign may change quickly. In principal this sensitivity is a local hint for the network operator using the optimization.

The global influence of the weight factor w on the optimal result can be seen in Fig. 7. It shows the relation between the weighting and the number of anchor points in the optimal solution. Generally the number decreases with a higher weight for the user traffic (increase of w). However the function is not strictly monotonic decreasing, because an anchor point dropped out in the upper level of the hierarchy is sometimes replaced by two or more anchor points in the lower levels. On the left hand side of the figure the results are not stable. Small changes at the weighting have significant effects on the optimal configuration. On the right hand side the results are relatively stable. This result stresses the need of a sensitivity analysis of the optimal configuration in order to use it in a real world network.

7   Conclusion and Outlook

In this paper the issue of the optimal placement of anchor points is examined. It consists of finding an optimal set of nodes for the placement of the micro-mobility functionality within a wireless access network. These anchor points accelerate handovers but slow down the forwarding of user traffic. The goal of the optimization is to balance these two characteristics.

A mathematical model for this issue for networks with and without cycles is presented, which can be used to construct an objective function and constraints for a non-linear optimization problem. This optimization problem can be solved via relaxation and standard mathematical optimization algorithms. The applicability of the model and of the optimization is demonstrated on a real world network of the city of Halle (Germany) containing more than 150 nodes. By means of different optimizations we were able to reduce the time needed to optimize this network from approx. 4400 seconds to approx. 10 seconds. The stability of the optimal network configuration against changes of the traffic data and the optimization parameters can be estimated with local sensitivity measurements. The sensitivity consideration improves the applicability of the model for real network scenarios. Moreover it supports the autonomic configuration of zero-touch networks.

In the future we plan to further extend our approach to improve the stability of the set of anchor points against traffic variations. Especially the differentiation of the mobile users based on their speed, their behaviour in the past and their assignment to different anchor point sets is expected to improve the performance of the optimization and its applicability to the real world. We expect large improvements of the performance of access networks due to the use of dynamic allocations of specific functionalities. The model and the optimization presented in this paper in connection with dynamic protocols like I-MPLS are the first major steps to bring this idea closer to reality.

References

1. REINBOLD, Pierre ; BONAVENTURE, Olivier: IP Micro-mobility Protocols. In: *IEEE Communications Surveys and Tutorials* 5 (2003). – http://www.comsoc.org/livepubs/surveys/public/2003/sep/reinbold.html
2. CHEW, Kar A. ; POLITIS, Christos ; TAFAZOLLI, Rahim: *Performance Evaluation of Mico-mobility Protocols for All-IP Based Infrastructures.* Wireless World Research Forum, December 2002
3. HSIEH, Robert ; SENEVIRATNE, Aruna ; SOLIMAN, Hesham ; EL-MALKI, Karim: Performance analysis on Hierarchical Mobile IPv6 with Fast-handoffoverEnd-to-End TCP. In: *GLOBECOM.* Taipei, Taiwan, 2002
4. GUSTAFSSON, Eva ; JONSSON, Annika ; PERKINS, Charles E.: *Mobile IP Regional Registration.* draft-ietf-mobileip-reg-tunnel-04.txt. 2000. – Internet Draft, Internet Engineering Task Force
5. BÖRINGER, René ; SAEED, Ahmad ; DIAB, Ali ; MITSCHELE-THIEL, Andreas ; SCHNEIDER, Matthias: I-MPLS: A Transparent Mico-Mobility-enabled MPLS Framework. In: *11th European Wireless 2005.* Cyprus, April 2005
6. SOLIMAN, Hesham ; CATELLUCCIA, Claude ; MALKI, Karim E. ; BELLIER, Ludovic: *Hierarchical Mobile IPv6 mobility management.* Network Working Group Draft, 2004. – <draft-ietf-mipshop-hmipv6-04.txt>
7. CAMERON, Craig W. ; H, Steven ; LOW, David X. W.: *High Density Model for Server Allocation and Placement.* ACMSigmetrics, 2002
8. DASKIN, Mark S.: *Network and Discrete Location: Models, Algorithms, and Applications.* Ney York : John Wiley & Sons Inc., 1995
9. EISELT, H. A. ; SANDBLOM, C.-L.: *Integer Programming and Network Models.* Heidelberg : Springer-Verlag, 2000
10. MathWorks: *Matlab 7 Online Help.* 2004

Robust Application-Level Multicast Tree Construction for Wireless/Mobile Hosts

Taku Noguchi[1] and Miki Yamamoto[2]

[1] College of Information Science and Engineering, Ritsumeikan University,
1-1-1 Nojihigashi, Kusatsu, Shiga, 525-8577, Japan
Tel: +81-77-561-5267
noguchi@is.ritsumei.ac.jp
[2] Faculty of Engineering, Kansai University,
3-3-35 Yamate-cho, Suita, Osaka, 564-8680, Japan

Abstract. IP multicast is an effective technology to distribute identical data simultaneously to multiple users. However, for technical and administrative reasons, IP multicast has not been globally deployed on the Internet. Another approach to multicast is *application-level multicast* (ALM). In ALM, multicast related features, such as group membership management, multicast routing and packet replication, are implemented at end-hosts instead of routers. Multicast delivery tree is constructed in the application layer, so all nodes in this tree are end-hosts. Packet transmission between end-hosts uses conventional IP unicast service. Therefore, ALM is a promising alternative to IP multicast. However, application-level multicast relying on end-hosts is more fragile than IP multicast relying on routers. Especially, when a mobile host forwards packets to downstream hosts, a handover causes performance degradations on downstream hosts. In this paper, to alleviate the impact of a handover, we propose a new tree building protocol which locates mobile hosts on leaves of multicast tree. A handover of the mobile host on a leaf does not affect other end-hosts. To investigate performance of our protocol, it is compared with existing application-level multicast protocols. Our simulation results show that our protocol outperforms existing protocols from the viewpoints of loss probability, throughput and delay performance.

1 Introduction

IP multicast [1] is an efficient way for one-to-many packet distribution at the network level. However, for technical and administrative reasons including reliability, scalable routing, security, group management and lack of business model, IP multicast has not been globally deployed on the Internet [2]. Today's IP multicast is limited to "island" of network domains under single administrative control or local area networks, and large parts of the Internet are still incapable of native multicast. As an alternative to IP multicast, ALM has drawn extensive attention recently [3]. ALM shifts multicast functionalities from routers to end-hosts. In ALM, multicast related features, such as group membership management, multicast routing and packet replication, are implemented at end-hosts. A multicast tree is constructed in the application layer, so all nodes in this tree are end-hosts, i.e. multicast members (the source and receivers). Packet transmission between members uses conventional IP unicast service. Since all packets are

T. Braun et al. (Eds.): WWIC 2006, LNCS 3970, pp. 108–119, 2006.

transmitted as unicast packets, the network infrastructure needs not support IP multicast.

Despite the above advantages, ALM has an inherent disadvantage compared to IP multicast: lack of robustness [4, 5]. Due to the dependency of the multicast tree on end-hosts (usually PCs or workstations), which are less stable than dedicated and well administered commercial routers, the multicast tree is intrinsically fragile. When the multicast tree is partitioned after a single end-host failure, e.g. OS/application crash or communication link failure, and so on, all downstream end-hosts from the failed end-host are forced to be decoupled from the multicast tree. As a result, multicast packet deliveries to these downstream end-hosts are interrupted and they suffer from burst losses. This problem may be more serious in the ALM session involving wireless/mobile hosts. A bad wireless connection and mobility of the mobile host relaying packets, i.e. *intermediate* node in the tree, causes temporary tree partitions and results in performance degradations on downstream hosts. Since mobile hosts may perform handover with higher probability than non-mobile host, i.e. wired fixed host, fails for some reasons, it is very important to address the handover of mobile hosts for commercial implementation of ALM. Existing ALM protocols have no means to address this handover problem. The majority of them detects tree partitions by periodic message exchanges between members and recovers tree partitions by tree reconstruction. This approach is hard to detect the temporary tree partitions caused by the handover, and if it can detect, it cannot respond them due to long tree reconstruction delay.[1] We would like to emphasize that the handover problem should be addressed rather by constructing the *robust tree* capable of avoiding tree partitions caused by the handover than by recovering tree partitions.

In this paper, we propose a new tree construction protocol that constructs a robust multicast tree against the handover by taking wireless mobile hosts into account. Our protocol locates mobile hosts on leaves of multicast tree. Our multicast tree can reduce the number of end-hosts affected by temporary tree partitions caused by the handover, namely the number of members which suffer burst losses during the period of interruption of multicast packet deliveries. To investigate performance of our protocol, it is compared with the existing application-level multicast protocol. Our simulation results show that our protocol outperforms the existing protocol from the viewpoint of throughput and delay performance.

Remainder of the paper is structured as follows. Section 2 provides a description of related work. In section 3, we present the handover problem in ALM. Section 4.1 shows the overview and the operation of our proposed protocol. In section 5, we study the performance of our proposed protocol, and compare it to existing ALM protocols through detailed simulation. Finally, Section 6 concludes the paper.

2   Related Work

Most studies of ALM have been focused on efficiency improvement and have not addressed the robustness aspect as a main focus. HBM [4,5] address this robustness aspect

---

[1] Tree reconstruction may take several tens of seconds due to exchange of control information between members.

by adding explicit redundancy in the distribution tree. In HBM, a rendezvous point (RP) gets all end-hosts' information, and instructs to build an optimal shared distribution tree based on the information. HBM enhances robustness against a single end-host failure by adding redundant links. However, this approach merely increases the redundancy of overlay networks and the tree without redundant links is fragile. Without increasing the redundancy, our protocol can enhance robustness against a single end-host failure, i.e. the handover.

3   Handover Problem in Application-Level Multicast

Delay and bandwidth penalties are unavoidable in ALM, because a packet may be replicated and forwarded on the same link more than once. A large number of previous studies of ALM have been focused on these ALM-specific efficiency problems [3, 6-13]. In this paper, we focus on another important problem in ALM, i.e. robustness aspect [4, 5].

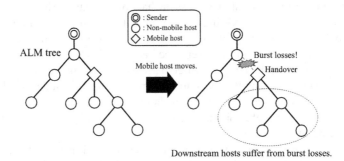

Fig. 1. The impact of the handover

When a multicast tree is partitioned after an end-host/link failure, all downstream end-hosts from the failed end-host are forced to be decoupled from the tree and suffer from burst losses until tree partitions are recovered. When a wireless mobile host participates the ALM session, its instability makes the robustness problem more serious. Due to a bad wireless connection and mobility, a wireless mobile host which is an intermediate node in the multicast tree may have an adverse affect on the performances of its downstream members. The handover of the intermediate wireless mobile host generates temporary tree partitions during the handover period,[2] and all downstream hosts from it suffer from burst losses (fig.1). The handover and wireless link failure occur more frequently than non-mobile end-host failures, e.g. wired link failure and continual congestion at an access link. Moreover, from the viewpoints of bandwidth, processing and battery power, wireless mobile hosts have relatively less capabilities than non-mobile hosts. Therefore, a wireless mobile host should be not an intermediate node, which is required to perform multicast forwarding functions, but a leaf node, which simply receives packets, in the ALM tree.

---

[2] In Mobile IP [14], this period may be long due to the complicated handover procedure consists of movement detection, new CoA configuration and binding update.

4   Construction of Robust ALM Tree

In this section, we propose a new tree construction protocol that constructs a robust multicast tree against the handover. The main idea is to have intermediate non-mobile hosts while wireless mobile hosts are moved to the leaves of the ALM tree.

4.1   Pure k-Tree Protocol

It is impossible to predict which wireless mobile host perform handover, at the time the multicast tree was built. Hence, the tree should be constructed to diminish the number of downstream end-hosts adversely affected by the handover, whichever wireless mobile host may perform handover. In order to improve the potential robustness of the multicast tree against the handover, we propose to use a degree-balanced tree, where all intermediate nodes have same outdegree k and all the levels are full except for the bottom level (fig.2), as the multicast tree. The regular tree shape of a degree-balanced tree can diminish the average number of downstream hosts affected by the handover of upstream mobile host, since each intermediate mobile host at same depth has much the same number of downstream nodes. We adopt pure k-tree protocol [15] to construct a degree-balanced tree. The brief operation description of pure k-tree protocol is as follows.

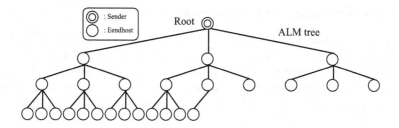

Fig. 2. Degree-balanced application-level multicast tree

Step 1) When a new member wishes to join an ALM session, it gets the source host's IP address by using the session directory functionalities [16].

Step 2) The new member sends a query to the source host (root) and gets following information: (i) a list of children; (ii) outdegree; and (iii) height[3], i.e. the length of the longest path from downstream leaves to the host. If the attachment to the root does not violate the degree constraint (k),[4] it sends a *JOIN_REQUEST* to the root.

Step 3) If the degree constraint (k) is violated, the new member sends a query to all listed children and gets information of the above listed (i), (ii), and (iii). From listed children, it selects the one with the smallest outdegree and sends a *JOIN_REQUEST* to the one. If there are more than two candidates, it measures RTTs to candidates and selects the closest one.

---

[3] Each member obtains its height by periodic exchanges of a control message between tree neighbors.

[4] The parameter of the degree-balanced tree. As an example, when k is 4, the 4-ary tree is built.

Step 4) If the new member cannot find a parent candidate among all children due to the degree constraint, it selects the one with the smallest height and sets the one as the potential grandparent.

Step 5) Similarly to step 3, the new member collects information from the potential grandparent's children, and selects the parent candidate among them. It sends a *JOIN_REQUEST* to the candidate.

Step 6) The new member repeats steps 4-5 until finds and sends a *JOIN_REQUEST* to the appropriate parent.

An example of the join process is shown in figure 3.

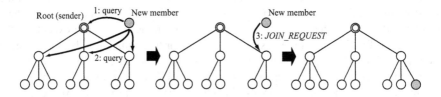

Fig. 3. Join process (degree constraint = 3)

4.2   New *k*-Tree Protocol for Wireless/Mobile Hosts

We propose new *k*-tree protocol which can locate mobile hosts on leaves of ALM tree by performing the position exchange between non-mobile host and mobile host. In pure *k*-tree protocol, new member is certainly a leaf node just after join an ALM session. Our new *k*-tree protocol recommends new member to connect to a non-mobile host for fear of creating an intermediate mobile host. The new operations added into pure *k*-tree protocol are as follows.

Step 1) A host in the tree notifies whether it is a mobile host or not by replying the query from the new member. If there are more than 2 parent candidates with same outdegrees and heights among the potential parents, the new member selects non-mobile one. If all candidates are mobile hosts, the new member measures RTTs to them and selects the closest one.

Step 2) If a mobile host participating an ALM session receives a *JOIN_REQUEST* from a new member, it checks whether the new member is a mobile host or not. To enable this action, the new member adds its host type information (non-mobile/mobile) to the *JOIN_REQUEST*.

   1. If a new member is a non-mobile host (fig.4), the candidate (mobile host) breaks up the relationship between itself and its parent by sending a *SWAP_LEAVE* to its parent. Subsequently, it attaches to the new member as child by sending a *SWAP_JOIN* including its old parent information to the new member (fig.4-②). Upon the receipt of this *SWAP_JOIN*, the new member resends a *JOIN_REQUEST* to the old parent of the source host of the *SWAP_JOIN* (fig.4-③). The old parent receiving a *SWAP_LEAVE* accepts the join request from the new member. Furthermore, it keeps forwarding multicast packets to the old

child, until the new parent-child relationship is established. This operation may constitute the degree violation at the old parent. Even if this violation occurs, the old parent accepts the join request because it is temporary and eliminated when the connection is established.

2. If a new member is a mobile host (fig.5), the candidate simply accepts the join request.

Step 3) A mobile host notifies its children of its host type information by periodical control messages. A mobile host's child performs tree optimization to change its position in the tree.

When a mobile new member selects a leaf mobile host as a parent candidate, it becomes an intermediate node in the tree (step 2-2). From the viewpoint of robustness, this situation is undesirable. This can be alleviated somewhat by performing position exchange between the intermediate mobile host and the non-mobile new member. This position exchange is performed when an intermediate mobile host receives a *JOIN_REQUEST* from a non-mobile new member (step 2-1). To further decrease the number of intermediate mobile hosts, our new *k*-tree protocol optimizes the multicast tree periodically by performing position exchange between hosts (step 3). The detailed tree optimization procedure is as follows.

Tree optimization. Each member which has a mobile parent host periodically tries to exchange its position with that of another member. An example of the tree optimization procedure is shown in fig.6. Member *i* first discovers another member *j* from the tree that is not its descendant and ancestor. This discovery is done by a random-walk on the tree, a technique proposed in [6]. In this technique, member *i* sends a *DISCOVER* message (fig.6-①) with a *time-to-live* (TTL) field to its parent on the tree.

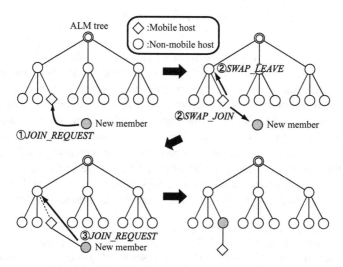

Fig. 4. Join process (The joined mobile host receives *JOIN_REQUEST* from new non-mobile member)

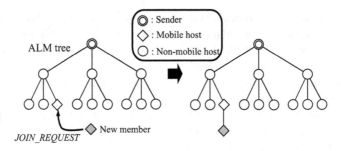

Fig. 5. Join process (The joined mobile host receives *JOIN_REQUEST* from new mobile member)

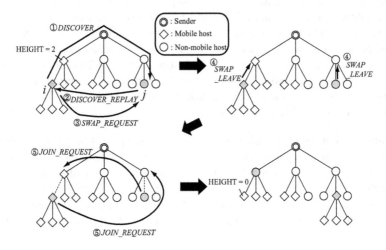

Fig. 6. Tree optimization

The message is randomly forwarded from neighbor to neighbor, without re-tracing its path along the tree and the TTL field is decremented at each hop. The member j at which the TTL reaches 0 is the desired random member. The member j notifies the member i of its own height and depth (this equals the number of entries in the path list[5]) by a *DISCOVER_REPLAY* message (fig.6-②). If members i and j are not descendant and ancestor of each other,[6] and if the position exchange between them can reduce the height of the member i's parent without increasing the height of the tree,[7] then the member i sends a *SWAP_REQUEST* message to the member j (fig.6-③). Members i and j break up the relationships between theirself and their parents by sending a *SWAP_LEAVE* to their parents (fig.6-④). Subsequently, they connect to

---

[5] Path list is the sequence of end-hosts comprising the path from the root to j. As well as height information, this information is obtained by periodic exchanges of a control message.

[6] A member can check whether another member is descendant/ancestor or not by looking up its own path list.

[7] Based on height and depth information received from j, the member i determines whether the heights of the tree and its parent increase or decrease after the position exchange.

the new parent by sending a *JOIN_REQUEST* (fig.6-⑤). Following this operation, in the example shown in fig.6, step 1 is performed because a mobile host (member i's old parent) receives *JOIN_REQUEST* from a non-mobile host (member j). Eventually, member j reattaches to the tree as the parent of the non-mobile host. In the tree optimization procedure, the position exchange between members i and j means the switch between subtrees rooted at these members. Note that in order to prevent tree partitions due to member's position exchange, the old parents of two members performing the position exchange should keep forwarding data to their old child until the position exchange is completed. If this operation constitutes the degree violation, it is admitted as a special case.

5   Performance Evaluation

In this section, we investigate performance of new k-tree protocol by comparing with existing ALM protocols.

5.1   Simulation Model

In our simulations, we used the BRITE model to generate network topologies (fig.7). All topologies in our simulations consist of one backbone network with 50 routers and 50 access networks with 20 routers (access points), i.e. the total number of routers in topologies is 1000. As multicast group members, non-mobile and mobile hosts are randomly attached to access network routers and access points, respectively. A mobile host can communicate with another host directly by using Mobile IPv6 with route optimization. The home agent for a mobile host is the router to which it attaches at the start of the simulation. Each mobile host moves toward a destination randomly selected in access points at a constant speed. A handover occurs when a mobile host moves out of the transmission range of current access point. A handover operation takes 1 [sec] and all downstream hosts from the handover host suffer from burst losses during this period. The packet loss probability at a virtual link of the ALM tree (excluding wireless links) is uniformly distributed between 0 and 2 [%]. Therefore, in our simulations, there is no correlation between the packet loss probability at a virtual link and its physical hop

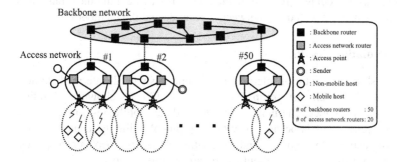

Fig. 7. Network topology for simulation (BRITE model)

Table 1. Simulation parameters

Link bandwidth (backbone network)	1 [Gbps]
Link bandwidth (access network, router - end-host)	100 [Mbps]
Link bandwidth (wireless link)	5 [Mbps]
Average link propagation delay (backbone network)	100 [msec]
Average link propagation delay (others)	1 [msec]
Link ropagation delay distribution	Exponential distribution
Data transmission rate at the sender	1 [Mbps]

count. In order to evaluate the performance degradation due to handover-caused loss, we assume that there is no wireless link packet loss. Other simulation parameters used are given in table 1.

Narada protocol [3], which is the famous ALM protocol, and pure k-tree protocol [15] are used as the targets for comparison. Narada protocol attempts to build a delay-optimized mesh interconnecting all members on which it runs a standard multicast routing protocol. The resulting tree is a sender-specific shortest path tree based on the underlying mesh. Each member has d neighbors on the mesh. This d is a protocol parameter and is similar to k which is degree constraint in new/pure k-tree protocol. We setup the intervals of control messages so that they have the same interval values in both new/pure k-tree protocol and Narada protocol. This means that the tree optimizations of new/pure k-tree protocol are performed with as much frequency as in Narada protocol.

5.2 Performance Metric

We compare the performance of new/pure k-tree protocol and Narada protocol along the following metrics:

- *Loss probability and throughput :* these metrics measure application level packet loss and throughput at the member, and are an indicator of the quality of ALM session.
- *Relative Delay Penalty (RDP) :* RDP is defined as $\frac{d'_i}{d_i}$, where d'_i is the multicast transmission delay perceived by member i in ALM communications, and d_i is the unicast shortest path delay between the source and the member i.

5.3 Simulation Results

Figure 8 shows the ratio of intermediate mobile hosts to all intermediate hosts in the ALM tree. The multicast group size is fixed at 300. As shown in this figure, new k-tree protocol reduces the number of intermediate mobile hosts in comparison with other protocols. This is because new k-tree protocol willingly locate mobile hosts on leaves of the tree. On the other hand, pure k-tree/Narada protocol constructs the degree-balanced/shortest path tree without any regard for mobile hosts.

Figures 9 and 10 show the average loss and throughput characteristics of all members. As shown in these figures, new k-tree protocol achieves the best performance of all

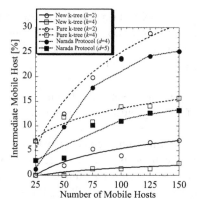

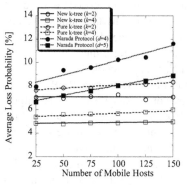

Fig. 8. Ratio of intermediate mobile hosts to all intermediate hosts (the number of members is 300)

Fig. 9. Average loss probability performance vs. Number of mobile hosts (the number of members is 300)

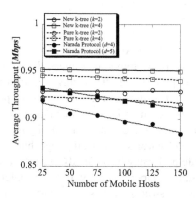

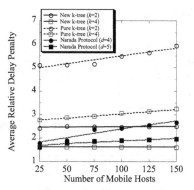

Fig. 10. Average throughput performance vs. Number of mobile hosts (the number of members is 300)

Fig. 11. Average RDP performance vs. Number of mobile hosts (the number of members is 300)

protocols. In new k-tree protocol, the number of intermediate mobile hosts is reduced and this reduction contributes to reduction of the average number of hosts suffering from burst losses due to intermediate mobile host's handover. The loss and throughput performance stabilities against increasing mobile hosts are another characteristics of new k-tree protocol. As shown in these figures, the loss and throughput performances in pure/new k-tree protocol remain stable independently of the number of mobile hosts. Generally, the loss and throughput performances in ALM are greatly affected by the number of application-level hops between the source and members. In pure/new k-tree protocol, the average number of these application-level hops is determined by the tree height, which is depended on the multicast group size. Therefore, when the multicast group size is fixed at 300, loss and throughput performances does not vary greatly with the number of mobile hosts.[8] On the other hand, Narada protocol constructs delay-optimized mesh, thus the number of application-level hops between the source and members varies depending on the number of mobile hosts, which are apt to suffer from high delay. Therefore, these performances are degraded with the increase of mobile hosts in Narada protocol.

Figure 11 shows average RDP between all pairs of the source and members. In fig.11, new k-tree protocol with $k = 4$ can outperform other protocols. The main reason for this is that there are fewer intermediate mobile hosts in new k-tree protocol than in other protocols. The intermediate mobile hosts which suffering from high delay by wireless communications have a negative impact on downstream hosts. In new k-tree protocol with $k = 4$, the tree height becomes shorter than with $k = 2$, thus the number of application-level hops between the source and members decreases. As a result, RDP performance are improved.

We have run other simulations with different multicast group size and wireless loss conditions. Although we had to omit graphs of these simulations due to space constraints, similar results were obtained in those simulations.

6   Conclusions

ALM lacks robustness. Due to the dependency of the ALM tree on end-hosts, which are less stable than dedicated and well administered commercial routers, the ALM tree is intrinsically fragile. When the ALM tree is partitioned after a single end-host failure, all downstream end-hosts from the failed end-host cannot receive multicast packet. It is very important to address this problem for commercial implementation of ALM. When a wireless mobile host participates the multicast session, its instability makes the robustness problem more serious. Due to a bad wireless connection and handover, a wireless mobile host which is an intermediate node may have an adverse affect on the performances of its downstream members. In this paper, to deal with this problem, we propose a new tree construction protocol that constructs a robust multicast tree against the handover by taking wireless mobile hosts into account. Our protocol locates mobile hosts on leaves of multicast tree. To investigate performance of our protocol, we compared our proposed protocol with pure k-tree protocol and Naraa protocol. Our simulation results show that our protocol outperforms other protocols from the viewpoints of robustness, loss probability, throughput and delay performance.

References

1. S. Deering and D. Cheriton, "Host Groups: A Multicast Extension to the Internet Protocol", RFC 966, Dec. 1985.
2. C. Diot, B. N. Levine, B. Lyles, H. Kassem, and D. Balensiefen, "Deployment Issues for the IP Multicast Service and Architecture", *IEEE Network*, Vol.1, No.14, Jan. 2000.
3. Y.-H. Chu, S. G. Rao and H. Zhang, "A Case for End System Multicast", *IEEE JSAC*, vol.20, pp.1456-1471, Oct. 2002.

---

[8] Due to intermediate mobile hosts, these performances are degraded slightly with the increase of mobile hosts in pure k-tree protocol.

4. A. El-Sayed, V. Roca, and L. Mathy, "A survey of Proposals for an Alternative Group Communication Service", *IEEE Network*, Special issue on "Multicasting: An Enabling Technology", Vol.17, No.1, Jan./Feb. 2003.

5. V. Roca, and A. El-Sayed, "A Host-Based Multicast (HBM) Solution for Group Communications", In Proc. of *1st IEEE International Conference on Networking (ICN'01)*, Colmar, France, July 2001.

6. P. Francis, "Yoid:Extending the Multicast Internet Architecture", 1999, white paper, http://www.icir.org
/yoid/.

7. S. Banerjee et al., "Construction of an Efficient Overlay Multicast Infrastructure for Real-time Applications", In Proc. of *INFOCOM'03*, San Francisco, USA, Mar. 2003.

8. Y. Chawathe, "Scattercast: An Architecture for Internet Broadcast Distribution as an Infrastructure Service", Ph.D.Thesis, Univ. of California, Berkeley, Dec. 2000.

9. S. Banerjee, B. Bhattacharjee and C. Kommareddy, "Scalable Application Layer Multicast", ACM SIGCOMM'02, pp.205-220, Pittsburgh, PA, Aug. 2002.

10. B. Zhang, S. Jamin, and L. Zhang, "Host Multicast: A Framework for Delivering Multicast To End Users", IEEE INFOCOM'02, pp.1366-1375, New York, NY, June 2002.

11. D. Pendarakis, S. Shi, D. Verma and M. Waldvogel, "ALMI: An Application Level Multicast Infrastructure", USENIX USITS '01, pp.49-60, San Francisco, CA, Mar. 2001.

12. Y. Chu, S. G. Rao, S. Seshan, and H. Zhang. "Enabling Conferencing Applications on the Internet Using an Overlay Multicast Architecture", ACM SIGCOMM'01, pp. 55-67, San Diego, CA, Aug. 2001.

13. Eli Brosh and Yuval Shavitt, "Approximation and Heuristic Algorithms for Minimum-Delay Application Layer Multicast Trees", IEEE INFOCOM'04, Hong Kong, Mar. 2004.

14. D. Johnson, C .Perkins, and J .Arkko, "Mobility Support in IPv6", Internet Draft, *draft-ietf-mobileip-ipv6-24.txt*, June 2003.

15. T. Noguchi and M. Yamamoto, "Construction of a Robust Multicast Tree for Application-level Multicast"CIn Proc. of IEEE ICC 2005, vo.1, pp. 130-135, Soul, Korea, May 2005.

16. M. Handley, "Session directories and scalable Internet multicast address allocation", ACM SIGCOMM '98, pp.105-116, Vancouver, Canada, Aug./Sept. 1998.

17. A. Medina, I. Matta, and J. Byers, "On the Origin of Power Lows in Internet Topologies", *ACM Computer Communication Review*, vol.30, no.2, pp.18-28, April 2000.

18. T. Pusateri, "Distance Vector Multicast Routing Protocol", Internet Draft, *draft-ietf-idmrdvmrp-v3-10.txt*, Aug. 2000.

Enhanced Fast Handover Mechanism
Using MIH Services in MIPv6

Yoon-Young An[1], Kang-Won Lee[2], Dong-Won Kum[2], Sung-Hyup Lee[2],
You-Ze Cho[2], Byung Ho Yae[1], and Woo-Young Jung[3]

[1] ETRI, Daejeon, Korea
{yyahn, bhyae}@etri.re.kr
[2] School of Electrical Engineering & Computer Science,
Kyungpook National University, Daegu, Korea
{kw0314, 80kumsy, tenetshlee, yzcho}@ee.knu.ac.kr
[3] DGIST, Daegu, Korea
wyjung@dgist.ac.kr

Abstract. In this paper, we propose an enhanced handover mechanism
with new additional primitives and parameters to the media independent handover (MIH) services as defined in IEEE 802.21. The proposed
scheme can reduce handover latency for MIPv6 (mobile IPv6) by removing the router discovery time. Moreover, when the proposed mechanism
is applied to a FMIPv6 (fast handovers for MIPv6), we can increase the
probability that FMIPv6 can be per-formed in a predictive mode by reducing the handover initiation time. As a result, we can get the reduced
handover latency in FMIPv6. In addition, with the proposed scheme,
we can design the cost-effective network by reducing cover-age overlap
between adjacent cells. This is due to the decreased handover initiation
time in FMIPv6. From simulation results, it is proven that the proposed
scheme can provide a higher goodput for UDP and TCP because it has
less service disruption during handovers.

1   Introduction

Mobile communication has become more popular due to the increased availability of portable devices and advanced wireless technology. Moreover, the core
network for heterogeneous wireless access is evolving into all-IP based network.
Accordingly, MIPv6 is recognized as a global solution that can support mobile
services in the Inter-net between various access networks[1][2]. The long handover
latency in the MIPv6 degrades the perceived quality of service (QoS) especially
in real-time services.

In order to reduce the handover latency in the MIPv6, FMIPv6 has been
proposed in the IETF. It reduces packet loss by providing fast IP connectivity,
as soon as a new link is established. It does so by fixing up the routing during
a L2 handover and bind-ing update, so that packets delivered to the old care
of address (CoA) are forwarded to the new. In addition, FMIPv6 performs the
CoA configuration by using the link information (such as the subnet prefix) of

T. Braun et al. (Eds.): WWIC 2006, LNCS 3970, pp. 120–131, 2006.

the new access router (nAR), while the mobile node (MN) is still attached to the old access router (oAR). FMIPv6 can reduce the CoA configuration time in the new subnet. However, the FMIPv6 only concentrates on the protocol operation while it does not consider other issues, such as radio access discovery and candidate access router discovery, which are critical to its hand-over performance. Moreover, during the handover initiation, the MN could lose its connectivity to the oAR due to a sudden disruption of the link. In this case, MN per-forms a normal handover procedure in the MIPv6 or a reactive FMIPv6, thus result-ing in a long handover latency[3].

IEEE 802 is developing standards to enable handover and interoperability procedures between heterogeneous networks. IEEE 802.21 specification, MIH, defines the method that provides the link layer intelligence and other related network information to the upper layer to optimize handovers. The existing MIH primitives, however, limit to optimize the handover latency and they hardly improve the performance of FMIPv6. This is because these are only used as link layer triggers.

In this paper, in order to reduce handover latency in MIPv6 and to increase the probability that FMIPv6 can be performed in predictive mode, we propose an enhanced handover mechanism with new primitives and parameters to MIH services in IEEE 802.21. By the newly-defined MIH primitives and parameters, we can improve the handover performance of MIPv6 and FMIPv6.

This paper is organized as follows. In Section 2, we describe the basic operation of the handover for MIPv6/FMIPv6. Then, we explain the overview of MIH services as defined in IEEE 802.21. In Section 3, we propose a new handover mechanism that uses MIH services with new primitives and parameters. In Section 4, we evaluate the performance of our mechanism as compared with that of MIPv6 and FMIPv6. In additionally, we analyze the correlation between the handover initiation time and cell coverage overlap. We also compare the performance of the proposed scheme with MIPv6 by NS-2 simulation. The conclusion is presented in Section 5.

2   Related Works

2.1   Handover in the MIPv6 Network

The MIPv6 supports a handover that changes its point of attachment to the network when a MN moves to a new IP subnet. The basic handover procedure for the MIP consists of two components, the L2 handover and L3 handover. The L2 handover denotes its support for roaming at the link layer level, while the L3 handover occurs in the network layer level. Usually, the L3 handover is independent of the L2 hand-over, although it must precede the L3 handover.

In Fig. 1, the MIPv6 handover procedure is illustrated. The MIPv6 consists of three operations and they may overlap each another: Movement detection, which includes the L2 handover, is a prerequisite procedure for other handover operations. The L2 handover, that must precede the L3 handover, performs channel scanning, authentication, and association. After the L2 handover, the

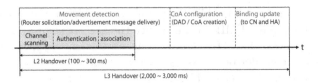

Fig. 1. The MIPv6 handover procedure

MN can detect movement to a new IP subnet by the operation of movement detection. In the basic MIPv6 specifications, during movement detection, the MN performs the unreachability detection. This is accomplished by finding a new and different available AR. Router discovery is achieved through the reception of a router advertisement (RA) message, which is sent from the new AR (nAR). The RA message contains router information such as its prefix, link layer address (MAC), MTU, and so on. The MN must configure a new IPv6 address that can be used on the new network in CoA configuration procedure. This will be the MN's new CoA (nCoA). The uniqueness of the configured addresses must be verified on the new link according to the DAD operation. Once the MN has moved to a new network, it obtains a new CoA that was granted during access to the new network. Then, the MN must perform the Binding Update operation by inform-ing its Home Agent (HA) and Correspondent Node (CN) of its new location.

The total handover latency in MIPv6 can be expressed as the sum of the L2 hand-over latency and L3 handover latency. The L2 handover latency is about between 100ms and 300ms. The L3 handover is about 2,000 to 3,000 ms. This handover latency is so long that MN can suffer from packet loss and service disruption.

2.2   Fast Handovers for MIPv6

The FMIPv6 addresses the following problems regarding the reduction of the hand-over latency: 1) how to allow the MN to send packets as soon as it detects a new subnet link, and 2) how to deliver packets to a mobile node as soon as its attachment is detected by the new access router[4][5]. In the FMIPv6, the MN is informed of a new AR's advertised prefix and it validates the duplication of nCoA on the new link prior to the movement of MN. So, the MN is already configured with nCoA before it is attached to the new link. In other words, the FMIPv6 is designed to eliminate de-lays associated with movement detection and CoA testing and the time that is introduced by the CoA configuration procedure.

FMIPv6 is designed to allow the MN to anticipate in its IP layer mobility. Link layer triggers are required for anticipation and handover initiation. They are delivered to network layer modules as events in order to report changes with respect to link and physical layer conditions. The link layer triggers for FMIPv6 are described in Table 1. Fig. 2 depicts the predictive FMIPv6 procedure that utilizes the link layer triggers in Table 1.

The FMIPv6 protocol, however, has several problems:

- The AR has to have the protocol to exchange information about their neighbors in order to construct the mapping table between the AP's MAC addresses and the corresponding AR. This table, however, is not defined in the IETF.
- Link layer triggers should be specified by organization of standards such as the IETF and IEEE 802.
- During the initiation of handover, the MN could lose its connectivity to the oAR due to a sudden degradation in the link. The MN processes a normal handover in MIPv6 or in a reactive FMIPv6. Therefore, the handover latency increases.

Table 1. Link layer triggers for the FMIPv6

Primitive	Description
link list	This trigger may be used to get a list of available link by AP scan.
link available	This trigger specifies that a new available link is detected.
link going down	A link down event will be fired in the near future so the network layer must initiate the handover procedure
link down	This indicates that the link cannot be used for data transmission any more.
link up	This is provided to L3 when a new link is connected

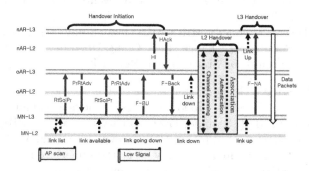

Fig. 2. The FMIPv6 procedure using MIH primitives

2.3   Media Independent Handover Function

Recently, IEEE 802 has been developing standards to enable handover procedures and interoperability between heterogeneous networks. IEEE 802.21 specification, MIH, defines a method that can provide link layer intelligence and other related net-work information to the upper layers. This is done so as to optimize handovers between heterogeneous media[6]. In FMIPv6, the network layer must detect an indication of a handover from the link layer in advance in order to achieve a seamless hand-over. Therefore, we need to introduce MIH services for link layer trigger in FMIPv6.

The MIH functions define asynchronous and synchronous services that enhance a handover between heterogeneous access links and service access points (SAPs), which is an interface between lower layers and upper layers. In the case of a system with multiple network interfaces of an arbitrary type, MIPv6 can use the event, command, and information services that are provided by the MIH to manage, determine, and control the state of the underlying interfaces. These services, which are provided by the MIH functions, help the MIPv6 and other protocols.

Information Service. The information service provides a framework and corresponding mechanisms by which a MIH function entity can discover and obtain network information, which exists within a geographical area, in order to facilitate handovers. The information service primarily provides a query/response type of mechanism for the transfer of information. This information may be stored within the MIH layer or it may be presented to an information server by which the MIH layer can get an access. The information service provides access to static information such as neighbor maps, helping network discovery. The service also may provide access to dynamic information which may optimize link layer connectivity with different networks. This could include link layer parameters such as channel information, MAC addresses, security

Event Service. The event service is used to facilitate handover detection within the MIP. Events inform the condition of the present network and the transmission behavior of the L2 data links, such as MAC, Radio resource management, etc. The MIP makes a registration to receive events from MIH layer using a request/confirm primitives.

The defined events include Pre-trigger (L2 Handoff Imminent), Link Available, Link Up, Link Parameters Change, Link Going Up, Link Down, Link Going Down, L2SDU Transmission Status, Event Rollback, etc.

Command Service. The command service refers to the commands that are sent from the higher layers to the lower layers. It includes commands from the upper layer to the MIH (e.g. upper layer mobility protocol to MIH services, or policy engine to MIH, etc), and from MIH to lower layer (e.g. MIH to MAC, or MIH to PHY). These commands mainly carry the upper layer decisions to the lower layer, and control the behavior of lower layer entities.

3   A Proposed Handover Mechanism

In general, the IP layer in FMIPv6 needs the L2 trigger in order to perform a hand-over initiation for the nCoA configuration before the L2 handover. In this case, MIH services are very useful for link layer triggers. With the existing MIH primitives, the handover performance of MIPv6 is very limited because MIH service is only used for detecting L2 layer information. In particular, it hardly improves the performance of the FMIPv6.

Table 2. Definition of primitives for the proposed mechanism

Primitive	Service	Parameters
MIH-PrefixInfo	CS	Interface ID, Prefix
MIH-LinkList	IS	Interface ID, Prefix, Mac Addr, BW, Quality Level
MIH-LinkAvailable	ES	Interface ID, Prefix, Mac Addr, BW, Quality Level
MIH-LinkGoingDown	ES	Interface ID, Mac Addr, BW, Quality Level
MIH-LinkDown	ES	Interface ID, Mac Addr
MIH-LinkUp	ES	Interface ID, Mac Addr

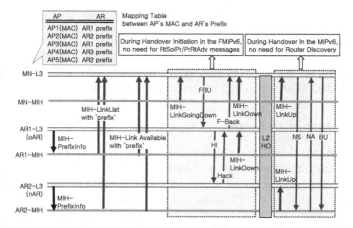

Fig. 3. The proposed fast handover mechanism using MIH primitives

In this session, we propose an enhanced handover mechanism with new additional primitives and parameters to the MIH services. As shown in Table 2, the new primitive "MIH-PrefixInfo" contains the prefix information of AR. The L3 module of the AR sends "MIH-PrefixInfo" to link layer to inform the subnet information when a new AP is attached or the prefix is exchanged. Therefore, the link-layer of the AR and AP can obtain the prefix information of its AR. The L3 module in MN gathers the information of neighbor APs using "MIH-LinkList" and "MIH-LinkAvailable". In this paper, we suggest that a "prefix" parameter be added to these primitives and thereby, the MN can obtain the prefix information of the new AP.

Fig. 3 shows the proposed mechanism by using the new primitives and parameters as defined in Table 2. In the proposed mechanism, whenever AR's subnet configuration is changed, the AR-L3 informs the prefix information of the AR-L2 through the AR-MIH. This is done by using the new primitive, MIH-PrefixInfo. The MN can obtain both AP and AR information as it receives "MIH-LinkList" and "MIH-LinkAvailable" primitive with AR's prefix parameter. Therefore, the

MN can make the mapping table between the AP's MAC and AR's prefix. In the original FMIPv6, ARs exchange information about their neighbors and have to reconstruct the mapping table for proxy advertisements with information on the neighboring subnets. In the proposed mechanism, since the MN has a mapping table regarding the new primitive and parameter in advance, the AR need not exchange information about their neighbors. Also, MN need not exchange RtSolPr/PrRtAdv messages or RS/RA messages for Router Discovery. This is because the router information is already contained in MIH primitives.

As a result, some steps in the CoA configuration procedure, which are related with router discovery or RtSolPr/PrRtAdv, can be reduced. Namely, with the proposed handover scheme, the MIPv6 can decrease the handover latency. The FMIPv6 can reduce the handover initiation by removing the Router Discovery procedure of hand-over procedure.

4   Performance Evaluation

This section compares the performance of the proposed handover scheme with that of MIPv6/FMIPv6 through analysis and simulation.

4.1   Performance Analysis

In this section, we show the performance from the viewpoint of two criteria, the handover latency and the handover initiation time. Table 3 shows the handover latency and the handover initiation time for MIPv6 and FMIPv6 with and without the proposed scheme. With MIPv6, the proposed mechanism can remove the time needed for router discovery (D_{RD}) from the handover latency. In the case of FMIPv6, the handover initiation time is reduced by removing the time for Proxy Router Discovery, D_{PrRD}.

Handover Latency. The handover latency affects the service disruption time, which is defined as the interval between the reception of the last packet through the oAR and the reception of the first packet through the nAR. It is an important criterion of the performance of real-time services. The handover latency in Table 3 can be expressed as follows:

$$D_{HO-MIPv6} = D_{L2} + \tau + \delta + 3RTT_{MN-nAR} + RTT_{nAR-HA} \quad (1)$$

$$D_{HO-ProMIPv6} = D_{L2} + \tau + 2RTT_{MN-nAR} + RTT_{nAR-HA} \quad (2)$$

$$D_{HO-FMIPv6} = D_{L2} + 2RTT_{MN-nAR} + RTT_{nAR-HA} \quad (3)$$

$$D_{HO-ProFMIPv6} = D_{L2} + 2RTT_{MN-nAR} + RTT_{nAR-HA} \quad (4)$$

where D_{L2} is the L2 handover latency, is the time for DAD, is D_{RD} for periodic RA, RTT_{MN-nAR} is the round-trip time between the MN and nAR, and RTT_{nAR-HA} is the round-trip time between the nAR and HA.

Fig. 4 compares the handover latency among MIPv6 and FMIPv6, and the pro-posed mechanism. We assume that is 1000 ms for RetransTimer (default

Table 3. Handover latency and handover initiation time for the MIPv6/FMIPv6 with and without the proposed scheme

Handover Mechanism	Handover Latency	Handover Init. Time
MIPv6	$D_{L2} + D_{DAD} + D_{RD} + D_{BU}$	
Proposed MIPv6	$D_{L2} + D_{DAD} + D_{BU}$	
FMIPv6	$D_{L2} + 2D_{MN-nAR} + D_{BU}$	$D_{PrRD} + D_{FMIP}$
Proposed FMIPv6	$D_{L2} + 2D_{MN-nAR} + D_{BU}$	D_{FMIP}

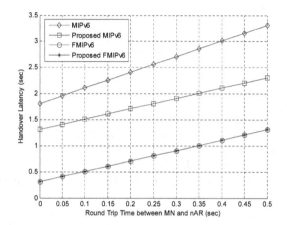

Fig. 4. A comparison of the handover latency of MIPv6/FMIPv6 with and without the proposed scheme

1000ms) and DupAddrDetectTransmits (default 1000ms), is rtAdvInterval/2 (500ms), and RTT_{nAR-HA} are 10ms. In the case of MIPv6, the proposed mechanism can obtain a better performance than that of the original MIPv6.

Handover Initiation Time. In the case of FMIPv6, it can not reduce the handover latency after the L2 handover but it can reduce the handover initiation time. During the handover initiation for FMIPv6, MN could lose its connectivity

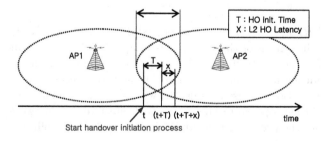

Fig. 5. The coverage overlap for handover initiation time

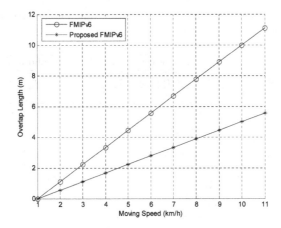

Fig. 6. Relationship between the coverage overlap legnth for handover initiation time and the moving speed of MN

to the oAR due to a sudden degradation of the link quality. In these failure cases, the FMIPv6 performs in a reactive FMIPv6 or in a normal MIPv6 and thereby, the handover latency is increased. The FMIPv6 with the proposed scheme can reduce the handover latency in the original FMIPv6 by the reducing the handover initiation time.

As shown in Fig. 5, coverage overlap is required for the MN to perform the hand-over initiation and link layer handover in FMIPv6. If the coverage overlap is too large, the coverage area is reduced, resulting in a capacity reduction of coverage. On the other hand, if it is too small, the MN does not have enough time for the handover initiation by which it predicts its movement between coverage. Thereby, the MN may proceed with a normal handover in MIPv6 or the reactive FMIPv6 [7]. The handover initiation time can be expressed as follows:

$$T_{FMIPv6} = D_{PrRD} + D_{FMIP} \tag{5}$$
$$= 2RTT_{MN-oAR} + (2RTT_{MN-oAR} + 2RTT_{oAR-nAR}) \tag{6}$$
$$= 4RTT_{MN-oAR} + 2\Delta \tag{7}$$
$$T_{ProFMIPv6} = 2RTT_{MN-oAR} + 2\Delta \tag{8}$$

where Δ and $RTT_{oAR-nAR}$ can be neglected due to very small values.

Fig. 6 shows the length of the coverage overlap according to the moving speed of the MN for the FMIPv6 and the proposed mechanism. Here, we can see that the handover initiation time has decreased and the size of the coverage overlap area has also decreased. Thus, the whole coverage capacity has increased. Consequently, the proposed mechanism is cost-effective for a network design. On the other hand, the proposed mechanism increases the probability that FMIPv6 can perform in predictive mode.

4.2 Simulation Results

We compare the UDP and TCP goodput of the proposed scheme with those of
MIPv6 by simulation using NS-2. Fig. 7 shows the network model for simulation.
We assume that the coverage area of an AR is 250 meters in radius, and the ARs
are 450 meters apart each other. Therefore, there is 50 meters overlapping area
between the adjacent ARs. In our simulation we consider the IEEE 802.11b as
the wireless LAN. The link characteristics, (the delay and the bandwidth), are
shown beside each link in the Fig. 7. We have simulated for two traffic types:
UDP and TCP. For UDP, the 512-byte packets were sent repeatedly at a constant
rate of 20 packets per second from the CN to a MN. For TCP, FTP traffic was
generated with a full window.

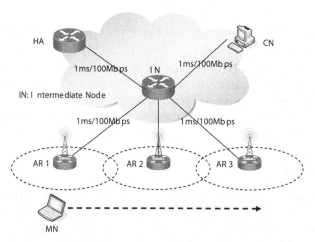

Fig. 7. Network model for simulation

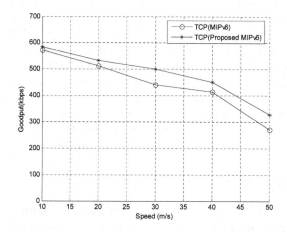

Fig. 8. TCP goodput behaviors between the proposed mechanism and the basic MIPv6

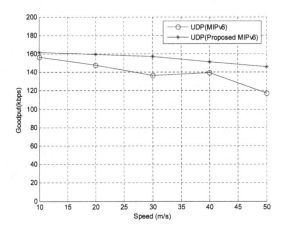

Fig. 9. UDP goodput behaviors between the proposed mechanism and the basic MIPv6

Goodput. Fig. 8 and 9 compare the TCP and the UDP goodput behaviors between the proposed mechanism and the MIPv6 basic, respectively. From these figures, we note that the proposed scheme can provide a higher goodput in both cases of the TCP and the UDP, because the proposed scheme has smaller service disruption during handovers.

5   Conclusion

In this paper, we proposed an enhanced handover mechanism with an improved performance, with MIH services as defined in IEEE 802.21. To do so, we defined a new primitive, "MIH-PrefixInfo", and added a parameter 'prefix' to the existing MIH primitives. By using MIH services with the new primitive, the MN can obtain the nAR's information without a router discovery or RtSolPr/PrRtAdv messages. There-fore, the proposed scheme can reduce the handover latency in MIPv6 by removing the router discovery time. Moreover, when the proposed mechanism is applied to the FMIPv6, we can increase the probability that FMIPv6 can be per-formed in a predictive mode by reducing the handover initiation time. As results, we can reduce the handover latency in the FMIPv6. In addition, with the proposed scheme, we can de-sign a cost-effective network by decreasing the coverage over-lap between the adjacent cells. This is because the handover initiation time in the FMIPv6 has decreased. Regarding the simulation results, we show that the pro-posed scheme can provide a higher goodput for the UDP and TCP because the proposed scheme has less service disruption during handover.

Acknowledgement

This work was supported in part by the MIC (Ministry of Information and Com-munication), Korea, under the ITRC (Information Technology Research Center) program, and the DGIST (Daegu Gyeongbuk Institute of Science and Technology).

References

1. Jian Ma, Zhigang Kan, "Role of of Mobile IPv6 for mobile networks and its remaining issues," APOC2001.
2. Douglas Howie, "Consequences of of using MIPv6 to achieve mobile ubiquitous multimedia," MUM2002.
3. Yoon-Young An, Chang-Min Park, Sung Back Hong, "The Method for Reducing Packet Loss in Handover Service of Mobile IPv6," AIC 29th Conference, Dec. 2003.
4. R. Koodli(Ed.), "Fast Handover for Mobile IPv6," IETF RFC 4068, July 2005.
5. Lila Dimopoulou, Georgios Leoleis, Iakovos S. Venieris, "Fast Handover Support in a WLAN Environment: Challenges and Perspectives," IEEE Networks, May/June 2005, 14-20.
6. IEEE 802.21 WG, "Draft IEEE Standard for Local and Metropolitan Area Networks : Media Independent Handover Services," IEEE P802.21/D00.05, January 2006.
7. Hesham Soliman, "Mobile IPv6 : Mobility in a Wireless Internet," Addison-Wesley, 2004.

NSIS-Based Quality of Service and Resource Allocation in Ethernet Networks

M. Carmo, B. Carvalho, J. Sá Silva, E. Monteiro, P. Simões,
M. Curado, and F. Boavida

University of Coimbra, Laboratory of Communications and Telematics,
DEI / CISUC, Polo II, 3030 Coimbra, Portugal
Tel: +351 239 790000, Fax: +351 239 701266
{maxweel, sasilva, edmundo, psimoes, marilia,
boavida}@dei.uc.pt, becarv@student.dei.uc.pt

Abstract. The definition of the IEEE 802.1Q and IEEE 802.1p standards provided Class of Service (CoS) capabilities to Ethernet networks and, consequently, allowed new QoS services to be deployed. This is used by the Subnet Bandwidth Management (SBM) protocol, an RSVP-based protocol that provides IntServ-like services at Ethernet level. This paper proposes an alternative way to quality of service provision and resource allocation in Ethernet networks, based on the emerging IETF NSIS framework. The proposed approach was validated as a proof of concept by simulation, showing the ability of NSIS to provide QoS differentiation in Ethernet scenarios.

1 Introduction

Ethernet is a network technology supported by a set of international standards that offer pragmatic solutions for communication. Its success is due not only to its low-cost but also to its simplicity.

Ethernet solutions are widely used in local area domains. However, with the development of Gigabit and 10 Gigabit variants, Ethernet seems to have gained a new momentum as a technology for use in all telecommunication networks. This, along with the fact that it is a flexible and switched technology, can be regarded as an omen of the success of Ethernet in future communication systems, especially when large networks are concerned. In fact, already nowadays Ethernet is not only used in Campus and LANs networks, but also in Small Office Home Office Networks, Metropolitan Area Networks (MAN) [1], Wide Area Networks (WAN) and MAN residential scenarios (Ethernet Passive Optical Networks - EPONs).

This paper presents a proposal for the support of QoS and resource allocation in Ethernet networks, developed in the scope of the EuQoS project (http://www.euqos.org).

EuQoS is an FP6 IST Integrated Project with the aim of proposing, developing and studying end-to-end QoS support for Internet applications. This will be achieved through the research, integration, testing, validation and demonstration of end-to-end QoS technologies that can support advanced QoS-demanding applications such as voice, video-conferencing, video-streaming, educational, tele-engineering and medical applications.

T. Braun et al. (Eds.): WWIC 2006, LNCS 3970, pp. 132 – 142, 2006.
© Springer-Verlag Berlin Heidelberg 2006

EuQos targets a wide range of network technologies, from access networks – including Ethernet, UMTS, and WiFi – to core networks. As such, one of the research lines of the EuQos project consists of the development of solutions that provide QoS in Ethernet networks.

The proposals presented in this paper were studied by simulation and are currently being refined in order to serve as a basis for prototyping. In order to adequately fundament and present the developed as well as the on-going work, the paper is organized as follows: the next section presents a global view of QoS in Ethernet, identifying the base standards and providing the motivation for extending QoS to such networks; Section 3 provides background and related work, by presenting the current approach to resource allocation in Ethernet, namely the RSVP-based Subnet Bandwidth Management protocol (SBM); Section 4 presents the main proposal of this paper, addressing the use of NSIS for resource allocation in Ethernet and presenting a simulation-based validation of this proposal; Section 5 summarizes the contributions and identifies the guidelines for further work.

2 Quality of Service in Ethernet

This section presents the base standards for QoS support in Ethernet and discusses the motivations for and support of such developments.

2.1 Standards Support

CSMA/CD is the media access control mechanism that was initially developed to give the possibility for two or more devices to share a common media. This mechanism worked well for 10 Mbps but revealed problems at higher data rates. Nowadays, CSMA/CD networks are hardly used. With the advent of full-duplex and switched solutions, it is possible to build collision-free tree and star topologies, connecting terminal equipment to switches.

Original Ethernet standards did not support QoS functionality. IEEE 802.1Q [2] can be considered a first step in this direction, by defining the operation of Virtual LAN (VLAN) Bridges.

Table 1. User priority values recommended by IEEE 802.1p standard

IEEE 802.1p User Priority	Traffic Type
7 (highest)	Network Management
6	Voice
5	Video
4	Controlled Load
3	Excellent Effort
0	Best Effort
2	Undefined
1 (lowest)	Background

The IEEE 802.1p standard (which is part of IEEE 802.1D [3]) supports the provisioning of expedited traffic in a LAN network, based on the use of VLAN tags. VLAN tags have two parts: the VLAN ID (12-bit) and the Prioritization field (3-bit). IEEE 802.1p defines this latter field, allowing the prioritization of traffic into 8 levels, thus providing the basic support for QoS differentiation in Ethernet.

The user priority values defined in the IEEE 802.1p standard are presented in Table 1. Each level is associated with a specific traffic type.

2.2 Rationale for QoS in Ethernet

It is important to distinguish the use and need of QoS mechanisms in the different types of Ethernet networks. Although the technology principles are the same, the purpose of implementing QoS policies can be different.

A SOHO, also called a *virtual office*, refers to the small office or home environment and the business culture that surrounds it. In this type of environment, the implementation of QoS mechanisms in order to differentiate traffic inside the network is not critical, as the number of active pieces of equipment is generally low.

Ethernet has found widespread acceptability in campus and small scale environments, and nowadays is the supporting technology of most LANs. With the use of different applications, with a wide range of requirements, it is crucial to differentiate the traffic and to manage it properly.

Current MAN infrastructures are built not only for a voice-centric world but also for data-centric world. However, in order to use Ethernet to implement MANs, it is necessary to offer and maintain the same level of QoS of traditional voice-based applications. The use of over-provisioned solutions, typical in some of the recent systems, leads to low resource utilization, high costs and poor scalability.

The main reason Ethernet is being considered in WANs is because of its low cost. Initially, Ethernet will be used as a switch-to-switch interconnection for multiplexing different traffic, offering inter operation between different vendors' implementations. The definition of new standards and policies is crucial to the mapping of traffic classes between different operators.

The high modularity and scalability of Ethernet solutions enables operators to supply broadband services to subscribers, including data, voice and video, through a cost effective architecture in residential networks, namely through the use of EPONs. However, in these networks, each link supports a set of subscribers, which produce very bursty traffic in contrast with MANs and WANs, where the bandwidth requirements are relatively smoother due to the aggregation of many traffic sources.

Given the variety of environments to which Ethernet is applicable, which nowadays covers the whole spectrum of networks, it is clear that if quality of service is to be provided to applications, it must be supported in this type of technology.

2.3 Support for QoS in Ethernet

Nowadays, there is a huge number of pieces of equipment, such as switches and network interface cards, that provide some level of IEEE 802.1p implementation. In addition, there are pieces of software, like device drivers and APIs that support the provisioning of QoS through the 802.1p standard.

Several network cards available in the market also support the 802.1p specification, allowing hosts to set the user priority of the frames, using appropriate operating system device drivers and routines.

Several operating systems provide traffic prioritization support at the application and host levels. Applications can use appropriate APIs to handle the 802.1p parameters, and network administrators can use traffic management tools to apply QoS requirements in applications that are not QoS-aware.

In [4] a MIB module related to the management of MAC bridges (IEEE 802.1D) is defined, specifying objects for the management of Traffic Classes (IEEE 802.1p) and Enhanced Multicast Filtering. [4] also defines a MIB module for the management of Virtual LANs, specified by the IEEE 802.1Q standard.

This diversity of implementations and support confirms the acceptance of the 802.1p specification by the market.

3 RSVP-Based Resource Allocation in Ethernet

The traffic class differentiation provided by the 802.1p, together with some signaling and admission control mechanisms, can provide a close approximation to the Integrated Services (IntServ) paradigm at the level of Ethernet.

The IETF Integrated Services over Specific Link Layers (ISSLL) Working Group [5] was responsible for the mapping of QoS mechanisms of upper layers into layer 2 (link layer). A direct result of this work was the definition of the Subnet Bandwidth Management protocol (SBM) [6], a signaling protocol for shared and switched IEEE 802-style networks, like Ethernet.

Specifically, the SBM protocol describes a method of performing the reservation of LAN resources for RSVP-enabled data flows along the path where switches and routers offer support to do it.

An important module of the SBM definition is the Designated SBM (DSBM), a protocol entity that resides in a switch/router and is responsible for the admission control in a network segment.

All the RSVP request messages crossing the Ethernet network are redirected to the DSBM entities that will check the availability of the required resources. Figure 1 presents a LAN where the router needs to forward an RSVP PATH message to the host. In case (a) the signaling message reaches the host without take into account details of the Ethernet network.

In case of a SBM scenario (b), the signaling message is sent to the DSBM entities, instead of the destination node. After processing the request and adding themselves to the path, the DSBMs forward the message until it reaches the host. In the same way, RSVP RESV messages, crossing the managed segment, also need to pass through the DSBMs entities.

Each DSBM entity maintains information about the available resources on a given segment, being responsible for sending a RESV_ERR message to the requester if the request cannot be granted.

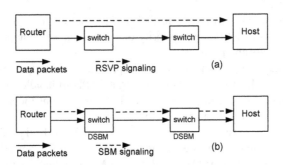

Fig. 1. RSVP and SBM signaling on Ethernet LAN scenarios

To ensure the existing of resources for the flows inside a LAN, [7] describes an approach to map the characterization parameters (e.g. bandwidth and delay bounds) [8] and services defined in the IntServ model (e.g. controlled load and guaranteed services) to the Ethernet traffic class parameters (Section 2.1). This mapping is performed in such a manner that different traffic flows requiring similar grade of service are aggregated into the same traffic class (with the same user priority value).

4   NSIS-Based Resource Allocation in Ethernet

This section presents the proposed resource allocation approach. As this approach is based on the use of Next Steps in Signaling (NSIS) [9], the section starts with a brief description of this IETF framework. Then, the basic proposal is presented and justified. The section ends with some results of a simulation-based evaluation.

4.1   Next Steps in Signaling

NSIS is a signalling framework being developed by the IETF, based on various signalling protocols, of which the RSVP is the corner stone. This framework is used for application signalling, in order to install and maintain flow state in the network, similar to other protocols such as the aforementioned RSVP.

NSIS can work on a per-flow basis, although it allows for flow aggregation based on the DSCP field of IP headers or on tunnels. In addition, NSIS works on a hop-by-hop basis (using NSIS-aware nodes in the network), as opposed to an end-to-end approach. The states related with the data flows are handled by NSIS-aware nodes, but this does not mean that every node in the network must support NSIS. NSIS has been specified in order to be usable in different parts of the Internet, for different needs, without requiring a complete end-to-end deployment.

NSIS considers two paradigms for resource reservation signalling, referred to as path-coupled and path-decoupled.

According to the path-coupled paradigm, the signalling messages are routed through NEs (NSIS Entities) that are on the data path only. These messages can use various addressing styles, with messages either explicitly addressed to adjacent NEs (normally referred to as NSIS hop) on-path, or addressed to an NSIS receiver with the

RAO option (Router Alert Option) in the data packets, allowing the messages to be intercepted by other NEs along the data path. This allows NEs to identify neighbours for future information exchange.

In the case of the path-decoupled paradigm, the messages are routed to nodes (NEs)   which are not assumed to be on the data path, but which are aware of it. The initial effort on NSIS development has been focused on the path-coupled paradigm, and some issues are still open in respect to the path-decoupled paradigm.

Figure 2 provides a simple scenario of NSIS path-coupled configuration. The NSIS messages are transparent to nodes that are NSIS-unaware, such as node R2 in the figure. A single message from Sender to Receiver establishes a session. On the way, nodes R1 and R3 will establish an association between them as adjacent NEs.

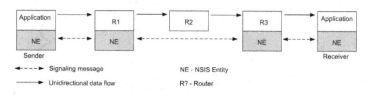

Fig. 2. Simple path-coupled signaling

NSIS decomposes the overall signalling protocol suite into a generic (lower) layer and specific upper layers for each specific signalling application. These are: NTLP (NSIS Transport Layer Protocol) and NSLP (NSIS Signalling Layer Protocol).

In the lower layer, NTLP (also known as GIST [10], General Internet Signaling Transport) offers transport services to higher layer signalling applications for two purposes: sending and receiving signalling messages between neighbouring hops (NSIS entities), and exchanging control and feedback information, through the use of *GIST-query*, *GIST-response* e *GIST-confirm* messages. NTLP messages can be delivered using existent transport protocols such as TCP, UDP, SCTP, HIP/IPsec, etc. By choosing the transport protocol to use, it is possible to guarantee security and reliability as needed.

Above the NTLP layer, there is the NSLP (NSIS Signalling Layer Protocol) layer, which generically stands for any protocol within the signalling application layer. Several NSLPs can be running independently of each other. This separation between transport and application allows NSIS to implement different QoS mechanisms, and extensibility even to non-QoS purpose. Although NSIS is used to QoS signalling in the first hand like in the QoS-NSLP specification [11], it should be possible to develop NSLPs for other signalling purposes that use different types of network control state, such as firewalls, NATs, and so on. NSLP uses GIST for message exchange.

4.2 NSIS in Ethernet

SBM, presented in Section 3, is RSVP-based. Although the NSIS protocol is quite similar to the RSVP protocol, namely in what respects support of unicast path-coupled signaling and soft state, NSIS has left out some complexities associated with RSVP like the multicast support. QoS NSLP also extends the set of reservation mechanisms like the support of sender or receiver-initiated reservations, bi-directional reservation and the support of reservations between arbitrary nodes. Thus, it makes sense to explore the use of NSIS for Ethernet resource allocation.

Exploring the usage of the NSIS over Ethernet makes even more sense if one considers that Ethernet is a widely spread technology, with more than 90% of today's data traffic originating from and terminating in it [12].

In the context of the EuQoS project, the authors propose the replacement of the SBM/RSVP solution by the NSIS approach for resource allocation in Ethernet networks. The basic approach is depicted in Figure 3, and is similar to the general NSIS approach.

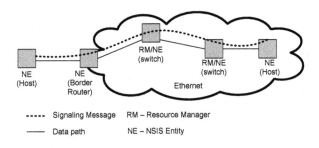

Fig. 3. Ethernet resource reservation through NSIS

The Resource Manager (RM) is the entity responsible for the admission control in the Ethernet domain, having similar functionality to the DSBM. This entity is NSIS-aware and includes a NSLP layer through which it is possible to receive signaling messages. These are used to install/maintain states along the Ethernet network.

Using this approach, it is possible to offer QoS guarantees even if the path between the sender and the receiver crosses an Ethernet network.

4.3 Validating NSIS in Ethernet

In order to validate the use of NSIS and its ability to support traffic differentiation in Ethernet, a preliminary simulation study was performed. Note that, at this stage, the objective of the study was not to compare NSIS with SBM/RSVP, but only to verify that NSIS is capable of supporting the required QoS functionality.

For the purpose of the study, the authors specifically developed several new modules for the NS-2 simulator, which allow the simulation of NSIS-based QoS provision over Ethernet networks. The modules, presented in [13], comply with the IEEE 802.1Q and IEEE 802.1p standards, implementing its traffic prioritization specifications.

Specifically, a queue object was developed that simulates an Ethernet switch/bridge and has the following properties:

- It can be configured to use up to eight virtual queues to group incoming LAN packets into separate traffic classes, according to IEEE 802.1p recommendations;

- The forwarding mechanism is implemented in such a way that packets from a given virtual queue are selected to transmit only if a higher order virtual queue is empty at the time of selection (strict priority queues).

To study the advantages of using priorities in Ethernet networks, the authors evaluated the transmission of heterogeneous signals in different topologies and with different traffic conditions. Next, one of these studies is presented, where a VoIP signal is transmitted over an overloaded Ethernet network, not using and using traffic priorities.

The topology of the referred scenario is depicted in figure 4. The link between the switch and Host 4 constitutes the bottleneck. The traffic from Host 1 to Host 4 is modeled as G.711 VoIP traffic without Voice Activity Detection (VAD) support. The other two traffic sources are modeled as exponential ON/OFF traffic.

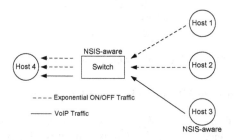

Fig. 4. Used LAN topology

A simplified NSLP layer implemented on the switch allows it to be signalled to process a flow with a certain priority (according to the priority levels listed on Table 1). Host 3 participates on the signalling process by sending to the switch a request asking for a highest priority for the VoIP traffic flow. The exponential on/off traffic packets are kept with a constant low priority along all the simulation time.

Figure 5 shows the one-way-delay (OWD) experienced by each of the traffic flows when no prioritization is performed in the switch. As expected, all the traffic presents similar behaviour, experiencing high delay in the face of network congestion.

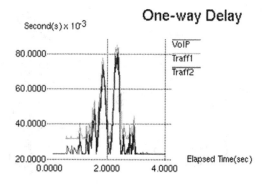

Fig. 5. Packet delay without traffic prioritization

Figure 6 presents the one-way-delay for the traffic flows, after the signaling message sent by Host 3 set the switch to prioritize the VoIP traffic in relation to the other two flows. The VoIP delay remains low during all of the simulation, as a result of the NSIS-based resource allocation.

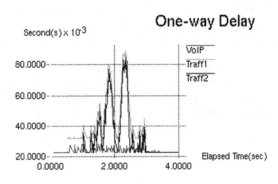

Fig. 6. Packet delay with traffic prioritization

4.4 NSIS-Based Resource Allocation in the EuQoS Project

Considering the current lack of Ethernet devices supporting NSIS protocol, two solutions have been envisioned to allow its deployment in the EuQoS project. However, the proposed solutions require some modification on the LAN's layout.

4.4.1 Centralized Resource Allocation

This solution considers the use of just one RM element, a standard computer, which will perform the resource allocation for flows trying to get access to the LAN (Figure 7). The RM element needs to be fed with details of the network topology including link information and assumptions about the switch capabilities. All the standard traffic (which did not explicitly ask for resource reservation) is aggregated on a lower priority queue by the edge switches to avoid disturbance of the flows which resources were reserved by the NSIS signaling. In this way, the RM does not need to be aware of each traffic flow present on the LAN.

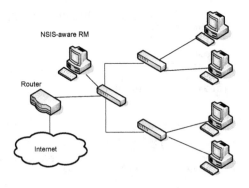

Fig. 7. Centralized resource allocation

4.4.2 Distributed Resource Allocation

In this case several RM elements are responsible for performing the resource reservation related tasks. As each RM manages a sub-set of resources (i.e. links), it is not necessary for them to know the entire network topology. As occurs on a standard IP NSIS signaling, it is necessary to establish a path inside the LAN by contacting the successive RM elements between the router and the destination node (Figure 8). Hosts inside the LAN can contact the closer RM to start the resource reservation process.

This solution is more flexible and allows a fine control over the traffic flows. By exploring the capabilities of some switches available on the market, it is possible to discover the RM elements between the sender and transmitter without a previous knowledge of the network topology. Naturally, this option demands more implementation effort.

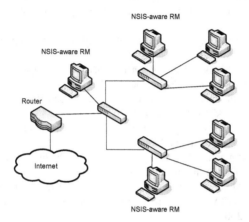

Fig. 8. Distributed resource allocation

5 Conclusion

As Ethernet becomes widely used in LAN, MAN and WAN scenarios, it is important to propose and study solutions for quality of service provision over this type of underlying network technology.

This paper proposed an approach to QoS provision in Ethernet, based on the emerging NSIS framework. In order to validate the proposal, simulation studies were performed which showed the potential of the proposed approach to differentiate traffic.

Following the promising simulation results, at the moment the authors are further analysing the overall issues related to the deployment of NSIS in Ethernet networks, and implementing the NSIS framework. Specifically, the GIST implementation is well under way and the NSLP protocol specification is being ultimated. Comparison of the SBM/RSVP-based solution with the NSIS solution will also be made in the near future, both by simulation and prototyping. Also, the analyses of the NSIS for QoS signaling purposes in heterogeneous scenarios involving Ethernet and WiFi is to be performed in future works.

References

1. Metro Ethernet Forum, http://www.metroethernetforum.org
2. 802.1Q, Standards for Local and metropolitan area networks; "Virtual Bridged Local Area Networks"; IEEE Computer Society 2003
3. 802.1D, Standards for Local and metropolitan area networks; "Media Acess Control (MAC) Bridges"; IEEE Computer Society 2004
4. A. Simt, P. Langille, A. Rijhsinghani, K. McCloghrie; "Definitions of Managed Objects for Bridges with Traffic Classes, Multicast Filtering and Virtual LAN Extensions"; RFC 2674; 1999
5. Integrated Services over Specific Link Layers (issll), http://www.ietf.org/html.charters/issll-charter.html; 2001
6. R. Yavatkar, D. Hoffman, Y. Bernet, and F. Baker; "SBM Subnet Bandwidth Manager): Protocol for RSVP-based Admission Control Over IEEE 802-style Networks"; RFC 2814; May 2000
7. M. Seaman, A. Smith, and E. Crawley; "Integrated Service Mappings on IEEE 802 Networks"; RFC 2815; May 2000
8. S. Shenker J. Wroclawski; "General Characterization Parameters for Integrated Service Network Elemens"; RFC 2215; September 1997
9. R. Handcock, G. Karagiannis, J. Loughney and S. van den Bosch; "Next Steps in Signaling (NSIS): Framework"; RFC 4080; June 2005
10. H. Schulzrinne, R. Hancock, "GIST: General Internet Signaling Transport draft-ietf-nsis-ntlp-09"; Internet Draft; February 2006
11. J. Manner, G. Karagiannis, A. McDonald, "NSLP for Quality-of-Service signalling draft-ietf-nsis-qos-nslp-09.txt"; Internet Draft; January 2006
12. M. McGarry, M. Maier and M. Reisslein, "Ethernet PONs: A Survey of Dynamic Bandwidth Allocation (DBA) Algorithms"; IEEE Communications Magazine, vol. 42, no. 8, pp. S8-S15, Aug. 2004
13. M. Carmo, et all; "Ethernet QoS Modelling in Emerging Scenarios"; Proceedings of 3rd International Workshop on Internet Performance, Simulation, Monitoring and Measurement, IPS-MoMe 2005, pp.90-96, IST MoMe Cluster

State of the Art Prepaid Charging for IP Services

Pascal Kurtansky[1] and Burkhard Stiller[1,2]

[1] Computer Engineering and Networks Laboratory TIK,
ETH Zurich, 8092 Zurich, Switzerland
[2] Department of Informatics IFI, University of Zurich, Switzerland,
{kurtansky, stiller}@tik.ee.ethz.ch

Abstract. The provisioning of IP services in the mobile telecommunication and the IP world differs in many aspects, especially with prepaid charging determining an important useability distinction. Thus, the state of the art of prepaid charging systems have been analyzed in detail, elaborating on their key capabilities and major limitations. Additionally, economic aspects in terms of operator's risks and major costs, addressing the technical overhead to implement prepaid charging, have been evaluated. Therefore, to enable prepaid charging for QoS-enabled and all-IP environments, key concerns for a future IP service provisioning have been determined, which remain infeasible with existing prepaid solutions, and the evaluation lead to a new scheme proposed.

1   Introduction

The Internet has evolved from a scientific and non-commercial network to an important and global economic domain, where commercial services are being offered on the basis of the Internet Protocol (IP). Important parts of any service level agreement (SLA), are the definition of service tariffs and the charging options to be applied—*e.g.*, pre- or postpaid. The postpaid option, is used throughout the whole telecommunication market, while prepaid is dominating the mobile telecommunication market. To make use of the Internet's global economic domain, providers base novel services on IP. Providers also aim to port the successful prepaid charging from non-IP mobile telecommunication systems into IP-based networks. Therefore, a prepaid charging option for these high-value IP services is required, ensuring an optimal economic and technical efficiency. The intersection of the mobile telecommunication and the IP world is moving away from being disjoint and is eventually ending up in an all-IP environment. This evolution towards all-IP introduces many interesting research issues.

This paper focuses at the particular issue of prepaid charging for IP services and gives an overview of existing solutions; a more detailed version can be found in [30]. Secondly, for prepaid charging in all-IP networks, open issues and concerns are identified, evaluated, and a solution to overcome them is outlined.

This paper is organized as follows. Based on available terminology in Sect. 2, an overview of prepaid charging systems in mobile telecommunication (Sect. 3) and in IP-based networks (Sect. 4) is presented. Sect. 5 contains discussion and evaluation of prepaid charging in an all-IP environment and Sect. 6 draws conclusions.

T. Braun et al. (Eds.): WWIC 2006, LNCS 3970, pp. 143 – 154, 2006.

2   Charging Terminology

The two worlds of mobile telecommunication and IP-based networks use different terminology with regard to charging and its associated processes. Based on [26], this paper uses a layered model and definition, where *charging* is positioned logically on top of metering and accounting, but below billing. The most important definitions are:

Charging calculates the charge for a given service consumption based on accounting records and the tariffs defined in the SLA. Charging acts as an umbrella term for charging *options* and charging *mechanisms*. This orthogonal seperation helps to emphasize either on the more technical or economic aspects of charging. Charging mechanisms are used to implement and realize charging options.

- With the *prepaid charging option*, the customer has to have a certain amount of credits prior to the service usage. Depending on the type service, periodical credit checks during service usage are performed. Prepaid charging influences the delivery of services to the customer, *e.g.*, service usage may be denied.
- With the *postpaid charging option*, service charges are aggregated on the user's account after service usage and the user is billed after a predefined period.
- With the *online charging mechanism,* charging (i.e. charge calculation) has to be performed in real-time. Note that online charging implies that accounting and metering have to be done in real-time as well.
- For the *offline charging mechanism*, no strict time constraints concerning the processing time of charging (i.e. charge calculation) are defined.

Billing is the process of consolidating charging information on a per customer basis and delivering a certain aggregate of it to a customer.

Tariff or tariff function, takes a set of accounting parameters as its input and outputs the *charge* to be paid for the particular value of those input parameters.

3   Prepaid Charging in 3G Mobile Telecommunication Networks

In 2/3G mobile telecommunication networks, prepaid charging has today a global average penetration of more than 50%, with the main revenue contribution resulting from circuit-switched voice and short message services [18]. For these classical services, the market penetration is currently around 90% and will reach complete saturation within the next years. In such a market situation, price differentiation has become the major marketing policy for Mobile network operators (MNO).Therefore, for these classical services prices are falling, hence MNO's are faced with a decline in ARPU (Average Revenue Per User). The only way to stabilize or even increase the ARPU is to increase the revenue made with packet-switched services. To further promote packet-switched services, MNO's aim to port the favorite prepaid charging from the circuit- to the packet-switched domain. Therefore, prepaid charging for IP services will play an important role in the future mobile market.

3.1 A Brief Overview of 3G Standards

Today's 3G systems in Europe are based on UMTS Release 99 [10]. Its pendant consists of CDMA2000 1x Release 0 [2] for circuit-switched services, together with CDMA2000 EV-DO Release 0 [4] for packet-switched services. The latest completely specified release in the pipeline of future UMTS releases, is UMTS Release 6 [11]. For CDMA2000 the pipeline consists of two possible branches, CDMA2000 EV-DO Release A [5] and CDMA2000 EV-DV Release D [3]. The terminology used in the specifications for the different 3G releases is correlated with the definitions of this paper in Tab. 1. The right column is based on 3GPP's vocabulary definitions [14], which are also used in 3GPP2's online charging specifications.

Table 1. Different terminology used in 3G mobile networks

All IP-based Network Proposal	3G Mobile Networks
Metering	Collecting charging information
Accounting	Charging
Accounting records	Charging Data Record (CDR)
Charging options	Billing arrangements, Payment methods
Prepaid/postpaid charging	Pre-paid/post-paid billing
Charging mechanism	Charging mechanism
Billing and parts of charging	Parts of Rating
Inter-/Multi-Domain Charging/Billing	Accounting

3.2 Existing Releases of 3G Networks

Initially, 2G mobile telecommunication networks were designed to offer only circuit-switched voice services and the short message service (SMS). Prepaid billing systems supporting these services are realized by one of the four techniques, [31]: (1) Service Node, (2) Intelligent Network (IN), (3) Handset-Based (SIM card-based), and (4) the concept of Hot Billing. In 3G networks, prepaid systems based on IN play the most important role. With UMTS R99, CAMEL Phase 3 [12] was introduced and current CDMA2000 networks use WIN Phase 2 [6]. Whereas the latter only supports prepaid charging for circuit-switched services, the former supports it also for packet-switched services. CAMEL 3 provides basically only rudimentary support for prepaid charging of IP services over GPRS, *e.g.*, it is unable to support content based charging.

3.3 Future Releases of 3G Networks

This rudimentary support of prepaid charging for IP services in existing 3G networks has been addressed by 3GGP and enhancements thereof were included in future releases of UMTS. The IP Multimedia Subsystem (IMS) [13], which has been defined with R5 of UMTS, plays *the* central role for delivery of advanced IP services. To support prepaid charging for IP-based services—especially for IMS services—3GPP specified a so-called online charging system (OCS) [15]. On the basis of 3GPP's IMS, 3GPP2 defined an IMS as well [9]. At the moment, its charging architecture, contains only a drafted OCS architecture and message flows are only specified for offline charging. Therefore, this section focusses on the OCS of 3GPP.

Prepaid charging is not addressed as such in 3GPP specifications, instead they deal with online charging. According to [1], full prepaid credit-control requires online charging. With offline charging, only a limited prepaid solution can be realized, e.g., only time-based tariffs are supported. Tab. 2 shows the relationship between the charging options and mechanisms.

Table 2. Combination of charging options with charging mechanisms

Charging Option	Charging Mechanism	
	Online	Offline
Prepaid	✔	(✔)
Postpaid	not useful	✔

To combine online with postpaid charging is not useful, due to the real-time overhead imposed by online charging. Thus, within 3GPP it exists a tight coupling between the prepaid charging option and the online charging mechanism. The logical architecture of 3GPP's OCS is shown in Fig. 1. Interfaces between the network entities in the middle an the OCS are used to deliver accounting records to the OCS and to exchange credit-control messages.

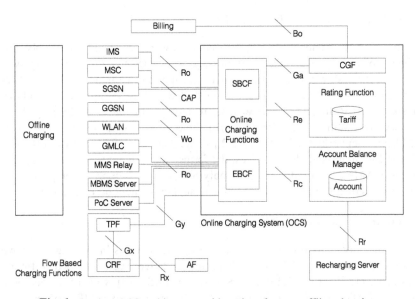

Fig. 1. Logical OCS architecture, without interfaces to offline charging

The *Ro* interface is based on DIAMETER Credit-Control Application (CCA) [25] and the *CAP* interface is used to realize online charging with CAMEL. The *Gy* and and *Wo* interfaces are based on CCA, too. Inside the OCS, the online Charging Functions (CF) are split to perform the credit-control for Session- and Event-Based services, i.e. SBCF and EBCF. From the charging functions, charging information is transported over the *Ga* interface towards the Charging Gateway Function (CGF) and then further over the *Bo* Interface to the operator's billing system. The charging functions have another interface—*Re*—towards the rating function to exchange price and tariff informations with the DIAMETER base protocol [19]. The rating function has the following tasks, (1) it returns the price for an event to the EBCF, or the tariff to be applied for a session to the SBCF, (2) it calculates the amount of non-monetary units for a given amount of monetary units, or it calculates the price (monetary units) to be paid for a given amount of non-monetary units. The functionalities of the account balance manager and its interface *Rc* are not yet specified.

To give an impression how reservation-based online charging is performed with the OCS, Fig. 2 shows a message sequence chart (MSC) for a session-based service, where the rating function is of class "B", i.e. counters are maintained by the rating function. In step 1, the mobile network forwards the service request to the SBCF. For every service, a predetermined amount of units is defined by the operator. The customer's balance must cover this initial amount of units otherwise he won't be allowed to use the service. To perform this coverage check, the SBCF requests the service tariff from the rating function, step 2. In this request, the initial amount of units is included as well. The rating function initializes the counter with the requested amount of units, gets the tariff and returns it, step 3.

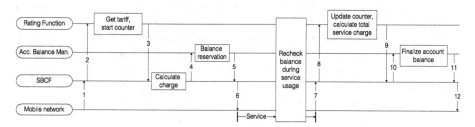

Fig. 2. Prepaid charging MSC for a session-based service

The SBCF calculates the initial service charge by evaluating the tariff function for the initial amount of units and requests service charge reservation, step 4. The account balance manager reserves the charge from the user's account and informs the SBCF (step 5), which grants the service usage, step 6. During service consumption, the granted units are monitored within the mobile network and upon their exhaustion, steps 1 to 6 are repeated. When the service session ends, a final credit check request is forwarded to the rating function, steps 7 and 8. According to the counter value, the total amount units consumed during the service session are determined and the total service charge is calculated and returned to the SBCF, step 9. The SBCF requests to debit the charge from the user's balance, step 10. The SBCF and the mobile network are informed about successful finalization of the user's account, step 11 and 12.

There are many more possible scenarios with regard to online charging, *e.g.*, a service session with multiple tariff switches. In [15], those basic scenarios are shown as MSC's, however they remain on the coarse-grained level as shown in Fig. 2. Therefore, important details of prepaid charging are left unanswered, for instance: (1) How are the units of a service (pre-)determined? What kind of optimality criteria is applied in order to minimize the network and economic costs for prepaid charging? (2) How is the balance administrated if multiple prepaid services are used at the same time, i.e. how are the credits apportioned among the services? (3) How are tariffs with more than one accounting parameter handled, *e.g.*, a service is charged per volume and per time? (4) How are non-linear tariff functions handled, *e.g.*, a logarithmic function?

4   Prepaid Charging in IP-Based Networks

In IP networks, charging is often referred to as pricing and the two terms are used interchangeably. Pricing—i.e. charging—in IP networks is on the research agenda since many years [36, 23, 28]. However, the focus was clearly on the postpaid charging option, making it therefore necessary to shift the attention towards prepaid charging.

4.1   Open Standards for IP Service Charging

In IP-based networks, RADIUS [34] with its extension for accounting [35] is still the most widespread protocol used for Authentication, Authorization, and Accounting (AAA). The IETF AAA [16] working group was working on a successor to RADIUS, which resulted in the DIAMETER base protocol [19] and CCA [25] to support prepaid charging. But since RADIUS is still widespread, another IETF working group —RADEXT [17]—is currently enhancing and extending RADIUS. Of special interest in this context is the RADIUS extension for prepaid [32]. Note that 3GPP2 added so-called Vendor Specific Attributes (VSA) to the base version of RADIUS [7] to support prepaid charging for packet-switched services. Compared to these VSA, the RADIUS extension for prepaid is based on CCA and has, therefore, more capabilities to support prepaid charging. Besides different protocol messages, RADIUS extension and CCA handle prepaid charging similarly and thus the focus here will be on CCA.

4.2   Prepaid Charging with DIAMETER CCA

DIAMETER CCA [25] is used to implement real-time credit-control (CC) for event- and session-based services. The standard defines a CC system architecture consisting of CC servers and CC clients. Typically, the CC server is part of an AAA server and the CC client is part of an accounting gateway (AG), i.e. CC server and CC client reside on physical different network elements (NE). The CC server is responsible for units determination by accessing the customer's account and applying service tariffs. Note that the determined units can be monetary or non-monetary, *e.g.*, volume. The CC client is responsible for monitoring the granted units by the CC server and is setting alarms in the metering components. These alarms represent thresholds of the granted units and are triggered when the units are exhausted. An example of the interactions between CC client and server can be deduced from Fig. 2, since an OCS can also be implemented using CCA. The CC client and the metering component are part of the mobile network and the functionalities of the CC server are split up into the SBCF and the rating function.

In a multi-service environment, multiple prepaid services can be used at the same time. Making it thus necessary to apportion the credits among these services—CCA suggests a solution with so-called *credit pools*: Instead of performing credit checks independently on a per service basis, it is done on a per pool basis. A credit pool consists of abstract credit units that are shared among all services belonging to the pool. The CC client is maintaining and monitoring credit pools. The CC server is responsible of (i) adding/removing services to/from a credit pool, (ii) defining the so-called service multipliers M_i and (iii) granting units. The CCA credit pool concept can only be applied for simple linear tariff functions of the form shown in Eqn. (1). The tariff f_i of service s_i is applied within a given tariff validity period, *e.g.*, from 08:00—17:00. The input parameter x_i represents any accounting parameter, *e.g.*, volume and the output of f_i is the charge to be paid.

$$f_i(x_i) = D_i x_i \quad \text{and} \quad \frac{d}{dx_i} f_i(x_i) = D_i \qquad D_i \in \mathbb{R} \qquad f_i : \mathbb{R} \curvearrowright \mathbb{R} \tag{1}$$

For these tariff functions f_i, the law of proportion is applied to weight the amount of units put into or withdrawn from the pool. The CC client is monitoring the credit pool and upon its exhaustion is requesting more quota from the CC server. With this credit pool concept, the amount messages exchanged between CC client and CC server is reduced. However there are some important drawbacks: (i) The credit pool concept cannot be applied for more complex and non-linear tariff functions depending on several parameters, *e.g.*, a combined abc-tariff as introduced by [27]. (ii) The workload imposed on the metering component is not reduced, i.e. metering data still has to flow in real-time towards the CC client. (iii) For usage based service charging, the thresholds to set the alarms in the metering component still need to be calculated on a per service basis—i.e. per accounting parameter x_i. Note that the M_i could only be used to calculate the thresholds, if the proportion of the amount of accounting data per service within a given time interval is the same as the proportion of their tariffs. Therefore, the credit pool concept doesn't solve the problem of calculating the thresholds, instead it shifts the problem from CC server towards CC client.

5   Prepaid Charging in All-IP — Discussion and Evaluation

An all-IP network architecture consists of separate IP multimedia domains interconnected and operating independently on IP. In order to deliver new and advanced IP multimedia services, the support of Quality of Service (QoS) is an important precondition to be met in all-IP network. Basically, any wired or wireless access technology supporting QoS can be used to access an all-IP network.

5.1 Evolution Toward All-IP

The evolution toward all-IP can be regarded from three angles. (i) *Research*: There are many emerging research issues in all-IP, which are for instance addressed by the Daidalos research project, [22]. (ii) *3G Evolution*: UMTS R6 [11] is extending the IMS, which was introduced with UMTS R5. Future CDMA2000 networks define an IMS as well and additionally an IP-based core network [8]. These steps are, thus, circumscribed as "All-IP in 3G" and are for instance addressed in [33, 37].

(iii) *Provider's view—Economics and Marketing*: With all-IP, the demand for IP-based equipment will increase and it is very likely that its prices will decrease eventually due to the economy of scale effect. Therefore, from the long-term perspective, all-IP yields to cost reductions for deploying a network infrastructure. Further more, with all-IP the development and integration of new services is facilitated. Saving development time and reducing the time-to-market, is essential in a competitive market. Another point is the ubiquitous nature of IP which gives operators all the flexibility needed to develop any kind of application services. Operators can emphasize on the service and content instead of the network technology used to deliver it.

5.2 Requirements on Prepaid Charging

Particularly important are these three angles of all-IP for prepaid charging for QoS-enabled IP services, cf. Fig. 3. Providers would like to make use of flexible tariffs with both the post- *and* prepaid charging option, [18, 24]. Especially in the multi provider all-IP environment, flexible tariffs are essential for a provider to delimit itself from its competitors. In such a multi provider environment, seamless roaming must be supported by the prepaid charging system. The main issues connected with roaming are the apportion of the credits and how prepaid billing information is exchanged between domains.

The intention behind flexible—and from a mathematical point of view more complex—tariff functions is to introduce a user incentive (prepaid) charging. Eqn. (2) shows the generalized tariff function from Eqn. (1). Accounting data of Eqn. (2) represents input as a vector with m elements. Vector $\underline{x}$ is partitioned to ensure that every tariff function $f_i(.)$ uses a different subset of $\underline{x}$ as its input. Note that $f_i(.)$ is represented by smooth or piecewise smooth functions and that $f_i(.)$ is monotonically increasing.

$$f_i(\underline{x}) \qquad \underline{x} \in \mathbb{R}^m \qquad f_i : \mathbb{R}^m \curvearrowright \mathbb{R} \tag{2}$$

An important economic driver for all-IP is the service cost reduction compared to existing telecommunication networks. The prepaid service costs, can be arranged into

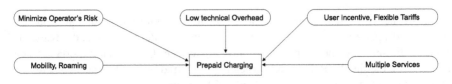

Fig. 3. Requirements arising in an all-IP environment on prepaid charging

two major parts: The expected cost for the real-time credit checks $E[C_c]$ and the expected revenue loss $E[R_l]$. The total service cost C_{tot}, is the sum of $E[C_c]$ and $E[R_l]$ plus a small ε for additional common and joint-costs, Eqn. (3).

$$C_{tot} = E[C_c] + E[R_l] + \varepsilon \qquad (3)$$

A prepaid charging system is working optimal, if C_{tot} is minimal. However, the dilemma is that minimizing $E[C_c]$ increases $E[R_l]$, as shown in [20, 21]. If too few credit checks are performed, then it is possible to overuse credits which yields to a revenue loss for the provider. Minimizing C_{tot} is not only important from an economic point of view, but also in terms of scalability. The scalability issues are crucial, if multiple prepaid services are used at the same time. A straightforward solution is to perform prepaid charging for all services independently. Thus, using n services in parallel means that up to n distributed processes are accessing and modifying the credits independently. If a providers has a big customer basis, the load imposed on the charging system increases dramatically and scalability is questionable.

5.3   TICA — Advanced Approach Proposed for Prepaid Charging in All-IP

In a QoS-enabled pure all-IP environment as being developed in [22], existing prepaid charging mechanisms need to be enhanced—a proposal is TICA as recently being presented in [29]. TICA consists of a server part residing on the AAA server and a client on the AG, whereas the communication protocol is left open on purpose in [29]. Additionnally, TICA introduces the concept of service bundles and uses the generalized tariff functions of the form in Eqn. (2). When the AG forwards a prepaid service request to the AAA server, TICA checks first, if sufficient credits are left to grant service usage. Then TICA calculates a time interval based on the estimated maximum resource consumptions for the whole service bundle. Being above a minimal threshold, the time interval is communicated to the AG, which grants service usage. The AG observes the time interval and upon its expiry, requests a new one, which is calculated on the basis of the real consumed resources of the past interval.

5.4   Evaluation of Existing Prepaid Solutions

Having identified all important requirements on prepaid charging in an all-IP environment, the next step is to evaluate the existing prepaid solutions fulfilling these requirements. Tab. 3 summarizes these requirements and indicates their support in existing 3G releases and future 3G releases. Note that the OCS of UMTS R6 can be implemented with DIAMETER CCA—which is likely to be used in future CDMA2000 releases as well. The third column represents TICA.

In existing 3G systems, multiple prepaid services are handled seperately. This is a straightforward solution, but scalability issues are a major conern of this approch. CCA or RadEXT introduce the concept of credit pools, where multiple services are belonging to. However, the credit pool concept does only support simple tariffs and does not solve the problem of apportioning credits, instead it shifts the problem toward the edge of the network. TICA solves this issue by calculating time intervals for IP service bundles, wherein any combination of services can be used. Therefore, even for a big number of multiple services, only one time interval needs to be observed.

Table 3. Comparison and evaluation of requirements for prepaid charging in all-IP

Requirements	Existing 3G Releases	DIAMETER CCA, RadExt	TICA
Multiple Services	Independent: (✔)	Credit Pool: (✔)	✔
Min. techn. Overhead	Single Service: ✔	— (Real-time CC)	✔
Min. Operator's Risk	Single Service: ✔	—	✔
User Incentive, Flex. Tariffs	—	—	✔
Mobility, Roaming	✔	✔	(✔)

Another important issue in all-IP, is the minimization of the technical overhead. Where existing 3G solutions can at least be optimized for single services, CCA uses explicitly online charging mechanisms, i.e. real-time CC. With TICA the technical overhead is minimized, such that as few as possible credit checks are needed. Other approaches reduce the real-time CC, but they introduce a possible fraud window, i.e. the MNO carries the risk of revenue loss. For the circuit-switched voice call service, 3G systems can be optimized, i.e. the best trade-off between technical overhead and revenue loss can be found. However, CCA does not even include such a optimization criteria for a single servcice. With TICA not only the number of CC are minimized but also the risk of revenue loss for an operator is minimized.

Today's tariffs are (often) not user incentive, *e.g.*, like soft tariffs which are adapted to the user's behaviour. Technically, neither existing 3G nor CCA support advanced mathematical tariff functions. TICA provides support for general tariff functions as specified in Eqn. (2). Within TICA only a few requirements to address such generalized tariff functions have to meet, [29]. Especially, in a multi-provider environment, mobility between MNO's and MVNO's is crucial. Here both standards—3G and CCA—are able to inter-domain mobility. In its current and first release, TICA supports inter-domain mobility in the sense of roaming—i.e. where accounting data from foreign domains is processed in the home domain.

6   Conclusions

The key goal of this paper is to define a detailed overview of existing prepaid charging solutions and to show major requirements as well as open issues arising from allIP networks. While the first part of existing solution focuses on 3G mobile telecommunication networks, the second part is dedicated to IP-based networks. The rudimentary prepaid support for IP-based services resulted in the development of OCS. The OCS supports CAMEL—an IN based approach present only in mobile telecommunications networks—or DIAMETER CCA, which was actually developed by the

IETF. This overlap of technologies forms the world of mobile telecommunication and IP-based networks; however, is not accidental—instead, it is another indication of the evolution toward all-IP. Concerning prepaid charging for QoS-enabled IP services within all-IP, requirements are arising which are not or only to a minor extend present today. Therefore, this paper outlined all open issues that need to be resolved in order to optimize the prepaid charging, both from the technical and economic point of view. The evaluation leads to the summary of the new approach proposed—TICA.

Acknowledgments. This work has been performed partially in the framework of the EU IST project Daidalos "Designing Advanced Interfaces for the Delivery and Administration of Location independent Optimized personal Services" (FP6-2002-IST-1-506997), where the ETH Zürich has been funded by the Swiss Staatssekretariat für Bildung und Forschung (SBF), Bern, under Grant No. 03.0141. The authors would like to extend many thanks to their Daidalos partners.

References

1. 3GPP TR 23.815 V5.0.0 (2002-03). Technical Specification Group, Services and System Aspects; Charging implications of IMS architecture (Release 5), 2002
2. 3GPP2 C.S0001-0. Introduction to CDMA2000 Standards for Spread Spectrum Systems, Release 0, Version 1.0 July 1999
3. 3GPP2 C.S0001-D. Introduction to CDMA2000 Standards for Spread Spectrum Systems, Release D. Version 1.0, February 2004
4. 3GPP2 C.S0024. CDMA2000 High Rate Packet Data Air Interface Specification, Release 0, Version 4.0, October 2002
5. 3GPP2 C.S0024-A. CDMA2000 High Rate Packet Data Air Interface Specification, Release A. Version 2.0, July 2005
6. 3GPP2 N.S0004-0 v 1.0. WIN Phase 2. Revision 0, April 2001
7. 3GPP2 X.S0011-005-C. CDMA2000 Wireless IP Network Standard: Accounting Services and 3GPP2 RADIUS Vendor Specific Attributes (VSA). Version 2.0, July 2005
8. 3GPP2 X.S0013-000-A. All-IP Core Network Multimedia Domain. Overview. Version 1.0, November 2005
9. 3GPP2 X.S0013-002-A v1.0. All-IP Core Network Multimedia Domain. IP Multimedia Subsystem—Stage 2. Version 1.0, November 2005
10. ETSI TS 123 002 V3.6.0 (2002-09). Digital cellular telecommunications system (Phase 2+); UMTS; Network Architecture (3GPP TS 23.002 version 3.6.0 Release 1999), 2002
11. ETSI TS 123 002 V6.7.0 (2005-03). Digital cellular telecommunications system (Phase 2+), UMTS, Network architecture (3GPP TS 23.002 version 6.7.0 Release 6), 2005
12. ETSI TS 123 078 V3.19.0 (2004-03). UMTS; customized Applications for Mobile network Enhanced Logic (CAMEL); Stage 2 (3GPP TS 23.078 Vers. 3.19.0 Rel. 1999), 2004
13. ETSI TS 123 228 V6.11.0 (2005-09). Digital cellular telecommunications system (Phase 2+); UMTS; IMS; Stage 2 (3GPP TS 23.228 version 6.11.0 Release 6), 2005
14. ETSI TR 121 905 V6.10.0 (2005-09). Digital cellular telecommunications system (Phase 2+); Vocabulary for 3GPP Specifications (3GPP TR 21.905 Ver. 6.10.0 Release 6), 2005
15. ETSI TS 132 296 V6.2.0 (2005-09). Online Charging System (OCS): Applications and interfaces (3GPP TS 32.296 vers. 6.2.0 Release 6), 2005

16. IETF AAA (Authentication, Authorization, and Accounting) Working Group. http://www.ietf.org/html.charters/aaa-charter.html, November 2005
17. IETF RADEXT (RADIUS Extensions) Working Group. http://www.ietf.org/html.charters/radext-charter.html, November 2005
18. Analysys Research and Consulting. http://www.analysys.com, November 2005
19. P. Calhoun, J. Loughney, E. Guttman, G. Zorn, J. Arkko. DIAMETER Base Protocol. IETF RFC 3588, September 2003
20. M. Chang, Y. Lin, Wei-Zu Yang. Performance of hot billing mobile prepaid service. Computer Networks, Vol. 36, No. 2-3, July 2001, pp. 269—290
21. M. Chang, W. Yang. Y. Lin. Performance of Service-Node-Based Mobile Prepaid Service. IEEE Transactions on vehicular technology, Vol. 51, No. 3, May 2002, pp. 597—612
22. DAIDALOS, an EU Framework Programme 6 Integrated Project, http://www.ist-daidalos.org, December 2005
23. M. Falkner, M. Devetsikiotis, I. Lambadaris. An overview of pricing concepts for broadband IP networks. IEEE Communications Surveys, Second Quarter 2000
24. F. Fulton. How do you rate IMS? Telecommunications International, October 2005, pp. 35—36
25. H. Hakala, L. Mattila, J-P. Koskinen, J. Loughney. DIAMETER Credit-Control Application. IETF RFC 4006, August 2005
26. M. Karsten, J. Schmitt, B. Stiller, L. Wolf. Charging for Packet-switched Network Communications—Motivation and Overview. Computer Communication, Vol. 23, No. 3, February 2000, pp. 290—302
27. F.P. Kelly. Charging and accounting for bursty connections. In Internet Economics, MIT Press, 1997, pp. 253—278. ISBN 0-262-13336-9
28. M. Koutsopoulou, A. Kaloxylos et a. Charging, Accounting and Billing Management schemes in Mobile Telecommunication Networks and the Internet. IEEE Communications Surveys & Tutorials, Vol. 6, No. 1, 2004, pp. 50—58
29. P. Kurtansky, B. Stiller. Time Interval-based Prepaid Charging of QoS-enabled IP Services. Workshop on Internet and Network Economics (WINE). LNCS, Springer, December 2005, Vol. 3828, pp. 325—335
30. P. Kurtansky, B. Stiller. State of the Art Prepaid Charging for IP Services. Computer Engineering and Networks Laboratory TIK, ETH Zurich. Technical Report No. 236, November 2005. ftp://ftp.tik.ee.ethz.ch/pub/publications/TIK-Report-236.pdf
31. Yi-Bing Lin; Ming-Feng Chang; Herman Chung-Hwa Rao. Mobile prepaid phone services. IEEE Personal Communications, Vol. 7, No. 3, June 2000, pp. 6—14
32. A. Lior, P. Yegani, K. Chowdhury, H. Tschofenig, A. Pashalidis. PrePaid Extensions to Remote Authentication Dial-In User Service (RADIUS). draft-lior-radius-prepaid-extensions-09.txt, October 2005
33. P. Newman. In search of the all-IP mobile network. IEEE Communications Magazine, Vol. 42, No. 12, December 2004, pp. S3—S8
34. C. Rigney, S. Willens, A. Rubens, W. Simpson. Remote Authentication Dial In User Service (RADIUS). IETF RFC 2865, June 2000
35. C. Rigney. RADIUS Accounting. IETF RFC 2866, June 2000
36. S. Shenker, D. Clark, D. Estrin, S. Herzog. Pricing in Computer Networks: Reshaping the Research Agenda; ACM Computer Communication Review, Vol. 26, No. 2, April 1996, pp. 19—43
37. D. Wisely, P. Eardley, L. Burness. IP for 3G. Wiley, December 2002.

Efficient Protection of Mobile Devices by Cross Layer Interaction of Firewall Approaches

Peter Langendoerfer[1], Martin Lehmann[2], and Krzysztof Piotrowski[1]

[1] IHP, Im Technologiepark 25, 15236 Frankfurt (Oder) , Germany
langendoerfer@ihp-microelectromics.com
[2] DFS Deutsche Flugsicherung GmbH, Langen, SH/IR,
Am DFS-Campus 2, 63225 Langen, Germany

Abstract. In this paper we discuss IP layer packet filtering and an application level gateway approach used to secure handheld devices when providing and using web services. We propose a firewall management plane as a means for cross layer interaction. In our approach the application level gateway updates the IP layer firewall rules based on its knowledge about whether or not a certain source is sending malicious packets. We show that such a cross layer interaction can significantly decrease the CPU load in case of attacks, i.e., if many malicious packets arrive at the handheld device. Our measurement results show that the additional overhead for IP layer filtering is less than 10 per cent, if the number of applied rule sets is less than 200. In addition our cross layer approach can reduce the CPU load caused by the application layer gateway by about 10 up to 30 per cent.

1 Introduction

Motivation. Mobile devices are becoming more and more powerful, e.g. current HP iPAQs are equipped with 400 MHz Xscale processors and 128Mbyte memory. In addition wireless modems are integrated into these devices. With theses increasing capabilities it becomes feasible to integrate mobile devices into e-commerce architectures, e.g. in business-to-consumer and in business-to-employee applications, too. As a result of this development the amount of sensitive data that is stored on mobile devices will increase tremendously. So, mobile devices will attract an increasing number of attackers, and since their integration will be done in an 'all-IP' approach, they are exposed to all typical Internet attacks. From our point of view mobile devices are tempting target due to the following facts:

1. The medium (air) can easily be accessed by anyone.
2. Mobile devices are not protected by additional hardware or software such as firewalls, which are normally deployed at the border of a company network.
3. Compared to a fully-equipped PC or laptop the mobile devices such as PDAs and mobile smart-phone still have very limited resources (calculation and battery power). Strong and exhaustive use of security means drains down the battery of the mobile device quite fast leading to inconvenient up times.

Thus, mobile devices are normally not as protected as more powerful devices are. The first two points cause the device to be immediately exposed to the attacker and the

T. Braun et al. (Eds.): WWIC 2006, LNCS 3970, pp. 155–165, 2006.

third one limits the ways to defend it. Our approach uses layer interaction in order to reduce the computational burden, caused by security mechanisms. This also leads to the fact that the mobile device is protected against malicious communication partners at the lowest possible layer, which in turn increases the security level of the mobile device.

Contribution and structure of this paper. In this paper we discuss the performance of IP layer personal firewalls running on a PDA as well as the performance of an application level gateway that does content inspection in order to secure Web Services. Our measurements clearly indicate that personal firewalls can be used without a significant degradation of the performance and up time of the mobile device. The Web Service Security approach [8] results in a much higher computational burden for the mobile device, which is due to its intensive use of cryptographic means.

In order to decrease the effort spent per malicious packet we realized a cross layer interaction between the IP netfilter and the Web Service security gateway. The latter updates the IP packet filter tables with new IP addresses as soon as it identifies a certain source as malicious. Our measurements show that this approach reduces the computational burden of the mobile device by 75 per cent in case of application layer attacks.

This paper is structured as follows. Section 2 provides a short state of the art. In the following section we discuss the idea of layer interaction that provides efficient but lightweight security architecture for mobile devices. In section 4 we present our measurement results. The paper concludes with a short summary and an outlook on further research.

2   Related Work

Security of mobile devices and related protocols such as 802.11x have attracted significant research effort. So, a lot of proposals have been made how to protect data during transmission etc. But to the best of our knowledge, protection means against network based attacks that attempt to hijack the mobile device, to render it useless or to steal information out of its memory have not been researched up to now. There are several solutions which provide firewall protection on the IP layer. For mobile devices running under Linux packet filters, such as netfilter [1] or nf-HiPAC [2] can be used. For PDAs running under MS Windows the first commercial packet filters by Bluefire [5] and Trust Digital [6][7] are available.

But since Web Services are becoming more and more widespread and commonly used, these mechanisms are no longer sufficient to protect mobile devices against attacks due to the fact that the related SOAP calls are tunnelling the IP packet filters. Potential attacks are SQL code injection to get access to confidential data and recursive payload of XML messages which consume the whole memory while being processed and thus render the mobile device useless [16]. While the first may not be very probable in the near future the latter is already feasible. A proper application of Web service security features as given in the WS-Security framework [8][9], and Security Assertion Markup Language (SAML) [14] helps to protect the mobile device against those attacks. But up to now there is no Web Service firewall solution for handheld devices available. Reactivity [10] and Forumsystems [11] are providing such solutions for server class systems.

3 Cross Layer Approach

In order to protect computers within company's network several specialized routers/computers are deployed. In such a network configuration a router does the IP packet filtering and on a separate computer, i.e. on a bastion, TCP- and application level gateways are executed. With such architecture it is possible to separate the external and internal world physically as well as logically. In contrast to this, the mobile device is exposed directly to attackers. Thus, it has to execute all protection mechanisms itself.

Providing a significant level of security enforces the use of packet filtering, gateway like approaches - and exhaustive use of cryptographic means. Due to the still limited resources of mobile devices, all these means have to be applied as efficient as possible.

From a security point of view as well as from efficiency point of view it is highly desirable to establish a defence line as close as possible to the network interface. This means that the malicious packet should be identified and blocked at the IP layer, whenever possible. This has the following benefits:

- All higher layers are protected from malicious packets.
- The mobile device does not spent battery and calculation power to process malicious packets at higher layers.

But IP filtering cannot detect whether an incoming packet is malicious or not, it just can check if the packet belongs to an existing connection and if the source address is already blocked etc. Http packets usually tunnel IP firewalls. Thus, application level gateways that do content inspection are needed to secure the mobile device. This task is very time consuming and should be done only if it is really necessary. In other words, it should be avoided whenever possible. If the application layer gateway is enabled to provide information about sources of malicious application layer packets to the IP packet filter, those packets can be blocked at the IP layer.

Cross layer communication. We propose the use of a firewall management plane (FMP). The FMP gathers data about malicious or at least suspicious packets. As soon as the suspicion is proven it updates the filtering rules available on lower layers. Whether a packet flow is considered to be malicious depends on the policy deployed at the mobile device. A single packet which is e.g. not well formed or which could not be validated may probably not be considered as an attack. But it should be recorded that such a packet was received together with its source address. If a sequence of suspicious packets coming from the same source is detected, it might still be caused by network errors not detected at lower layers, but it may also be a kind of attack. Thus, the source address should be marked as malicious and the firewall entries of the lower layers have to be updated. The maximal number of suspicious packets that are tolerated from a certain source, before this source is marked as suspicious or malicious, is specified in the policy file. So, the policy file reflects how cautious the user is.

In order to propagate information about malicious sources from high layers to lower layers the FPM needs to resolve e.g. URLs in order to get the corresponding IP address. This can be done using the already available mechanisms. Figure 1 shows the overall architecture and the interaction between the firewall management plane and the firewall solutions on different protocol layers.

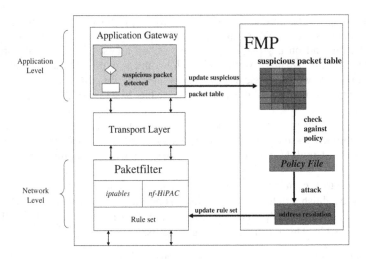

Fig. 1. Schematic view of the proposed cross layer architecture for a firewall management plane including content inspection on the application layer

4 Implementation

In order to evaluate the potential gain of our cross layer approach we realized a simplified version of the architecture discussed in the last section. We are using two kinds of IP packet filters namely nf-HiPAC and Netfilter in order to measure the performance of IP layer packet filtering. Here we investigated how the number of rules influences the performance of the packet filtering. This is important since due to our propagation strategy the number of filtering rules will increase constantly. As application level gateway we are using Xerces-c [12] to validate incoming XML packets, here SOAP calls or answers, and XML security for data integrity check, authentication etc. The cryptographic means as well as a rigorous verification of the SOAP packets against a strictly defined XML schema provides reasonable first step towards application level firewall functionality.

We developed our example Web Service using the gSOAP framework [15] that provides access to sockets also on application level. Thus, we did not include the address resolution in our first implementation. But compared to potential gain and the quite high effort to detect malicious packets on the application level, the additional effort for address resolution can be neglected. Figure 2 shows the current realization of the system, running on an HP iPAQ h5550.

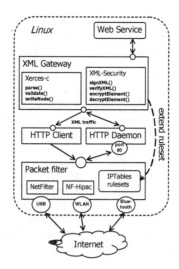

Fig. 2. Current implementation of FPM, displaying used software modules and cross layer interaction

5 Measurements

Measurement set-up. Figure 3 shows the network we used to run the measurements. As mobile device we used an HP iPAQ Pocket PC h5550 with a 400MHz Xscale Processor, 128 Mbyte SDRAM, 48 Mbyte flash ROM and an integrated 802.11b modem. The iPAQ is running the Familiar Linux distribution version 0.8 [13]. As communication partner we used an Acer 290 notebook, running SUSE Linux version 9.1. The wireless connection was set up using a D-Link DI-624 router providing an 802.11g wireless access point and four 100Mbit Ethernet interfaces. The wired connection was realized with USB1.1 cable attached to the notebook and to the iPAQ. We used the USB connection for the following reasons: first, it ensures that the computational load on the PDA is not limited by the available bandwidth and second, it is used to guarantee reproducible measurement results, due to the fact that no network errors occur in a wired connection[1].

On top of our sample network we realized a very simple Web Service client that does nothing else than accepting incoming "answers" from a Web service provider. In addition we realized a simple Web service provider, which accepts a request and sends back an answer that has a size of 1kbyte. Thus, the execution of the Web Service does not influence the measurement results. Our Web service client and our Web service provider have been realized using the gSOAP framework [15], and both can be executed on the PDA. In subsection 5.2 we present measurements done with the Web Service client running on the PDA. In this case we present measurements for different packet sizes, which may result from different requests to the service provider side. In subsection 5.3 we present measurements of the Web service provider running

---

[1] Due to space limitations, we do not provide results measured while USB was used. In addition we do not discuss the impact of the computational load of the PDA on usable bandwidth.

on the PDA. Here the size of the incoming packets is no longer of interest since we assume that normally the size of request is quite small, but a lot of request is sent to the service provider which will cause the major part of the effort at the provider side.

Experiments. We first measured the performance of IP packet filter approaches as a first simple step towards securing a handheld device against malicious communication partners. We altered the source address of the incoming packets on a per packet basis in order to ensure that all rules had to be checked before an incoming packet was recognized as malicious, i.e. our measurements presented later show the performance in a worst case scenario.

In the second step we measured the performance of an application level gateway that is securing a web service. Here we investigated the performance of several XML security issues such as encryption and digital signatures. In this experiment we used Web Service request with a size of 1Kbyte, 10Kbytes, 100Kbytes and 1000Kbytes.

In the last experiment we evaluated the performance of a combination of IP packet filters and our application level gateway. The interesting point in this experiment was up to which extend the computational load of the PDA can be reduced by applying our cross layer approach.

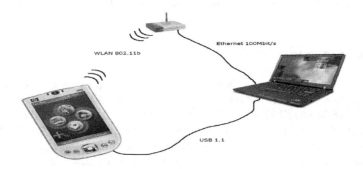

Fig. 3. Measurement set-up

5.1 IP Layer Packet Filtering

Filtering of packets at the IP layer is the first step to secure a handheld device. Our measurement results show that the additional CPU load is about ten per cent as long as the number of rules sets[2] applied is less than 200, see figure 4. Please note that the CPU load is about 20 per cent even without running any security function when a wireless connection is used, so additional 10 per cent of CPU usage seem to be an acceptable price for increasing the security of the mobile device. The situation changes when the number of rule sets is growing. But even then, more than 1000 rule sets have to be applied before the CPU load is about 50 per cent. So, as long as no really exhaustive use of rule sets is made packet filtering can be applied without turning the mobile device useless. If nf-HiPAC is used the additional effort for filtering is even less than 5 per cent, independent of the size of the rule set[3].

---

[2] Each rule set contains 2 outgoing (stateless + stateful) rules and 2 incoming rules.

[3] The independence of nf-HiPAC of the size of the applied rule set was already measured for PCs and presented in [17].

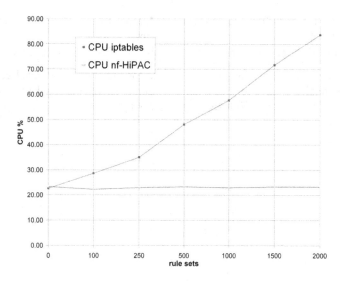

Fig. 4. CPU usage in per cent vs. size of the applied rules set for IP layer packet filtering using of IP tables and nf-HiPAC[4]; measurements done on HP IPAQ h5550; using a wireless connection via 802.11b

Our measurement results clearly indicate that IP layer filtering has some impact on the performance of the mobile device. But we with a reasonable number of rule sets, it is feasible to use IP packet filtering.

5.2 Web Service Gateway

In order to ensure secure operation at the application layer a lot of different techniques have to be applied. First, a certain packet containing SOAP requests has to be validated against the XML scheme of the corresponding Web Service. In addition, the XML security features such as en-/decryption and digital signatures have to be taken into account. The measurements discussed in this subsection present the client side of our simple Web service and have been measured on an iPAQ H5550.

In order to verify the computational load caused by the different security functions we have measured the following configurations:

- **Os**: Original set-up (mini-httpd and http) without any security functions used as benchmark and to calculate the overhead resulting from the security function used in other configurations.
- **Bc**: basic configuration XML packets are parsed and optionally serialized
- **BcV**: like Bc including the following addition: validation of incoming packets against corresponding XML scheme
- **BcS**: like Bc including the following additions: signature generation and verification (signXML at server, verifyXML at client)

---

[4] The constant CPU usage of nf-HiPAC is due to its mechanism for selecting the rule to apply. In principle it can be compared to calculation of a hash value for in coming packet which then immediately identifies the rule to apply.

- **BcE**: like Bc including the following additions: En-/decryption of XML packets (encryptXML at server, decryptXML at client)
- **BcES**: like BcE including the following additions: signature generation/verification.

Figure 5 shows the percentage of CPU usage for the application level gateway configurations explained above. For each configuration we measured requests with the size of 1Kbyte, 10Kbytes, 100Kbytes and 1000Kbytes.

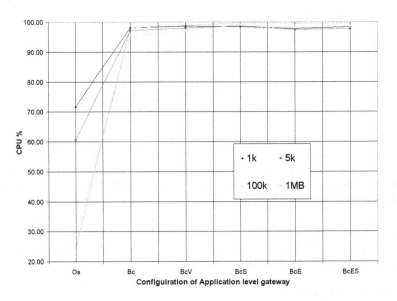

Fig. 5. CPU load of an iPAQ running our Web service client with diverse security settings applied for incoming Web service answers

The measurements depicted in Figure 5 show clearly that the additional security functions lead to a significantly increased CPU load. It is even increased significantly if the incoming packets are only parsed and validated. Figure 6 shows the load distribution in jiffies per scenario and size of requests in more detail. Comparing figure 5 and figure 6 shows that despite the CPU load in per cent is more or less equivalent for all sizes of requests, the absolute CPU load in scenarios with small packet sizes is relatively low. In addition, it can be seen that especially the XML security functions en-/decryption and the application of digital signatures increase the CPU load. The peak load in the BcS configuration results from the effort inhibited by the need to bring the request/answer packets in the canonical format, which is required to ensure proper signature verification at the receiver side. The effort for this operation is dramatically reduced if the packet is encrypted (see fig. 6 BcES scenario) since the encrypted data is in canonical form already, which ensures that less tokens have to be evaluated.

Depending on the Web Service and its configuration, at least parsing and validating have to be done in order to ensure proper operation of the running Web service client or service. Thus, the additional overhead caused by the application level gateway is quite low, i.e., the difference of the CPU load between the configuration BcV and BcS is less than 20 per cent. The performance penalty caused by the security functions can be minimized if the application level gateway passes the reference to the parsed tree and the result of the validation to the Web Service. So, these functions have to be executed only once.

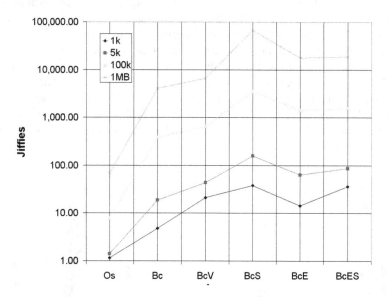

Fig. 6. CPU load in jiffies[5] for diverse settings of our application level gateway running on an iPAQ h5550; measurements displayed for the following packet sizes: 1000Kbyte, 100 Kbyte, 5Kbyte and 1Kbyte requests

5.3   Cross Layer Interaction

The effort to secure a handheld device is significant, as already shown earlier in this section. In order to reduce the total effort we propose to realize a vertical cross layer interaction between application level gateways doing content inspection and firewall solutions on lower layers. In order to evaluate the potential performance gain of our approach we measured the following scenarios:

- **Original:** no malicious packets
- **Original2:** all packets are malicious, and the detection is done at the application level
- **Original3:** like original2 but only 50 per cent of the packets are malicious
- **iptables1:** 50 per cent of the packets are malicious; the first malicious packet of a certain source is detected at the application level, then the IP netfilter is updated and all following malicious packets from the same source are detected and dropped at the IP layer
- **ipables2:** like iptables1, but all packets are malicious.

---

[5] Jiffies denote the number of hardware clock ticks that were counted in a certain time interval.

Figure 7 shows the CPU load for all scenarios. Comparing the scenarios *Original2* and *iptables1* clearly indicates that updating the IP netfilter rule sets helps to reduce the CPU load significantly. In our example the CPU load is reduced by about 10 per cent, in case that 50 per cent of the incoming packets are malicious. If the number of malicious requests is increased the benefit resulting from our approach increases too. In addition to the reduced CPU load our approach enables the Web service to serve more requests within the same time interval. The scenarios *original3* and *IPtables1* have been executed under the same conditions, i.e., half of the incoming requests have been malicious. Due to the application of our cross layer approach about 300 additional requests more have been processed in the latter scenario. Please note that the benefit resulting form our approach is due to the fact that all incoming packets in scenario *iptables2* are malicious, which means they are processed only once by the application level gateway, and afterwards they are blocked by the IP layer firewall.

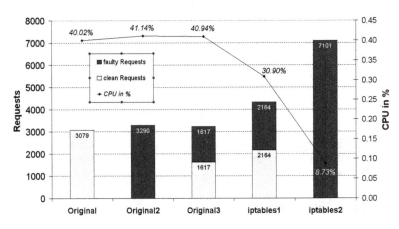

Fig. 7. CPU load caused by Web service provider with and without using cross layer interaction in scenarios with different percentage of malicious request; measurements done on an iPAQ h5550

6   Conclusions and Outlook

In this paper we have investigated the performance of IP layer firewalls as well as the performance of application level gateways for Web Services on handheld devices. Our measurements indicate that it is feasible to use firewalls on mobile devices. The CPU load caused by IP layer filtering is less than 10 per cent, even if about 200 rule sets are applied. We have proposed to use a cross layer interaction to reduce the performance penalty that results from the use of application level gateways on handheld devices. Our experiments show that layer interaction can reduce the CPU load by about 30 per cent. How much the CPU load is reduced depends however on the number of malicious packets as well as on the security means applied.

In our next research steps we will evaluate:

- power consumption which stems from the security functions running on a handheld devices
- performance of firewalls on handheld devices, in case hardware accelerators are used to execute the cipher mechanisms.

Acknowledgements

This work was partially funded by the German Ministry of Education and Research under grant 01AK060B.

References

[1] Netfilter/iptables Project Homepage. www.netfilter.org
[2] nf-HiPAC: High Performance Firewall for Linux Netfilter. http://www.hipac.org
[3] Extensible Markup Language (XML) 1.0 (Third Edition). http://www.w3.org/TR/2004/REC-xml-20040204
[4] http://webservices.xml.com
[5] Wireless Security Software for Handheld Mobile Devices from Bluefire Security Technologies. http://www.bluefiresecurity.com/
[6] Trust Digital - Solutions - TRUST Mobile Device Applications, http://www.trustdigital.com
[7] Security Basics for PDAs and Handheld PCs, http://www.smallbusinesscomputing.com/webmaster/article.php/10732_3400641_2
[8] Web Services Security (WS-Security), http://www-106.ibm.com/developerworks/webservices/library/ws-secure/
[9] XML Encryption Syntax and Processing. http://www.w3.org/TR/xmlenc-core/
[10] Reactivity: The Secure Web Services Deployment System. http://www.reactivity.com/
[11] Forum Systems, Inc. - The Leader In Web Services Security. http://www.forumsystems.com
[12] XML-Security-C. http://xml-security-c.sourceforge.net
[13] Handhelds.org - Open Source Operating Systems for Handheld Devices. www.handhelds.org
[14] OASIS, Security Assertion Markup Language (SAML) V2.0 available at http://www.oasis-open.org/committees/tc_home.php?wg_abbrev=security#samlv20
[15] Robert van Engelen, gSOAP 2.7.2 User Guide, available at: http://gsoap2.sourceforge
[16] Forum Systems: Anatomy of a Web Services Attack: A Guide to Threats and Preventive Countermeasures, 2004 available at: http://forumsystems.com/papers/Anatomy_of_Attack_wp.pdf
[17] Michael Bellovin: nf-HiPAC High Performance Packet Classification High Performance Packet Classification for Linux Netfilter, 2005, available at: http://www.hipac.org/documentation/nf-hipac-nfws2005.pdf

Scalability of Name Resolution for Ambient Networks

Pekka Pääkkönen[1], Nadeem Akhtar[2], Rui Campos[3], Cornelia Kappler[4],
Petteri Pöyhönen[5], and Di Zhou[6]

[1] VTT Technical Research Centre of Finland,
Kaitoväylä 1, 90571 Oulu, Finland
{Pekka.Paakkonen}@vtt.fi
[2] University of Surrey, Guildford, United Kingdom
{N.Akhtar}@surrey.ac.uk
[3] INESC Porto, Porto, Portugal
{RCampos}@inescporto.pt
[4] Siemens Communications, Berlin, Germany
{Cornelia.Kappler}@siemens.com
[5] Nokia Research Center, Helsinki, Finland
{Petteri.Poyhonen}@nokia.com
[6] PSE/Siemens, Vienna, Austria
{Di.Zhou}@siemens.com

Abstract. The convergence of mobile domain and data networks has been under focus in the standardization forums. However, dynamic interworking of wired infrastructure, wireless access systems and small scale Personal Area Networks has been challenging due to their heterogeneous nature. One of the most important problems to be solved is name resolution between different terminals and networks. This paper presents a new mechanism for name resolution, which relies on existing naming mechanisms. In particular the focus is on the scalability of the solution from signaling load and latency point of view.

1 Introduction

Ambient Networks (AN) is an integrated project of the Wireless World Initiative (WWI) financially supported by EU in its FP6 program. It presents a new networking concept enabling automatic, dynamic, flexible and on-demand cooperation of heterogeneous networks belonging to different operator and technology domains [1]. From a more pragmatic viewpoint this would mean the integration between devices, heterogeneous networks, and multiple accesses, which is a challenging goal due to the lack of a common control layer [1]. To overcome the problem the Ambient Control Space (ACS) concept has been introduced, which comprises of all the control functions (Connectivity, Mobility, QoS etc.) in a network domain and can be dynamically composed of several Ambient Networks to form a new AN [1]. To enable the cooperation between different ANs and connecting of functions between ACSs of the ANs, a Generic AN Signaling Protocol (GANS) stack has been developed [16]. GANS should support multiple access systems, user terminals and network domains. Therefore it is important that GANS is scalable for the heterogeneous environments. One of the most important properties of GANS is name resolution support for addressing and

T. Braun et al. (Eds.): WWIC 2006, LNCS 3970, pp. 166–177, 2006.
© Springer-Verlag Berlin Heidelberg 2006

resolving endpoint(s) between the ACSs of the communicating ANs. GANS uses the services provided by a Destination Endpoint Exploration Protocol (DEEP) for name resolution, which is independent of the AN context. DEEP is a distributed name resolution protocol, which relies on existing naming mechanisms [17].

The most widely applied name resolution mechanism in the Internet infrastructure has been the Domain Name System (DNS), which enables resolution from a name to an IP address [9]. Measurements at two different locations in the Internet indicate that the median DNS latencies are below 100 ms, but the 90th percentile varies between 447 ms to 1176 ms [10]. Due to the problems of high latency, DNS server and gateway bottlenecks, implementation errors, misconfigurations, load imbalance, and update propagation a new name service for the Internet has been proposed [11]. It uses proactive caching with a Beehive replication framework, automatic load-balancing and fast propagation of updates, and should be compatible with legacy DNS and able to fully replace the existing DNS infrastructure.

The Session Initiation Protocol (SIP) [13] uses name resolution at the application level from a SIP URI to an IP address. SIP has been originally developed for the initiation and control of end-to-end sessions between SIP user agents, but in addition has other applications such as instant messaging and games [14]. SIP messages are transmitted to the destination via SIP servers, which are capable of resolving the SIP URI to an IP address of the endpoint. Usually DNS is used for finding the SIP server based on the SIP URI, but also local policies can be applied [13, 14].

Host Identity name space has been proposed to fill the gap between IP and DNS namespaces, to separate the IP layer from the transport, and to offer a basis for end-host mobility and multi-homing security problems [15]. The HIP name space consists of Host Identifiers (HI), which are used for identifying hosts. A HI is a public key of an asymmetric key-pair, and may be published with DNS or may be unpublished. Communication between HIP-nodes may be established peer-to-peer or via a Rendez-vous-server [15].

Ambient Networks should be able to be applied in a wide context: in the fixed and mobile domain networks to Personal Area Networks, (PAN) which may not have access to the infrastructure. In this context DEEP is proposed as a generic name resolution mechanism, which relies on existing naming mechanisms, such as DNS, SIP and HIP, but is not targeted to replace them. DEEP is needed for several reasons: (1) Existing name resolution schemes have heterogeneous architectures and may be executed in different networking domains. DEEP is designed as a unified name resolution mechanism, which provides interworking between the existing name resolution schemes and hides the heterogeneity related to them [17]. (2) Infrastructure support from DNS is not always possible in mobile access networks or ad hoc networks, and other solutions such as DHT [18] might need to be applied. This brings more complexity to the naming schemes, which should be able to interwork. (3) With the concept of moving networks in the AN context, the configuration of local name resolution information may need to be stored privately in an external name resolution system [17]. In this case updates to the global name resolution infrastructure (DNS) may not be needed when the local name-to-address mapping is changed. Thus it cannot be assumed that DNS can be applied in all the different networking environments of Ambient Networks. (4) Internet Multimedia Subsystem (IMS) is a signaling framework enabling end-to-end signaling between cellular terminals in heterogeneous networks. In the AN context the SIP based name resolution scheme of IMS cannot be seen to be sufficient (consider ad hoc networks as an example), given that it even has problems with interworking with the terminals in the WLAN domains [19].

The contribution of this paper is the presentation of DEEP in the AN context, and the scalability of DEEP. In particular DEEP has been analysed from the signaling load and name resolution latency point of view, which are important aspects of any protocol being developed for the Internet scale.

The results show the dependency of signaling load on the number of ANs and independency on the number of sessions in the AN context. In addition updating of sessions has been focused on. DEEP latency evaluation shows quite good scalability for name resolution delays smaller than 100 ms up to 10 intermediate DEEP-nodes. For bigger name resolution delays at the intermediate DEEP-nodes, the scalability of DEEP latency worsens.

The organization of the paper is as follows. An overview of DEEP name resolution design in the AN context is presented in Chapter 2, while Chapter 3 describes the implementation and simulation model used for the scalability study. The results, validation and evaluation of DEEP scalability are presented in Chapter 4. The conclusions made are stated in the last Chapter.

2   DEEP Name Resolution

DEEP enables symbolic name resolution to a locatable IP address of any remote Communication Endpoint (CEP). It is not dependent on the GANS protocol stack, and can be used outside the AN context. However, DEEP is presented with GANS, because it is important to understand that DEEP requires name resolution mechanism support from the framework it is being applied in (DNS, SIP etc.).

The structure of the Generic AN Signaling (GANS) protocol stack (Figure 2) follows the two-layer approach for generic signaling currently being defined by the NSIS working group in the IETF [5]. NSIS is a signaling protocol suite for manipulating control state in network elements on the data path of a flow. In the NSIS scope a signaling layer protocol (NSLP) is a generic term referring to any protocol within the application layer, which supports a specific signaling application [5]. The role of the NSIS Transport Layer Protocol (NTLP) is to transport signaling messages in the network independently of the particular NSLP [5].

The main differences between the GANS approach and the NSIS framework are in the addressing and routing of messages. In the NSIS scope it is assumed that the next NTLP signaling peer has knowledge of routing flow-based messages towards a destination, and a Router Alert Option [7] is used to enable NTLP-aware routers along a path to intercept packets. In GANS, the signaling is not always flow related, and the IP address of the signaling peer is not always known either. Rather, both symbolic names and IP addresses may be used for addressing the Communication Endpoint (CEP) in the destination AN. When the destination is addressed with a symbolic name, DEEP name resolution is performed. The Generic Internet Signaling Transport (GIST) as the instance of NTLP has been extended in order to support symbolic names in the Message Routing Information (MRI) [6], which is the main difference between GIST and EGIST. EGIST is a backwards compatible version of GIST, which means that GIST implementations in the network are able to interoperate with EGIST implementations despite of the modification. Generic Transport Layer Protocol (GTLP) refers to the combination of EGIST and DEEP protocols, which offers a transport service for GSLP (NTLP is the NSIS scope).

DEEP relies on sequential name resolution via one or more intermediate DEEP-nodes (Figure 2). The DEEP-nodes rely on existing local name resolution (NR) mechanisms (DNS etc.). DEEP is a stateless protocol, and follows the query-response messaging paradigm by using an EXPLORE message in the downstream and a RESPONSE is the upstream direction. DEEP can be run on top of any transport such as UDP or TCP.

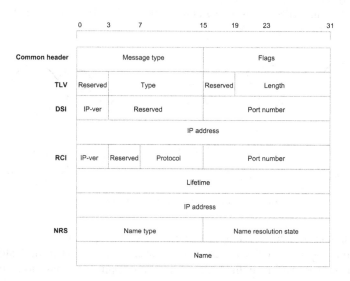

Fig. 1. DEEP message structure

All DEEP messages have a common header and objects (DSI, RCI, NRS), each of which has a Type-Length-Value (TLV) header (see Figure 1) [17]. The common header expresses the type of the message, and has a flags field for extensions. Both EXPLORE and RESPONSE messages contain a Name Resolution State (NRS) object. NRS type indicates the syntax and semantics of the name, and NRS state expresses the part(s) of the name, which have been resolved. EXPLORE has a DEEP Source Info (DSI) object, which includes the IP-version, port and IP address information of the source. RESPONSE has a Remote Contact Info (RCI) object, which includes the same information of the destination as the DSI object, but in addition lifetime of the name binding state is included. A binary format was selected for DEEP as opposed to a text-based format (e.g. XML) in order to minimize protocol overhead.

Figure 2 describes DEEP name resolution as part of GANS. GSLP at AN1 requests the sending of a message to AN2 with a symbolic name (CEP@AN2) (1). GSLP provides session-ID, GSLP-ID and MRI (symbolic name included) as parameters, which are used to identify a GTLP session and is saved by EGIST to the Message Routing State (MRS) table [6] (2). DEEP is used for name resolution, because a symbolic name is used for addressing the CEP (3). In this case only part of the name is resolved and a DEEP EXPLORE is sent towards the next intermediate DEEP-node (4). The intermediate DEEP-node uses its local name resolution service (5) in order to resolve the IP address of the gateway at AN2 and forwards the EXPLORE (6). The gateway in AN2 (gateway@AN2) receives the EXPLORE message and resolves the address of the final CEP, and forwards the message to it (7). The CEP (CEP@AN2) replies with a RESPONSE, which is sent back to AN1 (8). Finally AN1 receives the RESPONSE, and informs EGIST of a successful name resolution. EGIST adds a new entry to the MRS table, and sends further messages directly to the CEP in AN2.

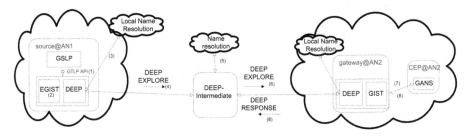

Fig. 2. An example of DEEP name resolution

The mapping between a symbolic name and the corresponding IP address is called name binding state, which is included inside every MRI-object in the entries representing the GTLP sessions in the MRS table. The mapping may have to be updated in some circumstances, for example, because GSLP is willing to extend the lifetime of the binding. The updating may involve the execution of DEEP, which depends on local configuration or policies to be deployed in the AN context, both of which may vary. For example the destination DEEP-node may only be authorized to confirm the length of the lifetime to be extended.

3 Simulation Model

The experiments performed in the simulation model tries to follow the principles discussed in [3] and [4] by varying a number of scalability variables in the network model and keeping the invariants unchanged. In the output other parameters are measured, based on which conclusions can be made.

The simulation model was synthesized in Network Simulator NS-2 [8] for the validation purposes of signaling load models in name resolution and update procedures. In addition the contribution of the procedures to the total signaling load was under study. The rationale and model for DEEP latency evaluation has been described in section 4.5.1. The GTLP protocol stack described in Figure 1 was implemented and consisted of the EGIST and DEEP protocols, which were executed on top of UDP. In addition a GSLP application and the required Tcl scripts were implemented in order to generate input over the GTLP API for the simulation scenario.

The simulation setup has been described in Figure 3. In the beginning of the scenario a different number of ANs perform name resolution and establish GTLP sessions with the destination AN (ANr) randomly within a 10 second time interval. This leads to the exchange of EXPLORE/RESPONSE messages (Name Resolution), and the sending of EGIST Data messages to AN-R (GTLP session setup). Finally each of the GTLP sessions is updated during a time period of 2 seconds at a random interval. ANi acted as a forwarder of traffic in the simulation setup.

The number of ANs (10,100,300), number of GTLP sessions (10,30,100) and probability of using DEEP in the update procedure (0;0,5;1) were used as input variables and simulations were executed with all combinations of them (3^3 cases). The above-mentioned variables were selected, because they were most obviously affecting the scalability aspects of DEEP in the hypothesized models. The number and sizes of DEEP messages were measured during the execution of the cases.

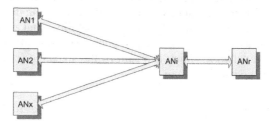

Fig. 3. The simulation setup

4 Evaluation of Results

4.1 Name Resolution Signaling Load

The signaling load as bytes on the network from the point of view of an AN performing name resolution is given by equation (1). numberOfCEPs describes the number of CEPs in the destination AN identified by a different symbolic name. E and R express the size of EXPLORE and RESPONSE messages. The total signaling load as bytes on the network is given by equation (2), which is the sum of signaling loads of the individual ANs performing the name resolution process (K = number of ANs). The model is applicable for a name binding lifetime.

The model described with equations (1) and (2) was validated with the name resolution phase in the simulation scenario, and show that the signaling load on the network is dependent on the number of ANs and doesn't depend on the number of sessions, when multiple ANs perform name resolution to an AN with a single CEP. Further results may be derived from the model by assuming that the overhead increases linearly to the number of CEPs to be contacted, since DEEP messages have to be exchanged when contacting the CEPs with different symbolic names. When a different number of destination ANs are considered, this would increase the load as a multiple of the CEPs and ANs to be contacted.

$$NR\_signaling\_load\_AN = \sum_{i=1}^{numberOfANs} numberOfCEPs_i * (E + R) . \quad (1)$$

$$NR\_signaling\_load\_total = \sum_{j=1}^{K} NR\_signaling\_load\_AN(j) \quad (2)$$

4.2 Update Procedure Signaling Load

The updating of a GTLP session may involve the execution of DEEP as was explained in Chapter 2. Equation (3) describes the signaling load as bytes on the network, when an AN is performing the update procedure for a number of GTLP sessions. numberOfSessions describes the number of GTLP sessions to be updated with the remote AN, and P the probability of using DEEP in the update procedure or of updating a number of sessions with DEEP. A probability is taken into account, because DEEP may be used with the update procedure. Equation (4) describes signaling load as bytes on the network, which is a sum of the signaling loads produced by K ANs performing the update procedure.

$$UPD\_sig\_load\_AN = \sum_{i=1}^{numberOfANs} numberOfCEPs_i * P * (E + R) * numberOfSessions \cdot \quad (3)$$

$$UPD\_sign\_load\_total = \sum_{j=1}^{K} UPD\_sig\_load\_AN(j) \cdot \quad (4)$$

The model was validated with the update phase in the simulation scenario by comparing it to the results generated with equations (3) and (4). Based on the validated equation it can be seen that signaling load on the network increases linearly with the number of GTLP sessions to be updated and the number of ANs performing the update. Further results can be derived from the model, when the number of ANs to be communicated with is increased. In this case the signaling load should multiply as its function.

4.3 Total Overhead

The total signaling load as bytes on the network is the sum of the signaling loads from the name resolution and update procedures and given by equation (5).

$$Tot = \sum_{i=1}^{K} NR\_signaling\_load\_AN(i) + UPD\_sig\_load\_AN(i) \quad (5)$$

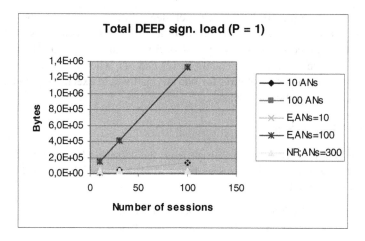

Fig. 4. Total *signaling load* on the network as measured in the simulation scenario and graphs drawn by the model (E=equation 5). In addition *signaling load* from the NR with 300 source ANs has been described.

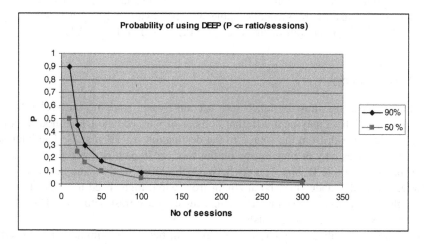

Fig. 5. The *probability of using DEEP* in the update procedure when the load from the update procedure is lower than 90% or 50% of the total signaling load

The total signaling load on the network based on equation (5) was validated with the results measured in the simulation scenario. When comparing the load from the name resolution (Figure 4) to the total load, it can clearly be noticed that the load from the update procedure is dominating if each of the sessions are updated at least once during the lifetime of the name binding state. However it is not known at the moment how frequent the updates are or is DEEP involved in the update procedure. Because of this, further results on the probability of using DEEP in the update proce dure have been described in Figure 5, which depicts the threshold for the probability of using DEEP in the update procedure in order to keep the share of signaling load from the update procedure lower than 90% or 50% of the total load. The equation in the figure has been derived from equations (2) and (4), when it is considered that an AN would perform name resolution for one AN and would execute the update procedure for a varying number of sessions.

4.4 DEEP Message Size

The size of DEEP messages is important from the signaling load point of view. The model (6) for DEEP message sizes as bytes were developed based on the message structure described in Figure 2.

$$
\begin{aligned}
EXPLORE &= 20 + symbolicname + IPaddress \\
RESPONSE &= 24 + symbolicname + IPaddress
\end{aligned}
\tag{6}
$$

In the EXPLORE and RESPONSE messages the symbolic name and IP address consume most of the space in the message. If the symbolic name is assumed to be structured based on the Fully Qualified Domain Name (FQDN) [10], its maximum size is 255 bytes. An IPv4 address is 4 bytes and an IPv6 address 16 bytes long. In the simulations the size of the symbolic name was 100 bytes and an IPv4 address was used, which led to the following sizes: EXPLORE=124 bytes, RESPONSE=128 bytes.

4.5 DEEP Latency

A number of factors must be taken into account, when studying the scalability of DEEP latency. There may be a different number of intermediate DEEP-nodes on the name resolution path from the source to the destination AN (Figure 1). The intermediate DEEP-nodes may or may not be on the shortest IP path between the peers, and there may be multiple IP hops/routers between the DEEP-nodes. The networks used between the DEEP nodes may be anything from wired high speed networks to wireless high-latency access systems. The name resolution infrastructure used by DEEP may be DNS or any other mechanism.

The model described by equation (7) was used, because in simulations a specific L1/L2 technology would have been selected. The simulations would have produced results only suitable for the selected L1/L2 technology. The goal was to determine scalability in terms of different RTTs between endpoints, and not focus on a particular lower layer. It has been assumed that DEEP name resolution is executed in the initiator and intermediate DEEP-nodes. The NR_delay describes the delay of the particular name resolution mechanism to be performed at intermediate DEEP-nodes, which has been assumed to be equal in each of the intermediate-nodes along the path. Interm_DEEP_nodes is the amount of intermediate DEEP-nodes on the name resolution path. RTT describes the time required for the EXPLORE/RESPONSE message exchange. Simulations were not executed for the latency evaluation, because RTT estimates would have become dependent on the L1/L2 solution, which was not the purpose of the study. The goal of the study is to explore the scalability of DEEP latency-for networks with different RTTs, when the number of intermediate nodes and name resolution delay is varied. Figure 6 describes the latency of DEEP for a RTT of 300ms. The graphs with other RTTs follow a similar shape.

$$DEEP\_lat = (Interm\_DEEP\_nodes + 1) * NR\_delay + RTT \ . \qquad (7)$$

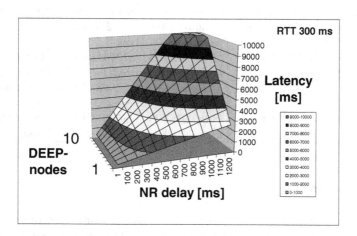

Fig. 6. DEEP latency as a function of the number of intermediate DEEP-nodes and NR delays when RTT of DEEP messages is 300 ms

The results of DEEP latencies with RTTs up to 1500 ms, and their equations have been described in Table 1 (the equations have been derived based on (7) and the higher NR delay values in Table 1). DNS was considered as a name resolution mechanism in the study, and in particular the delays reported in [10] were used as a basis. Both median and 90th percentile of DNS latencies were considered and applied with model (7).

DEEP NR latency depends on the delay of the name resolution mechanism and topology of DEEP nodes in the Internet both of which are not known at the moment. Thus different RTT values, NR delays and number of intermediate nodes were explored with the proposed model. If DNS is considered to be used with DEEP as an existing name resolution mechanism supporting DEEP, and DEEP NR delay in intermediate nodes is assumed to be within the median DNS delays [10] (40-100 ms), the latency is expected to be under 2.6 seconds for all RTTs when intermediate DEEP-nodes up to 10 are considered. In fact based on the equations it can be stated that the NR delay share is smaller than 60% of the total delay ((10DEEP-nodes*100ms)/2600ms). However, when the typical median DNS delays [10] are considered, the results show that DEEP latencies up to 10 intermediate DEEP-nodes are significantly bigger (maximum between 13.5-57.6 seconds), because the NR delay share begins to dominate in the total latency.

Table 1. DEEP latencies and equations with different RTTs and number of intermediate DEEP-nodes

RTT	300 ms	600 ms	1000 ms	1500 ms
NR delay				
40-100 ms (DNS median)	380-1400 ms (*100*DEEP-nodes+400*)	680-1700 ms (*100*DEEP-nodes+700*)	1080-2100 ms (*100*DEEP-nodes+1100*)	1580-2600 ms (*100*DEEP-nodes+1600*)
100-1200 ms (DNS 90th percentile)	500-13500 ms (*1200*DEEP-nodes+1500*)	800-13800 ms (*1200*DEEP-nodes+1800*)	1200-14200 ms (*1200*DEEP-nodes+2200*)	1700-14700 ms (*1200*DEEP-nodes+2700*)
1200-5000 ms	2700-56356 ms (*5000*DEEP-nodes+5300*)	3000-56656 ms (*5000*DEEP-nodes+5600*)	3400-57056 ms (*5000*DEEP-nodes+6000*)	3900-57556 ms (*5000*DEEP-nodes+6500*)

5   Conclusions

This paper presented the DEEP protocol for symbolic name resolution in Ambient Networks, and the results of a scalability analysis. In particular signaling load and latency aspects of the solution were focused on. The results show that DEEP name resolution signaling load on the network is directly proportional to the number of ANs and doesn't depend on the number of GTLP sessions. However, if multiple CEPs are to be contacted, then the load increases linearly, when contacting the CEPs with different symbolic names. Results in the DEEP update procedure show that signaling load on the network increases linearly with the number of GTLP sessions to be updated and the number of ANs performing the update. The overall DEEP signaling load on the network is the sum of the loads from the name resolution and update procedures. The results show that updating becomes a dominating factor in the total load, if the frequency of session updates or the number of sessions to be updated is high during the lifetime of the name binding state. It should however be noticed that the requirement for updating was derived from the AN context, and may not be needed in other frameworks. Models developed based on DEEP specification and implementation indicates that symbolic name and IP address form a major share of the DEEP message sizes, and determine the final size of the messages.

DEEP latency evaluation results show quite good scalability for name resolution delays smaller than 100 ms up to 10 intermediate nodes. In fact according to the previous studies, median DNS delays are lower than 100 ms. In this case the latency would be under 2.6 seconds for RTTs up to 1500 ms, and the share of the name resolution performed at the intermediate DEEP-nodes should be lower than 60% in the total latency. However if NR delays bigger than 100 ms are considered for RTTs up to 1500 ms, the results show that NR delays begin to dominate the total latency, which increases in direct proportion to the number of intermediate DEEP-nodes. Based on these results it can be stated that the scalability of DEEP depends in large part on the NR mechanism providing support for DEEP.

References

1. Niebert, N., et al. : Ambient Networks: An Architecture for Communication Networks Beyond 3G. IEEE Wireless Communications. 2 (2004) 14–22
2. Brunner, M.: Requirements for Signaling Protocols. IETF RFC 3726, (April 2004)
3. Floyd, S.,Paxson, V. : Difficulties in Simulating the Internet. IEEE/ACM Transactions on Networking. 4 (2001) 392–403
4. Floyd, S.,Kohler, E. : Internet Research Needs Better Models. SIGCOM Computing Communications Review. 1 (2003) 29–34
5. Hancock, R. et al.: Next Steps In Signaling (NSIS): Framework. IETF RFC 4080, (June 2005)
6. Schulzrinne, H., Hancock, R. : GIST General Internet Signaling Transport. IETF draft <draft-ietf-nsis-ntlp-08>, (September 2005)
7. Partridge, C. Jackson, A..: IPv6 Router Alert Option. IETF RFC 2711, (October 1999)
8. NS-2 website, URL: http://www.isi.edu/nsnam/ns/
9. Mockapetris, P. : DOMAIN NAMES-IMPLEMENTATION AND SPECIFICATION. IETF RFC 1035, (November 1987)
10. Jung, J., Sit, E., Balakrishnan H., Morris, R. : DNS Performance and the Effectiveness of Caching. IEEE/ACM Transactions on Networking. 5 (2002) 589–603
11. Ramasubramanian, V., Sirer, E.G. : The Design and Implementation of a Next Generation Name Service for the Internet. 2004 Conference on Applications, technologies, architectures, and protocols for computer communications. (2004) 331–342
12. Mockapetris, P.: Domain Names-Concepts and facilities. IETF RFC 1034, (November 1987)
13. Rosenberg, J et al.: SIP: Session Initiation Protocol. IETF RFC 3261, (June 2002)
14. Schulzrinne, H., Rosenberg, J. : The Session Initiation Protocol:Internet-Centric Signaling. IEEE Communications Magazine. 10 (2000) 134–141
15. Moskowitch, R., Nikander, P.: Host Identity Protocol Architecture IETF draft <draft-ietf-hip-arch-03>, (August 2005)
16. Akhtar, N.,et al. : GANS: A Signaling Framework for Dynamic Interworking between Heterogeneous Networks. submitted to VTC 2006
17. Pöyhönen, P.,et al. : DEEP - A Generic Name Resolution Protocol for Heterogeneous Networks. to appear in ICTTA'06
18. Araujo, F., et al. : CHR: a distributed hash table for wireless ad hoc networks. 25th IEEE International Conference on Distributed Computing Systems Workshops. (2005) 407-413
19. Marquez, F. G., et al. : Interworking of IP Multimedia Core Networks between 3GPP and WLAN. IEEE Wireless Communications. 3 (2005) 58–65

Urban Cellular Planning Optimisation of Multi-service Enhanced UMTS Based in Economic Issues

Orlando Cabral, Fernando J. Velez, Cátia Franco, and Ricardo Rei

IT-DEM, University of Beira, Interior Calçada Fonte do Lameiro,
6201-001 Covilhã, Portugal
`OCabral@e-projects.ubi.pt, fjv@ubi.pt,`
`{c_franco, rrei}@megamail.pt`

Abstract. Results for Enhanced UMTS (E-UMTS) cost/revenue optimisation are obtained, as a function of the coverage distance, R. E-UMTS traffic generation and activity models are described and characterised in an urban scenario based on population and service penetration values. By using a System Level Simulator results were obtained for blocking and handover failure probabilities. Models for the supported fraction of active users and for the supported throughput, as a function of active users, were obtained. When one amplifier is used, the maximum throughput per BS is around 600kb/s. However, it achieves values up to 2000kb/s when three amplifiers per BS are considered. Generally, the profit in percentage is a decreasing function with R. The use of three amplifiers per BS is strongly advised in order to get cheaper communications, with prices that vary from 0.016 to 0.07 €/min, for R=250 and 1075m, respectively.

1 Introduction

UMTS (Universal Mobile Telecommunications System) has an enormous potential in answering to the challenge of supporting heterogeneous traffic like data, video, audio, and multimedia communications together with voice in all kind of environments. However, because of limitations of the first releases of UMTS, innovations have to be sought, e.g., for making higher data rates available in both links. HSDPA/HSUPA (High speed downlink/uplink packet access) seek for these solutions, and IST-SEACORN (Simulation of Enhanced UMTS Access and Core Networks) proposed a so-called, E-UMTS (Enhanced UMTS), which is a UMTS evolution step that provides bit rates higher than 2 Mbit/s in the uplink and downlink directions over a 5 MHz frequency carrier [1]. It enables the provision of new wideband services and a significant reduction of the price per bit, running over flexible Quality of Service (QoS) enabled IP based access and core networks, and making possible an effective end-to-end packet based transmission. E-UMTS will allow for expansion in both down- and uplink directions, e.g., by using higher order modulations or advanced coding schemes. Hence, it will support wideband real-time (RT)/time-based (TB) mobile applications with a very high system capacity, and will set the ground for an initial introduction of actual broadband mobile applications, an important step towards 4G. Since the proposed enhancements have not yet been implemented, the only practical way to evaluate their effect is by means of simulation.

T. Braun et al. (Eds.): WWIC 2006, LNCS 3970, pp. 178–189, 2006.

From the SEACORN scenarios [2], in this work only the urban scenario, with two BSs (Base Stations) configuration is explored, with slightly different assumptions for service usage, Table 1. The data rate, R_b, and average duration, τ, are also defined in Table 1. The traffic model is based on population and service penetration values, in order to determine call generation rates for the constituent services within the scenario. Service characteristics of the corresponding applications, i.e., intrinsic time dependency, delivery requirements, directionality, and symmetry/asymmetry were extracted from [3], [4]. Examples of sound, high interactive multimedia (HIMM), narrowband (NB), and wideband (WB) applications are VOI (Voice), VTE (Video-telephony), MWB (Multimedia, MM, Web Browsing), and ATR (Assistance in Travel), respectively.

Table 1. Applications Usage in the Urban Scenario

Services	R_b [kb/s]	Usage [%]	τ [min]	Distribution of activity/inactivity	Activity duration ON [s]	Activity duration OFF [s]
Sound Voice (VOI)	12.2	82.5	3	Exponential	1.4	1.7
High Inter. Multimedia Video-telephony(VTE)	144	11.0	3	-	10	10
Narrowband MM Web browsing (MWB)	384	2.0	15	Pareto	10	13
Wideband Assistance in travel (ATR)	768	4.5	15	Weibull/Pareto	10	10

Session activity parameters describe the detailed aspects of traffic within a call. This is accomplished by means of an alternating ON/OFF state model. The activity within a call can be modelled by defining an average duration of each period, together with an adequate statistical distribution (e.g., reflecting long-range dependence).

The purpose of this work is to optimise the cellular planning process for multi-service E-UMTS in urban scenarios by using results for system capacity as an input for a cost/revenue function, e.g., to choose the best coverage distance of cells. Similar results are presented in [5] for the offices scenario.

In Section 2, the urban scenario is characterised and the main features of the system level simulator are described. Section 3 presents results for the blocking and handover failure probabilities when one amplifier per tri-sectorial BS is used. In Section 4, the process of determination of system capacity is addressed for both BS configuration, one and three amplifiers per BS. In Section 5, a cost/revenue model is proposed and described, and its particular application to the urban scenario is presented. Section 6 discusses results regarding costs/revenues, and the optimisation of the coverage distance (that maximises the profit in percentage). Finally, conclusions are presented in Section 7.

2 Traffic Modelling and Simulations

The activity within a call is modelled by defining an average duration of each active/inactive period, together with an adequate statistical distribution. For example, the basic model for data applications normally uses a Web session as a paradigm, although the model may be used for all types of data. A session is composed of a set of active periods made of packet sequences (packet calls) separated by inactivity periods. A packet call is a sequence or burst of packets, corresponding, e.g., to a Web page or other data item. Inactivity periods between packet call arrivals are often called reading or inactivity time.

A simulation approach is being considered, and the SEACORN SLS (System Level Simulator [6], [7], [8]) is used. It captures the dynamic end-to-end behaviour of the whole network, including the dynamic user behaviour (e.g., mobility and variable traffic demands), radio interface, radio access network, and core network. The SLS is separated into three modules: mobile environment, control mechanisms, and performance evaluation, Figure 1.a). This separation is made according to their functionality. Control mechanisms involve PC (power control), CAC (call admission control), handover control, load control, and packet scheduling. PC consists of open-loop PC and inner-loop PC, outer-loop PC in both UL (uplink) and DL (downlink) directions, and slow PC applied to the DL common channels. When a new call is required, the CAC checks if there is an OVSF (Orthogonal Variable Spreading Factor) code, and PC checks if there is enough power. Hard handover is the only one supported by the simulator. The scheduling algorithm is the Drop Tail (FIFO) queuing one. Details on load control and packet scheduling are given in [8].

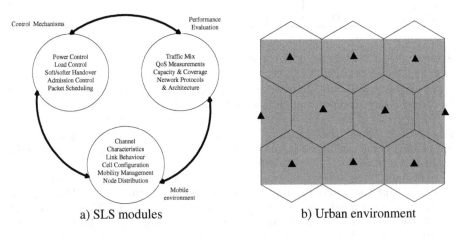

a) SLS modules   b) Urban environment

Fig. 1. Modular View of the System Level Simulator and cellular topology

The mobile environment category contains the methods of generating a topology for a scenario as well as the initialization or redefinition of node properties. Node Bs and user equipments (UEs) are distributed in a predefined grid that represents the simulation area. For the basic simulator the cells are initially assumed to be circular with equal radius but it can be extended to hexagonal (or other) patterns.

Performance evaluation will consider the network traffic model, the network protocols and architecture from the network and transport level simulations, and scenarios for traffic services and applications. Network performance must enable the evaluation of coverage, capacity, Radio Resource Management (RRM) mechanisms, protocols, architectures, and QoS (using metrics such as call blocking, call/packet dropping, and end-to-end packet delay).

Several factors influence the performance including the coverage and capacity, i.e., mobility, QoS demands, radio environment, plus radio and core network control mechanisms. For example, the distance between the User Equipment (UE) and the Node-B, the path loss, and the power control mechanisms affect the coverage. Capacity is affected by traffic and handover mechanisms. Interference affects both coverage and capacity. QoS is affected by the different network architectures, protocols, and Radio Resource Management (RRM) mechanisms. These factors are addressed by simulations at network and transport levels. The basic algorithm for system level simulations is presented in [9]. Enhancements are mainly applied to the radio link, and to the IP infrastructure. These enhancements include Multi-path Interference Canceller, MPIC, Space Time Transmit Diversity, STTD, and MIMO systems [8].

The topology of the urban scenarios consists of several BSs, using tri-sectored antennas, and two different hypothesis are considered: one and three wideband amplifiers. Several values were tested for cell radius so that a 4km^2 area is covered in an efficient way, Figure 1.b).

The mobility model used for the urban vehicular environment is the Gauss-Markov mobility one. This is an entity mobility model as it defines individual but not group movement patterns. The pattern is confined within the predefined grid area. As in all mobility models, the users are confined within this area and return to a point inside the topology when they reach the boundaries. The Gauss-Markov model is defined to be between the random walk (slow speeds) and the fluid flow (very high speeds) models. The two models, random walk and fluid flow, are labelled as extremes. Most of the nodes move somewhere in-between those speeds. Parameters for the Gauss-Markov model include the mobile speed at 50km/h (13.89m/s), and a random seed, a number that is fed into a random number generator, which allows that this model can assign pseudorandom paths to the mobile users. The Radio Propagation model is the Hata propagation one [7].

The traffic mix model defined for this environment generates traffic according to predefined usage percentages, Table 1 and assigns an application to each user accordingly. Each user in the urban scenarios has a probability to be active. This is determined by the Busy Hour Call Attempts (BHCA) provided as a set of bounds for the percentage of active users in a simulation run. Busy hour call attempt represents in this case the total number of call attempts by all users considered in one simulation

$$BHCA_j = \frac{Usage_j}{\tau_j} \cdot M_T \cdot \rho , \qquad (1)$$

where M_T is the number of users in the cell, τ_j is the average call/session duration, and ρ is the average traffic per user, which can vary from 0 to 1. In simulations, one considers one fourth of the user density given in [2], i.e., 0.012/4; this reduction is owing to limitations of the simulator, which did not support higher user densities. Hence, in an area of 4000000m^2, M_T =4000000m^2×0.012/4=12000. The fraction of active users, f, is obtained from the average traffic per user as $f = \rho/(\rho+1)$. In the urban scenario, one considers the following values: f=0.7, 0.8, 1.7, 2.3, 3.4, 4.3, and 5.2%.

3 Results for Quality of Service

Quality of service results were obtained by using the SEACORN SLS for a maximum transmitted power of 16dBW. The aim is to get the best cell radius in order to guarantee a certain grade of service (GoS). The considered QoS measures are blocking probability, P_b, and handover failure probability, P_{hf}. The first set of results include the blocking probability, where an analysis of all classes of services together, a so-called "total services" approach, is considered. While in this analysis the results for the various applications are not distinguished, a "detailed services" one can be defined, which discriminates the classes of services. Figure 2 presents results for the "total services" approach.

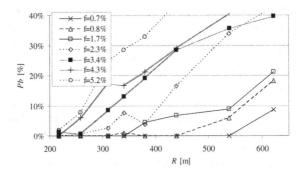

Fig. 2. Blocking probability for f=0.7, 0.8, 1.7, 2.3, 3.4, 4.3 and 5.2%, "total services"

It is a worth noting that the mechanisms involved in new calls blocking are CAC (Call Admission Control) and PC (Power Control), which test the power thresholds, and the existence of OVSF codes. In the context of an all IP network, the most common way to treat users is to queue them instead of blocking. However, for services with real time QoS requirements, an admission control algorithm has to be implemented. It is necessary to maintain desired QoS, especially for RT/TB services. Regarding GoS, the blocking probability has to be lower than 2% [2]. By analysing Figure 2, the acceptable radius, R_a, is obtained by using a linear intersection with P_b=2%. Figure 3 presents results for each individual class of service in the "detailed services" approach. By using the same procedure as for the "total services" approach, one obtains the correspondence between f and R_a, the acceptable cell radius for a given P_b. Table 2, presents results for both approaches. Although the results for ATR are presented in Figure 3, these results are not considered in Table 2, as ATR is a Non-RT application, and the simulation algorithm obtains it in an almost straightforward way. For NRT applications, blocking probability has low influence in QoS since establishing a connection will be transparent for users, and will not be delay sensitive.

HO (Handover) is one of the major characteristics of mobile systems. Its influence in QoS is proportional to its intensity/ rate. The smaller is the cell radius and the higher is the user mobility, the higher is the handover intensity/rate. The SEACORN SLS only considers hard handover. Besides, it considers three base stations in the active set; a user is dropped only after six unsuccessful attempts to make handover. Figure 4 presents results for P_{hf} as a function of the cell radius, and also for P_{hfmax}, the handover failure probability threshold, for the "total services" approach. Figure 5 presents results for P_{hf} as a function of the cell radius for the "detailed services" approach.

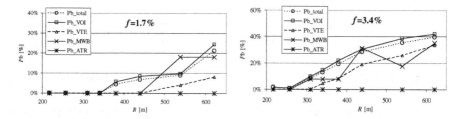

Fig. 3. Blocking probability, example for f=1.7 and 3.4%, "detailed services"

Table 2. Acceptable cell radiuses considering P_b constraints

$f_{[\%]}$	Pb_total	Pb_VOI	Pb_VTE	Pb_MWB
0.7	557	552	621	621
0.8	472	473	550	447
1.7	358	354	488	458
2.3	293	285	317	385
3.4	266	264	323	271
4.3	230	228	280	274
5.2	218	217	269	267

The variation of the maximum allowed P_{hf}, P_{hfmax}, with the coverage distance, is also presented in each case, it being different for each application. P_{hfmax} is computed from the simulation results by using $P_{hfmax}=P_{dmax}/Nb\_HO_j$, where Nb_HO_j is the number of handovers per application j call/session, and the value of the maximum call dropping probability is P_{dmax}=1% [10]. By adding BSs to the topology, although the network capacity increases, the number of handovers per call also increases. Then, small cell radius may not be the solution which better satisfy handover failure probability requirements. This is true in particular for RT/TB calls/sessions, like VOI, VTE and MWB, as a call being dropped causes extreme dissatisfaction to the users.

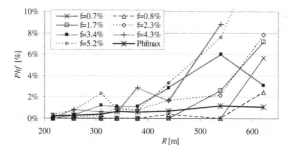

Fig. 4. Handover failure probability for f=0.7, 0.8, 1.7, 2.3, 3.4, 4.3 e 5.2%, "total services"

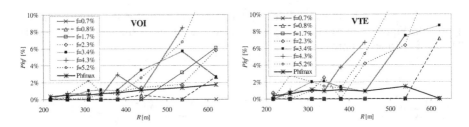

Fig. 5. P_{hf} for VOI and VTE, f=0.7, 0.8, 1.7, 2.3, 3.4, 4.3 e 5.2%, "detailed services"

Hence, when analysing Figures 4 -5 for several values of f, the most appropriate cell radiuses, R_{ap}, agreeing with handover failure constraints, have to be chosen, Table 3.

Table 3. The most appropriate cell radius agreeing considering P_{hf} constraints

$f_{[\%]}$	Phf_total	Phf_VOI	Phf_VTE	Phf_MWB
0.7	555	621	621	621
0.8	577	588	552	621
1.7	471	476	621	538
2.3	322	350	395	341
3.4	256	271	247	258
4.3	227	239	239	311
5.2	217	238	224	256

4 System Capacity

Although results for QoS were only presented when one amplifier is considered, the same analysis was performed for three amplifiers, and the respective results for system capacity will be presented in this Section. Only the "detailed services" approach is being addressed since it seems to be the most accurate one. Taking a worst case situation between P_b and P_{hf} GoS constraints into account, by using an inversion procedure, the most suitable f was found for each value of R, Figure 6. By using a curve fit approach, curves for the supported f were found:

- one amplifier f=1/(-0.38192+0.00072·$R^{1.24156}$),
- three amplifiers f=1/(-0.15486+1.27916·10^{-04}·$R^{1.34116}$).

By considering these results for $f(R)$, the system throughput, $thr_{[Mb/s]}$, can be extracted from simulation results, for the same values of R, Figure 6.

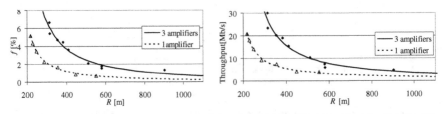

Fig. 6. Supported fraction of active users and total throughput as function of cell radius, R

Once more, by using a curve fit approach, the curve for the supported throughput can be found (downlink), which presents a decreasing behaviour:

- one amplifier $thr = 1/(-0.22620 + 0.00790 \cdot R^{0.65905})$,
- three amplifiers $thr = 1/(-6.42541 \cdot 10^{-02} + 1.61696 \cdot 10^{-04} \cdot R^{1.10393})$.

Hence, as the cell radius increases system capacity decreases. This decreasing behaviour of system capacity is the normal trend, although it can be noticed that there is a high decreasing tendency up to 400-500m, after this coverage distances there is a tendency for the throughput to be constant. By doing an analysis of the throughput per BS, Figure 7, each base station reaches maxima of 600kb/s and 2000kb/s, for $R \approx 217$ and 250m, for one and three amplifiers, respectively. When the cell radius is low the high value of the throughput per BS can be explained due to the fact of users being closer to the BS can easily be served; they transmit with low power (by using Power Control algorithms) causing low interference to each other. However, for cell radius higher than 400m, if the same power were used, owing to the higher distance from users to BSs, more blocks would occur; hence, users have to transmit with a high power level, causing higher interference. As a consequence, BSs have to make more power available for each user, and resources vanish more rapidly [11].

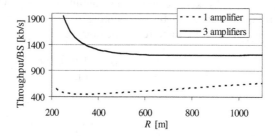

Fig. 7. Throughput per BS as function of R

5   Cost/Revenue Model

In this work, we consider the operator/service provider's point of view [12]. In urban scenarios, a cost/revenue function was developed taking into account the cost of building and maintaining the infrastructure, and the way the number of channels available in each cell affects operators' revenues. Fixed costs for licensing and bandwidth auctions should also be taken into account. Although one considers a project duration of five years as a working hypothesis, one will analyse costs and revenues on an annual basis. Furthermore, the analysis is made under the assumption of null discount rate [13]. Note however that appropriate changes would be needed to perform a complete economic analysis based on discounted cash flows (e.g., to compute the net present value).

The system costs includes a fixed term that represents the fixed costs, C_f, and one term proportional to the number of base stations, C_b (although there is a term proportional to the number of carrier of a base station, in this work approach, only one carrier is considered, and this is incorporated in C_b).

The total cost per unit area is given by

$$C_{[€/km^2]} = C_{f[€/km^2]} + C_{b[€]} \cdot N_{cell/km^2} , \quad (2)$$

where N_{cell/km^2} is the actual number of cells per square kilometre in the simulated geometries. The revenue per cell per year, $(R_v)_{cell}$ can be obtained as a function of the throughput per BS, $thr_{BS\ [kb/s]}$, and of the revenue of a channel with a data rate $R_{b[kb/s]}$, $R_{Rb[€/min]}$,

$$\left(R_v\right)_{cell\ [€]} = \frac{thr_{BS[kb/s]} \cdot T_{bh} \cdot R_{R_b}[€/min]}{R_{b[kb/s]}} , \quad (3)$$

where T_{bh} is the equivalent duration of busy hours per day. The revenue per square kilometre per year, R_v, is obtained by multiplying the revenue per cell by the number of cells per square kilometre

$$R_{v[€/km^2]} = N_{cell/km^2}(R_v)_{cell\ [€]} = N_{c/km^2} \cdot \frac{thr_{BS[kb/s]} \cdot T_{bh} \cdot R_{R_b}[€/min]}{R_{b[kb/s]}} . \quad (4)$$

By considering six busy hours per day, 240 busy days per year [13], $T_{bh}=6 \cdot 240 \cdot 60$min, and the revenue/price of a 144kb/s "channel" per minute (corresponding to information truly transferred, i.e., obtained by discounting the off periods of the traffic), $R_{144[€/min]}$, the revenue per square kilometre can be obtained as

$$R_{v[€/km^2]} = \frac{1}{-0.0168 + 2.7729 \cdot 10^{-5} \cdot R^{1.3674}} \cdot \left(\frac{thr_{BS[kb/s]} \cdot 60 \cdot 6 \cdot 240 \cdot R_{144[€/min]}}{144_{[kb/s]}} \right), \quad (5)$$

where

$$N_{c/km^2} = \frac{1}{-0.0168 + 2.7729 \cdot 10^{-5} \cdot R^{1.3674}} , \quad (6)$$

gives the number of cell in a 4km^2 area. Three hypothesis have been considered for the revenue/price of a 144kb/s channel: $R_{144[€/min]}=0.01$, $R_{144[€/min]}=0.05$ and $R_{144[€/min]}=0.10$. As the transfer of 1 MB of information lasts 56s at 144 kb/s, R_{144} corresponds approximately to the price of a 1 MB transfer. Two different assumptions (hypothesis A [14], and B) were also considered for the cost of tri-sectorial BSs with one and three wideband amplifiers, Table 4. One also assumes that the maximum lifetime of BS is five years.

Table 4. Assumptions for costs

Parameters	Macrocell (three amplifiers)		Macrocell (one amplifier)	
	A	B	A	B
Initial Costs:				
BS price, C_{BS} [€]	50 000	25 000	20 000	10 000
Installation, C_{Inst} [€]	30 000	2 500	30 000	2 500
License fees, C_{fl}[€/km^2]	1 590	1 590	1 590	1 590
Annual Cost:				
Operation and maintenance, $C_{M\&O}$	3 000	750	3 000	750

6 Optimisation

The left hand side of Figure 8 presents costs/revenues per km^2 as a function of R for the three hypotheses for prices and for the two hypothesis for costs, for the case of one wideband amplifier. For $R_{144[\text{€/min}]}=0.01$, in case A costs are always higher than revenues, while in case B cost are equal to revenues; while in the first case the network profit is negative, in the second case it is null. For $R_{144[\text{€/min}]}=0.05$, while in case B there is clearly profit, for case A the profit is approximately zero. For $R_{144[\text{€/min}]}=0.10$, the network is always being profitable since revenues always overcome costs.

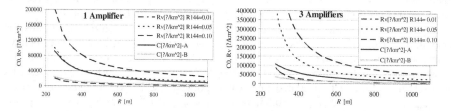

Fig. 8. Costs/revenues per km^2 as a function of R, one and three amplifiers per BS

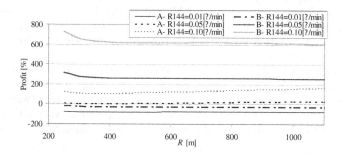

Fig. 9. Profit per km^2 as a function of R (one amplifier)

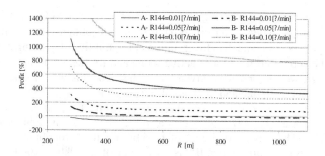

Fig. 10. Profit per km^2 as a function of R (three amplifiers)

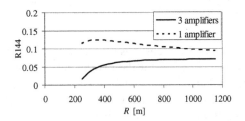

Fig. 11. Required $R_{144[\text{€/min}]}$ to obtain a profit of 250%

The right hand side of Figure 8 presents costs/revenues per km^2, as a function of R, when three wideband amplifiers are used. The same hypotheses are considered for prices and costs. The case $R_{144[\text{€/min}]}=0.01$ is the only one with negative profit.

Figure 9 presents the dependence of the profit in percentage on the cell radius for one amplifier per BS. It can be observed that the curves present a decreasing behaviour for case B and an increasing behaviour for case A. Hence, for one amplifier the most profitable cell radius will be 217m (the lowest simulated one) for hypothesis B, and 621m (the highest simulated one) for hypothesis A. By varying the price from $R_{144[\text{€/min}]}=0.01$ up to $R_{144[\text{€/min}]}=0.05$, or to $R_{144[\text{€/min}]}=0.10$, a variation in the profit from -78% up to 9%, or to 119% is obtained in hypothesis A (for R=621m) .

Figure 10 presents the dependence of the profit in percentage on the cell radius for three amplifiers per BS. In this case, it can be observed that the curves have a decreasing behaviour. The most profitable radius will be 257m (the lowest simulated one). By varying the price from $R_{144[\text{€/min}]}=0.01$ to $R_{144[\text{€/min}]}=0.05$, or to $R_{144[\text{€/min}]}=0.10$, a variation in the profit from -18% up to 308%, or to 716% is obtained (in hypothesis A).

If the objective is to obtain a profit of 250% for both configurations, the respective price, R_{144}, presents the variation from Figure 11. When the coverage distance varies from 217 to 1075m, the values of $R_{144[\text{€/min}]}$ converge to a limit between 0.07-0.09 €/min. However, for the smallest cell radius, $R_{144[\text{€/min}]}$ can be very low when three amplifiers are used, meaning that the amount of traffic required has to be high to provide low cost services.

7 Conclusions

The SEACORN System Level Simulator incorporates a E-UMTS traffic generation model, which was applied to an urban environment to obtain Quality of service results, such as blocking and handover failure probabilities. By using these results, models for the supported fraction of active users, and for the supported throughput, as a function of R, were found for a given GoS. These models were found for different BS configurations: with one and three amplifiers per tri-sectorial BS.

When the cell radius decreases, the supported traffic and the corresponding throughput increases. However, it occurs at the cost of a significant increase in the number of BSs. There is an optimum of 600kb/s for the throughput per BS around R=217m when one amplifier per BS is used, and of 2000kb/s around 250m when three amplifiers per BS are used.

By using a cost/revenue model, where revenues depend on the throughput, one concludes that the profit is generally a decreasing function with R. The use of three amplifiers per BS is strongly advised in order to get cheaper mobile network access with prices that vary from 0.016 €/min, for R = 250m, up to 0.07 €/min, for R=1075m.

Acknowledgements

This work was partially funded by MULTIPLAN, and CROSSNET (Portuguese Foundation for Science and Technology POSI and POSC projects with FEDER funding), and by "Projecto de Re-equipamento Científico" REEQ/1201/EEI/ 2005 (a Portuguese Foundation for Science and Technology project).

References

1. http://seacorn.ptinovacao.pt
2. J. Ferreira and F.J.Velez, "Deployment Scenarios and Applications Characterisation for Enhanced UMTS Simulation", in *Proc. of 3G 2004 - 5th IEE International Conference on 3G Mobile Communication Technologies*, London, UK, Oct. 2004.
3. F.J. Velez and L.M. Correia, "Mobile Broadband Services: Classification, Characterisation and Deployment Scenarios," *IEEE Communications Magazine*, Vol.40, No. 4, Apr. 2002, pp. 142-150.
4. Eva R. San José and F.J. Velez, "Enhanced UMTS Services and Applications: a perspective beyond 3G", in *Proc. of EPMCC' 2003 – 5th European Personal Mobile Communications Conference*, Glasgow, Scotland, Apr. 2003.
5. O. Cabral, F.J. Velez, G. Hadjipollas, M. Stylianou, J. Antoniou, V. Vassiliou and A. Pitsillides, "Enhanced UMTS Cost/revenue Optimisation in Offices Scenarios," in *Proc. of 3G2005 - 6th IEE International Conference on 3G & Beyond*, London, UK, Nov. 2005.
6. http://seacorn.cs.ucy.ac.cy/eumtssim/
7. J. Antoniou, *A System Level Simulator for Enhanced UMTS Coverage and Capacity Planning*, MSc Thesis, Department of Computer Science, University of Cyprus, Nicosia, Cyprus, June 2004.
8. N. Vlotomas and J. Antoniou (editors), *Final Public Report*, IST SEACORN CEC Deliverable 34900/UCY/DS/047/ a1, IST Central Office, Brussels, Belgium, Aug. 2004.
9. O. Cabral, F.J. Velez, G. Hadjipollas, M. Stylianou, J. Antoniou, V. Vassiliou and A. Pitsillides, "Enhanced UMTS Simulation-based Planning in Office Scenarios," in *Proc. of EW2006 - 12th European Wireless Conference*, Athens, Greece, April. 2006.
10. B. Jabbari, "Teletraffic Aspects of Evolving and Next Generation Wireless Communication Networks," *IEEE Personal Communications Magazine*, Vol. 3, No. 6, Dec. 1996, pp. 4-9.
11. H. Holma, A. Toskala, *WCDMA for UMTS*, John Wiley and Sons, Chichester, West Sussex, UK, 2004.
12. B. Gavish and S. Sridhar, "Economic Aspects of Configuring Cellular Networks", *Wireless Networks*, Vol. 1, No. 1, Feb. 1995.
13. F.J. Velez and L.M. Correia, "Optimisation of mobile broadband multi-service systems based in economics aspects", *Wireless Networks*, Vol. 9, No. 5, Sep. 2003, pp. 525-533.
14. Klas Johansson, Anders Furuskär, Peter Karlsson, and Jens Zander, "Relation between cost structure and base station characteristics in cellular systems," in *Proc. of PIMRC' 2004 - 15th IEEE International Symposium on Personal, Indoor and Mobile Radio Communications*, Barcelona, Spain, Sep. 2004.

Traffic Modeling and Characterization for UTRAN

Xi Li, Su Li, Carmelita Görg, and Andreas Timm-Giel

Communication Networks, University of Bremen, FB1,
Otto-Hahn-Allee NW1, 28359 Bremen, Germany
{xili, lisu, cg, atg}@comnets.uni-bremen.de

Abstract. This paper presents an analytical approach for characterizing the aggregated traffic carried in the UMTS Terrestrial Radio Access Network (UTRAN). The characteristic of the incoming traffic stream of UTRAN is studied based on the measured trace traffic from the simulations. The main idea of the aggregated traffic modelling is to employ Batch Markov Arrival Process (BMAP) model as an analytically tractable model, which considers different lengths of packets and batch arrivals. In this paper, the setup and customization of the BMAP model for characterizing the aggregated traffic in UTRAN is presented. The accuracy of the BMAP model is demonstrated by comparing with simulations and Poisson traffic model. At the end the potential application of the presented approach and its advantages is briefly discussed.

1 Introduction

The Universal Mobile Telecommunication Systems (UMTS) network, as a third generation of mobile communication networks, provides high-speed mobile access to a great variety of services in a world-wide scope, including voice, data, video, etc. Nowadays high-speed data transferring becomes the major trend in UMTS network. More and more mobile subscribers access UMTS network to request Internet services such as email, file downloading or web browsing. Therefore, UMTS is characterized by a migration from voice-only network to an integrated services IP network. In this paper, we focus on studying the pure IP traffic. For designing the UMTS network, in addition to fulfill the QoS at the user level, in the UTRAN the Iub interface, which is between the NodeB and the RNC, also has to fulfill the strict delay requirements to guarantee the radio frames to be delivered on time to the air interface. Therefore, the QoS at the UTRAN is also a very critical issue to be specifically considered in UMTS network. An essential step to predict the network performance and the achievable QoS in the UTRAN is to study the properties of the aggregated traffic on the Iub link. In UMTS, a number of mobile users are active in a base station area, i.e. NodeB, each of the users generating different traffic streams related to different applications. The traffic from all users served by the same base station is aggregated and then transported via AAL2/ATM at the Iub link. This aggregated traffic can be seen as superposition of traffic streams of all users. The fundamental idea of traffic modeling lies in building models that can capture the important statistical properties of the underlying measured trace data. For this purpose, an analytically tractable model is preferred to accurately capture the properties of the aggregated traffic on the Iub link.

T. Braun et al. (Eds.): WWIC 2006, LNCS 3970, pp. 190–201, 2006.

However, the characterization of the aggregated traffic can not be represented with the simple Poisson traffic model any more, since the Poisson model is typically used for studying the classical telephone networks and it is not able to capture any burstiness or self-similarity properties of the IP traffic.

Several approaches for traffic modeling and characterization for UMTS have been outlined by 3GPP [1]. However, these traffic models are not derived from real measurements or simulations and are not analytically tractable. Recently, Alexander Klemm proposes the BMAP model for the aggregated traffic of UMTS in [2]. However, the parameters of the BMAP model are not derived from the measurements of the existing UMTS system, but obtained by the measured Internet traffic at the ISP dial-in modem/ISDN link with certain scaling procedure, which is used to adapt the bandwidth of the dial-in modem/ISDN links to different bandwidth classes with respect to different radio access bearers available in UMTS. Therefore, this approach is only based on investigating the incoming IP packets but does not take into consideration of the influence of the radio aspects on the air interface and the lower layer protocols like FP, and AAL2/ATM layer in UTRAN. The contribution of this paper is two-fold: First, the characteristic of the aggregated traffic of UTRAN network is analyzed on the basis of the trace data measured from the simulations using a UMTS simulation model built with OPNET. The simulation model comprises all basic radio aspects of UMTS and the measured trace data is the observation of arrivals of radio frames of all users to the UTRAN. Second, the BMAP model is implemented and customized to analyze the aggregated traffic of the UMTS network, which considers the different length of radio frames and arrivals. For customizing the model, the Expectation Maximization (EM) method is used to estimate parameters for the BMAP model.

The remainder of the paper is organized as follows: the next section will give a detailed analysis of the characteristics of the aggregated traffic carried in the UTRAN. Section 3 gives an introduction of the BMAP model. Afterwards we will describe the setup and customization of the BMAP model for single user and multiple users, individually. In section 5, the main results of the aggregate traffic model of UMTS using BMAP are presented and a comparison with simulations and Poisson traffic model is given. The end gives an outlook of potential applications of the presented analytical approach and a discussion on the benefit of using the BMAP model.

2   Aggregated UMTS Traffic Characteristics

The protocol structure of the UTRAN is given in Figure 1. After the data arrives at the RNC from the network, the Radio Link Control (RLC) layer will segment the IP packet into appropriate RLC Packet Data Unit (PDU)s and then pass them to the Medium Access Control (MAC) layer. The MAC layer in the RNC schedules the traffic to the UEs for the air interface. Because data loss and excessive delay at the Iub link will result in retransmissions which leads to a waste of radio resources or capacity, all traffic scheduled for the air interface or received from the air interface has to obey real-time QoS requirements. For the purpose of air interface traffic scheduling, the MAC controls the characteristics of the traffic, i. e. transmission time interval (TTI) and the amount of user data to be sent per TTI. The TTI determines the time between two consecutive radio frames that is sent to the air interface. TTI value and the amount of user data per TTI are based on the Radio Access Bearer (RAB).

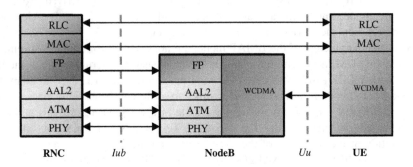

Fig. 1. UTRAN Protocol Stack

Each user traffic stream (voice, video or data) is carried by a so-called Dedicated Transport Channel (DCH) between RNC and Node B. The Frame Protocol (FP) provides for adaptation and exchange of control information for each DCH. The DCH traffic stream is handed over from the FP layer to the Transport Network Layer (TNL) in the form of FP PDUs. Due to the MAC scheduling, the FP PDUs arrive periodically and each FP PDU carries the amount of user traffic to be sent on the air interface for one TTI. In UMTS release 99, ATM constitutes the current TNL technology in the UTRAN. The AAL2 segments the FP PDUs into AAL2 packets. These AAL2 layer packets are then packed into ATM cells before being transmitted to the Iub link.

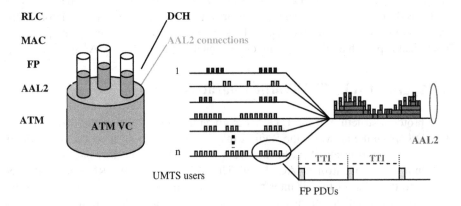

Fig. 2. Aggregated Traffic on the UTRAN Iub Link

As shown in Figure 2, the DCH traffic stream from each user is aggregated at the AAL2 layer. Since the FP PDUs of each user periodically arrives at the common AAL2 layer, the aggregated traffic is seen as superposition of arriving FP PDUs streams of all users.

In the last decade, there are already many researches on the characterization of measured IP traffic in local and wide area networks. The most important result of these studies is that the IP traffic has fractal-like behavior, which indicates the burstiness, long-range dependence and self-similarity. That means, the measured IP traffic rates look statistically the same in all time scales, i.e. both small and large time scale (i.e. "self-similarity" [10]), in both LAN and WAN environments. Usually, the degree of self similarity is mathematically represented by Husrt Parameter. The self similarity of IP traffic can be caused by the heavy tail file size distributions at the application layer, the other possible reasons are the TCP congestion control and TCP retransmission scheme for reliable transportation.

In the UTRAN, the FP PDU is sent every TTI due to the MAC scheduling. When transferring IP traffic, the IP packet arrival is converted into corresponding shaped FP PDU streams. Each Round Trip Time, one or several TCP packets will be sent in a time, which cause the burst of the traffic. However, because N* TTI << RTT, the arrival of FP PDUs at the AAL2 layer still behaves bursty, as seen in Figure 3.

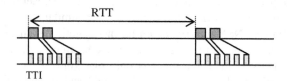

Fig. 3. Characteristics of FP PDU Stream

From the above analysis, the aggregated traffic, i.e. the superposition of FP PDU streams of all users, inherit the bursty and self-similarity property of the IP traffic. This will be proved in section 5.

3   Introduction of BMAP Model

The Batch Markovian Arrival Process (BMAP) is the generalization of Phase-type (PH) distribution [3]. PH distribution is usually used to analyze an absorbing Markov chain, i.e. a Markov chain that includes at least one absorbing state. For example, an absorbing Markov chain with states (1, 2 ... N, N+1), where the states (1, 2...N) are transient states and state (N+1) is the absorbing state. It is possible to transit from each non-absorbing state to the absorbing state in one or more time-steps. The distribution of time from transient state i to absorbing state (N+1) is called PH distribution. The infinitesimal generator of PH distribution is given by:

$$Q = \begin{pmatrix} T & T^0 \\ 0 & 0 \end{pmatrix} \quad (1)$$

Here, matrix T is an N*N matrix which represents the transitions among the transient states. Matrix T^0 is a column vector of size N which represents the transitions from the transient states to the absorbing state (N+1).

BMAP is the generalization of PH distribution. It is characterized by a finite and absorbing Markov chain [4]. Considering a two-dimensional Markov process {P(t),J(t)} with state space {(i,j); i≥0,1<=j<=N}, here P(t) counts the number of arrivals in the interval (0,t), and J(t) represents the underlying Markov chain. An infinitesimal generator Q has the following structure:

$$Q = \begin{Bmatrix} D(0) & D(1) & D(2) & D(3) & \dots \\ 0 & D(0) & D(1) & D(2) & \dots \\ 0 & 0 & D(0) & D(1) & \dots \\ 0 & 0 & 0 & D(0) & \dots \\ \dots & \dots & \dots & \dots & \dots \end{Bmatrix} \tag{2}$$

Here, D(0), similar to matrix T in PH distribution, is an N*N matrix (the dimension equals to the number states of J(t)), which has negative diagonal elements and nonnegative off-diagonal elements. D(0) represents a transient state transitions without packet arrivals. D(m) (m≥1), similar to matrix T^0 in PH distribution, is an also N*N matrix, which has nonnegative elements representing a state transition with an packet arrival of batch size m. In case m=1, it is Markovian Arrival Process (MAP), in which there is only one kind of batch arrivals. If π is defined as the initial probability vector of the underlying Markov chain {J(t)}, π should satisfy

$$\pi \cdot D = 0, \pi \cdot 1 = 1 \tag{3}$$

Here $D = \sum_{m=0}^{\infty} D(m)$, and the 1 is a column vector of ones.

The basic characteristics of a BMAP are described by the following equations:

- Probability density function:

$$f_m(t) = e^{D(0)t} \cdot D(m) \tag{4}$$

- Complementary cumulative distribution function (CCDF):

$$F^c(t) = e^{D(0)t} \tag{5}$$

- The cumulative distribution function of the inter-arrival time for the batch size m is [5]:

$$F(t) = \pi \left(1 - e^{D(0)t}\right)\left(- D(0)\right)^{-1} D(m)1 \tag{6}$$

Here, I is the unit matrix and 1 is the 1 is a column vector of ones.

- The arrival rate of the process is

$$\rho = \pi \sum_{m=1}^{\infty} mD(m)1 \tag{7}$$

The BMAP model is characterized by parameters D(0), which represents the transition probability between the transient states without arrivals, and D(m), which is the transition probability within an arrival of packet with batch size m. The BMAP can capture the packet arrival process and packet length process. In the previous researches, the BMAP model has been applied to analyze the aggregated traffic modeling of IP networks [9]. In this paper, BMAP model is proposed to use to analyze the UMTS traffic:

- UMTS provides different RAB types for transmission the user data. For different RAB types, the TTI and the amount of user traffic to be sent on the air interface for one TTI (i.e. FP PDU size) is different.
- BMAP model defines D(0) and D(m) (m≥1). D(m) represents the packet arrival process. And m corresponds to the different length of the packet of measured traffic., e.g. when m = 3, that means there are three different packet lengths, i.e. FP PDU size corresponding to three different RAB types in the UMTS network.

4 Setup of the BMAP Model

This section gives a brief description of how to setup and customize the BMAP model for single user and multiple users, individually.

4.1 BMAP Model for Single User

As explained above, the UMTS user traffic is aggregate at the AAL2 layer. More specifically, the FP PDU streams of all users arrive at the common AAL2 buffer and then multiplexed into an AAL2 path which corresponds to an ATM VC. Due to the shaping applied on the ATM VC, i.e. using a fixed rate according to Peak Cell Rate of the VC, the service time is deterministic. Thus, the system can be modeled as BMAP/D/1 model. The content of the AAL2 buffer content is increased by new arrival of FP PDU from certain user, and decreased by the regular departure to the ATM layer. This means, the changes of the buffer contents can indicate the new arrival of FP PDU from the aggregated FP PDU streams of all users.

When there is only one user in the system, we can set up a 2 states- BMAP model as an example, as shown in Figure 4. Here, state 1 and 2 correspond to high buffer content state and low buffer content state, respectively.

With the above state transitions, we get $D(0) = \begin{pmatrix} -r & r \\ 0 & -\lambda \end{pmatrix}, D(1) = \begin{pmatrix} 0 & 0 \\ \lambda & 0 \end{pmatrix}$. Then the arrival rate can be calculated with equation (7).

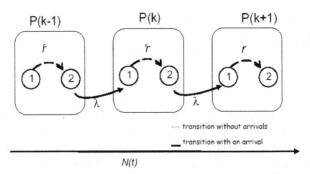

Fig. 4. States Transitions for BMAP Model (2 states) for Single User

4.2 BMAP Model for Multiple Users

For multiple users, the system becomes much more complex to obtain D(0) and D(m) with the above approach. Usually, parameter estimation method is used for estimating the model parameters based on the observations of the packet inter-arrival time and packet size from the measured traffic. There are a few current studies on the parameter estimation for the BMAP model. Ryden has employed Expectation Maximization (EM) algorithm for the MMPP model [6]. Breuer and Lindermann developed the method of EM algorithm for the BMAP [7] [8]. In this paper, the EM for BMAP is implemented based on the above two methods from Ryden and Lindermann. In principle, the EM algorithm is divided into E-step (Expectation) and M-step (Maximization). The E-step is to compute the expectation of likelihood function for the observed data; the M-step is to estimate the parameter by maximizing the expectation of the likelihood function from the E-step. These two steps are repeated until a predefined maximum number of iterations is reached or until a convergence criteria holds.

For setting up the BMAP model for multiple users, first problem is to determine how many states should be created in the BMAP model to reach an acceptable accuracy. The likelihood represents the accuracy of the BMAP model. Figure 5 gives a comparison of the likelihood of the BMAP model with 2, 3 and 4 states. As seen in Figure 5, when the number of states grows the likelihood increases. There is a big gap between the likelihood of using 2 states 2 and 3 states. On the other hand, further increase on the number of states (i.e. N > 4) will only lead to slight increase on the likelihood ([9]). It can be seen that the results using 3 states is close to using 4 states, and the likelihood is almost stabilized. As a compromise of computation effort and accuracy of the results, 3 states are chosen for setting up the BMAP model.

Another question of the BMAP model is the selection of initial parameter set. The initial parameter set is determined by the simple random initialization. That means the initial parameter D(0) and D(m) is generated randomly. Figure 6 shows the likelihood of BMAP model with 3 different random initial estimates. It can be seen that, with different random initial values, the final convergence trend tend to be almost identical, though their likelihoods differ at the early iteration steps. On the other hand, with different initial parameters, the iteration steps that the likelihood value reach the

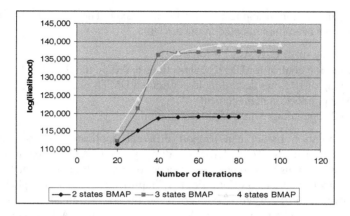

Fig. 5. Likelihood for different number of states

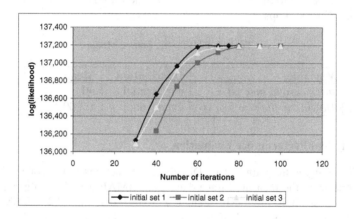

Fig. 6. Likelihood for different initial parameter sets

convergence is not identical. For example, the blue line reach the convergence up to 60 iterations and the purple line reach the same convergence up to 80 iterations. In a word, the initial parameters don't have impact on the final convergence but on the iteration steps reaching the similar convergence. In our estimations, the convergence is reached when the likelihood values of consequent steps differs up to 10^{-3}.

5 Results Analysis

5.1 Simulation Model and Traffic Source Model

The simulation model, which is used for generating the traces, was built according to UTRAN release 99 using the OPNET simulator (version 10.0). The UTRAN models were set up based on the OPNET ATM workstation/server model, which allows a flexible configuration of applications on the user layer. The following UMTS specific functions have been implemented in the model:

1) Modeling of RLC, MAC, FP for UMTS
2) Admission control for UMTS connections based on the flow level
3) Shaping of IP flows according to configured UMTS rates
4) AAL2 connection management
5) AAL2 scheduling with QoS differentiation.

This simulation model can support different application types and transport technologies such as TCP, UDP or directly over ATM. For different QoS requirements, various RAB types are available for transmitting different applications.

In this paper, we focus on IP traffic. For simplification, the user application is FTP running over TCP/IP, where the distribution of the download file size and their average value are given in Table 1. And all users use the RAB 128kbps to transfer data. That means, only one FP PDU length will be considered in this paper. Only one NodeB is connected to the RNC with a PVC on the Iub link with a reserved maximum bandwidth of 1500[1] kbps.

Table 1. FTP Traffic Source Model

Variable	Distribution	Mean
Inter-arrival time (s)	exponential	30
Download file size(bytes)	exponential	10000

5.2 Analytical Performance Evaluation

Figure 7 compares the Cumulative Distribution Functions (CDF) of FP PDU inter-arrival time from the measured trace data, from BMAP using EM algorithm and the Poisson process. It is obviously seen in Figure 7 that the CDF of BMAP model accurately matches the CDF of the measured traffic; while the CDF of Poisson process behave much more smooth than the measured traffic, which means the Poisson process conceals the bursty property of the traffic. It shows the advantages of using the BMAP model compared with Poisson process to analyze the aggregated UMTS traffic.

Figure 8 plots sample paths of the aggregated UMTS traffic stream taken from the simulations (left) and sample paths of the aggregated traffic stream applying the parameterized BMAP model (right). The figure shows that the customized BMAP captures the average transferred data volume within 1 second. The burstiness of the measured FP PDU rate and the analytical FP PDU rate obtained by the BMAP are similar. The mean arrival FP PDU rate of the measured traffic is 703.90packet/sec, while the mean arrival FP PDU rate of BMAP is 722packets/sec. The standard deviation of arrival FP PDU rate of the measured traffic is 7657.9packets/sec and from BMAP is 7520.5packets/sec.

---

[1] The remaining bandwidth of the modeled E1 line (420 kbps) is consumed for general signaling purposes and dedicated control channels.

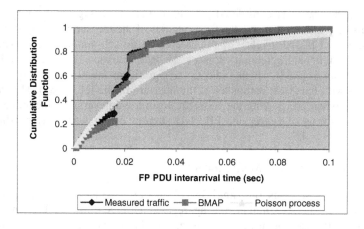

Fig. 7. CDF of FP PDU inter-arrival time

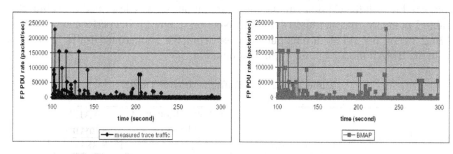

Fig. 8. Sample paths of the measured user traffic (left) and the customized BMAP (right)

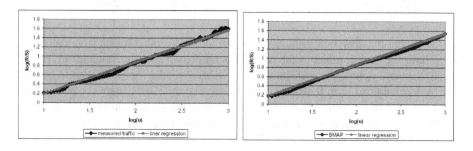

Fig. 9. R/S statistic plot of the measured user traffic (left) and the customized BMAP (right)

These observations are emphasized by the analysis of traffic burstiness, i.e. self-similarity, which is expressed in terms of the Hurst parameter H, which is calculated

as $E\left[\left(\frac{R}{S}(u)\right)\right] \to c \cdot u^H$, where R/S is rescaled adjusted range statistics. When

0.5<H<1, the traffic is considered as self-similar. This is generally referred as the Hurst effect. Figure 9 presents the R/S statistics of the measured user traffic (left) and the customized BMAP (right). The degree of traffic self-similarity can expressed by the slopes of linear regression plots of the R/S statistics. The value of H for the BMAP model is 0.68, which indicates a significant amount of traffic burstiness, compared with the Hurst parameter of the measure traffic (H = 0.69). This result also shows that when transferring the IP traffic from the uplayers, the incoming traffic of UTRAN in forms of aggregated FP PDU streams at the AAL2 layer exhibits self-similarity as H > 0.5.

5.3 Application of the BMAP Model

One of the applications of using BMAP model in simulation is to generate the background traffic to simulate the aggregated UMTS traffic at Iub link and then combined with the explicit traffic from the simulation model. This hybrid simulation method can greatly improve the simulation efficiency and save the simulation time. Following gives an example of using the BMAP trace as the background traffic and compared it with the explicit simulations. Simulation setup is described in section 5.1. Table 2 compares the measured Transport Network Layer (TNL) performance such as AAL2 delay and ATM throughput obtained from the background traffic generated from the BMAP model and the explicit simulation.

Table 2. Measured Traffic vs. BMAP Traffic

		ATM VC Throughput (bits/sec)	AAL2 delay(ms)
mean	Measured traffic	142.721	15.381
	BMAP	134.923	15.533
deviation	Measured traffic	66.787	3.414
	BMAP	49.926	2.849

It is seen that the analytical simulations using the background traffic from the BMAP trace have the similar effect as the real traffic on the network performance in terms of throughput and delay. This indicates that the BMAP model can be applied to generate the background traffic in the simulations to achieve the similar network performance but save a lot of the simulation effort and enhance the simulation speed. The further application of the BMAP model is to use it as an analytical model to directly calculate the performance for such system as BMAP/D/1.

6 Conclusions and Outlook

The characteristic of the aggregated UMTS traffic is discussed at the beginning of the paper. It implies that the aggregated traffic of UMTS network exhibits the self-similarity, which is proved in the results. In order to analytically capture the property of the aggregated traffic of UMTS, the BMAP model is presented and implemented.

This paper shows how to describe the system's behavior aiming at analytical tractable BMAP model for source traffic and radio link characterization. The obtained results from the BMAP model is shown to match very well with the measured trace traffic, which gives the first demonstration that the BMAP model is able to accurately capture the characteristics of the aggregated traffic carried in the UTRAN. And therefore the BMAP model can be used an appropriate analytical method to represent the aggregated traffic for UMTS. However, this paper only gives the first result of using the BMAP method for single RAB type in UMTS, i.e. there is no batch since all packets have the same length. The further work is to validate the BMAP model for multiple RAB types with different packet sizes, as well as different applications. Furthermore, it will be important to validate the BMAP approach with the traces from the real-world system to improve the reliability of the results.

References

1. 3GPP, http://www.3gpp.org
2. A. Klemm, C. Lindemann, and M. Lohmann, Traffic Modeling and Characterization for UMTS Networks, Proc. of the Globecom, Internet Performance Symposium, San Antonio TX, pp. 1741-1746, Nov. 2001
3. Alma Riska, "Aggregate Matrix-analytic Techniques and their Applications"
4. D. M. Lucantoni, New Results on the Single Server Queue with a Batch Markovian Arrival Process, Comm. in Statistics: Stochastic Models 7, 1-46, 1991.
5. SH Kang, YH Kim, DK Sung, and BD Choi, "An application of Markovian Arrival Process (MAP) to modeling superposed ATM cell streams," IEEE Trans. Commun., vol.50, no. 4, pp. 633-642, Apr. 2002
6. T. Ryden, An EM Algorithm for Parameter Estimation in Markov Modulated Poisson Processes, Computational Statistics and Data Analysis 21, 431-447, 1996
7. Lothar Breuer: An EM algorithm for Batch Markovian Arrival Processes and its comparison to a simpler estimation procedure, Annals of Operations Research 112 (2002), pp.123—138
8. C. Lindemann, and M. Lohmann, "Numerical Robust Parameter Estimation for the Batch Markovian Arrival Process Using Randomization
9. A. Klemm, C. Lindemann, and M. Lohmann, Modeling IP Traffic Using the Batch Markovian Arrival Process (extended version), Performance Evaluation, 54, pp. 149-173, 2003
10. W. Willinger, V. Paxson, and M.S. Taqqu, Self-similarity and Heavy Tails: Structural Modeling of Network Traffic, In: A Practical Guide to Heavy Tails, 27-53, Chapman &Hall 1998.

On the Optimal Allocation of Downlink Resources in OFDM-Based Wireless Networks

Patrick Hosein*

Huawei Technologies,
10180 Telesis Court, Suite 365, San Diego, CA 92121, USA
phosein@huawei.com

Abstract. Orthogonal Frequency Division Multiplexing (OFDM) is used in both 802.11 and 802.16 [1] wireless network standards and is being evaluated for Fourth Generation (4G) networks. Its tolerance to frequency selective fading has made it an attractive choice for these broadband wireless networks. In both downlink and uplink directions, resources can be allocated in three dimensions, frequency, time and power. In both cases the resource allocation is performed primarily by the BS. In this paper we focus on the allocation of downlink resources when such a network is used for Quality of Service (QoS) applications. We formulate and solve the corresponding optimization problem and use the solution to design simple, practical algorithms. In doing so we take into account practical details that have not been addressed in previous work.

1 Introduction

The recently defined 802.16 standards use OFDM for the physical layer transmissions because it has been shown to be robust against frequency selective fading. These networks will provide users with high data rates with a much wider coverage than WiFi networks (802.11). They will also support QoS services and 802.16e will provide support for limited mobility. In OFDM networks, resources are scheduled in the frequency, time and power domains. In the downlink, the rate achieved by a user increases with the number of sub-channels (frequency domain) assigned, the number of time slots (time domain) assigned and the fraction of base station (BS) power allocated. The same is true for the uplink except that there is a limit on the total transmission power of each subscriber station (SS). Both uplink and downlink resource allocation is performed by the BS.

Several papers have been published on the downlink scheduling problem (e.g., [2], [3], [4], [5]). However those papers focused on maximizing the sum rate capacity while we will focus on maximizing a more general utility-based objective function for which sum-rate capacity is a special case. Note that [3] does consider optimization over utility-based objective functions but their formulation does not take into account the fact that each frame transmission

---

* This work was performed while the author was employed with Ericsson Inc.

T. Braun et al. (Eds.): WWIC 2006, LNCS 3970, pp. 202–213, 2006.

consists of multiple time slots and their proposed solutions are too compute intensive for practical purposes. In addition we take into account finite queue size situations.

Our paper is different in several aspects. We assume that sub-channels, made up of multiple sub-carriers, are assigned to users in discrete time slots. Each sub-channel/time-slot pair will be referred to as simply a slot. Therefore the number of available slots is the product of the number of sub-channels and the number of time-slots. In practice, some of these slots are needed for control and signaling information. In that case the approach herein described should be applied only to those slots available for data. We assume that each slot can be assigned to at most one user. Secondly, we assume each user is assigned a utility function of their throughput and the objective is to maximize the total utility over all users. Note that throughput maximization is a special case in which the utility function is simply the average throughput. However, we are interested in more sophisticated utility functions such as the logarithm function which provides proportionally fair user throughputs [6] and those containing Barrier functions for QoS support [8].

In this paper we assume that the sub-carriers of a sub-channel are chosen randomly over the allocated frequency spectrum (i.e., the distributed permutation option in the 802.16 standard [7]). The sub-channnel SINR is therefore an average of the SINRs of its sub-carriers. In light of this, we assume that for each user the forward link path gain as well as the intercell interference experienced by the SS is the same for all sub-channels assigned to that SS. Note that since the forward link transmissions are orthogonal in the frequency domain then there is no intra-cell interference. This implies that the received Signal to Interference and Noise ratio (SINR) for a given sub-channel transmission power is the same for all sub-channels. The total power allocated over all sub-channels must also not exceed the power available at the BS for data transmissions.

Finally we take into account a constraint imposed by the 802.16 standard for the Partially Used Subchannelization (PUSC) mode of operation. With this mode each user is allocated slots sequentially along the sub-channel dimension before being allocated slots in the subsequent time-slot. This is best illustrated pictorially as in Figure 1. Although we do not explicitly include this constraint, we show how the solution we obtain can conform to it.

The optimization must be performed over two dimensions, the assignment of slots to users and the allocation of power to slots. It has been shown in [5] that the performance gain (over a static allocation) obtained from the latter optimization is small compared to the gain from the former optimization. Therefore we use the following approach. We first assume that the power is equally spread over all sub-channels in each time slot and solve the resulting slot allocation problem. Once this solution is obtained we then solve the power allocation problem given this slot allocation. This does not provide the optimal solution but since we solve the slot allocation problem first we expect the solution to be close to optimal. In the next section we formulate the slot allocation problem, present the optimality conditions and then provide a simple algorithm that can be used to determine optimal user slot allocations.

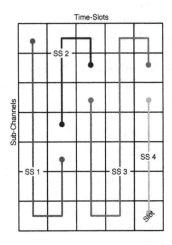

Fig. 1. Slot Allocation Pattern

2   The Slot Allocation Problem

We assume N users and M sub-channels with T time slots per frame. The BS can allocate at most P watts for the downlink sub-channels in each time-slot. We denote the power allocated to each slot by $p = P/M$. For each user we assume that the SINR of the signal received by a particular SS is the same for all sub-channels (i.e., they experience the same path losses, shadow fading and intercell interference). We denote the SINR of the signal received at the BS per unit transmission power by g. Hence if a transmission power of p is used to transmit a packet over a sub-channel then the SINR of the received signal is pg.

We assume that the channel state of each sub-channel is reported by each SS and used to compute the SINR of each sub-channel. Given this, together with the transmission power allocated to the sub-channel, we can then compute the maximum payload for that transmission. This mapping depends on several factors such as the modulation and coding scheme. However, in [8] it is shown that the shape of this mapping function between SINR and rate closely follows the Shannon capacity function with some effective bandwidth B. We also assume that the overhead percentage is constant for all modulation and coding schemes and include this factor in B so that the Shannon function provides the data payload rate. In addition, the factor B takes into account the logarithm factor since we will be using natural logarithms instead of base 2 logarithms. We will denote the Shannon rate, normalized to the effective bandwidth B, by d and hence we have $d = \ln(1 + pg)$.

Note that a similar approach is taken in [9]. In their approach they discount the SINR of the received signal by an amount β that depends on the required bit error rate (BER) using the following formula

$$\beta = \frac{1.5}{-\ln(5BER)}.$$

This takes into account the efficiency of the modulation and coding scheme used. In this case the normalized rate is given by $d = \ln(1 + \beta pg)$. Our methodology can also be used with this model by normalizing the received SINR values g with the constant β instead of using an effective bandwidth approach.

Note that the achievable slot rate of a SS is the same for all slot positions since the power and SINR are the same for all slots. Therefore we need only determine the number of slots that should be allocated to a user. Once this number is determined we can then allocate the user's slots in the specific manner as depicted in Figure 1. We denote the number of slots allocated to SS i by x_i. Therefore the total (normalized) rate achieved by the SS is given by $d_i(x_i) = x_i \ln(1 + pg_i)$. where p is the slot transmission power, and g_i is the per slot SINR for all slots within the frame.

The average throughput of a user at the start of the frame being scheduled is denoted by r. We assign a throughput dependent utility function to each user. This function, which may be different for different SSs, represents the utility to that user of the corresponding throughput achieved. It is denoted by $U(r)$. Note that utility functions that are dependent on other metrics (such as queue size, delay, etc.) are also covered by the approach described in this paper but will not be discussed due to space limitations.

Let r_i and $\tilde{r}_i$ denote the SS's average throughput before and after the frame transmission respectively. This throughput is updated based on x_i as follows:

$$\tilde{r}_i(x_i) = \alpha r_i + (1 - \alpha)d_i(x_i) = \alpha r_i + (1 - \alpha)x_i \ln(1 + pg_i), \quad 0 < \alpha < 1, \quad (1)$$

where α is the filter constant that is chosen based on the desired time frame over which the utility requirement is averaged.

The size of the data queue of a user before transmission of the concerned frame is denoted by q. The final constraint that we consider is the fact that the amount of data queued for each user is finite. Therefore we need to ensure that a user is only scheduled slots when data is available to fill them. For a given allocation x_i, the achievable rate is $Bd_i(x_i)$ kbps. If we denote the total service duration by τ then the queue constraint becomes $Bd_i(x_i)\tau \leq q_i$. For simplicity we assume that the amount of data, q_i, can exactly fit in an integer number of SS i's slots. This can be satisfied by padding the queued data accordingly. Let us summarize the notation that has so far been introduced and then formulate the optimization problem.

N	= number of SSs
M	= number of downlink sub-channels
T	= number of time-slots per frame
P	= BS transmission power available for data sub-channels
B	= effective Shannon bandwidth per sub-channel
g_i	= forward link SINR (per unit transmission power) of SS i
r_i	= average throughput of user i before the frame transmission
$\tilde{r}_i$	= average throughput of user i after the frame transmission
$U_i(r)$	= utility function of user i as a function of throughput r
q_i	= queue size of user i before frame transmission

x_i = total number of slots allocated to user i

$\boldsymbol{x}$ = $[x_1, \ldots, x_N]$

τ = duration of a downlink frame

The optimization problem can be stated as follows:

$$\max_{\boldsymbol{x} \in \{0,1,\ldots,MT\}^N} F(\boldsymbol{x}) \equiv \sum_{i=1}^{N} U_i(\tilde{r}_i(x_i)) \tag{2}$$

$$\text{s.t.} \quad \tilde{r}_i(x_i) = \alpha r_i + (1 - \alpha)x_i \ln(1 + pg_i) \quad 0 \le \alpha \le 1,$$

$$\text{with} \quad \sum_{i=1}^{N} x_i \le MT \quad \text{and} \quad Bx_i \ln(1 + pg_i)\tau \le q_i.$$

Note that this is an integer programming problem. We instead consider the following close approximation. We relax the integer constraint and use a modified utility function. Let $\hat{U}(x)$ denote the function that is equal to $U(x)$ at integer values of x and piecewise linear between integer values. Note that when we write $U(x)$ we actually mean $U(\tilde{r}(x))$ but use the simpler notation for convenience.

$$\hat{U}(x) \equiv U(\lfloor x \rfloor) + (x - \lfloor x \rfloor)[U(\lceil x \rceil) - U(\lfloor x \rfloor)].$$

We replace $U(x)$ with $\hat{U}(x)$ in 2 and relax the integer constraint. We will also use the following fact. If we assume that $U(x)$ is non-decreasing in x then the objective function $F(x)$ is also non-decreasing in x. Therefore suppose that the optimal solution $\boldsymbol{x}^*$ is such that $\sum_{i=1}^{N} x_i^* < MT$ then we can increase the number of slots allocated to one or more SSs without decreasing the objective function value. Hence there exists a solution for which this constraint is binding (i.e. $\sum_{i=1}^{N} x_i^* = MT$) and so we use equality for this constraint. Note that this requires the implicit assumption that sufficient data is available in all data queues to fill the frame. In Figure 2 we plot the piecewise linear function $\hat{U}(\tilde{r}(x)) - \hat{U}(\tilde{r}(0))$ together with $U(\tilde{r}(x)) - U(\tilde{r}(0))$ for the proportional fair utility function. Notice that the approximation is good especially for large values of x. The resulting optimization problem is give by

$$\max_{\boldsymbol{x} \in [0,MT]^N} F(\boldsymbol{x}) \equiv \sum_{i=1}^{N} \hat{U}_i(\tilde{r}_i(x_i)) \tag{3}$$

$$\text{s.t.} \quad \tilde{r}_i(x_i) = \alpha r_i + (1 - \alpha)x_i \ln(1 + pg_i) \quad 0 < \alpha < 1,$$

$$\text{with} \quad \sum_{i=1}^{N} x_i = MT \quad \text{and} \quad Bx_i \ln(1 + pg_i)\tau \le q_i.$$

Next we show that there exits an optimal solution to this problem in which all user allocations are integral. Suppose that only one SS has a non-integer allocation then, because the equality $\sum_{i=1}^{N} x_i^* = MT$ must hold, the solution is not feasible. Therefore at least two SSs must have non-integer allocations. For convenience suppose that SSs one and two have non-integer allocations. For

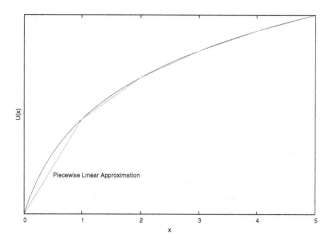

Fig. 2. Utility Function and it Piecewise Linear Approximation

non-integer values of x, $\hat{U}(x)$ has a unique derivative. Let $U_1'(x_1^*)$ and $U_2'(x_2^*)$ denote the utility function derivatives for users 1 and 2 at their optimal allocations. If these derivatives are not equal then the total utility can be increased by increasing the allocation of the user with the larger derivative and decreasing by the same amount the allocation of the user with the smaller derivative. However this is a contradiction since we assumed that the allocations were optimal. The only other possibility is that the derivatives are equal. In this case we can increase the allocation of one of them and decrease the allocation of the other up to the point where at least one of the two allocations is integral. Note that since the derivatives are both constant throughput this range (since $\hat{U}(x)$ is linear between integral values of x) then the total utility remains constant and hence the objective function remains at its optimal value. We can repeat this for all pairs of non-integer allocations until we obtain integer allocations for all users.

2.1   Optimality Conditions

Note that the derivative of $\hat{U}(x)$ is discontinuous at integer values of x. Hence let $\hat{U}'(x)_+$ denote the right sub-gradient and $\hat{U}'(x)_-$ denote the left sub-gradient (i.e., all sub-gradients supported at this point lie between these two values) at x. The gradient is unique at all points other than at integer values of x. At integer values, with $x > 0$, the left and right sub-gradients are given by

$$\hat{U}'(x)_+ = U(x+1) - U(x)$$
$$\hat{U}'(x)_- = U(x) - U(x-1).$$

Therefore we have shown that Problem 3 is the maximization of a concave function (i.e., the sum of piecewise linear, concave utility functions) over a compact set. We can therefore use Lagrange Multiplier methods to determine the optimal solution. If we denote the optimal vector by $\boldsymbol{x}^*$ then there exists some $\gamma > 0$ such that

$$\gamma \in [\hat{U}_i'(x_i^*)_+, \hat{U}_i'(x_i^*)_-] \quad \text{iff} \quad 0 < B\tau d_i(x_i^*) < q_i, \tag{4}$$

$$\gamma < \hat{U}_i'(x_i^*)_- \quad \text{iff} \quad B\tau d_i(x_i^*) = q_i, \tag{5}$$

$$\gamma > \hat{U}_i'(x_i^*)_+ \quad \text{iff} \quad x_i^* = 0. \tag{6}$$

These are necessary and sufficient conditions for optimality for maximization of a concave function over a compact set.

We illustrate the optimality conditions with a simple example. We consider the case $N = 4$, $M = 4$, $T = 2$ and hence 8 slots must be assigned to the 4 users. In Figure 3 we illustrate a possible solution. The optimal allocations are listed along the x-axis while above the plot we provide the queue lengths, q_i, (in terms of number of slots) for each user. $x_1 = 0$ because the gradient of the user is not growing fast enough even at the origin. $x_2 = 1$ and is limited by its queue size. $x_3 = 3$ and $x_4 = 4$ so that the total number of slots allocated is 8 as required. Note that for x_3 and x_4 there exists sub-gradients of value γ.

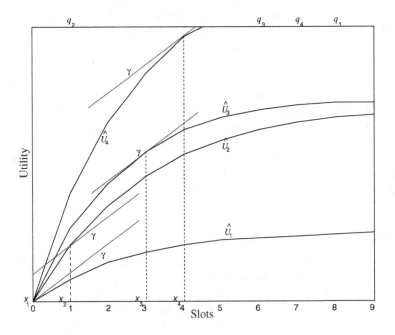

Fig. 3. Example of an Optimal Slot Allocation Solution

2.2   Optimal Solution Computation

We will allocate one slot at a time and show by induction that the solution obtained when all slots are allocated is optimal. Let k denote the number of slots that have so far been allocated. Note that if $k = 0$ then the optimal allocation is $x_i^* = 0$ for all users i and this allocation satisfies 6 since, if we assume $q_i > 0$ for all i, we can choose $\gamma = \infty$.

Let us now assume that the optimal allocation, x_i^*, for k sub-channels is known and we show how the optimal allocation for $k + 1$ sub-channels can be determined. Let $\gamma(k)$ denote the corresponding γ for the case of k sub-channels. Let $\mathcal{S}$ denote the set of users that still have data for transmission (i.e, for which $q_i > B\tau x_i^* \ln(1 + pg_i)$). We choose $\gamma(k + 1)$ as follows:

$$\gamma(k + 1) = \max_{i \in \mathcal{S}}\{\hat{U}_i'(x_i^*)_+\}. \tag{7}$$

and denote the SS for which this condition holds by i^*. We assign the new slot to user i^*. Observe that $\gamma(k) \geq \gamma(k + 1)$ since the utility function is concave. Consider those SSs $i \neq i^*$. For those users obeying condition 4 we have $\gamma(k + 1) \leq \gamma(k) \leq \hat{U}_i'(x_i^*)_-$ where the last inequality holds because we assume optimality for the case of k slots. Also $\gamma(k + 1) = \hat{U}_{i^*}'(x_{i^*}^*)_+ \geq \hat{U}_i'(x_i^*)_+$ and so these SSs continue to satisfy 4. If an SS obeys condition 5 then again this condition holds for the $k + 1$ case because $\gamma(k + 1) \leq \gamma(k) < \hat{U}_i'(x_i^*)_-$. If an SS obeys 6 then $\gamma(k + 1) = \hat{U}_{i^*}'(x_{i^*}^*)_+ \geq \hat{U}_i'(x_i^*)_+$ and so this condition holds for those users for the $k + 1$ slots case. Now consider the chosen user i^*. If it previously obeyed condition 4 then note that $\hat{U}_i'(x_{i^*}^*)_+ = \hat{U}_i'(x_{i^*}^* + 1)_-$ and so this user still obeys 4. Note that it could not have obeyed 5 since it would not have been included in $\mathcal{S}$. Finally if it had obeyed 6 then an argument similar to that used for condition 4 can be used to show that it will now obey condition 4.

We repeat this process until $k = MT$ or no more data is available from any SS for transmission. Once the number of slots for each SS is determined, the specific slot assignments (sub-channel/time-slot pairs) can be made following the method outlined in Figure 1.

2.3 Numerical Examples

In this section we will consider two well known utility functions. First consider the function $U_i(r) = \theta_i r$ for some constant θ_i which may, for example reflect the importance of the SS. Suppose that all users have an infinite backlog of data then we have

$$\hat{U}_i'(x_i)_+ = (1 - \alpha)\theta_i \ln(1 + pg_i).$$

Therefore using the criterion in 7 to choose a user, the user with the largest weighted (by θ_i) rate will be chosen in each iteration and hence will be allocated all slots. Note that this reduces to the maximum sum-rate capacity problem when we set $\theta_i = \theta$ for all i. In this case the user with the largest achievable rate is allocated all slots and this provides the maximum throughput.

Next let us consider the Proportional Fair utility function $U_i(r) = \ln(r)$. In this case we have

$$\hat{U}_i'(x_i)_+ = \ln(\alpha r_i + (1 - \alpha)(x_i + 1)\ln(1 + pg_i)) - \ln(\alpha r_i + (1 - \alpha)x_i \ln(1 + pg_i))$$

Therefore

$$i^* = \arg\max_{i \in S}\{\hat{U}_i'(x_i)_+\} = \arg\max_{i \in S} \frac{(1-\alpha)\ln(1+pg_i)}{\alpha r_i + (1-\alpha)x_i\ln(1+pg_i)} = \arg\min_{i \in S}\{x_i + \kappa_i\}$$

where $\kappa_i \equiv \frac{\alpha r_i}{(1-\alpha)\ln(1+pg_i)}$ is an allocation independent, SS dependent variable.

In the limit as α goes to 1 (i.e., long term memory), this user will always be the user for which $\frac{\ln(1+pg_i)}{r_i}$ is largest. In other words the user with the largest slot rate to throughput ratio is allocated to all slots. In the limit as α goes zero (i.e., short term memory), the user for which x_i is smallest is chosen at each iteration. One can see that this attempts to divide the slots evenly among all users (i.e. for any two users the difference in their number of slot allocations is at most one). Each user then achieves a throughput proportional to its achievable slot rate in that frame. A value of α close to unity provides long term fairness but with a high throughput while the inverse is true for α close to zero. In general the solution will lie between these two extremes. In Figure 4 we provide an example of pseudo-code for the case of the proportional fair utility function. In this code we take into account another practical detail which is that there is a minimum rate below which transmissions are not allowed. Under the assumption that the power is evenly spread this minimum rate requirement can be stated in terms of a constraint on the minimum supportable gain (i.e., $g \geq g_{min}$).

```
S = ∅
for (i = 1 : N) {
    x_i = 0
    κ_i ≡ αr_i / ((1−α) ln(1+pg_i))
    if ((q_i ≥ Bτ ln(1 + pg_i)) && (g_i ≥ g_min))   {S = S ∪ {i}}
}
for (k = 1 : MT) {
    i* = arg min_{i∈S} {x_i + κ_i}
    x_{i*} = x_{i*} + 1
    if (q_{i*} < Bτ(x_{i*} + 1) ln(1 + pg_{i*}))   {S = S \ {i*}}
    if (S == ∅) {exit}
}
```

Fig. 4. Pseudo-code for the Slot Allocation Problem with Proportional Fair Utilities

3   The Power Allocation Problem

So far we have addressed the slot allocation problem under the assumption that the same power is assigned to each slot transmission. In general, the increase in performance obtained by optimizing over power is small so instead of performing the joint optimization problem (power and slot allocation) we will determine the optimal slot allocation using the method described in the previous section and then find the optimal power allocation.

Assume that users have been allocated to slots using the previously specified methodology. Denote the power allocated to the slot corresponding to sub-channel j in time-slot t by p_{jt} and let $\boldsymbol{P}$ denote the corresponding $M \times T$ matrix. Let $a_{jt}(i) = 1$ if user i is allocated to sub-channel j in time-slot t and zero otherwise. Also let u_{jt} denote the index of the user allocated to that slot. The optimization problem is given by:

$$\max_{\boldsymbol{P}} F(\boldsymbol{P}) \equiv \sum_{i=1}^{M} U_i(\tilde{r}_i(\boldsymbol{P})) \tag{8}$$

$$\text{s.t.} \quad \tilde{r}_i(\boldsymbol{P}) = \alpha r_i + (1-\alpha) \sum_{j=1}^{M} \sum_{t=1}^{T} a_{jt}(i) \ln(1 + p_{jt} g_i), \quad 0 \le \alpha \le 1,$$

$$\text{with} \quad \sum_{j=1}^{M} p_{jt} \le P \quad \text{for} \quad t = 1, \ldots T.$$

We ignore the queue size constraint since we assume that the power allocation optimization has a relatively small effect on the total rate of each SS and hence the carried payload is approximately equal to that for the slot allocation case.

Again using Lagrange Multiplier methods we can show that for each time-slot t the following must hold for all j:

$$\left. \frac{\partial F(\boldsymbol{P})}{\partial p_{jt}} \right|_{\boldsymbol{P}=\boldsymbol{P}^*} = \gamma \quad \text{iff} \qquad 0 < p_{jt} < P$$

$$\left. \frac{\partial F(\boldsymbol{P})}{\partial p_{jt}} \right|_{\boldsymbol{P}=\boldsymbol{P}^*} > \gamma \quad \text{iff} \qquad p_{jt} = P$$

$$\left. \frac{\partial F(\boldsymbol{P})}{\partial p_{jt}} \right|_{\boldsymbol{P}=\boldsymbol{P}^*} < \gamma \quad \text{iff} \qquad p_{jt} = 0.$$

Next note that

$$\frac{\partial F(\boldsymbol{P})}{\partial p_{jt}} = \left. \frac{dU_{u_{jt}}}{dr} \right|_{r=\tilde{r}_{u_{jt}}} \frac{d\tilde{r}}{dp_{jt}}$$

where $\tilde{r}$ is the total rate achieved by user u_{jt}. This can be closely approximated by the value that was obtained when optimizing the slot allocations. Denote the solution for that problem by $\boldsymbol{x}^*$ then we can approximate the rate after optimization over power by

$$\tilde{r}_{u_{jt}} \approx x^*_{u_{jt}} \ln(1 + g_{u_{jt}} P/m).$$

For convenience let us denote the derivative of $U_{u_{jt}}(\tilde{r})$ with respect to $\tilde{r}$ (evaluated at this approximation to $\tilde{r}$) by $\lambda_{u_{jt}}$ since it's value is dependent solely on the user (given the previously obtained allocations). Next note that $\tilde{r}$ depends on all the transmissions of user u_{jt}. However, its partial derivative with respect to p_{jt} depends only on the concerned slot. Hence we have

$$\frac{d\tilde{r}_{u_{jt}}}{dp_{jt}} = \frac{(1-\alpha)g_{u_{jt}}}{1 + p_{jt}g_{u_{jt}}}$$

and so the optimality conditions for $0 < p < P$ is given by

$$\lambda_{u_{jt}} \frac{g_{u_{jt}}}{1 + p_{jt} g_{u_{jt}}} = \gamma$$

where for convenience we have included the factor $(1 - \alpha)$ in a modified constant γ. Therefore

$$p_{jt} = \frac{\lambda_{u_{jt}}}{\gamma} - \frac{1}{g_{u_{jt}}}. \tag{9}$$

We now use the fact that $\sum_{j=1}^{M} p_{jt} = P$. Note that this constraint must be binding (i.e., hold with equality) otherwise the total utility can be increased by increasing the power of any of the transmissions in the time-slot which would be a contradiction to optimality. We have

$$P = \frac{1}{\gamma} \sum_{k=1}^{M} \lambda_{u_{kt}} - \sum_{k=1}^{M} \frac{1}{g_{u_{kt}}}.$$

Solving for γ and substituting back into 9 we obtain

$$p_{jt} = \frac{\lambda_{u_{jt}}}{\sum_{k=1}^{M} \lambda_{u_{kt}}} \left(P + \sum_{k=1}^{M} \frac{1}{g_{u_{kt}}} \right) - \frac{1}{g_{u_{jt}}}. \tag{10}$$

Hence we can directly obtain the optimal power allocation. Note that if we determine that $p_{jt} < 0$ for any slot then zero power should be used for that slot and the problem should be resolved with this constraint. We do not expect this to be the case for practical problems.

We can evaluate this allocation for different utility functions. In the case of the maximum sum-rate objective we have $\lambda_{u_{jt}} = 1$ for all sub-channels. Using this in 10 we get

$$p_{jt} = \frac{1}{M} \left(P + \sum_{k=1}^{M} \frac{1}{g_{u_{kt}}} \right) - \frac{1}{g_{u_{jt}}}$$

and so if all allocated users in the time-slot have similar SINR values then approximately P/M power is used for each sub-channel.

For the Proportional Fair utility function we have $\lambda_{u_{jt}} = 1/\tilde{r}_{u_{jt}}$. Using this in 10 we get

$$p_{jt} = \left[\sum_{k=1}^{M} \frac{\tilde{r}_{u_{jt}}}{\tilde{r}_{u_{kt}}} \right]^{-1} \left(P + \sum_{k=1}^{M} \frac{1}{g_{u_{kt}}} \right) - \frac{1}{g_{u_{jt}}}.$$

Hence the power allocations also take into account the throughputs of the SSs in addition to taking into account their channel conditions. In Figure 5 we show an example of pseudo-code for the power allocation algorithm in the case of proportionally fair utilities.

```
Let x denote slot allocations obtained by algorithm in Figure 4
t = 1;   j = 1
for (i = 1:N) {
    while (x_i > 0) {
        u_jt = i
        if (j < M)  {j = j + 1}   else   {j = 1; t = t + 1}
        x_i = x_i - 1
    }
}
for (t = 1 : T) {
    λ = 0;   μ = 0
    for (k = 1 : M)   {λ = λ + 1/r_{u_{kt}};   μ = μ + 1/g_{u_{kt}}}
    for (j = 1 : M)   {p_jt = (P+μ)/(r_{u_{jt}}λ) - 1/g_{u_{jt}}}
}
```

Fig. 5. Pseudo-code for the Power Allocation Problem with Proportional Fair Utilities

4   Conclusions and Future Work

We have formulated the downlink resource allocation problem for a OFDM-based wireless network and presented a simple solution that can be used to determine the optimal allocation in a practical system. Although we proved optimality for the slot allocation algorithm, we plan to simulate the algorithm to compare it with sub-optimal approaches.

References

1. A. Ghosh, et. al., "Broadband wireless access with WiMax/802.16: Current performance benchmarks and future potential," *IEEE Commun Mag.* Feb. 2005.
2. G. Munz, S. Pfletschinger and J. Speidel, "An efficient waterfilling algorithm for multiple access OFDM", *IEEE Globecom*, 2002.
3. G. Song and Y. (G). Li, "Cross-layer optimization for OFDM wireless network – part I and part II," *IEEE Trans. Wireless Commun.*, vol.4, no. 2, Mar. 2005.
4. J. Jang and K. Bok Lee, "Transmit power adaptation for multiuser OFDM systems," *IEEE J. Select. Areas Commun.*, vol. 21, Feb. 2003.
5. G. Song, Y. (G). Li, L. J. Cimini and H. Zheng, "Joint channel-aware and queue-aware data scheduling in multiple shared wireless channels," in *Proc., IEEE Wireless Commun. Networking Conf.*, Mar. 2004.
6. F. Kelly, "Charging and rate control for elastic traffic," *European Trans. On Telecommunications*, vol. 8, 1997.
7. IEEE Std. 802.16-2004, "IEEE Standard for Local and Metropolitan Area Networks – Part 16: Air Interface for Fixed Broadband Wireless Access Systems," Oct. 2004.
8. P. Hosein, "Capacity of Packetized Voice Services over Time-Shared Wireless Packet Data Channels," *Proc. IEEE INFOCOM*, March, 2005.
9. X. Qiu and K. Chawla, "On the performance of adaptive modulation in cellular systems," *IEEE Trans. Commun.*, vol. 47, no. 6, Jun. 1999.

Scheme for Joint Optimization of MAP Overhead and System Throughput in Message Based MIMO-OFDM Systems

Chung Ha Koh, Kyung Ho Sohn, Ji Wan Song, and Young Yong Kim

Dept. of Electrical and Electronic Engineering,
Yonsei University, Seoul, Korea 120-749
{ski244, heroson7, wanbabo, y2k}@yonsei.ac.kr

Abstract. We propose a novel resource allocation scheme, which can reduce MAP overhead and maximize the throughput in the MIMO-OFDM systems. Message based broadband access systems are needed to minimize the MAP overhead since the excessive MAP overhead causes degradation of system throughput. Increasing the size of resource allocation unit can reduce MAP overhead. However, multiuser diversity gain becomes smaller as the size of resource allocation unit increases. Therefore, we investigate joint optimization between multiuser diversity gain and MAP overhead size. The proposed scheme can reduce the MAP overhead size as well as achieve high throughput.

1 Introduction

Message based multiplexing is becoming more prominent than channel based multiplexing in the next generation communication systems like 802.16 Broadband Wire-less Network [1]. Channel based multiplexing systems give each user monopolistic rights to use the channel resource when the session is opened. Channel based multiplexing employs pre-divided area as the resource allocation unit. In contrast, message based multiplexing systems allocate the resource using flexible resource allocation unit as shown in Fig. 1. Message based multiplexing is well matched with the burst nature of data traffic, and it makes the system exploit radio resources efficiently.

Message based multiplexing systems have to inform all users of the resource allocation results in every frame since the base station allocates the resource differently in each frame considering users' channel state and required rate. In the Broadband Wireless Network system, the base station (BS) broadcasts a MAP message which is appended to the front part of each frame in order to transfer the allocation information. All the users are needed to receive the MAP message reliably because it is an essential control message which indicates the location of data information. Therefore, the MAP message must be transmitted with the low order modulation and the heavy coding. It causes the degradation of the system throughput since the transmission time of the MAP message becomes longer.

T. Braun et al. (Eds.): WWIC 2006, LNCS 3970, pp. 214–223, 2006.
© Springer-Verlag Berlin Heidelberg 2006

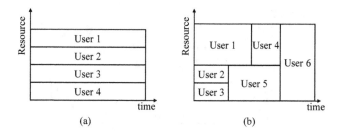

Fig. 1. (a) Channel based multiplexing (b) Message based multiplexing

In this paper, we propose a novel resource allocation scheme, which can reduce MAP overhead and maximize the throughput in the MIMO-OFDM systems. The current resource allocation algorithms in MIMO-OFDM systems do not consider the MAP overhead. To shrink MAP overhead size, our work focuses on the allocation unit of frequency resource. We assume that a subband consists of several subchannels and regard it as a frequency resource allocation unit. Note that the subband size means the number of subchannels in it. When the subband size becomes larger, the MAP overhead size becomes smaller since the number of allocation is decreased. On the other hand, as the subband size gets larger, the multiuser diversity gain decreases because the capacity of a subband is determined by minimum channel capacity of subchannels in it. Therefore, the potential to exploit higher data throughput introduces a tradeoff problem between the size of the MAP message and multiuser diversity gain.

Our main focus is on determining the optimum subband size to maximize the system throughput using knowledge about users' subchannel capacity distribution. Our simulation results shows that the proposed algorithm tends to outperform in terms of maximizing throughput. Our scheme can be easily applied to MIMO-OFDM systems.

The rest of this paper begins with the description of the downlink single-cell model of MIMO-OFDM system in Section II. This is followed by the trade-off performance analysis between multiuser diversity gain and MAP overhead in Section III. Section IV shows simulation results, and conclusions are drawn with some final remarks in Section V.

2   System Model

We consider MIMO-OFDM downlink system where each user transmits simultaneously via t antennas and reception is via r antennas. Let K be the number of users supported by the system and N be the number of subchannels. The subchannel is defined as the group of subcarriers which are close enough to be within coherent bandwidth. Therefore, we can assume that each subchannel of a user is independent from other subchannels of the same user. This MIMO-OFDM system employs the user selection scheduling scheme rather than the substream selection in order to reduce the complexity of resource allocation. In

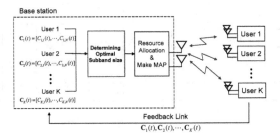

Fig. 2. MIMO-OFDM system model

addition, the instantaneous channel capacity of user k' subchannel n, the maximum achievable data rate of a single user MIMO system with channel matrix $\mathbf{H}_{k,n}$, is given as follows.

$$C_{k,n}(t) = \log_2 \left[\det \left(I_r + (\frac{P}{t})\mathbf{H}_{k,n}(t) \cdot \mathbf{H}_{k,n}(t)^H \right) \right] \tag{1}$$

P denotes the signal to noise ratio (SNR) of user k and is assumed a deterministic value. $\mathbf{H}_{k,n}$ indicates the (r x t) channel gain matrix of user k' subchannel n. At a given time slot t, $C_{k,n}(t)$ can be considered as a random variable because $\mathbf{H}_{k,n}(t)$ is a random matrix. Based on the result of [4], this random variable is shown to be approximated as a Gaussian random variable when the number of antennas is sufficiently large [2], [5].

The BS is able to estimate the instantaneous channel state information of all BS-to-mobile links based on the received uplink transmission as long as the channel varies relatively slowly. Using channel state information (CSI), the BS allocates subbands to users under the policy of Max C/I, in which the system gives a resource to the best channel capacity user in each subband. As well as the instantaneous channel capacity, capacity distribution can be estimated in the BS [5]. Using channel distribution information and CSI, the BS can determine the optimal subband size in order to minimize the MAP message size, and obtain higher throughput while allocating resources to all users with a determined subband size.

3   Problem Formulation and Analysis

In this section, we find the optimum subband size which maximizes the system throughput considering trade-off relationship between multiuser diversity gain and the MAP overhead size. Firstly, to simplify our analysis we assume that the all subchannels have an independent and identical distribution (i.i.d.) channel capacity. Then, we expand the results to the situation in which each user has different channel capacity and propose the heuristic algorithm for that case.

3.1   I.I.D. Channel Capacity Case

To simply our analysis, we consider i.i.d. subchannel capacity distribution and best user selection scheduling scheme. Let us assume $X_{k,n}$ is an i.i.d. sequence of random variable for the capacity given subchannel n, user k. If we make a subband by binding p subchannels and use it as a unit of resource allocation, Y_k, a subband capacity of user k, is

$$Y_k = mean\{X_{k,1}, X_{k,2}, \cdots, X_{k,p}\} \tag{2}$$

X has a Gaussian distribution under the condition of sufficient number of antennas in the MIMO system, so the average value of an X sequences and Y have also a Gaussian distribution. If the mean value of X is μ_X and the variance value is σ_X^2, then the mean value of Y, denoted as μ_Y, is μ_X, and the value of variance Y, denoted as σ_Y^2, is $(\sigma_X/p)^2$. When we consider the best user selection scheduling that allocates the subband to maximum subband capacity user, the average throughput is calculated as follows [5].

$$M = \max\{Y_1, Y_2, \cdots, Y_K\} \tag{3}$$

$$E[M] = \mu_Y + \sqrt{2\sigma_Y^2 \log K} = \mu_X + \frac{\sqrt{2\sigma_X^2 \log K}}{p} \tag{4}$$

Here, $\sqrt{2\sigma_X^2 \log K}/p$ is the multiuser diversity gain from scheduling leading to high increase of throughput. When the value of p gets larger, the amount of multiuser diversity gain gets smaller. This is because selecting max capacity in each subchannel can obtain larger scheduling gain than selecting max capacity among the mean capacity of several binding subchannels.

The transmission time for the MAP message is formulated as follows. Downlink MAP message consists of various elements as Fig. 3 shows [1]. In Fig. 3, the DL-MAP is specified by the MAP IE, which represents the allocating result that exploit the same modulation order and coding rate. MAP message transmission time depends on the number of MAP information elements (IEs) which indicate the number of allocated users in a frame.

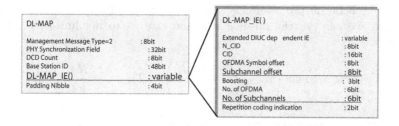

Fig. 3. Downlink MAP information in 802.16e Broadband system

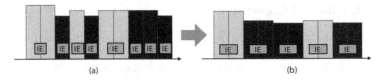

Fig. 4. Comparision of the number of IEs using (a) subband size=1 and (b) subband size=2

When we allocate resources in subbands which is the binding of several sub-channels, the number of IEs decreases as shown in Fig. 4. Under our assumption that all the subchannels are independent and identical, the probability for selecting user k in one subband, Pr_k, is all the same for all users, $1/K$, where K is the number of total users. Therefore, the number of IEs is derived as follows, where N is the total number of subchannels and p is the subband size.

$$E[No. \ of \ IE] = \sum_{k=1}^{K} \frac{N}{p} \cdot Pr_k = \frac{N}{p} \qquad (5)$$

Let r be the constant value for transforming units from bit to sec, which influences on the modulation order and coding rate. If we ignore the fixed number of bits of DL-MAP, we can obtain T_{MAP}, the MAP transmission time by multiplying the number of IE by constant r. Since one frame length, T_{frame}, can be divided into overhead transmission time and data transmission time, the data transmission time, T_{data}, is calculated by subtracting T_{MAP} from T_{frame}.

$$T_{data} = T_{frame} - \frac{N}{p} \cdot r \qquad (6)$$

Therefore, we can derive the total throughput, S, in a frame while considering the subband size, p, as follows.

$$S = \left(\mu_X + \frac{\sqrt{2\sigma_X^2 \log K}}{p} \right) \cdot \left(T_{frmae} - \frac{N}{p} \cdot r \right) \qquad (7)$$

The value of optimum subband size, p^*, can be obtained by differentiating the total throughput in (7). However, the closed form solution is very complex, and other relaxation process for getting the optimum integer value is needed. Therefore, we can get the optimal subband size p^* to maximize the system throughput.

$$p^* = \arg\max_{p} \left(\mu_x + \frac{\sqrt{2\sigma_x^2 \log K}}{p} \right) \cdot \left(T_{frmae} - \frac{N}{p} \cdot r \right) \qquad (8)$$

3.2   Different Capacity of Each User Case

In the previous subsection, we showed that optimum subband size in the case of i.i.d. subchannel. We now present numerical results in the more practical case where each user's subchannel has a different capacity distribution from other user's subchannel capacity. In this situation, it is advantageous to determine subband sizes that are different from each other. Let us assume p_k is a subband size of user k, and Y_k is the subband capacity of user k, $Y_k = mean\{X_{k,1}, X_{k,2}, \cdots, X_{k,p_k}\}$. Then, we can obtain the multiuser diversity gain as follows [6].

$$
\begin{aligned}
E[M] &= \sum_{k=1}^{K} E[Y_k | Y_k \text{ is maximal}] \\
&= \sum_{k=1}^{K} \left\{ \int_{-\infty}^{\infty} y \frac{Pr(Y_k \text{ is maximal} | Y_k = y)}{Pr(Y_k \text{ is maximal})} \frac{1}{\sqrt{2\pi}\sigma_k/p_k} e^{-\frac{(y-\mu_k)^2}{2(\sigma_k/p_k)^2}} dy \right\} \\
&= \sum_{k=1}^{K} \left[\frac{1}{Pr_k} \int_{-\infty}^{\infty} \frac{y}{\sqrt{2\pi}\sigma_k/p_k} e^{-\frac{(y-\mu_k)^2}{2(\sigma_k/p_k)^2}} \prod_{\substack{i=1 \\ i \neq k}}^{K} \left\{ 0.5 + 0.5 erf\left(\frac{y-\mu_i}{\sqrt{2}\sigma_i/p_i}\right) \right\} dy \right]
\end{aligned}
\tag{9}
$$

Alike notation of previous section, M is the random variable of the selected user who has the largest subband capacity, and μ_k, σ_k^2 represents the mean and variance value of user k' subchannel capacity respectively. Then, data transmission time is like below.

$$
T_{data} = T_{frame} - \left(\sum_{i=1}^{K} \frac{N}{p_i} \cdot Pr_i \right) \cdot r
\tag{10}
$$

Given (9) and (10), the total throughput of this system is given by

$$
S = \sum_{k=1}^{K} \left[\frac{1}{Pr_k} \int_{-\infty}^{\infty} \frac{y \cdot e^{-\frac{(y-\mu_k)^2}{2(\sigma_k/p_k)^2}}}{\sqrt{2\pi}\sigma_k/p_k} \prod_{\substack{i=1 \\ i \neq k}}^{K} \left\{ 0.5 + 0.5 erf\left(\frac{y-\mu_i}{\sqrt{2}\sigma_i/p_i}\right) \right\} dy \right] \cdot \left\{ T_{frame} - \left(\sum_{i=1}^{K} \frac{N}{p_i} \cdot Pr_i \right) \cdot r \right\}
\tag{11}
$$

Where Pr_k is defined as the probability which user k is selected, Pr_k can be written as

$$
\begin{aligned}
Pr_k(\mu, \sigma) &= Pr(Y_k \text{ is maximal}) \\
&= \int_{-\infty}^{\infty} \frac{1}{\sigma_k/p_k \sqrt{2\pi}} e^{-\frac{(x-\mu_k)^2}{2(\sigma_k/p_k)^2}} \prod_{\substack{i=1 \\ i \neq k}}^{K} \left(0.5 + 0.5 erf\left(\frac{x-\mu_i}{\sqrt{2}\sigma_i/p_i}\right) \right) dx
\end{aligned}
\tag{12}
$$

To find the optimum solution which maximizes (11), $\overrightarrow{p}^* = [p_1^*, p_2^*, ..., p_K^*]$, is difficult because it is a non-linear optimization problem. Therefore, obtaining an optimal solution is very difficult. That is why we proposed heuristic algorithm MAP Reduced Resource Allocation (MRRA)

3.3   MAP Reduced Resource Allocation (MRRA)

We assume the Gaussian MIMO channel capacity with mean vector $\overrightarrow{\mu} = [\mu_1, \mu_2, ..., \mu_K]$ and standard deviation vector $\overrightarrow{\sigma} = [\sigma_1, \sigma_2, ..., \sigma_K]$. In the MRRA algorithm, pre-calculated values of the optimum subband size according to the capacity distribution are used. It is impossible to get the maximized global solution of (11), so we consider the i.i.d. channel assumption in order to simplify the problem. Namely, we assume that other users' channel capacity are the same as user k, and then calculated the optimum subband size of user k, p_k.

$$p_k = \arg\max_p \left(\mu_k + \frac{\sqrt{2\sigma_k^2 \log K}}{p} \right) \cdot \left(T_{frame} - \frac{N}{p} \cdot r \right) \qquad (13)$$

We can determine the optimum subband size using (13). It is effective because the multi-dimensional search is not necessary. In addition, the adaptive scheme according to various capacity distributions can be exploited. However, if the subband size of each user is different from each other, a problem may occur in the resource allocation steps since the general resource allocation schemes are based on the same allocation unit size. Therefore, we consider integrating each user's subband size to one value by averaging. We have also proved the performance of this heuristic algorithm by simulation.

4   Simulation Results

We now describe some simulation experiments which were conducted to quantify the performance gains from proposed subband size determining scheme. Consider a 4x4 MIMO-OFDM system operating with 40MHz bandwidth and 256 subchannels under Rayleigh flat fading channel. Each time frame is 1ms in length, and single-cell MIMO-OFDM system model is used.

In order to evaluate the performance of the proposed MRRA scheme, it is compared with other resource allocation scheme. Here, we consider the comparison with Max C/I resource allocation method. In the Max C/I resource allocation scheme, the system allocates a subband to the user who has the best channel capacity of that subband (It is as same as the best user scheduling in [5]). The two schemes are compared via com-puter simulation using the same single-cell OFDM system model. Users' positions are all random, so that the capacity distribution of all users is different from each other.

Let α be the initial MAP loading parameter that the proportional value of MAP message transmission time over a frame length when the subband size is fixed to one. Accordingly, the initial MAP loading α is a real value between zero to one.

$$\alpha = \frac{T_{MAP,p=1}}{T_{Frame}} \qquad (14)$$

Fig. 5 shows the total system throughput for change number of users, K, assuming that an initial MAP loading of α is 0.5 and SNR is -8dB in all users, namely i.i.d. channel capacity case. The results are presented in terms of the throughput per unit time obtained by each user, normalized by the system bandwidth. The figure shows that the throughput of all cases is maximum throughput

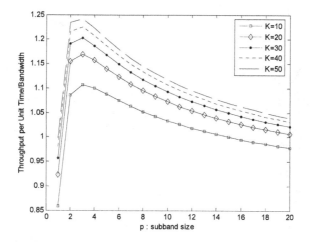

Fig. 5. Normalized throughput vs. subband size (i.i.d. case)

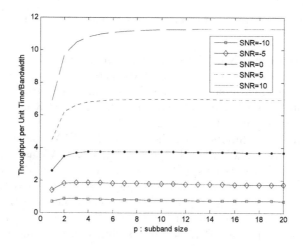

Fig. 6. Normalized throughput vs. subband size (i.i.d. case)

at $p = 3$. The throughput of all cases is invariant with the subband size since it affects only the MAP overhead size and data transmission time. Furthermore, the throughput increases with the number of users because the multiuser diversity gain is proportional to the number of users. Note that the optimum subband size p^* is equal to all cases, so it is independent of the number of users.

Fig. 6 plots the basic throughput as a function of subband size. In this experiment, we assume there are $K = 20$ users in a cell, the initial MAP loading α is 0.5, and all users have same SNR. As noted earlier, SNR is the important factor for deciding the channel capacity distribution, so that all users have the i.i.d. channel capacity. In Fig. 6, while the SNR of users increases, the throughput goes

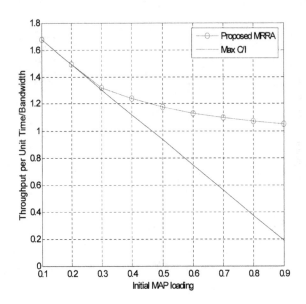

Fig. 7. Normalized throughput vs. initial MAP loading

up. It is because larger SNR brings the higher channel capacity. Moreover, the optimum subband size gets larger as the SNR increases since the users with the good SNR channel environment have smaller channel variance. In other words, the capacity difference between subchannels of the good SNR users is relatively small comparing with that of other users.

Fig. 7 presents throughputs under the proposed MRRA scheme and max C/I scheme, respectively as the initial MAP loading increases. We assume 20 users in a cell, and all users have various SNR randomly chosen between -13 and -3 dB. The proposed scheme achieves higher throughput when the MAP overhead get larger. We observe that using proposed MRRA scheme increases the throughput by more than 17% comparing with using MAX C/I scheme $\alpha = 0.5$. In addition, when α is 0.8, the proposed MRRA scheme exhibits twice the throughput of Max C/I scheme. This throughput gain results from joint optimization of multiuser diversity and MAP transmission time.

In general, we observed that the performance gains from the MRRA scheme depend on the initial MAP loading. When there is heavy initial MAP loading, proposed scheme may help considerably improve performance.

5   Conclusions

In this paper, we have considered maximizing downlink throughput for MIMO-OFDM systems by exploiting joint optimization between multiuser diversity and the MAP overhead. In particular, we focused on determining the optimum sub-band size to maximize the system throughput. Simulation results show that the proposed MRRA scheme outperforms a Max C/I scheme in terms of throughput due to the optimality of our scheme. In the future MIMO-OFDM systems, the proposed MRRA algorithm should take into account specific resource allocation scheme in order to guarantee the QoS, which needs further investigation.

References

1. IEEE 802.16-2004,"IEEE Standard for Local and Metropolitan Area Networks - Part 16: Air Interface for Fixed Broadband Wireless Access Systems," Oct.01, 2004
2. Peter J Smith and Mansoor Shafi, "On the Gaussian Approximation to the Capacity of Wireless MIMO System," Proceedings of IEEE ICC 2002, pp. 406-410, New York, May 2002
3. G.J. Focshini, "Layered Space-Time Architecture for Wireless Communication in a Fading Environment When Using Multi-Element Antennas," Bell Labs Technical Journal, pp.41-59, Oct.1996.
4. V.L. Girko, "A Refinement of the Central Limit Theorem for Random Determinants," The-ory of Probability and its Application, vol.42, no.1, pp.121-129, 1997.
5. B.W. Hochwald, T.L.Marzetta, and V. Tarokh, "Multi-Antenna Channel-Hardening and its Implications for Rate Feedback and Scheduling," IEEE transactions on Information Theory, vol. 50, no.9, pp.1893-1909, Sep. 2004
6. Athanasios Papoulis and S. Unnikrishna Pillai, "Probability, Random Variables and Stochastic Processes," 4th ed. Mc Graw Hill

A Novel IEEE 802.11e-Based QoS Protocol for Voice Communications over WLANs*

José Villalón, Pedro Cuenca, and Luis Orozco-Barbosa

Instituto de Investigación en Informática de Albacete,
Universidad de Castilla-La Mancha,
02071 Albacete, Spain
{josemvillalon, pcuenca, lorozco}@info-ab.uclm.es

Abstract. Voice over WLAN (VoWLAN) is widely acknowledged as one of the key, emerging applications for wireless LANs. As with any multi-service network, there is the need to provision the WLANs with the QoS mechanisms capable of guaranteeing the requirements of various services. The upcoming IEEE 802.11e (EDCA) standard is on the way to define the required QoS mechanisms into the protocol architecture of IEEE 802.11 WLANs. However, recent studies have shown that EDCA performs poorly when the medium is highly loaded. This situation has led many researchers to design techniques aiming to improve the performance of EDCA. Unfortunately, the main deficiency of many of the proposed mechanisms to date comes from their inability to properly interoperate with legacy IEEE 802.11 (DCF) systems. Moreover, the implementation of many of the proposed QoS mechanisms requires important and incompatible changes to the IEEE 802.11e specifications. In this paper we introduce a novel IEEE 802.11e-based QoS protocol capable of providing QoS support to voice communications, and able to properly interoperate with legacy DCF based stations. Our design has been based on an in-depth analysis of the several operation modes of both standards. This should ensure full compatibility of operation: an important feature since the transition from the IEEE 802.11 to the IEEE 802.11e will take some time making more likely the existence of hybrid scenarios where both standards will have to coexist. Our results show that the proposed mechanism outperforms the IEEE 802.11e standard by offering better QoS guarantees to the voice service over a wider range of load conditions and traffic mix scenario.

1 Introduction

A wide range of enterprise organizations have realized significant productivity increases by deploying mobile data applications using WLAN networks. Motivated by the success, the organizations are now looking to further enhance the productivity of their mobile workers and leverage their WLAN network investments by deploying more applications into their networks. Voice communications is one of the leading applications that benefit from the mobility and increasing bit rates provided by current

---

* This work was supported by the Ministry of Science and Technology of Spain under CICYT project TIC2003-08154-C06-02, the Council of Science and Technology of Castilla-La Mancha under project PBC-03-001 and FEDER.

T. Braun et al. (Eds.): WWIC 2006, LNCS 3970, pp. 224–235, 2006.

and emerging WLAN technologies. Voice over WLAN (VoWLThis work was supported by the Ministry of Science and Technology of Spain under CICYT project TIC2003-08154-C06-02, the Council of Science and Technology of Castilla-La Mancha under project PBC-03-001 and FEDERAN) is widely acknowledged as one of the most important applications for WLANs.

Nowadays, users expect toll-quality service regardless of the medium (wired vs. wireless) and the switching technology employed. Multi-Service networks require special prioritization protocols to ensure good voice performance. The upcoming IEEE 802.11e draft standard [1], is on the way of defining the mechanisms to meet the QoS requirements of various applications, such as, voice and video services.

In the near future, it is expected that the IEEE 802.11e interface cards will take over the WLAN market, replacing the use of legacy IEEE 802.11 [2] interface cards in most WLAN applications. The complete migration to the new IEEE 802.11e standard will take several years given the wide scale use of legacy IEEE 802.11 in the market place today. This creates an important number of networking scenarios where legacy IEEE 802.11 based stations and IEEE 802.11e based stations will be required to interoperate.

However, the ratification of the IEEE 802.11e standard is becoming a very challenging task. It is observed that the IEEE 802.11e (EDCA) performs poorly as the network load increases: mainly due to the higher probability of collision. This reason has led many researchers to design techniques aiming to improve the performance of EDCA [3], [4]. The two main drawbacks of such proposals are: 1) their implementation requires important modifications to the IEEE 802.11e specifications in a moment in which IEEE 802.11e is in its final stage of ratification; and 2) their inability to meet the multimedia applications QoS requirements in the presence of legacy DCF based stations: these stations have greater priority than the video flows.

In this paper, we address the two aforementioned issues by introducing a novel IEEE 802.11e-complaint mechanism capable of providing QoS guarantees to voice services even under scenarios where legacy DCF based stations are present. Our main objective has been to design a scheme compatible with the IEEE 802.11 standards, including the DCF and EDCA mechanisms. Our simulation results show that our new scheme outperforms EDCA.

The paper is organized as follows. Section 2 provides an overview of the IEEE 802.11 WLAN standard. In Section 3, we overview the upcoming IEEE 802.11e QoS standard. Section 4 describes our new proposed IEEE 802.11e-based QoS mechanism. In Section 5, we carry out a comparative performance study of our proposal and EDCA. Towards this end, we consider various system configurations and network load conditions. Finally, Section 6 concludes the paper.

2   The IEEE 802.11 DCF and QoS Enhancements

The basic access function in IEEE 802.11 is the *Distributed Coordination Function* (DCF) and is based on a *Carrier Sense Multiple Access with Collision Avoidance* (CSMA/CA) algorithm supplemented by a contention (*backoff*) algorithm. Under this scheme, a station may start transmitting after having sensed the channel idle during an interval of time longer than the *Distributed InterFrame Space* (DIFS):

$$DIFS = 2 \text{ x } Slot\_time + SIFS \tag{1}$$

where *SlotTime* is a parameter that depends on the physical layer being used and *SIFS* is the *Short InterFrame Space*. Otherwise, if the channel is sensed busy, the station should wait for the ongoing transmission to finish. The station will then wait a random interval of time (*the backoff time*) before attempting to transmit:

$$Backoff \_ Time = \lfloor CW \times rand\,() \rfloor \times aSlotTime \tag{2}$$

where *rand()* is a random function with uniform distribution within the range (0,1); *CW* is the *Contention Window* ($CW_{min} \leq CW \leq CW_{max}$). *CW* is initially set to CW_{min}.

As long as no activity is detected in the channel, the transmitting station makes use of a backoff counter, initially set to *Backoff_Time*. This counter is decremented on a *SlotTime* by *SlotTime* basis. Whenever activity is detected, the backoff counter is stopped and reactivated as soon as the channel is sensed idle during an interval of time not shorter than *DIFS*. The station can start transmitting as soon as its backoff counter reaches zero. Upon receiving the data, the destination station sends an *Immediate Positive Acknowledgement* (ACK) to the source station after having sensed the channel state during a time interval equal to the *Short InterFrame Space* (*SIFS* <*DIFS*) from the time instant the data frame has been received.

In case of an unsuccessful transmission attempt, the backoff procedure is invoked. The station updates its *CW* as $CW_{new} = 2(CW_{old} + 1)$. If, after repeated updates *CW* reaches CW_{max}, the contention window is maintained unchanged till a successful transmission occurs or the maximum number of retries is reached. After a successful transmission, *CW* is reset once again to CW_{min}. The use of this simple procedure helps to considerable reduce potential access conflicts with other active (waiting) stations. Figure 1 depicts the state diagram of the IEEE 802.11 mechanism.

Even though DCF is a simple and effective mechanism, DCF does not comprise the differentiation mechanisms allowing it to guarantee bandwidth, packet delay, packet loss-rate and/or jitter bounds for high priority stations or multimedia flows. DCF has been basically designed for providing a best-effort service. For this reason, many research efforts are currently focusing on the design of QoS mechanisms for DCF. Two approaches have been mainly undertaken. The first approach is based on priorities, giving access preference to those stations that have been assigned higher priority. This is done by assigning different values to the parameters used to access the medium, namely the *DIFS* and *CW* parameters. Due to the characteristics of the DCF, the shorter *DIFS* is set, the earlier the station is able to start transmitting. Moreover, a shorter *CW* translates into a shorter backoff period. The schemes based on the assignment of priorities do not work well when the number of active stations is large. The second approach is based on the use of fair scheduling algorithms for sharing the resources according to pre-assigned weights. For this purpose, a large number of researchers have proposed the use of well-known algorithms having given good results when applied to wired networks. A complete overview of the different QoS enhancements mechanisms for IEEE 802.11 can be found in [5]. In that work, the authors have summarized and classified a large number of the proposed techniques. A comparative performance evaluation of some of them can be found in [6], [7].

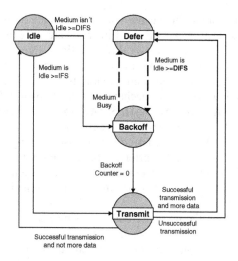

Fig. 1. IEEE 802.11 DCF State Diagram

3   The IEEE 802.11e Draft Standard

The IEEE 802.11e draft standard [1] aims to specify the mechanisms enabling the provisioning of QoS guarantees in IEEE 802.11 WLANs. In the IEEE 802.11e standard, distinction is made among those stations not requiring QoS support, known as *nQSTA*, and those requiring it, *QSTA*. In order to support both Intserv and DiffServ QoS approaches in an IEEE 802.11 WLAN, a third coordination function is being added: the *Hybrid Coordination Function* (HCF). The use of this new coordination function is mandatory for the QSTAs. HCF incorporates two new access mechanisms: the contention-based *Enhanced Distributed Channel Access* (EDCA), known in the previous drafts as the *Enhanced DCF* (EDCF) and the *HCF Controlled Channel Access* (HCCA). In the HCCA mechanism a central node is used for coordinating the access to the channel: the *Hybrid Coordinator* (HC). When the HC takes control over the channel during the *Contention Period* (CP), it is said that a *Controlled Access Phase* (CAP) has been generated. It is worth noting that the HC should at all times hold the highest priority allowing it to initiate the CAP.

One main feature of HCF is the definition of four *Access Categories* (AC) queues and eight *Traffic Stream* (TS) queues at MAC layer. When a frame arrives at the MAC layer, it is tagged with a *Traffic Priority Identifier* (TID) according to its QoS requirements, which can take values from 0 to 15. The frames with TID values from 0 to 7 are mapped into four AC queues using the EDCA access rules. The frames with TID values from 8 to 15 are mapped into the eight TS queues using the HCF controlled channel access rules. The TS queues provide a strict parameterized QoS control while the AC queues enable the provisioning of multiple priorities. Another main feature of the HCF is the concept of *Transmission Opportunity* (TXOP), which defines the transmission holding time for each station.

EDCA has been designed to be used with the contention-based prioritized QoS support mechanisms. In EDCA, two main methods are introduced to support service differentiation. The first one is to use different IFS values for different ACs. The second method consists in allocating different CW sizes to the different ACs. Each AC forms an EDCA independent entity with its own queue and its own access mechanism based on an DCF-like mechanism with its own *Arbitration Inter-Frame Space* defined by *AIFS[AC]=SIFS+AIFSN[AC]×SlotTime* and its own CW[AC] (*CWmin[AC] ≤CW[AC] ≤ CWmax[AC]*), where *AIFSN[AC]* is the *Arbitration Inter Frame Space Number*. If an internal collision arises among the queues within the same QSTA, the one having higher priority obtains the right to transmit. It is said that the queue getting the right to access to the channel obtains a transmission opportunity (TXOP). The winning queue can then transmit during a time interval whose length is given by *TXOPLimit*.

The 802.11e Working Group is currently working hard towards the ratification of the draft standard. However, there are still many open issues and concerns regarding the poor performance exhibited by the proposed standard related to the support of time-constrained services, such as voice and video services. Moreover, any attempt to successfully define a QoS-aware standard for IEEE 802.11 WLANs, such as EDCA, has to take into account that compatibility with legacy IEEE802.11 based stations. These reasons have led to us to design a new IEEE 802.11e-based QoS protocol for voice communications over WLAN.

4 B-EDCA: A New IEEE 802.11e-Based QoS Mechanism

Due to the large number of legacy IEEE 802.11 infrastructure already in place, the IEEE 802.11e-based systems will be required to properly interoperate with the existing mechanisms, such as DCF. Under such scenarios, EDCA has shown to be unable to meet the QoS of time-constrained services, in particular voice communications. Based on these limitations and under the constraint that assuring compatibility with existing mechanism is a key element for its successful deployment, we propose a new IEEE 802.11e-based QoS mechanism capable of providing QoS support to time-constrained applications.

Table 1. Parameter settings specified in standards [1], [2]

		IFS	CW_{min}	CW_{max}
DCF		2 x Slot_time + SIFS	CW_{min}	CW_{max}
	AC	**AIFSN**	CW_{min}	CW_{max}
EDCA	Vo	2	$(CW_{min}+1)/4 -1$	$(CW_{min}+1)/2 -1$
	Vi	2	$(CW_{min}+1)/2 -1$	CW_{min}
	Be	3	CW_{min}	CW_{max}
	Bk	7	CW_{min}	CW_{max}

Table 1 shows the parameters as currently specified by the DCF and EDCA standards. The values of *AIFSN[AC]* and *CW* parameters used by EDCA have been set bearing in mind compatibility with the DCF standard. It is clear that the setting of the *AIFSN[AC]* to 2-2-3-7 enables the provisioning of a higher priority to the voice and video services over the best-effort and background services. Furthermore, this setting avoids the conflict between the time-constrained services and the HCCA mechanism. Recall that the HCCA mechanism requires holding the highest priority. As shown in Table 1, the main difference between the high-priority flows in EDCA (voice and video) and the DCF stations is the use of a shorter contention window by the former. However, one of the main problems with this setting is that the voice service may badly degrade in the presence of video services and DCF-based stations.

Based on the results obtained in one of our previous studies [8], we have found out that the IFS (denoted AIFS in the EDCA draft standard) is the most important and critical parameter enabling the provisioning of QoS to multimedia applications. This is particular true when a large number of stations attempt to gain access to the channel, since under these conditions, the stations will often have to stop decrementing their backoff counters. Recall that every time that a station stops decrementing its counter, the station must wait an AIFS before resuming the count down.

One possible solution will be to set up AIFSN=1 for the voice applications. In this way, it will increase his chances to gain access to the channel. However, setting up AIFSN=1 to this service is incompatible with the HCCA. As already explained, the HC should be able to take the control of the channel at any time. This is to say, the HCCA should hold the highest priority over all the services to be supported by the standard.

In order to introduce our proposal, we take a closer look at the mode of operation of the DCF and EDCA schemes, and particularly on the role played by the IFS (AIFS) parameter. The IFS (AIFS) is used in the following two cases:

1. In the **Idle** state: when the station becomes active has to sense the channel during an interval whose length is determined by IFS: If the channel is sensed free, the station can initiate the packet transmission. Otherwise, the station executes the backoff algorithm.
2. In every transfer from the **Defer** state to the **Backoff** state. In other words, every time after having sensed the channel free during an interval of length IFS.

According to the current DCF and EDCA standards, the same values for the IFS parameter should be used regardless of the state in which the station is (see Table 1). Based on the previous observation, we then propose to use a different set of IFS values depending on the state in which the station is. We have however to ensure not to compromise the operation of the HC, and in particular to ensure that it holds at all times the highest priority. We then propose the following parameter setting:

1. In the **Idle** state. The stations will use the IFS values as specified in the IEEE 802.11e draft standard (see Table 1) including the Hybrid Coordination Function. This also ensures compatibility with the IEEE 802.11 (DCF) mechanism.
2. In every transfer from the **Defer** state to the **Backoff** state, we propose to use a different parameter, equivalent to the IFS, denoted from now on by B-AIFSN (*Backoff*-AIFSN). We then propose setting up this parameter to one, i.e., *B-AIFSN[Vo] = 1*, for the voice service. In this way, we improve considerably the performance of voice applications, increasing their priorities with respect to other flows (included the traffic generated by DCF-based stations). This setting also

ensures that the HC will keep the highest priority. This can be explained by examining the state diagram of the channel access mechanism (see Figure 1). According to this mechanism, the stations must wait at least one additional slot during the backoff procedure before being allowed to transmit since the backoff interval is set within the [1, CW+1] range. In turn, the HC is allowed to take the control at the end of the IFS. To improve further the provisioning of QoS guarantees to the time-constrained applications when the network is highly loaded, we propose increasing the assigned value to *B-AIFSN* used by the Best-Effort traffic, with respect to the specified in [1]. We then propose using the set of values for *B-AIFSN[AC]* to 1-2-4-7 for voice, video, best-effort and background traffics, respectively.

Table 2 depicts the parameter setting of our proposal that proves to be fulfilling the requirement of the voice services while avoiding any interference with the HCCA mechanism. It is clear that the parameter setting to be used depends on the state of the communication. This is essentially the major change with respect to the current EDCA standard. Our proposal essentially reduces to the minimum acceptable value, the waiting time required to continue decrementing the backoff counter used by the time-constrained applications. This minimum value is fully compatible with the operation modes of the DCF and HCCA functions.

Table 2. Parameter settings proposed for B-EDCA

	AC	AIFSN Idle	AIFSN Defer
	Vo	2	2
EDCA	Vi	2	2
	Be	3	3
	Bk	7	7
	Vo	2	1
B-EDCA	Vi	2	2
	Be	3	4
	Bk	7	7

5   Performance Evaluation

In this section, we carry out a performance analysis on the effectiveness of our proposed mechanism. We show that our proposed scheme assigns the highest priority to the voice service over any other of the three services: video, best-effort and background, and over the legacy IEEE 802.11 (DCF) stations. Throughout our study, we have made use of the OPNET Modeler tool 11.0 [9], which already integrate the IEEE 802.11 DCF simulator. We have integrated into the simulator the EDCA and B-EDCA mechanisms.

5.1   Scenarios

In our simulations, we model an IEEE 802.11a WLAN consisting of several wireless stations and an access point that also serves as sink for the flows coming from the wireless stations. All the stations are located within a *Basic Service Set* (BSS), i.e., every station is able to detect a transmission from any other station. The use of three different types of wireless stations is considered: DCF-complaint stations and QoS-aware, EDCA and B-EDCA, stations. The EDCA and B-EDCA-based stations support four different types of services: voice(Vo), video(Vi), best-effort(BE) and background (BK). This classification is in line with the IEEE802.1D standard specifications.

Each wireless station operates at 36 Mbit/s IEEE 802.11a mode and transmits a single traffic type to the access point. We assume the use of constant bit-rate voice sources encoded at a rate of 16 kbits/s according to the G.728 standard [10]. The voice packet size is equal to 168 bytes including the RTP/UDP/IP headers. For the video applications, we have made use of the traces generated from a variable bit-rate H.264 video encoder [11]. We have used the sequence *mobile calendar* encoded on CIF format at a video frame rate of 25 frames/sec. It is clear that these types of sources exhibit a high degree of burstiness characterized by a periodic traffic pattern and a high variance bit rates. The average video transmission rate is around 1.1 Mbits/s with a packet size equal to 1064 bytes (including RTP/UDP/IP headers). The best-effort, background and DCF traffics have been created using a *Pareto* distribution traffic model. The average sending rate of best-effort and background traffic is 256 kbit/s, using a 552 bytes packet size (including TCP/IP headers). The average sending rate of DCF traffic is 512 kbit/s, using a 552 bytes packet size (including TCP/IP headers). All the traffic sources are randomly activated within of the interval [1,1.5] seconds from the start of the simulation. Throughout our study, we have simulated one minute of operation of each particular scenario. When choosing the parameter settings to use for the DCF and EDCA mechanisms under study, we have used the settings specified in the standards [1], [2] (see Table 1, using $CW_{min} = 15$ and $CW_{max} = 1023$). The modified parameter settings with respect to EDCA used for the B-EDCA proposed mechanism are given in Table 2.

In order to limit the delay experienced by the video and voice applications, the maximum time that video packet and voice packet may remain in the transmission buffer has been set to 100ms and 10ms, respectively. These time limits are in line with the values specified by the standards and in the literature. Whenever a video or voice packet exceeds these upper bounds, it is dropped.

Our measurements started after a warm-up period (about three seconds) allowing us to collect the statistics under steady-state conditions. Each point in our plots is an average over thirty simulation runs, and the error bars indicate the 95% confidence interval.

For the first scenario (refer from now on as *Scenario 1*), we have assumed that one fifth of the stations support one of the four kinds of services (Vo, Vi, BE, BK) and DCF-complaint stations. We start by simulating a WLAN consisting of five wireless stations, each one supporting a different type of traffic and one DCF-complaint station. We then gradually increase the *Total Offered Load* of the wireless LAN by increasing the number of stations by five. In this way, the stations are always incorporated into the system in a ratio of 1(Vo):1(Vi):1(BE):1(BK):1(DCF). We increase the number of stations 5 by 5 starting from 5 and up to 65. In this way, the normalized offered load is increased from 0.08 up to 1.06. We have preferred to evaluate a normalized offered load, rather than the absolute value. The normalized offered load is determined with respect to the theoretical maximum capacity of the 36 Mbit/s IEEE 802.11a mode, i.e. 26.9 Mbit/s (corresponding to the use of the maximum packet size used by the MAC layer and in the presence of a single active station).

For the second scenario (refer from now on as *Scenario 2*), we start simulating from a *Total Offered Load* of 0.65. This load corresponds to the maximum load supported by the EDCA scheme in the first scenario. We then gradually increase the *Total Offered Load* of the wireless LAN by increasing the number of stations by six. In this way, only voice stations are always incorporated into the system. We increase the number of stations 6 by 6 starting from 8 and up to 32. In this way, the *Total Offered Load* is increased from 0.65 up to around 0.665. This will allow determining the number of additional voice load that can be supported by both schemes.

In the same way, in a third scenario (refer from now on as *Scenario 3*), we start by simulating the first scenario when the *Total Offered Load* of the wireless LAN is 0.65. We then gradually increase the *Total Offered Load* of the wireless LAN by increasing the number of the video stations by two. We increase the number of stations from 8 and up to 16. In this way, the total load is increased from 0.65 up to around 0.98.

5.2   Results

To be able to compare the graphs from different levels of load (traffic patterns of different applications), we have preferred plotting the normalized throughput rather than the absolute throughput. The normalized throughput is calculated as the percentage of the offered data that is actually delivered to the destination. Figure 2 shows the voice, video, best-effort, background, DCF and Global normalized throughput obtained when using the EDCA and B-EDCA methods. In the case of the voice service, our proposed scheme, B-EDCA, is able to provide better QoS guarantees than EDCA. Taking into account that the maximum acceptable loss rate for the voice service is 5%, it is clear from the results that EDCA is unable to provide such guarantees for load exceeding 65% of the network nominal rate: B-EDCA is able to provide such guarantees for load up to 90%. Figures 2.b to 2.e show that our proposal does not penalize the rest of the traffics. In fact, it is able to slightly improve the throughput of them. In the case of the BE and BK traffics (figures 2c and 2d), these are severely affected as the network load is increased. Figure 2f shows the overall throughput for all the services under study. It is clear that the B-EDCA exhibits the highest normalized throughput. This is due to the reduction of the collision rate with respect to EDCA mechanism (see figure 3).

Figure 3.a shows that by setting up the *B-AIFSN[Vo]=1*, the proposed scheme is able to considerably reduce the number of retransmission required to successfully transmit the voice packets. In other words, B-EDCA is able to reduce the number of collisions and in turn assign a higher priority to the voice service over any other service, including the video service. This reduction is the result of assigning a different value of B-AIFSN to the voice and video flows. This reduces the probability of collision between the voice and video packets. Figure 3.b also shows that the overall number of retransmissions is lower for the B-EDCA than for EDCA.

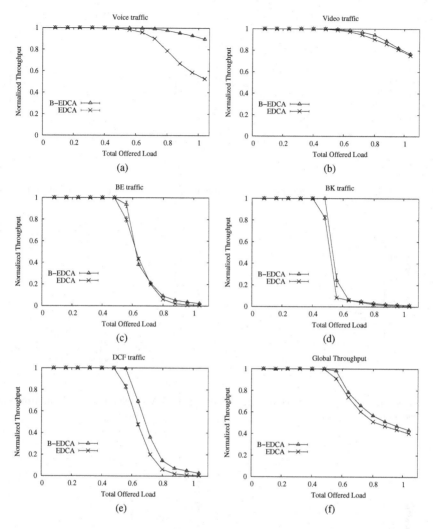

Fig. 2. Scenario 1: Average Normalized Throughput a) Voice, b) Video, c) Best-Effort d) Background e) DCF Traffic and f) Total Traffic

The second scenario, Scenario 2, allows us to evaluate the performance of the proposed scheme as the number of voice sources is increased. Figure 4 shows that B-EDCA is able to provide better QoS guarantees to the voice service than EDCA. It is clear that while EDCA is unable to guarantee a loss rate below the 5% mark, B-EDCA can support up to 12 additional voice stations. However, it is clear that the normalized throughput degrades, limiting the number of voice sources that can be effectively supported. Even though, the voice sources are characterized by their low-bandwidth requirement, their high activity rate increases the probability of collisions. Therefore, the number of necessary retransmissions increases rapidly resulting in an increasing number of losses.

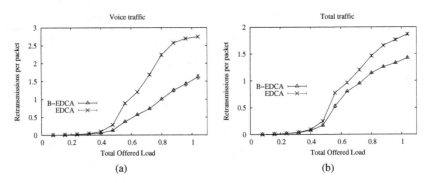

Fig. 3. Scenario 1: Average number of Attempts per packet. a) Voice, b) Total Traffic.

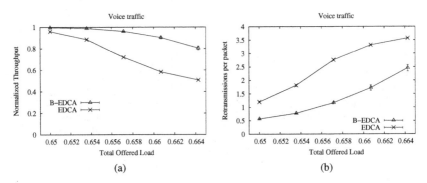

Fig. 4. Scenario 2. a) Average Normalized Throughput, b) Average number of Retransmissions per packet for voice traffic.

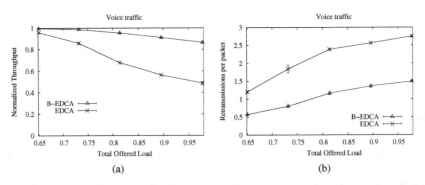

Fig. 5. Scenario 3. a) Average Normalized Throughput, b) Average number of Attempts per packet for voice traffic.

Figure 5 shows the results for Scenario 3. In this case, the maximum load supported by the network is far above the one supported in the previous case. This can be explained by the fact that the video sources have higher bandwidth requirements. This limits the number of additional video sources that can be incorporated. Similarly to the previous case, EDCA is unable to guarantee a loss rate below 5%, while B-EDCA can support four additional video stations.

6 Conclusions

In this paper, throughout an in-depth analysis of the IEEE 802.11 DCF and EDCA standards, we have been able to design B-EDCA. B-EDCA is a novel scheme offering the highest service level to voice services. Throughout our analysis, we have also shown that our proposal is fully compatible with the IEEE 802.1 DCF and HCCA schemes. This ensures the interoperability with the large number of already deployed DCF-complaint stations and the upcoming HCCA mechanism. Our results show that B-EDCA outperforms EDCA providing better QoS guarantees not only for the voice service but as well to the video service. B-EDCA is able to reduce the number of collisions encountered by the voice traffic by half with respect to the EDCA mechanism. We have also shown that B-EDCA outperforms EDCA under different traffic scenarios providing better QoS guarantees to the voice service.

References

1. IEEE 802 Committee of the IEEE Computer Society, IEEE P802.11e/D13.0 Draft Amendment to IEEE Std 802.11, "Part 11: Wireless LAN Medium Access Control (MAC) and Physical Layer (PHY) Specifications: Medium Access Control (MAC) Quality of Service (QoS) Enhancements", April 2005.
2. LAN MAN Standards Committee of the IEEE Computer Society, ANSI/IEEE Std 802.11, "Part 11: Wireless LAN Medium Access Control (MAC) and Physical Layer (PHY) Specifications", 1999 Edition.
3. Y. Kwon, Y. Fang and H. Latchman, "Design of MAC Protocols with Fast Collision Resolution for Wireless Local Area Networks". IEEE Transactions on Wireless Communications, Vol. 3, No.3. pp. 793-807, May 2004.
4. M. Malli, Q. Ni, T. Turletti and C. Barakat "Adaptive Fair Channel Allocation for QoS Enhancement in IEEE 802.11 Wireless LANs", Proceedings of IEEE ICC, Paris, June 2004.
5. F. Mico, P. Cuenca and L.Orozco Barbosa "QoS Mechanisms for IEEE 802.11 Wireless LANs". Lecture Notes in Computer Science. Vol. 3079. pp. 609-623, 2004.
6. A. Lindgren, A. Almquist and O. Schelén, "Quality of Service Schemes for IEEE 802.11 Wireless LANs - An Evaluation", Journal of Special Topics in Mobile Networking and Applications (MONET), Vol. 8, No. 3, pp. 223-235, June 2003.
7. W. Pattara-Atikom, P. Krishnamurthy and S. Banerjee, "Distributed Mechanisms for Quality of Service in Wireless LANs", IEEE Wireless Communications, Vol. 10, No. 3, pp. 26-34, June 2003.
8. J. Villalón, P. Cuenca, L. Orozco-Barbosa, "On the Effectiveness of IEEE 802.11e QoS Support in Wireless LAN: A Performance Analysis". Lecture Notes in Computer Science. Vol. 3726. pp. 605-616, 2005.
9. Opnet.Technologies.Inc. OPNET Modeler 10.0, 1987-2004. http://www.opnet.com
10. ITU-T Recommendation G.728, "Coding of Speech at 16 kbit/s using Low-Delay Code Excited Linear Prediction", Std., September 1992.
11. ITU-T Recommendation H.264, "Advanced Video Coding For Generic Audiovisual Services". May 2003.

A Live Harmonic Broadcasting Scheme for VBR-Encoded Hot Videos

Hung-Chang Yang[1], Hsiang-Fu Yu[2], Zeng-Yuan Yang[1], Li-Ming Tseng[1], and Yi-Ming Chen[3]

[1] Dep. of Computer Science and Information Engineering,
National Central University, Jung-Li, Taiwan
{cyht, yzy}@dslab.csie.ncu.edu.tw, tsenglm@csie.ncu.edu.tw
[2] Computer Center, National Central University, Jung-Li, Taiwan
yu@dslab.csie.ncu.edu.tw
[3] Dep. of Information Management, National Central University, Jung-Li, Taiwan
cym@im.mgt.ncu.edu.tw

Abstract. With the growth of broadband networks, Video-on-Demand (VoD) has become realistic. Most of the significant broadcasting schemes have been proposed to reduce the server bandwidth requirement for Constant Bit-Rate (CBR) encoded videos. The few existing proposals, which support of the bandwidth-efficient Variable Bit-Rate (VBR) encoded videos, smooth and minimize the server bandwidth requirement at the cost of data losses. The lossless and bandwidth efficient (LLBE) scheme states that minimization of the server bandwidth as a shortest path problem on a directed acyclic graph, and uses a dynamic programming method to solve the problem. However, it cannot be used for support live video broadcasting. In this paper, we propose a live harmonic broadcasting (LHB) scheme to support VBR-encoded live video broadcasting. The ideas behind the scheme are (1) support VBR-encoded videos by asynchronous downloading and playing, and hybrid division by length and size, and (2) support live videos by postponing recasting process. It is simple and effective. Using data from real videos, we conduct a simulation to evaluate our scheme. The experiment results indicate that the LHB scheme requires slightly higher server bandwidth than LLBE scheme.

1 Introduction

Video-on-Demand (VoD), a subset of Media-on-Demand (MoD), allows clients to watch a video of their choice at the time of their choice. With the advancement of broadband networking technology and the growth of processor speed and disk capacity, there are many researches have been stimulated in the recent years. A VoD system is typically implemented by a client-server architecture, and may easily run out of bandwidth because the growth in bandwidth can never keep up with the growth in the number of clients. This results in tremendous demand for computing power and communication bandwidth on the system.

To alleviate the stress on the bandwidth and I/O demands, many alternatives have been proposed by sacrificing some VCR functions, or known as near-VoD services. One way is to distribute the top ten or twenty so-called "hot" videos more efficiently

T. Braun et al. (Eds.): WWIC 2006, LNCS 3970, pp. 236–246, 2006.
© Springer-Verlag Berlin Heidelberg 2006

[3]. An efficient category is the segment based broadcasting [2]. It transfers each video according to a fixed schedule and consumes a constant bandwidth regardless of the number of requests for that video. That is, the number of clients watching a given video is independent of their bandwidth requirements.

The idea behind segment based broadcasting schemes is to divide the video into a series of segments and broadcast each segment periodically on dedicated server channels. In some schemes, a segment is further divided into sub-segments. The schemes [1,4-24,27-29] share a similar arrangement and substantially reduce the bandwidth requirement for hot video. The first channel always transmits the first segment. The other channels transmit the remaining segments according to a schedule predefined by the scheme. When viewers want to watch a video, they first wait for the beginning of the first segment or wait a fixed amount of time until the entire first segment is buffered. Furthermore, the viewers' set-top boxes (STB) or computers are necessary to download enough data from the other channels, so they will be able to play the segments of the video in turn.

Most of the significant broadcasting schemes have been proposed to reduce the server bandwidth requirement for Constant Bit-Rate (CBR) encoded videos. The few existing proposals [9,17,27-29], which support of the bandwidth-efficient Variable Bit-Rate (VBR) encoded videos, smooth and minimize the server bandwidth requirement at the cost of data losses. The lossless and bandwidth efficient (LLBE) [10] scheme states that minimization of the server bandwidth as a shortest path problem on a directed acyclic graph, and uses a dynamic programming method to solve the problem. It must employ off-line calculating to get optimal solution and its time complexity of the segmentation algorithm is $O(Nm^2)$, where N is the number of segments and m is the number of frames. In the real world, however, some real time events are very hot, for example, the collision of the comet Shoemaker-Levy with Jupiter, US Open final, and USA NBA final, etc. The LLBE scheme cannot be used for support VBR-encoded live video broadcasting. In order to overcome this obstacle, this paper proposes a live harmonic broadcasting (LHB) scheme to support VBR-encoded live video broadcasting. The ideas behind the scheme are (1) support VBR-encoded videos by asynchronous downloading and playing, and hybrid division by length and size, and (2) support live videos by postponing recasting process. Further, the time complexity is $O(m)$. It is simple and effective. Using data from real videos, we conduct a simulation to evaluate our schemes. The experiment results indicate that the LHB scheme require slightly higher server bandwidth than LLBE scheme.

The rest of this paper is organized as follows. In Section 2, we provide an overview of the existing schemes and comment on their performance. In Section 3, we present the transmitting and receiving scheme of VBR-encoded live video segments scheduled by LHB scheme. Some analysis and simulation results are presented in Section 4. We make brief conclusions in Section 5.

2   Related Works

The simplest broadcasting scheme is the staggered broadcasting [1] scheme. The server allocates K channels to transmit a video. Its maximum viewers' waiting time is L/K, where L is the video length. The pyramid broadcasting [20] scheme divides a video into increasing size of segments and transmits them on multiple channels of the same bandwidth. It requires less viewers' waiting time than the staggered broadcasting scheme. The fast broadcasting (FB) [7] scheme divides a video into a geometrical series of 1, 2, 4, ..., 2^{K-1}. Its maximum waiting time is $L/(2^K - 1)$. In comparison with staggered broadcasting and pyramid broadcasting scheme, the FB scheme obtains less viewers' waiting time. An implementation of the FB scheme on IP networks was reported in [26]. Based on the pagoda broadcasting (PB) [13] scheme, the new pagoda broadcasting (NPB) [14] scheme divides a video into fixed-size segments and maps them into data channels of equal bandwidth at the proper decreasing frequencies. Accordingly, the NPB scheme obtains less viewers' waiting time than the FB scheme. In fixed-delay pagoda broadcasting scheme with parameter q (FDPB(q)) [16], the viewer initially downloads for qd seconds from all channels before he starts displaying the video, where q is a positive integer, d is the length of time slot. When parameter q is increased, the viewers' waiting time decreases. The FDPB(q) scheme requires less viewers' waiting time than the NPB scheme. The recursive frequency splitting (RFS) [18] scheme further improves the waiting time to approach theoretical lower bound by using a more complex segment-to-channel mapping.

The harmonic broadcasting (HB) [6] and enhanced harmonic broadcasting (EHB) [8] schemes first divide a video into several segments equally, and further divide the segments into horizontal sub-segments according to the harmonic series. Yang, Juhn, and Tseng [25] have proved that the HB scheme requires the least viewers' waiting time under the same bandwidth. However, to ensure the data delivery on time, the scheme partitions each video frame into smaller parts. Such partition is too complex to be practical. The cautious harmonic broadcasting (CHB) [11], quasi-harmonic broadcasting (QHB) [11] and poly-harmonic broadcasting (PHB) [12] schemes divide the segments into vertical sub-segments to solve the problem. The greedy equal bandwidth broadcasting (GEBB) [4] scheme uses the same construction as PHB scheme exception of equal bandwidth of all channels. Both the PHB and GEBB schemes provide almost the same performance result as HB scheme. The staircase broadcasting (SB) [5] scheme was proposed to reduce buffer requirements on client end. The scheme requires a client to buffer only 25% of a playing video. However, like the HB scheme, the SB scheme is too complex to be practical. In the interleaving harmonic broadcasting (IHB) [23] and interleaving staircase broadcasting (ISB) [24] schemes, they use the interleaving technology to significantly improve the perceived quality of a video and solve the problem. Furthermore, they have almost the same performance as the HB and SB schemes.

The above schemes assume that videos are encoded in constant-bit-rate (CBR). Accordingly, they cannot support variable-bit-rate (VBR) videos well. Some schemes were proposed to address this problem. The periodic broadcasting with VBR-encoded video (VBR-B) [17] integrates the pyramid broadcasting scheme with the techniques of the GoP smoothing, server buffering, and client prefetchig to transmit VBR videos. Based on the VBR-B, the trace adaptive fragmentation (TAF) scheme [9] takes the trace of each video into account to predict the bandwidth requirements, and then uses complex techniques to smooth the bandwidth consumption. A more simple and effective approach is the variable bandwidth harmonic broadcasting (VBHB) [15], which divides a VBR video into fixed length segments.

The first and second segments are broadcasted at the transmission rate guaranteeing on time delivery of all frames. All other segments, which are distributed in the way of the cautious harmonic broadcasting (CHB) scheme, are completely downloaded before their display starts. Based on the FB scheme, Yu et al proposed smooth fast broadcasting (SFB) [27] scheme to reduce the variance of required bandwidth. A video server divides a VBR video into multiple equal-length segments by time, and then transmits each segment at constant bit rate. The order of the segments on each channel is further changed to smooth the total required bandwidth. In the smooth recursive-frequency splitting (SRFS) [28] scheme, it uses similar concept as SFB scheme and further improve the total required bandwidth. In the lossless and bandwidth efficient (LLBE) [10] scheme, it states that minimization of the server bandwidth as a shortest path problem on a directed acyclic graph, and uses a dynamic programming method to solve the problem.

3 Live Harmonic Broadcasting Scheme

3.1 VBR-Encoded Videos Support

Figure 1 shows the data consumption rate of a MPEG-2 video, Jurassic Park III. The variance of the rate is very large, and so is its required bandwidth. If we directly partition a VBR video into multiple segments, and then distribute the segments using the HB scheme. Video servers may easily stop their video services because the disk transfer rate and bandwidth requirements exceed their capabilities. In addition, clients probably cannot receive the video data in time when the networks cannot satisfy the peak bandwidth requirements

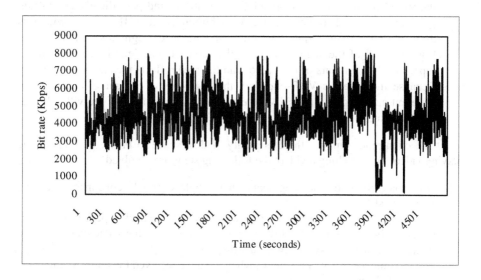

Fig. 1. The data consumption rate of the video, Jurassic Park III

.To eliminate the variance of bandwidth requirements for VBR videos, we propose two different areas compare with the conventional HB scheme.

- Asynchronous download and playback for a segment. The data consumption rate of a VBR video varies with time so the rate is probably larger than its data transfer rate. In the HB scheme, a client receives and plays a segment concurrently; thus, the video playback may be blocked when the consumption rate is larger than the transfer rate. To ensure the continuous playback, the LHB scheme requires a client to buffer a segment completely before playing it. That is the client cannot receive and play a video segment concurrently.
- Hybrid division by length and size. The LHB scheme divides a VBR video into segments by playing length, and then further divides the segments into sub-segments by file size. The scheme transmits each sub-segment on each channel at constant bit rate. Thus, the variance of required bandwidth is zero.

On the server side, the LHB scheme involves the following steps.

1. A video is divided into N segments by equal length. Thus the length of each segment is $d=L/N$. We also call such time length a time slot. Suppose S_i is the ith segment of the video, and its size is x_i. The concatenation of all the segments constitutes the whole video, $S = S_1 \bullet S_2 \bullet S_3 \bullet ... \bullet S_N$. Further, we divide the segment S_i into i equal-size sub-segments. Suppose $S_{i,j}$ is the jth sub-segment of S_i. The concatenation of all the sub-segments constitutes the whole segment, $S_i = S_{i,1} \bullet S_{i,2} \bullet S_{i,3} \bullet ... \bullet S_{i,i}$. The size of $S_{i,j}$ is x_i/i.
2. After preparing the video segments for broadcasting, we allocate N channels, from C_1, C_2 to C_N, to convey each video segment. The video server broadcasts the sub-segments of S_i on channel C_i sequentially and periodically at constant bit rate. Figure 2 illustrates the distribution of a VBR video, which is divided into seven equal-length-but-unequal-size segments, as indicated Fig. 2(a). All of the segments are of the same playing length. The rectangles represent the segments of the video, and the area reflects the size of a segment. Because the video is VBR-encoded, the segments of the same length are of different size. Figure 2(b) shows the segment arrangement of the video by the LHB scheme.

At the client end, suppose there is plenty of disk space to buffer portions of the playing video. For watching a video, the following steps are involved:

1. Download all of the sub-segments on multiple channels concurrently during each time slot.
2. To ensure continuous video playing, we delay the playback a period of time. If the client begins to download the video segments at T_0, the video can be played in the order of $S_1 \bullet S_2 \bullet S_3 \bullet ... \bullet S_N$ at T_0+L/N.
3. Stop loading data from channel C_i when we have received the entire segments S_i from that channel.

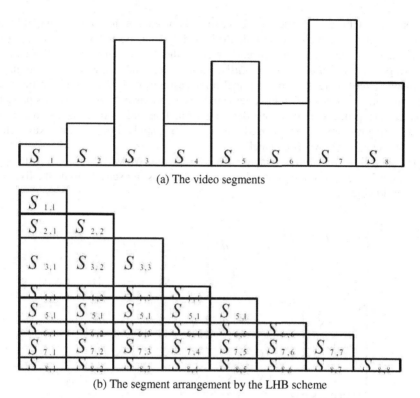

(a) The video segments

(b) The segment arrangement by the LHB scheme

Fig. 2. An example for video distribution by the LHB scheme

3.2 Live Videos Support

Since the scenes of a live video are broadcasted with video progress; the broadcasting schemes can not transmit the posterior and unavailable segments of live video in advance. Herein, we capture a live video on the fly and postpone the recasting process of segments. When server receives the video segment completely, it begins scheduling the deferred segment S_i as conventional harmonic broadcasting scheme does. That

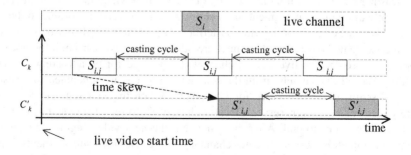

Fig. 3. The time skew scheduling strategy

is to say, everything is identical to conventional one except the starting time of broadcasting on each channel is deferred. Besides deferring the recasting process, at the client sides, viewers must concurrently receive the ongoing live video. We call this deferring process as *time skew scheduling* strategy and show in Figure 3. In Figure 3, Channel C_k represents the conventional broadcasting process to broadcast the video sub-segment $S_{i,j}$. Because video segment S_i is non-existent, we must postpone the broadcasting process until S_i broadcasting from live video site. As the result, the broadcasting process of the deferred video piece $S'_{i,j}$ applied by our time skew scheduling strategy are shown as channel C'_k.

The time skew scheduling strategy is a general rule. We will describe how to apply this strategy to enhance the generic harmonic broadcasting scheme to be the live ones in the following.

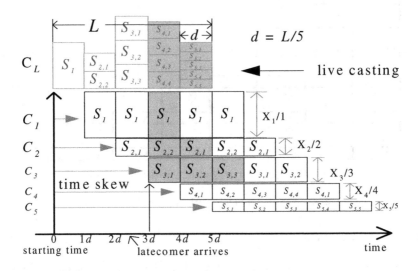

Fig. 4. Live harmonic broadcasting scheme

Suppose there is a live video with pre-defined length L, and we want to divide the video into five segments. First, in order to conform to the conventional harmonic broadcasting scheme, we not only equally divide a whole video into five segments but also evenly divide the *i*th segment into *i* sub-segments. Second, according to the rules of time skew scheduling policy, the posterior video segments will not be recast until they are existent. Two types of channel are adept by our live harmonic broadcasting scheme (Figure 4). The live casting channel (C_L) is used for broadcasting live video on time. The other channels, from the channels C_1 to C_5, are scheduled to recast the recorded segments of live video for latecomers. When the first segment S_1 is completely received by server, server allocates channel C_1 to recast segment S_1 cyclically until the video goes to end. After one time slot, the next video segment S_2 has been received completely, server allocates channel C_2 to recast video sub-segments $S_{2,1}$ and $S_{2,2}$ repetitively. After another one time slot, server will schedule channel C_3 to recast video sub-segments $S_{3,1}$, $S_{3,2}$ and $S_{3,3}$ repeatedly. The same process will apply for video segment S_4 and S_5 again. Figure 4 shows this example of live harmonic broadcasting scheme.

In addition to the deferred process applied on server, latecomers of live harmonic scheme must take following steps to participate the live video virtually on time. Latecomers wait for the first frame of live video to appear on channel C_1. On occurrence of the first frame, we must:

1. Begin to download data segments from live casting channel C_L absolutely. In addition, concurrently download all of channels on which the video segment has been broadcast. We call these channels that have been conveyed the recasting video segments as *active channels*.
2. Right after the first frame of the live video is downloaded completely, latecomers can start to watch an entire video from the beginning.
3. Stop downloading from active channel C_i when we have received all of video sub-segments of segment S_i from that channel. Moreover, stop downloading from the live channel C_L when the live video goes to end.

Figure 4 also shows the case of live harmonic broadcasting scheme that a latecomer arrives between time $2d$ and $3d$. He/she can start to watch his/her missing video completely at time $3d$. He/she receives the live video segments S_4 and S_5 from C_L and receives his missing video segments S_1, S_2 and S_3 from channels C_1 to C_3 respectively.

4 Analysis and Comparison

Suppose the client has enough disk space to buffer portions of the playing video on disk. The viewer's waiting time comes from the access time of video segments on networks. However, when we just miss the start of certain time slot, we must wait for the start of next time slot to download the video data. Thus, the maximum viewers' waiting time δ is

$$\delta = \frac{2L}{N}.$$ (1)

Because the video server broadcasts the sub-segments of S_i on channel i sequentially and periodically, the required bandwidth B_i on channel i is equal to $\frac{x_i}{\delta * i}$. The total required bandwidth is

$$\sum_{i=1}^{N} B_i = \frac{1}{\delta} \sum_{i=1}^{N} \frac{x_i}{i}.$$ (2)

According to (1) and (2), we can readily obtain the relation between the viewers' waiting time and the bandwidth that we need to allocate for the video.

Figure 5 depicts the maximum bandwidth requirements for real videos, Jurassic Park III and Star Wars II. These videos are encoded by MPEG-2. The length is 6067 and 8400 seconds respectively. Assume the live video data is known, we can compare to the LLBE scheme, which gives the minimum bandwidth. The experiment results indicate that the LHB scheme requires slightly higher server bandwidth than LLBE scheme for the real videos

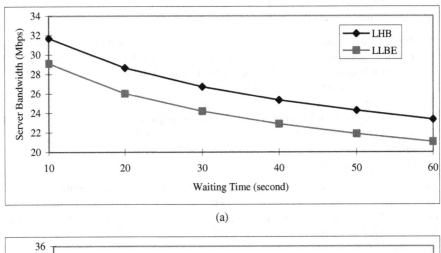

(a)

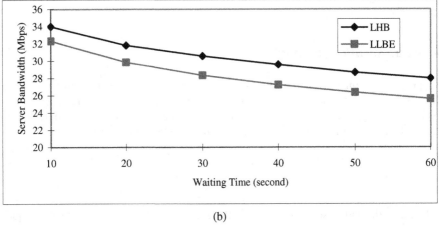

(b)

Fig. 5. The required bandwidth versus waiting time, (a) Jurassic Park III (b) Star Wars II

5 Conclusions

The video broadcasting service is already popular on Internet. The few existing proposals, which support of the bandwidth-efficient Variable Bit-Rate (VBR) encoded videos, smooth and minimize the server bandwidth requirement at the cost of data losses. The lossless and bandwidth efficient (LLBE) scheme states that minimization of the server bandwidth as a shortest path problem on a directed acyclic graph, and uses a dynamic programming method to solve the problem. However, it cannot be used for support live video broadcasting. In this paper, we proposed a live harmonic broadcasting (LHB) scheme to support VBR-encoded live video broadcasting. The ideas behind the scheme are (1) support VBR-encoded videos by asynchronous downloading and playing, and hybrid division by length and size, and (2) support live videos by postponing recasting process. It is simple and effective. A simulation that broadcasted real MPEG-2 videos was conducted to evaluate the LHB scheme. The experiment results indicate that the LHB scheme requires slightly higher server band-width than LLBE scheme.

Acknowledgement. The authors would like to thank the National Science Council of the Republic of China for financially supporting this research under Contract No. NSC 94-2213-E-008-026.

References

[1] K. C. Almeroth and M. H. Ammar, "The use of multicast delivery to provide a scalable and interactive video-on-demand service," *IEEE Journal on Selected Areas in Communications*, 14(50):1110-1122, Aug. 1996.

[2] Steven W. Carter and Darrell D. E. "Stream tapping:a system for improving efficiency on a video-on-demand server," *Technical Report UCSC-CRL-97-11*, University of California,Santa Cruz,April 1997.

[3] Asit Dan, Dinkar Sitaram, Perwez Shahabuddin, "Dynamic batching policies for an on-demand video server," *Multimedia Systems*, vol. 4, no. 3, pp. 112–121, June 1996.

[4] Ailan Hu, "Video-on-Demand Broadcasting Protocols: A Comprehensive Study," *IEEE INFOCOM*, pp. 508-517, 2001.

[5] L.S. Juhn and L.M. Tseng, "Staircase data broadcasting and receiving scheme for hot video service," *IEEE Transactions on Consumer Electronics*, vol. 43, no. 4, pp. 1110-1117, Nov 1997.

[6] L.S. Juhn and L.M. Tseng, "Harmonic broadcasting for video-on-demand service," *IEEE Transactions on Broadcasting*, vol. 43, no. 3, pp. 268-271, Sep 1997.

[7] L.S. Juhn and L.M. Tseng, "Fast data broadcasting and receiving scheme for popular video services," *IEEE Transactions on Broadcasting*, vol. 44, no. 1, pp. 100-105, Mar 1998.

[8] L.S. Juhn and L.M. Tseng, "Enhanced harmonic data broadcasting and receiving scheme for popular video service," *IEEE Transactions on Consumer Electronics*, vol. 44, pp. 343-346, 1998.

[9] F. Li, and I. Nikolaidis, "Trace-adaptive fragmentation for periodic broadcasting of VBR video," in *Proceedings of 9th International Workshop on Network and Operating System Support for Digital Audio and Video* (NOSSDAV'99), June 1999.

[10] I. Nikolaidis, F. Li and A. Hu, "An Inherently Loss-Less and Bandwidth-Efficient Periodic Broadcast Scheme for VBR Video," in *Proceedings of ACM SIGMETRICS*, 2000.

[11] J.-F. Paris, S. W. Carter, and D.D. E. Long, "Efficient broadcasting protocols for video on demand," in *Proceedings of the 6th International Symposium on Modeling, Analysis and Simulation of Computer and Telecommunication Systems*, Montreal, Canada, pp. 127-132, July 1998.

[12] J.-F. Paris, S. W. Carter, and D. D. E. Long, "A low bandwidth broadcasting protocol for video on demand," *Proc. Int'l Conf. on Computer Communications and Networks*, pp. 690-697, Oct. 1998.

[13] J-F. Paris, S. W. Carter and D. D. E. Long, "A Hybrid broadcasting protocol for video on demand," *Proc. 1999 Multimedia Computing and Networking Conference*, San Jose, CA, pp. 317-326, Jan 1999.

[14] J-F. Paris, "A simple low bandwidth broadcasting protocol for video on demand," *Proc. 7th Int. Conf. on Computer Communications and Networks*, pp. 690-697, Oct 1999.

[15] J. F. Paris, "A broadcasting protocol for compressed video," in *Proceedings of Euromedia'99 Conference*, Munich, Germany, pp 78-84, Apr 1999.

[16] J-F. Paris, "A fixed-delay broadcasting protocol for video-on-demand," *Proc. of Int'l Conf. on Computer Communications and Networks*, pp. 418-423, 2001

[17] D. Saparilla, K. Ross, and M. Reisslein, "Periodic broadcasting with VBR-encoded video," *IEEE INFOCOM 1999*, pp 464-471, 1999.

[18] Yu-Chee Tseng, Ming-Hour Yang and Chi-He Chang, "A Recursive Frequency-Splitting Scheme for Broadcasting Hot Videos in VOD Service", *IEEE Transactions on Communications*, vol. 50, issue:8, pp. 1348-1355, Aug 2002.

[19] Yu-Chee Tseng, Ming-Hour Yang, Chi-Ming Hsieh, Wen-Hwa Liao, and Jang-Ping Sheu, "Data broadcasting and seamless channel transition for highly demanded videos," *IEEE Transactions on Communications*, vol. 49, no. 5, pp. 863-874, May 2001.

[20] S. Viswanathan and T. Imielinski, "Pyramid Broadcasting for video on demand service," in *Proceedings of IEEE Multimedia Computing and Networking Conference*, vol. 2417, pp. 66-77, San Jose, California, 1995.

[21] Hung-Chang Yang, Hsiang-Fu Yu and Li-Ming Tseng, "Adaptive Live Broadcasting for Highly-Demand Videos," *Journal of Information Science and Engineering*, vol. 19, no. 3, pp. 531-549, May 2003.

[22] Hung-Chang Yang, Hsiang-Fu Yu, Li-Ming Tseng and Yi-Ming Chen, "A Segment-Alignment Interactive Broadcasting Scheme," *International Conference on Advanced Communication Technology*, Feb. 2004.

[23] Hung-Chang Yang, Hsiang-Fu Yu, Li-Ming Tseng and Yi-Ming Chen, "Interleaving Harmonic Broadcasting and Receiving Scheme with Loss-Anticipation Delivery," *Proceedings of IEEE Symposium on Computers and Communications*, June 2004.

[24] Hung-Chang Yang, Hsiang-Fu Yu, Li-Ming Tseng and Yi-Ming Chen, "Interleaving Staircase Broadcasting and Receiving Scheme with Loss-Anticipation Delivery," *Proceedings of International Conference on Internet Computing*, June 2004.

[25] Z.-Y. Yang, L.-S. Juhn, and L.-M. Tseng, "On Optimal Broadcasting Scheme for Popular Video Service," *IEEE Transactions on Broadcasting*, vol. 45, no. 3, pp. 318-322, September 1999.

[26] Z.-Y. Yang, "The Telepresentation System over Internet with Latecomers Support," *Ph.D. Dissertation*, Department of Computer Science and Information Engineering, National Central University, Taiwan, 2000.

[27] Hsiang-Fu Yu, Hung-Chang Yang, Yi-Ming Chen, Li-Ming Tseng and Chen-Yi Kuo, "Smooth Fast Broadcasting (SFB) for Compressed Videos," *Lecture Notes in Computer Science*, 2957, pp. 272-283, Jan. 2004.

[28] Hsiang-Fu Yu, Hung-Chang Yang, Yi-Ming Chen, and Li-Ming Tseng, "Smooth Recursive Frequency-Splitting Scheme for Compressed Videos," *Lecture Notes in Computer Science*, 3079, pp. 950-960, Sep. 2004.

[29] Hsiang-Fu Yu, Hung-Chang Yang, Li-Ming Tseng, and Yi-Ming Chen, "Simple VBR Staircase Broadcasting (SVSB)," *Computer Communications*, vol. 28, no. 17, pp. 1903-1909, Oct. 2005.

A Novel Design and Analysis of Cross-Layer Error-Control for H.264 Video over Wireless LAN

Jeong-Yong Choi and Jitae Shin

School of Information and Communication Engineering,
Sungkyunkwan University, Suwon, 440-746, Korea
{eldragon, jtshin}@ece.skku.ac.kr

Abstract. Efficient H.264 video transmission over wireless/mobile networks, which is used as a dominant video coding standard in Digital Multimedia Broadcasting (DMB) and in other advanced video conferencing, becomes dominant. However, wireless video transmission suffers from deficient wireless channel conditions such as high bit error rate, error bursts due to channel fading and bandwidth limitations. In this paper, a novel design and analysis of unified error-control with cross-layer interaction over IEEE 802.11e Wireless LAN, in order to improve error protection performance, is proposed. This framework combines cross-layer error protection techniques, i.e., error correction code in the link/MAC layer, erasure code in the application layer and automatic retransmission across the link/MAC layer and the application layer. The performance of the proposed scheme in comparison to the generic scheme is demonstrated by simulation.

1 Introduction

In Korea, Satellite Digital Multimedia Broadcasting (S-DMB) and Terrestrial Digital Multimedia Broadcasting (T-DMB) services have been widely standardized on a national basis. S-DMB was launched as a test-service in January and as a main-service in May 2005, respectively, and T-DMB commenced service in December 2005. The T-DMB system [1] adopts the European Digital Audio Broadcasting (DAB) system known as Eureka-147 [2] as its base, and adds various coding, networking and error correcting tools to process multimedia content. While S-DMB and T-DMB services have a different system, the associated video coding techniques are based on the H.264/Advanced Video Coding (AVC) baseline profile [3]. The H.264/AVC video coding standard provides for coding efficiency and network friendliness, splitting the Video Coding Layer (VCL) and Network Adaptation Layer (NAL).

In the trend of broadcasting communication convergence, multimedia content is supplied via various communication channels. IEEE 802.11-based Wireless LANs (WLANs) can be one of a great communication channel, supplying users with portability. IEEE 802.11e [4] has been developed and standardized to

T. Braun et al. (Eds.): WWIC 2006, LNCS 3970, pp. 247–258, 2006.
© Springer-Verlag Berlin Heidelberg 2006

support QoS of Audio/Visual (AV) data. In contrast to wired networks, since wireless channels suffer from restrictions such as bit-error and bandwidth, video transmission over wireless channels is a challenging task.

There has been considerable research invested, to overcome such inferior channel conditions. Many hybrid ARQ (HARQ) techniques combine various error-control schemes [5][6][7][8]. They include error detection code, Forward Error Correction (FEC) and Automatic Repeat reQuest (ARQ). Although aforementioned error-control-related research proposes efficient error protection schemes, there have been few concrete cross-layer frameworks in WLANs.

In this paper, a novel cross-layer error-control framework in IEEE 802.11e wireless LAN is proposed to improve error protection performance. This framework combines cross-layer error protection schemes, i.e., error correction code (Reed-Solomon code) in the link/MAC layer, erasure code in the application layer and ARQ across both the link/MAC layer and the application layer. The proposed cross-layer approach conforms to IEEE 802.11e MAC standard for retransmission, which means modification of de facto standard, is not required, and better transmission efficiency is shown both in the amount of overhead and in error rate, since related cross-layers cooperate with each other. The performance of the proposed scheme in comparison with the generic scheme is demonstrated by simulation.

The remainder of this paper is organized as follows. A brief overview of H.264 video transmission in wireless channels and a review of error-control techniques are provided in Section 2. Section 3 describes the proposed unified cross-layer error-control framework. In Section 4, the performance of proposed framework is evaluated. Lastly, conclusions and further works are presented in Section 5.

2   Related Works on Key Error-Control Components

2.1   H.264 over Wireless Channel

H.264/AVC standard [3][9] introduces a conceptual separation between VCL which provides the core high-compression representation of video picture content, and NAL which packages a representation for efficient delivery over particular types of networks. The H.264 NAL design provides the ability to customize the format of VCL data for delivery over a variety of particular networks. In this relationship, a unique packet-based interface between the VCL and the NAL is defined. The two design goals, compression efficiency and network friendliness, motivate differentiation between the VCL for coding efficiency and the NAL to take care of network issues. The overview on packetization issues and the error-resilience tools of H.264 coded video over IP networks, using RTP as the real-time transport protocol [10] is well described in [11].

For transmission of video over wireless networks with limited bandwidth and transmission power resources, high compression efficiency is required. In addition, adaptation of video data to network fluctuation is an additional important task, due to special properties of the wireless channel. The issues of H.264/AVC with RTP encapsulation, generic forward error correction, delayed feedback information, and error concealment in the IP-based wireless environment are discussed in [12]. In Section 2.3, the error-control techniques for video transmission will be reviewed.

2.2   Error-Controls for Video Transmission

FEC and delay-constrained ARQ are the main error-control techniques in video transmission. FECs, which are based both on the error correction code and on the erasure code, realize a proactive error-control mechanism. The sender generates redundant data and transmits these data with the original data. Then, the receiver recovers the erroneous bits or packets with redundant data. In order to prevent confusion, FECs are classified into two categories, i.e., error correction code-based FEC (namely Symbol-level FEC, S-FEC) and erasure code-based FEC (namely Packet-level FEC, P-FEC). While both S-FEC and P-FEC provide proactive solutions, ARQ is driven by reactive feedback information. ARQ spends less overhead in comparison with constantly rate-wasteful FECs, because ARQ is driven only when the received packet is erroneous. However, ARQ tends to result in greater delay than FECs.

In order to alleviate error resilience, hybrid techniques were attempted, and type-I [13] and type-II HARQ [14] were introduced. H. Liu et al. proposed a HARQ technique that combines the benefit of type-I and type-II techniques, and showed its efficacy for video transmission over wireless networks [5]. Y. Shan et al. presented a priority-based error protection scheme in the sense of the cross-layer approach [7]. Lastly, P. Ferré et al. attempted to modify the IEEE 802.11 legacy MAC to improve the throughput efficiency [15]. The article includes composition of an MAC frame and modification of MAC-level retransmission.

This paper is dominantly motivated by [15], to move the wireless channel to IEEE 802.11e, and makes use of the FEC option and BlockAck mechanism of IEEE 802.11e MAC.

2.3   IEEE 802.11e MAC-Level Error-Control Techniques

Symbol-Level Forward Error Correction (S-FEC) [16]: Fig. 1 shows the MAC Protocol Data Unit (MPDU) format defined in the draft specification of IEEE 802.11e [16]. Basically, a (224, 208) shortened Reed Solomon (RS) code, defined in GF(256), is used. Since an MAC Service Data Unit (MSDU), from the higher layer, can be much larger than 208 octets, an MSDU may be split into (up to 12) multiple blocks, and then each block is separately encoded by the RS encoder. The final RS block in the frame body can be shorter than 224 octets, using a shortened code. A (48, 32) RS code, which is also a shortened RS code, is used for the MAC header, and CRC-32 is used for the Frame Check Sequence (FCS). It is important to note that any RS block can correct up to 8 byte errors. The outer FCS allows the receiver to skip the RS decoding process if the FCS is correct. The inner FCS (or FEC FCS) allows the receiver to identify a false decoding by the RS decoder.

MAC Header	Frame Body MSDU		FCS
32	$208 \times (N-1)+1 \sim 208 \times N$		4

(a) Without the optional FEC

MAC Header		Frame Body (N Blocks)							FCS
Header	Header FEC	MSDU₁	FEC	MSDU₂	FEC	....	MSDU_N + FEC FCS	FEC	FCS
32	16	208	16	208	16	....	208	16	4

(b) With the optional FEC

Fig. 1. IEEE 802.11e MPDU format

MAC Header						
Frame Control	Duration	Receiver Address	Transmitter Address	BAR Control	BlockAck Starting Sequence Control	FCS
2	2	6	6	2	2	4

(a) BlockAck-request frame format

(a) BlockAck-request frame format

MAC Header							
Frame Control	Duration	Receiver Address	Transmitter Address	BAR Control	BlockAck Starting Sequence Control	BlockAck Bitmap	FCS
2	2	6	6	2	2	128	4

(b) BlockAck frame format

(b) BlockAck frame format

Fig. 2. IEEE 802.11e BlockAck-request and BlockAck frame format

ARQ [17]: The legacy MAC of IEEE 802.11 is based on the simple Stop-and-Wait ARQ (SW-ARQ) scheme. This involves a lot of overheads due to the immediate transmissions of acknowledgements (ACKs). In 802.11e, a new Selective-Repeat ARQ (SR-ARQ) mechanism named block acknowledgement (BlockAck) is introduced. In this mechanism, a group of data frames can be transmitted one by one with SIFS interval between them. Then, a single BlockAck frame is transmitted back to the sender to inform ACKs how many packets have been received correctly. Obviously, this scheme can improve channel efficiency. There are two kinds of BlockAck mechanisms used in 802.11e: *immediate* and *delayed*.

In the case of immediate BlockAck, the sender transmits a BlockAck-request frame after transmitting a group of data frames; the receiver has to transmit back the BlockAck after a SIFS interval. If the sender receives the BlockAck frame, it retransmits frames that are not acknowledged in the BlockAck frame, either in another group or individually. Immediate BlockAck is very useful for applications that require high-bandwidth and low-latency. However, it is very difficult for implementations to generate the BlockAck in SIFS interval. On the other hand, the delayed BlockAck does not require the strict timing limit.

In delayed BlockAck mechanism, the receiver is permitted to transmit a normal ACK frame first to acknowledge the BlockAck-request. The receiver can then transmit the BlockAck back at any other time less than the delayed Block-AckTimeout. The delayed BlockAck scheme is useful for applications that can tolerate moderate latency. If the sender does not receive the BlockAck or ACK frame from the receiver, it will retransmit the BlockAck-request frame. When the maximum BlockAck-request retransmission limit number is reached, the whole group of data frames will be deleted. Corresponding frame formats for BlockAck-request and BlockAck are specified in Fig. 2.

3 Unified Cross-Layer Cooperating Error-Control Framework

In this section, a unified error-control framework with cross-layer interactions is proposed, and the role of each layer and cross-layer cooperation are described. The overall structure of the proposed framework is depicted in Fig. 3.[1] The techniques and schemes previously explained in Section 2 are combined, in order to achieve an efficient framework.

3.1 Link/MAC Layer

As explained in Section 2.3, the link/MAC layer performs S-FEC. On the sender side, the MAC header and all MSDUs are encoded using $(48, 32)$ and $(224, 208)$ RS codes, respectively, and then composed into an MAC frame. After S-FEC encoding, the whole MAC frame is calculated and the CRC-32 and FCS field are generated.

On the receiver side, prior to S-FEC decoding, the FCS check is performed. If the FCS is correct, the S-FEC decoding procedure is unnecessary, and is therefore not performed. However, if the FCS is incorrect, all S-FEC blocks are decoded and erroneous blocks are corrected. If MAC header is erroneous and uncorrectable, all of the MSDUs belonging to the MAC header will be dropped. If an FEC block of MSDUs is uncorrectable, the block is marked as erroneous and then passed to a higher layer. The uncorrectable S-FEC block is determined whether to be retransmitted in the application layer.

In addition to S-FEC, the link/MAC layer provides ARQ scheme for the erroneous MSDUs, as explained in Section 2.3. Since the uncorrectable S-FEC block is passed to higher layers, not immediately requested for retransmission, the delayed BlockAck scheme is used, rather than the immediate BlockAck scheme. The sequence numbers of the uncorrectable S-FEC blocks determined to be retransmitted are bitmapped in the BlockAck frame.

---

[1] Since, in this paper, the range of the implementation is restricted, the implemented components are marked as shadow in Fig. 3.

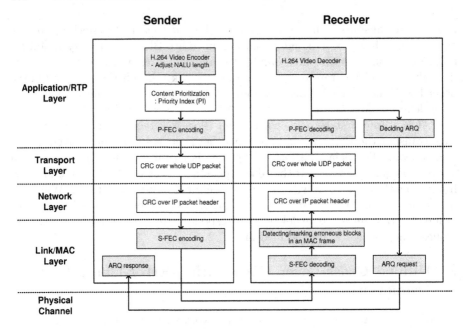

Fig. 3. Overall structure of the unified error-control framework with cross-layer interactions

3.2 Application Layer

In the proposed cross-layer framework, the application layer is responsible for *packet-level adaptation* and *cross-layer interaction*. Packet-level adaptation includes H.264 encoding, priority indexing (PI), RTP packetization and P-FEC. In this procedure, the H.264 encoder should consider the maximum length of an MSDU at the link/MAC layer. This implies that if one RTP packet is not fragmented into greater than one MSDU at the link/MAC layer, so as not to deteriorate error resilience, the maximum length of an RTP packet, including the P-FEC header attempted by G. Lieble et al. [18], should not exceed 180 bytes, as presented in Fig. 4. Size-adjusted H.264 NAL Units (NALUs) are P-FEC-encoded and packetized into an RTP packet. Priorities of each NALUs

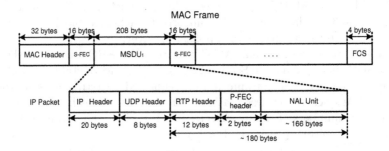

Fig. 4. Structure of an MAC frame

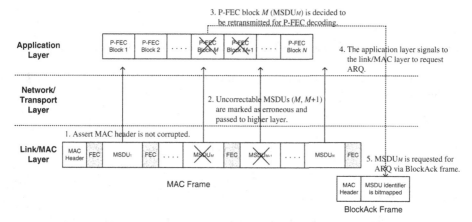

Fig. 5. Cross-layer error-control process at the receiver

are estimated and indexed, while NALUs are simultaneously encoded. The PI method which is used in [19][20] may be extended for H.264.[2] The PI-values can be criteria for Unequal Error Protection (UEP) strategy.

Next, consider the cross-layer interaction. The proposed framework complements S-FEC with P-FEC and ARQ. First, S-FEC protects all symbols in a packet. Next, if S-FEC proves to be uncorrectable, P-FEC recovers the erroneous data blocks. Lastly, if P-FEC fails, the application layer requests retransmission of the necessary data blocks by signaling to the link/MAC layer, to ensure that cross-layer cooperation is completed. The detailed error-control process is depicted and explained in Fig. 5. Compared with the proposed cross-layer framework, in the generic error-control framework which does not consider the cross-layer interaction, each layer will make best-effort for the best quality within underlying resources. For example, if uncorrectable bit-errors are detected in an MAC frame at the link/MAC layer, the link/MAC layer will attempt to request ARQ for a whole MAC frame, within the allowable maximum ARQ count. Such a framework requires wasteful bandwidth, whereas it can improve quality. To conclude, the application layer adapts the video content to the underlying structure of the link/MAC layer, and decides the error-control strategy, whereas the link/MAC layer provides the application layer with the transport information of the packets and a means for retransmission. In Section 3.3, the mathematical analysis of the proposed cross-layer framework is provided.

3.3 Mathematical Analysis

For mathematical analysis, some fundamental notations as presented in [16], are defined. At the link/MAC layer, given Bit Error Rate (BER), p_b, the probability of error in a block of l-bit length, $p_e(l)$, is determined by

---

[2] Although we include PI in the proposed framework, it is out of scope in this paper because of page limit.

$$p_e(l) = 1 - (1 - p_b)^l \qquad (1)$$

where p_s is the corresponding 8-bit symbol error probability, expressed as $p_s = p_e(8)$.

For (n_s, k_s) S-FEC, the error probability of an S-FEC block, $P_{\text{SFEC}}(n_s, k_s)$ is given by

$$P_{\text{SFEC}}(n_s, k_s) = \sum_{i=\lfloor (n_s - k_s)/2 \rfloor + 1}^{n_s} \binom{n_s}{i} p_s^i (1 - p_s)^{(n_s - i)}$$

$$= \sum_{i=t_s+1}^{n_s} \binom{n_s}{i} p_s^i (1 - p_s)^{(n_s - i)} \qquad (2)$$

where t_s is the error correction capability, expressed as $t_s = \lfloor (n_s - k_s)/2 \rfloor$.

Given symbol error probability, p_s, the error probability of MSDU with N coded blocks in the frame body, $P_{\text{MSDU}}(N)$, is

$$P_{\text{MSDU}}(N) = 1 - (1 - P_{\text{SFEC}}(48, 32))(1 - P_{\text{SFEC}}(224, 208))^N \qquad (3)$$

where $P_{\text{SFEC}}(48, 32)$ is the error probability of the 48-byte MAC header encoded with RS(48, 32) and $P_{\text{SFEC}}(224, 208)$ is the error probability of the 224-byte MSDUs encoded with RS(224, 208).

S-FEC decoded MSDUs are error-marked and passed to higher layers, eventually arriving at the application layer in the form of RTP packets. At the application layer, error-marked P-FEC blocks whose source blocks are RTP packets, are P-FEC decoded. For (n_p, k_p) P-FEC, the error probability after P-FEC decoding is given by

$$P_{\text{PFEC}}(n_p, k_p) = 1 - \sum_{i=0}^{n_p - k_p} \binom{n_p}{i} P_{\text{pkt}}^i (1 - P_{\text{pkt}})^{(n_p - i)} \qquad (4)$$

where P_{pkt} is the average error probability of a P-FEC block (i.e., an RTP packet), which corresponds to the expectation of $P_{\text{MSDU}}(N)$, $P_{\text{pkt}} = E[P_{\text{MSDU}}(N)]$ of the P-FEC block.

If P-FEC is not decodable, i.e., more than $(n_p - k_p)$ packets are erroneous, retransmission is requested by the application layer. Thus, the overall packet error probability with P-FEC parameters and ARQ parameter at the application layer, $P_{\text{Total}}(n_p, k_p, n_r)$, is given in Eq. (5). In order to simplify the expression, it is assumed that the BlockAck messages of IEEE 802.11e MAC except for the video MAC frames, be error-free.

$$\begin{aligned} P_{\text{Total}}(n_p, k_p, n_r) &= \Pr[\text{ARQ fails} \mid N_e \text{ packet errors}] \\ &= \frac{\Pr[\text{ARQ fails} \cap N_e \text{ packet errors}]}{\Pr[N_e \text{ packet errors}]} \\ &= \frac{P_{\text{pkt}}^{(n_r+1)(N_e - (n_p - k_p))}}{P_{\text{PFEC}}(n_p, k_p)} \end{aligned}$$

$$= \frac{P_{\text{pkt}}^{(n_r+1)(N_e-(n_p-k_p))}}{1 - \sum_{i=0}^{n_p-k_p} \binom{n_p}{i} P_{\text{pkt}}^i \left(1 - P_{\text{pkt}}\right)^{(n_p-i)}} \qquad (5)$$

where n_r is the maximum retransmission count, and N_e $(> n_p - k_p)$ is the number of erroneous packets.

4 Simulation

In this section, the performance of the proposed cross-layer error-control framework is demonstrated over IEEE 802.11e WLAN, by performing simulations under several BER conditions. The "Foreman" sequence (CIF, 352x288) was encoded using H.264 with encoding parameters, as presented in Table 1, and then transmitted through the Gilbert-Elliott channel model. The performance of the generic error-control scheme and the proposed error-control scheme are compared. Both schemes consist of (24, 20) P-FEC at the application layer, (224, 208) S-FEC at the link/MAC layer and ARQ with maximum ARQ count of 2.

Fig. 6 and Fig. 7 present the simulation results for the generic isolated-layer scheme and the proposed cross-layer scheme. Fig. 6(a) and Fig. 6(b) present the MSDU overhead rate required for ARQ in the number of MSDUs, and the NALU error rate, both as a percentage. From graphical results, it is demonstrated that the proposed cross-layer scheme results in less NALU error rate with dramatically less overhead. The simulation result, presented in Fig. 7, shows that the proposed cross-layer error-control scheme outperforms the isolated-layer error-control scheme, with regard to end-quality. In the isolated-layer scheme, since even an uncorrectable MSDU in the MAC frame results in retransmission of the whole MAC frame, the isolated-layer scheme experiences higher bit error probability than the cross-layer scheme. Thus, greater retransmission overhead is required, and high MAC frame error probability deteriorates throughput, eventually, producing degradation of objective video quality.

Table 1. Video encoder parameters and channel settings used in the simulation

Parameter settings	
Video encoder	H.264 (JM 10.1)
Sequence name	Foreman
Image format	CIF (352×288)
Number of encoded frames	1200
Encoding method	1 IDR-frame followed by 1199 P-frames with CBR (384kbps), 20 random intra MB update every P-frame, fixed packet size shorter than 180 bytes.
Channel settings	
Channel model	Gilbert-Elliott channel model
Bit error rate	$3 \times 10^{-3} \sim 1 \times 10^{-2}$

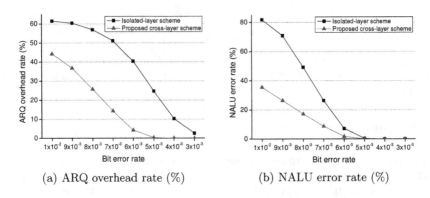

(a) ARQ overhead rate (%)   (b) NALU error rate (%)

Fig. 6. The performance comparison of ARQ overhead rate and NALU error rate

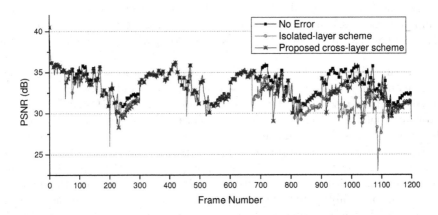

Fig. 7. PSNR distribution of Y-component of transmitted sequences (BER=5×10^{-3}): (a) No error, (b) Isolated-layer error-control scheme, and (c) Proposed cross-layer error-control scheme

From simulation results, it can be inferred that the proposed cross-layer error-control scheme presents excellent performances from the viewpoint of both end-quality and transmission efficiency.

5   Conclusions and Future Works

In this paper, a novel design and analysis of unified cross-layer error-control framework was proposed, and the performance of the framework was demonstrated. In the proposed error-control framework, the cross-layer controls between S-FEC/ARQ at the link/MAC layer and P-FEC/ARQ decision at the application layer are incorporated and can obtain obvious gain with comparison of simple combinations of isolated layers, thus unnecessary operations can be avoided. From simulation results, it can be inferred that the proposed cross-layer error-control scheme demonstrates excellent performance from the viewpoint of both end-quality and transmission efficiency.

For further works, in order to maximize the performance of FEC and ARQ, combined with packet-level interleaving and symbol-level interleaving can be considered. Moreover, mathematical analysis with assumed Gilbert-Elliott bit error-prone channel can be used to estimate optimal S-FEC parameters (i.e., n_s and k_s) and to change such parameters adaptively in order to enhance error protection performance.

Acknowledgements

This research was supported by the Ministry of Information and Communication (MIC), Korea, under the Information Technology Research Center (ITRC) support program supervised by the Institute of Information Technology Assessment (IITA) (IITA-2005-(C1090-0502-0027)).

References

1. "Digital Multimedia Broadcasting," Telecommunications Technology Association, 2003SG05.02-046, 2003.
2. "Radio Broadcasting System: Digital Audio Broadcasting (DAB) to mobile, portable and fixed receivers," ETSI EN 300 401 v1.3.3, May, 2001.
3. Draft ITU-T Recommendation and Final Draft International Standard of Joint Video Specification (ITU-T Rec. H.264 — ISO/IEC 14496-10 AVC), Document: JVT-G050r1, May. 2003.
4. IEEE 802.11e/D3.0, "Draft Supplement to Part 11: Wireless Medium Access Control (MAC) and Physical Layer (PHY) specifications: Medium Access Control (MAC) Enhancements for Quality of Service (QoS)," May, 2002.
5. H. Liu and E. Zarki, "Performance of H.263 Video Transmission over Wireless Channels Using Hybrid ARQ," IEEE Journal on Selected Areas in Communications, Vol. 15, No. 9, Dec. 1997.
6. I. Rhee and S. R. Joshi, "Error Recovery for Interactive Video Transmission over the Internet," IEEE Journal on Selected Areas in Communications, Vo. 18, No. 6, Jun. 2000.
7. Y. Shan and A. Zakhor, "Cross Layer Techniques for Adaptive Video Streaming over Wireless Networks," International Conference on Multimedia and Expo, Lausanne, Switzerland, Aug. 2002, pp. 277-280.
8. P. de Cuetos and K. W. Ross, "Unified Framework for Optimal Video Streaming," IEEE INFOCOM 2004, Hong Kong, Mar. 2004.
9. T. Wiegand, G. J. Sullivan, G. Bjøntegaard, and A. Luthra, "Overview of the H.264/AVC Video Coding Standard," IEEE Trans. on Circuits and Systems for Video Technology, Vol. 13, No. 7, July 2003.
10. H. Schulzrinne, "RTP: A Transport Protocol for Real-Time Applications," RFC 3550, IETF, Jul. 2003.
11. S. Wenger, "H.264/AVC over IP," IEEE Trans. on Circuits and Systems for Video Technology, Vol. 13, No. 7, July 2003.

12. T. Stockhammer, M. M. Hannuksela, and T. Wiegand, "H.264/AVC in Wireless Environments," IEEE Trans. on Circuits and Systems for Video Technology, Vol. 13, No. 7, July 2003.

13. H. Deng and M. Lin, "A Type I Hybrid ARQ System with Adaptive Code Rates," IEEE Trans. Communications, vol. 46, pp. 733-737, Feb. 1995.

14. S. Lin and D. Costello, "Error Control Coding: Fundamentals and Applications," Englewood Cliffs, NJ: Prentice-Hall, 1983.

15. P. Ferré, A. Doufexi, A. Nix, D. Bull, and J. Chung-How, "Packetisation Strategies for Enhanced Video Transmission over Wireless LANs," Packet Video Workshop (PV2004), Irvine, CA, USA, 13 14 Dec. 2004.

16. S. Choi, "IEEE 802.11e MAC-Level FEC Performance Evaluation and Enhancement," IEEE Global Telecommunications Conference, 2002.

17. Q. Ni, L. Romdhani and T. Turletti, "A Survey of QoS Enhancements for IEEE 802.11 Wireless LAN," RFC 3550, IETF, Jul. 2003.

18. G. Liebl, T. Stockhammer, M. Wagner, J. Pandel, G. Baese, M. Nguyen and F. Burkert "An RTP Payload Format for Erasure-Resilient Transmission of Progressive Multimedia Streams," Internet Draft, IETF, Feb. 2001 (http://www3.ietf.org/proceedings/01mar/I-D/avt-uxp-00.txt).

19. J. Shin, J. G. Kim, J. W. Kim and C.-C.J. Kuo, "Dynamic QoS mapping control for streaming video in relative service differentiation networks," European Transactions on Telecommunications, Vol. 12, No. 3, May-June 2001, pp. 217-230.

20. J.-Y. Choi and J. Shin, "Content-Aware Packet-Level Interleaving Method for Video Transmission over Wireless Networks," Springer-Verlag LNCS3510 (WWIC05), May 2005.

WLAN Service Coverage Based on PixelFlow Predictions

Nicolas Echenard[1] and Jean-Frédéric Wagen[2]

[1] Swiss Federal Institute of Technology, Lausanne, Switzerland
[2] Ecole d´Ingénieurs et d´Architectes de Fribourg, Switzerland
nicolas.echenard@epfl.ch, jean-frederic.wagen@eif.ch

Abstract. Increase of WLAN network deployments lead to the need of developing tools to predict coverage in terms of available service. In this paper we propose to establish service coverage based only on approximate floor plans by using the so-called PixelFlow algorithm. This algorithm is based on discrete version of the Huygens principle and appears to be rather robust to approximation in the floor plan. Measurements of service performances have been undertaken and used to calibrate the prediction results. Since the conventional calibration based on prediction errors is not the goal of service coverage prediction, a new metric has been developed to quantify differences between predicted and measured boundaries of the service coverage. Despite the complex impact of inaccuracies related to floor plan, wall material, radio propagation and WLAN protocols, it appears that the service coverage prediction proposed here is suitable to ease the radio network design of indoor Wi-Fi system.

1 Introduction

Increasingly many "hotspots" are deployed to provide Internet access on public buildings such as airports, schools, libraries, shopping centers or restaurants by using Wi-Fi technology. Generally those buildings have larger dimensions than the maximum range of a WLAN access point and thus require many access points to be fully covered. Finding optimal positions of the access points is a non trivial task and cannot be done efficiently without the use of a coverage prediction tool or lengthy measurement surveys. The number of academic or commercial coverage tool is too large to be properly referenced here but an overview of these works shows that most prediction software tools produce coverage maps in term of received signal strength intensity which must be interpreted with a strong knowledge in radio propagation and radio system performance. In order to provide a tool that can be used and understood by network users as well as network administrators, we propose to produce coverage in term of available service instead of power levels.

In most indoor environments where an exact description is too tedious to model, it is assumed that the main propagation phenomena can be captured by a 2D simulation while neglecting the floor attenuation in this work. It is also assumed that over the short distances involved in typical office environment, the error between 2D and 3D path loss can be approximately mitigated by a scaling factor. Furthermore, it is desired to only capture the essence of the propagation phenomena to predict service coverage. The exact prediction of the received signal strength is not the aim of this work.

T. Braun et al. (Eds.): WWIC 2006, LNCS 3970, pp. 259–274, 2006.

Although, the algorithm presented here has a sound basis for propagation predictions [JOH71, HOE85, LUT95, LUT98], the PixelFlow algorithm defined here is used only to predict user service coverage, i.e., to predict whether or not "it works" as most users care to know. A given threshold for the throughput measured at the application level for a single user is used to quantify the user service coverage: in this work a threshold of 2 Mbit/s and 5 Mbit/s has been chosen as an example. The multi-user service coverage is out of scope of this paper. However, the Wi-Fi radio resource being a shared resource it can be assumed that the multi-user throughput is the single user throughput divided by the number of simultaneous users served by a given Wi-Fi acces points [WJF04]. Lower throughput due to interference between access points with the same carrier frequency is not taken into account here. Manual and automatic frequency planning [GWR03] can be used to mitigate this effect.

Section II introduces the PixelFlow algorithm on which the service predictions are based. Section III describes the measurements of WLAN service. Section IV introduces a new metric to compare the predicted and measured coverage results. Section V explains the calibration of the model and the last section VI concludes this paper.

2 Service Coverage Prediction: An Overview of the PixelFlow Algorithm

The main prediction algorithm, called here PixelFlow, is based on a 2D discretization of the indoor floor plan. Therefore, only a bitmap version of the floor plan is required. The bitmap can be obtained electronically from many specialized software or by simply scanning the floor plan (hand-drawn or printed). The bitmap of the floor plan is used to define a lattice whose nodes are separated by a distance Δr as represented in Fig. 1. A node is either a source node, or a free-space node or an obstacle node. The obstacle nodes represent mainly the building walls. However, writings or other features on the scanned floor plan could be taken as obstacles. These spurious obstacles nodes do not affect significantly the prediction in most cases. Care should be taken to avoid too dirty floor plans or the ones with too many inscriptions on them.

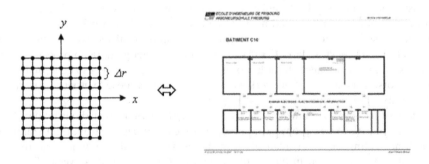

Fig. 1. 2D lattice applied on the bitmap of the floor plan for PixelFlow computations

The PixelFlow algorithm applies the Huygen's principle on each node of the lattice. The only difference between the free-space and obstacle nodes is their parameters β and γ as described hereafter.

Each node on the lattice is connected to its four neighbors by straight edges. The wave propagation is modeled by flows f running on those edges. Fig. 2 defines the eight flows f along the edges. The sum of the four out-going flows can be shown to satisfy the discrete wave equation [LUT98, HOE85]. The relations between out-going and in-coming flows for different nodes are given below.

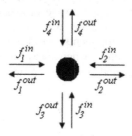

Fig. 2. Definition of the flows along each of the four edges

Considering the lattice of nodes representing a floor plan, three types of nodes are considered:

- **source node:** flows are forced to a given value. For an isotropic harmonic source located at (x, y) and with an amplitude $\tilde{a}$ and a period T, the out-going flows are:

$$f_i^{out}(x, y, k\Delta t) = \frac{\tilde{a}}{4} \sin\left(\frac{2\pi}{\tilde{T}} k\right) \quad i = 1,...,4. \tag{1}$$

The in-coming flows are equal to the appropriate out-going flows from the adjacent nodes (see Fig. 2).
The normalized period $\tilde{T}$ is given by

$$\tilde{T} = \frac{T}{\Delta t} \tag{2}$$

where Δt is the discrete time interval chosen in the PixelFlow computations. Considering an isotropic source emitting in free space, [JOH71] showed that the smaller the value of $\tilde{T}$ is, the less circular the wave fronts are. This is due to the fact that the wave speed along the axial directions is slower than the wave speed along the diagonal directions by a factor approaching one when $\tilde{T}$ >> 4.

- **free space nodes:** according to Huygen's principle, a free space node acts as an isotropic radiator. All incident energy is scattered. Thus we use $\beta = 1$ and $\gamma = 0$ in equation (4) given below.

It is shown in [LUT95] that the solution given by equation (4) with $\beta = 1$ and $\gamma = 0$ is the solution found by solving the discrete wave equation under the conditions (3). Thus, the sum φ of the four in-going flows satisfies the discrete wave equation. Thus, for free space propagation in 2D or 3D, the attenuation is proportional to the distance from the source or the square of the distance, respectively [e.g., LUT98, GAR04].

$$\varphi(x, y, k\Delta t) = \sum_{i=1}^{4} f_i^{in}(x, y, k\Delta t) \tag{3}$$

- **obstacle (wall) nodes** : in previous works [LUT95, LUT98] a PixelFlow like algorithm was used to compute wave propagation in micro-cells located in urban environment. The building walls were modeled by considering only reflection. In indoor environments transmission and scattering must also be taken into account. Therefore, when a wave reaches an obstacle, a part β of its energy is scattered and another part γ is reflected.

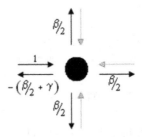

Fig. 3. Example of the output flows of Fig.2 corresponding to a unitary input flow ($f_1^{in} = 1$) for an obstacle or building wall node with transmission coefficient β and reflection coefficient γ

In this case, by noticing that output flows of a node are input flows of the adjacent nodes in the next time iteration and abandoning the in/out distinction, the time evolution of flows can be written as follows:

$$\begin{pmatrix} f_1(x + \Delta r, y, t + \Delta t) \\ f_2(x - \Delta r, y, t + \Delta t) \\ f_3(x, y + \Delta r, t + \Delta t) \\ f_4(x, y - \Delta r, t + \Delta t) \end{pmatrix} = \frac{\beta}{2} \begin{pmatrix} 1 & -1 & 1 & 1 \\ -1 & 1 & 1 & 1 \\ 1 & 1 & 1 & -1 \\ 1 & 1 & -1 & 1 \end{pmatrix} + \gamma \begin{pmatrix} 0 & -1 & 0 & 0 \\ -1 & 0 & 0 & 0 \\ 0 & 0 & 0 & -1 \\ 0 & 0 & -1 & 0 \end{pmatrix} \begin{pmatrix} f_1(x, \\ f_2(x, \\ f_3(x, \\ f_4(x, \end{pmatrix} \tag{4}$$

As an example, the geometry presented in Fig. 4 is considered: a wall is placed at 10 meters in front of the source. Theoretical and computed attenuations are compared in Fig. 5 for some values of the "reflection" (γ) and "transmission" (β) coefficients. The wall attenuation A_{wall} in dB is defined as the difference between the received power without and with the wall. In case of 2D propagation, the received power is proportional to the inverse of the distance d. Thus we define the normalized distance attenuation $A(d)$ as follows:

$$A(d)[dB] = 10 \cdot \log(d / d_1) \tag{5}$$

with d_1 as an arbitrary constant.

For distance d on the other side of the wall from the source $(d > d_{wall})$, the attenuation is increased by the wall attenuation A_{wall} :

$$A(d > d_{wall})[dB] = 10 \cdot \log(d / d_1) + A_{wall} \tag{6}$$

In the following figure, comparisons are made between the results from the theoretical equations (5) and (6) and the results (7) from the PixelFlow computation scaled using A_o such that the choice of d_1 and the choice of the amplitude $\tilde{a}$ of the source in the PixelFlow computations are irrelevant.

$$A_{PixelFlow}(d(x, y))[dB] = A_o - 10 \cdot \log\left(\sum_k |\varphi(x, y, k\Delta t)|^2\right) \tag{7}$$

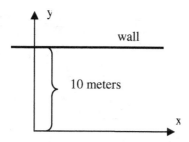

Fig. 4. Geometry with a wall placed at 10 meters in front of the source to investigate the wall attenuation. Results are presented in Fig. 5

As expected from the interference between the incident and reflected wave, the PixelFlow attenuation, oscillates when measured between the source and the wall, i.e, for distance smaller than 10 meters. Beyond the wall (for d > 10m), the attenuation is linear with respect to distance as it should be for a 2D free-space propagation. The influence of γ's value is clearly seen in Fig. 5: the greater the value γ, the greater the wall attenuation A_{wall}. A graph of the desired wall attenuation versus γ is out of the scope of this paper but is available in [ECH05].

Observing that free space propagation and wall reflections could be approximated by the PixelFlow computations, the following figure (Fig. 6) shows the results of the PixelFlow computations applied to a typical floor plan. In Fig. 6, the thick black line represents the walls. The PixelFlow results (7) are plotted in Fig. 6 using a grey scale allowing the visualization of the interference pattern. These results could be compared to path loss measurements but in this paper, comparisons will be made with service coverage instead.

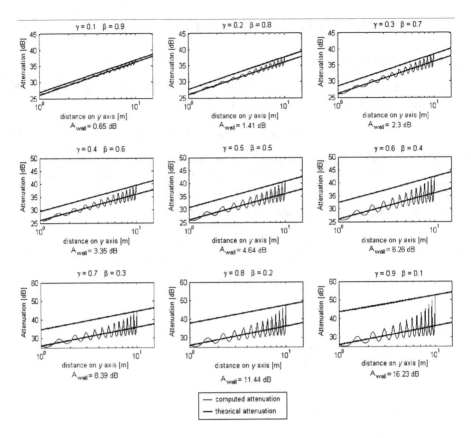

Fig. 5. Fitted free-space attenuation (thick line) and PixelFlow attenuation (thin line) for nine different values of β and γ satisfying the relation $\beta + \gamma = 1$. The wall attenuation A_{wall} is the difference between the two thick lines. Different wall attenuations (0.65 to 16.23 dB) can be obtained by adjusting the parameters β and γ.

Conventional radio coverage map provides some information about network performance but are quite complex to interpret because of multipath effects, signal and receiver characteristics, protocols used and enhancements such as [CSN04]. It is assumed that most end-user of Wi-Fi equipment and many IT or WLAN managers are only interested in knowing whether "it works or not", i.e., whether or not the offered service is acceptable. Thus, we aim to provide this required information in term of service coverage prediction instead of received power level.

To quantify the definition of acceptable service, we choose the rate at which user data can be transferred through the network. In other word, our goal is to predict whether or not the latency felt by a single user while browsing the web is acceptable or not when the main bottleneck is due to the radio path. Furthermore, real time applications like streaming, voice over IP, network games and some distributed services require a larger data rate to work properly. Those reasons lead to produce map in terms of service performance instead of path loss or signal strength. Therefore, the

PixelFlow algorithm is tuned to predict service coverage maps. These service coverage maps indicate only whether or not the user throughput is above a given threshold. In the following and as an example, we arbitrarily choose to define two services:

- *Business service:* the user throughput for web surfing, file transfer, server access, etc. which lead to a required user throughput of at least 2 Mbit/s on the Wi-Fi radio link.
- *Interactive service*: the user throughput should be at least 5 Mbit/s.

The throughputs are defined over the WLAN radio link at the application level. More details are provided in the following section describing the measurements used for the calibration of the model proposed here.

Fig. 6. Radio coverage obtained by applying PixelFlow to a typical floorplan. In this figure, the grey scale applied with respect to the received power level in dBm is irrelevant here. Specular reflection and scattering can be observed.

3 Measurements

A measurement campaign was undertaken to collect service performance measurements at many locations in one classroom/office environment and in one home. The results were used to adjust the PixelFlow parameters by a point matching like method to minimize the difference between the predicted and measured WLAN service coverage. This section describes the measurements. The new metric used in this work is presented in the next section.

The measured service performance is defined as the measured user throughput between a client and a server. The client (a laptop PC: DELL) was connected to the server (another laptop PC: ASUS) via a Wi-Fi access point (Cisco Aironet 1100, IEEE 802.11b/g protocol in infrastructure mode) as shown in Fig. 7 (the access point is the left most device, the PC server is in the middle and the PC client is on the right). Only the case for a single user was considered as discussed in the introduction (Section 1).

Analyzing typical IP traffic, most data are transmitted by using the following protocols: HTTP/TCP, FTP/TCP, TCP or UDP. Thus, the service performance measurements have been conducted for these four protocols. The service performance is defined as the protocol throughput measured for data transfer lasting about 10 seconds. These measurements were aimed to capture the satisfaction of a typical user in a simplified and objective way.

The main measurement campaign took place in an office/laboratory environment at the EIA-FR (Ecole d'ingénieurs et d'architectes de Fribourg, Switzerland, www.eif.ch). A typical floor was chosen to perform a complete measurement survey at 94 different locations (the square dots in Fig. 10). The floor plan delimits five large laboratories/classroom and seven offices of smaller size. Fig. 8 illustrates the floor at the EIA-FR. At each of the 94 locations, 15 throughput and signal level measurements were taken per protocol.

Fig. 7. The measurement equipments set-up used to conduct the measurements: the WLAN access point on the left is linked to the leftmost PC via a cross-over Ethernet cable. The right most PC is the client with our own survey software.

Fig. 8. Example of an office room where the measure-ments have been undertaken

Although not presented here, measurement results at fixed location at the EIA-FR exhibit a variation over time of about 2 to 5 dB in received power level. In some cases up to 10 dB variations had been recorded and attributed to persons moving in the hallways. Thus, others measurements were performed in a locative flat to determine the time dependence of the measurements. For the long-term measurements presented here, the measurement client was left at the same place for 24 hours and 15 distinct transfers for each protocol were measured every 30 minutes. The measurement client was placed in a bedroom and the measurement server and Wi-Fi access point in another room (corridor), with one wall between the two rooms. The two graphs in Fig. 9 show the average received signal strength intensity (RSSI) measured during the HTTP tests and the measured HTTP throughput with respect to "time of the day".

Fig. 9 shows that the RSSI measured values are quite stable (~2 dB) during the night whereas the RSSI values fluctuate during the day (up to 10 dB). Variations in the received power are expected to come from changes in the environment: people are moving and perhaps switching on or off devices that can generate electromagnetic interferences (e.g., microwave ovens, Bluetooth devices ...). However throughput values are quite stable for the whole day. This shows that it is difficult to find a correlation between the measured received power (RSSI) and the measured throughput. For instance, a decrease of 10 dB in RSSI is observed between 11h and 11h30. But this does not lead to a drastic diminution of the measured throughput.

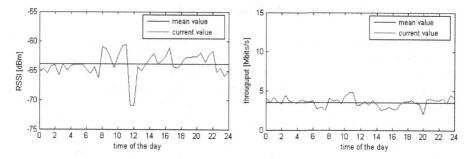

Fig. 9. Measured RSSI and HTTP throughput during a whole day

Although not shown here, comparing measurements for HTTP and TCP, we observe that for a given RSSI, the HTTP throughput values have smaller standard deviations from its mean value than results using TCP. Usually the maximum throughput is achieved at ~8 Mbit/s for HTTP transfers and at ~17 Mbit/s for TCP transfers. The measured values for HTTP takes into account the time to load a test page after the user requests it: this explains the lower throughput. TCP transfers accounts only for the data transmission. Thus the HTTP throughput is not used for the calibration of the service performance prediction, but the TCP throughput was found to be an effective measurement of service quality.

Fig. 10 shows the measured service coverage when a minimal user rate of 2 Mbit/s is required (*Business service* [section 1]). Because of the random fluctuations observed above, it is reasonable to suppose that values measured at a given position will be valid over an area. How large this area can be, has been roughly investigated. Our measurements tend to show limited fluctuations over an area of about $1m^2$. Thus, position error of the order of 1 meter should be acceptable.

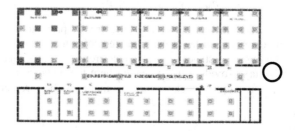

Fig. 10. Measured service coverage for *Business service* (user throughput threshold = 2 Mbit/s, 94 locations): the light grey squares are the locations where the service coverage is acceptable; the dark grey squares are the location where the service coverage is below threshold. The access point is located at the center of the circle.

The following section introduces the metric used to compare measured and predicted service coverage. The comparison is designed to determine the PixelFlow parameters such that differences between the predicted and computed coverage maps are minimized.

4 Prediction Accuracy: The Distance Metric

Usually the quality of a prediction is quantified by computing the standard deviation of the difference between the predicted and measured values. Here, a new approach is proposed to express in meters the average difference between the measurement points and the predicted coverage map. Since the predicted and measured coverage maps can both be seen as "bitmaps", comparison can be done pixel by pixel. A prediction error is introduced each time a pixel has not the same value in the two maps. The distance metric defined here is computed over all measured pixel for which a prediction error occurred. The distance metric is the average distance of these erroneous predictions. The distance considered for the distance metric is the distance to the nearest coverage border. The mathematical description of the distance metric is defined in this section.

The following notation for the service coverage "bitmaps" is used:

- The superscript X is the service threshold level. In the results presented here, $X = 2$ Mbit/s (*Business service*) or 5 Mbit/s (*Interactive service*). The subscript differentiates the measurements (M) from the PixeFlow predictions (PF).
- $C_M^X(x, y)$: represents the measured coverage at location (x, y),
- $C_{PF}^X(x, y)$ represents the predicted coverage (predicted pixel) at location (x, y),

The distance $\delta_M(x, y)$, in pixel unit, from a pixel located at (x, y) in the measured coverage C_M^X to the border of the predicted coverage C_{PF}^X is defined as the number of single pixel layers required to be added to, or removed from, the border of the predicted coverage in order to reach the (x, y) pixel. Only location (x, y) where the measurements disagree with the prediction are taken into account. Thus, with Δr the width of a pixel in meters, the following distance:

$$d_M(x, y) = \delta_M(x, y) \cdot \Delta r \tag{8}$$

indicates the distance in meters between an incorrectly predicted measurement point and the nearest pixel on the border of the predicted coverage map (see also Fig. 11).

Computing the mean distance for all measurements locations (x, y) where a prediction error occurs provide a metric called here the distance metric or prediction accuracy $M(C_M^X, C_{PF}^X)$ which is expressed in meters. The prediction accuracy is expressed by:

$$M(C_M^X, C_{PF}^X) = \frac{1}{N} \sum_{\{(x,y)|C_M^X(x,y) \neq C_{PF}^X(x,y)\}} d_M(x, y) \tag{9}$$

with N is the number of location with a prediction error.

Note that:

$$M\left(C_1^X, C_2^X\right) \neq M\left(C_2^X, C_1^X\right) \tag{10}$$

i.e., the order in the notation used here is important since the reference border is defined by the second coverage "bitmap", that is by C_2^X in $M\left(C_1^X, C_2^X\right)$.

To illustrate the distance metric introduced here, a simple case is shown in Fig. 11. Pixels with predicted coverage are colored in light grey whereas pixels without coverage are colored in dark grey. Let us consider two locations (A and B) where the measurements indicate a prediction error. The numbers (1, 2, or 3) in Fig. 11 indicate the normalized distance $\delta_M(x, y)$ to the border of the predicted coverage C_{PF}^{coverage} (light grey).

In Fig. 11, the pixel A has a normalized distance equal to 4 and pixel B has a normalized distance equal to 3, the distance metric is thus given by

$$M\left(C_M^{cov\,erage}, C_{PF}^{cov\,erage}\right) = \frac{1}{2}(4+3)\Delta r = 3.5\Delta r$$

Assuming a grid with $\Delta r = 0.5\ m$, the distance metric or the prediction accuracy would be of $\sim 1.8\ m$.

The distance metric M defined above has the following properties:

- M is always greater or equal to zero since the normalized distance is taken as a positive integer (at least one pixel layer must be added or subtracted to the predicted coverage border to reach the pixel ($x,\ y$) with a measurement erroneously predicted).

- M equals 0 if and only if all pixels in the measured coverage C_M^X are predicted correctly in C_{PF}^X, i.e., if there is no prediction error.

When taking measurements it cannot be avoided to obtain measured values with uncertainties (Fig. 9). To illustrate another practical example of the computation of the distance metric M, it is assumed that the uncertainties can be modeled with a log-normal shadowing. Assuming a free-space propagation, theoretical coverage for a given service threshold is given by a disk, as shown in Fig. 12 (a). The service threshold is taken as an arbitrary power level: $-65\ dBm$, for example. The measured coverage maps are simulated by adding a log-normal shadowing with a given standard deviation σ to the theoretical coverage. A standard deviation of $\sigma/4 = 1.25\ dB$ and $\sigma = 5\ dB$ is used for Fig.12 (b) and Fig.12 (c), respectively. The pixel size Δr is $0.25\ m$.

The distance metric M for the simulated measurements is computed by:

$$M_\sigma = M\left(C_{TH}^{-65dBm} + N(0, \sigma), C_{TH}^{-65dBm}\right).$$

The results gives $M_{1.25dB} \sim 3.7\ m$ (Fig.12 (b), $\sigma/4 = 1.25\ dB$) and $M_{5dB} \sim 19.6\ m$ ($\sigma = 5\ dB$). These results illustrate the distance inaccuracies to be expected as a result from imprecision in the measurements. As usual averaging the measurements helps to avoid inaccuracies. Further theoretical and experimental results related to the distance metric can be found in [ECH05]. For example, considering a given reference

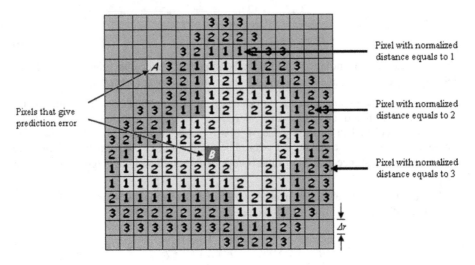

Fig. 11. Illustration of the normalized distance $\delta_M(x,y)$ for the calculation of the distance metric M

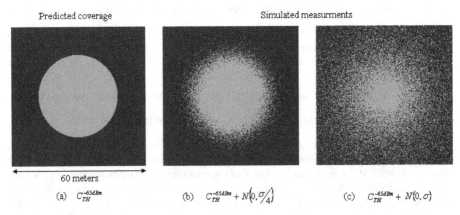

Fig. 12. Theoretical and simulated coverage bitmaps used to quantify uncertainties in measurements

coverage threshold (e.g., -65 dBm) and a simulated measurement given by a "wrong" threshold (e.g., -60 dBm) leads to a distance metric that can be computed analytically to verify the computations [ECH05]. For the example mentioned here, the distance metric is about 3.7 m, i.e.,

$$M\left(C_{TH}^{-60dBm}, C_{TH}^{-65dBm}\right) \cong 3.7 \text{ m.}$$

These results show that the distance metric (9) is to be interpreted, as expected, as the average distance between the prediction and the prediction errors. Thus, the distance metric defined above (9) quantifies in meters the prediction accuracy of the service coverage boundary.

5   Calibration

The calibration of the PixelFlow parameters to optimize the prediction of the service coverage of the WLAN network is performed by minimizing the distance metric described above. The optimization of the PixelFlow parameters achieved by computing predictions for several parameters, computing the distance metric for the proposed services (Business and Interactive services as an example) and choosing the best parameters. The identification of the best parameters remains a manual process that could be automated in the future and based only on a few measurements or on a particular description of the environment.

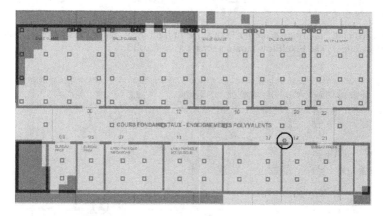

Fig. 13. Predicted *"Business service"* coverage in light grey. The access point is at the center of the black circle. The PixelFlow parameters are $T\bullet = 16$, $\beta = 0.41$, $\gamma = 0.59$ and $\tilde{a} = 0.3672$.

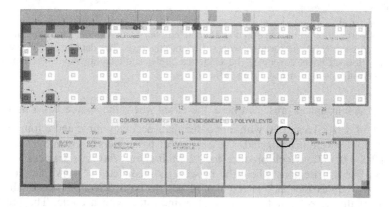

Fig. 14. Superposition of the measured and predicted *"Business service"* coverage maps. The white squares represent the location with sufficient coverage. The dark square regions represent the locations with insufficient coverage. The 5 dotted circles show the only locations where prediction errors occurred.

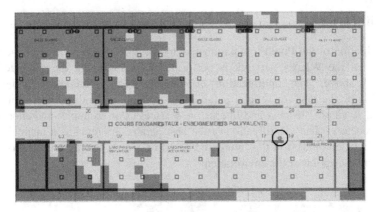

Fig. 15. Predicted *"Interactive service"* coverage in light grey. The access point is at the center of the black circle. The PixelFlow parameters are as in Fig. 13.

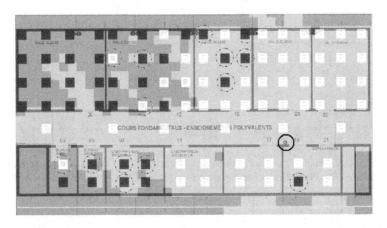

Fig. 16. Superposition of the measured and predicted *"Interactive service"* coverage maps. The white squares represent the location with sufficient coverage. The dark squares represent the location with insufficient coverage. The 11 dotted circles show the locations where prediction errors occurred (out of 94 measurement points).

For the environment presented here, the cases where the source has a normalized period $\tilde{T}$ of 8, 10, 16 and 20 with a two decimals accuracy for β and a four decimals accuracy for $\tilde{a}$, were investigated. The best set of parameters is given by $\tilde{T} = 16$, $\beta = 0.41$ and $\tilde{a} = 0.3672$, which produce the "2 Mbit/s" or *"Business services"* coverage shown in Fig. 13. Regions where the network is predicted to "work" are colored in light grey whereas the dark grey color represents insufficient service quality. The position of the access point (the source) is indicated with a circle. The prediction accuracy M is equal to ~$1.2\ m$.

The figure below (Fig 14) shows a superposition of the predicted and measured coverage maps. To illustrate the prediction error, the five locations where a prediction error occurred are marked with dash-doted circles in Fig. 14.

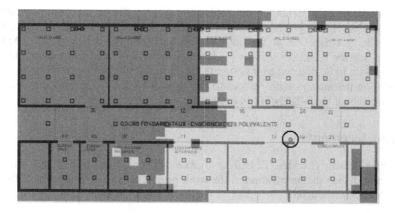

Fig. 17. The worst predicted "Business service" coverage found during the manual optimization process.

Predicted service coverage for a "5 Mbit/s" or *"Interactive service"* is given in Fig. 15. The superposition with the *"Interactive service"* coverage measurements is shown in Fig. 16. The prediction accuracy M for the *"Interactive service"* equals ~1,2 m as for the other service.

As expected using the wrong set of parameters for the prediction lead to erroneous results. To quantify the errors, the worst simulation obtained during the optimization process has been obtained with the following parameters $\tilde{T} = 20$, $\beta = 0.33$, $\gamma = 0.67$ and $\tilde{a} = 0.1613$. The resulting service coverage map is shown in Fig. 17 (*"Business service"*). The resulting metric is about *5 m*, i.e., about the size of an office or a room. Since the results are not entirely wrong, this result can be interpreted as an illustration of the robustness of the approach presented in this paper.

6 Conclusion

Although theoretically sound for 2D propagation, the PixeFlow algorithm inspired from [JOH71, HOE85, LUT95, LUT98] is not used here to predict signal strength but to predict Wi-Fi service coverage in indoor environments. The service coverage is defined in term of measured user throughput which might not be uniquely related to the signal strength due to the complexity of the protocols used [e.g., CSN04]. Optimization of the prediction parameters to simulate Wi-Fi coverage is undertaken based on measurements of the HTTP and the TCP protocols. The measurements were performed in a typical indoor office and classroom environment. Time and location dependence were investigated. The experimental results showed that a fluctuation of 10 dB can be recorded in the measured signal level depending on when measurements are taken. The values measured at a given position tend to be valid over an area of about 1m².

A new metric was defined to compare service coverage maps with measurements by averaging the distance between the predicted and measured results in meters. The new distance metric was used because the conventional mean error and its standard deviation were not useful to compare service coverage maps. The distance metric defined here might also be useful in other areas where predicting a boundary is the main goal.

Although measurements for the calibration were performed in only one building, the preliminary results presented here are promising [ECH05]. The resulting prediction accuracy is less than *1.5 m* for the two service investigated here, i.e., "2 Mbit/s – *Business service*" and "5 Mbit/s – *Interactive service*". Measurements in other buildings should be planned to investigate the expected independence of the PixelFlow computation parameters with respect to the characteristics of the building and to the characteristics of the WLAN/Wi-Fi system.

Acknowlegements

Prof. Juan Mosig (LEMA, EFPL) is thanked for his support and the interesting discussions during the preparation of the work presented here. The support of the EIA-FR is also acknowledged.

References

[CSN04]   S. Ci, H. Sharif, and G. Noubir. *Improving Goodput of the IEEE 802.11 MAC Protocol by Using Congestion Control Methods*. International Journal on Wireless and Optical Communications (IJWOC), Vol. 1, No.2 (2004) 1-9, World Scientific Publishing.

[HOE85]   W. J. R. Hoeffer. *The transmission-line matrix method theory and applications*. IEEE Trans. on Microwave Theory and Techniques, MTT-33(10):882–893, October 1985.

[LUT95]   P. O. Luthi, B. Chopard, and J.-F. Wagen. *Wave Propagation in Urban Microcells: a Massively Parallel Approach Using the TLM Method*. Lecture Notes In Computer Science; Vol. 1041 archive Proceedings of the Second International Workshop on Applied Parallel Computing, Computations in Physics, Chemistry and Engineering Science. Ed. Springer-Verlag, 408 – 418, 1995. ISBN:3-540-60902-4.

[LUT98]   P.O. Luthi. *Lattice Wave Automata: from radio wave to fracture propagation*. PhD thesis, Computer Science Department, Univ. of Geneva, 24 rue General-Dufour, 1211 Geneva 4, Switzerland, 1998.

[JOH71]   P.B.Johns and R.L.Beurle, *Numerical solution of 2-dimensional scattering problems using a transmission-line matrix*. Proc. of IEEE, Vol. 118, Sept 1971.

[ECH05]   N. Echenard, *Logiciel de prédiction des couvertures pour les réseaux sans fil*. Master Thesis, Swiss Federal Institute of Technology (www.epfl.ch), Oct 2005.

[GAR04]   F. Gardiol, *Électromagnétisme*, Traité d'Électricité Vol. 3, PPUR, 2004. ISBN 2-88074-508-X.

[GWR03]   Gamba, Fiorenzo. Wagen, Jean-Frédéric. Rossier, Daniel. Towards Adaptive WLAN Frequency Management Using Intelligent Agents. Lecture Notes in Computer Science. 2865 / 2003. Ad-Hoc, Mobile, and Wireless Networks: Second International Conference,ADHOC-NOW2003. October 8-10 2003, Montreal, Canada. Springer-Verlag Heidelberg . ISBN 3-540-20260-9, p. 116 – 127.

[WJF04]   Wagen, Jean-Frédéric, Unpublished results obtained during a practical classroom work using the *netperf* software with eight laptops served by a single access points, Nov. 2004.

State Description of Wireless Channels Using Change-Point Statistical Tests

D. Moltchanov

Institute of Communication Engineering,
Tampere University of Technology,
P.O. Box 553, Tampere, Finland
moltchan@cs.tut.fi

Abstract. We consider the state of the wireless channel in terms of the covariance stationary signal-to-noise ratio (SNR) process and parameterize it using the probability distribution function of SNR and lag-1 autocorrelation coefficient of associated autocorrelation function (ACF). In order to discriminate the state of the wireless channel we apply methods of statistical process control. Particularly, we use exponential weighted moving average (EWMA) change-point statistical test to detect shifts in the mean of the SNR process. The proposed approach is verified using SNR measurements of IEEE 802.11b wireless channel.

1 Introduction

Due to movement of a mobile user and movement of different objects in a radio channel, the propagation path between the transmitter and the receiver may vary from simple line-of-sight (LOS) to very complex ones. As a result, any metric used to represent the quality of the wireless channel is characterized by time-dependent stochastic behavior. Insufficient signal-to-noise ratio (SNR) at a certain instant of time may result in incorrect reception of the channel symbol possibly leading to an erroneously received bit. Techniques such as forward error correction (FEC) and automatic repeat request (ARQ) may allow to recover from these errors locally. However, bit errors may still propagate to higher layers resulting in loss of protocol data units (PDU) at those layers.

To ensure acceptable quality of the wireless channel, some wireless access technologies incorporate features allowing to control power of the transmitter such that the target bit error rate (BER) is maintained. This capability, known as power control, may lead to various undesirable effects including 'cell breathing' in CDMA systems, increase in interference with neighbor cells in TDMA systems, etc. These effects should be avoided when possible.

The another way to maintain the acceptable quality of the wireless channel is to dynamically change correction capability of FEC schemes at the data-link layer. FEC procedures use proactive approach eliminating the influence of bit errors in advance introducing error correction redundancy. This redundancy is efficiently exploited at the receiver to recover from bit errors. The major advantage of FEC techniques is that they do not introduce delays allowing some

T. Braun et al. (Eds.): WWIC 2006, LNCS 3970, pp. 275–286, 2006.

information to be lost. There are a number of papers exploring the correcting effect of FEC codes for different conditions of wireless channels [1, 2].

The state of the wireless channel is usually represented in terms of the stochastic process, where the stochastic variable of interest is either SNR or a certain function of it. There are two types of processes widely used to describe the state of the wireless channel. These are SNR process or PDU error processes. The latter models aim at determining the performance of a wireless channel at a certain layer of the protocol stack. Although PDU error models can be directly measured, the major advantage of these models is that they can be derived from the SNR model at the physical layer [1, 3]. From this point of view, PDU error models are seen as an extension of SNR models. Due to this reason, to represent the state of the wireless channel, SNR process is used.

Most papers that considered performance of information transmission over wireless channels either implicitly or explicitly assumed covariance stationary property of wireless channel statistics. Recently, important observations of wireless channel characteristics have been published in [4]. Authors found their GSM bit error traces to be non-stationary and proposed an algorithm to extract covariance stationary parts. They further used doubly-stochastic Markov processes to model these parts separately. The modeled trace is finally obtained by concatenation. Among other conclusions, authors suggested that a given bit error trace can be divided into a number of concatenated covariance stationary traces. Since the bit error probability is a function of the SNR value, we can expect the same property for SNR observations too. Despite of important conclusions made in [4], authors failed to develop theoretical basis for their change detection algorithm. In this paper in order to discriminate the state of the wireless channel in terms of the covariance stationary SNR segments, we propose to use well-known sequential change-point statistical test.

The rest of the paper is organized as follows. In Section 2 we review propagation characteristics of wireless channels and models used to capture them. Setup of experiments is described in Section 3. Model for SNR process is introduced in Section 4. Sequential statistical tests for detecting changes in parameters of the stochastic process are reviewed in Section 5. The EWMA statistical test is also proposed there. Numerical results are given in Section 6. Conclusions are drawn in the last section.

2   Description of Wireless Channels

2.1   Ergodicity and Stationarity

To determine parameters of a stochastic process, such as mean and variance, based on only one, sufficiently large realization we usually assume ergodicity for stochastic observations. The sufficient condition for a stochastic process to be ergodic is $\lim_{i \to \infty} K(i) = 0$, where $K(i)$, $i = 0, 1, \ldots$, is its ACF. The concept of stationarity is an advantageous property of ergodic stochastic processes. It is of paramount importance in context of modeling of stochastic observations and further applications. Practically, if some observations are found to be non-stationary, their stochastic modeling is rarely feasible. A process is said to be strictly stationary if its all M-dimensional distributions are the same. Only few real-life processes are strictly stationary. A process is said to be weak (covariance) stationary if mean of its all sections is the same and ACF depends on the time shift only, i.e. $K(t_1, t_2) = K(i)$, $i = t_2 - t_1$.

3   Setup of Experiments

In this paper we use SNR observations from IEEE 802.11b wireless local area network (WLAN) connection operating according to distributed coordination function (DCF) of IEEE 802.11 in DSSS mode at 11Mbps. In order to gather SNR statistics we carried out a number of experiments. In this section setup of experiments is described, statistical characteristics of SNR observations are shown and the model for covariance stationary SNR process is proposed.

According to the setup experiments shown in Fig. 1, there were two entities involved in communication. These are the mobile node, called *tester node*, and the access point (AP). An SNR capturing software was installed on mobile node. The communication between AP and the tester node was of interest. The tester and AP were in non-LOS (NLOS) and LOS environments as explained below. To capture SNR traces we used Network Stumbler software (version 0.4.0, [5]). This program is capable to capture SNR value averaging it over 0.5 second intervals.

All experiments were carried out in office environment under different mobility patterns as shown in Fig. 1, where reference points denote the stationary places where measurements were carried out, AP denotes the placement of AP transceiver. Note that the mobile station in points 1 and 3 are in NLOS environment with respect to the transceiver of AP. The distance between reference point 1 and AP is shorter than that between reference point 3 and AP. Point 2 corresponds to LOS environment. The experiments were carried out as follows. Mobile station was at a certain reference point for some time and then was moved to another reference point. SNR was uninterruptedly measured during the course of each experiment.

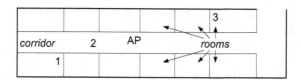

Fig. 1. Testbed for SNR measurements

4   Model for SNR Process

4.1   Statistical Characteristics

Let us consider statistical characteristics of the SNR process when a mobile station is in stationary position. We concentrate our attention on two statistical

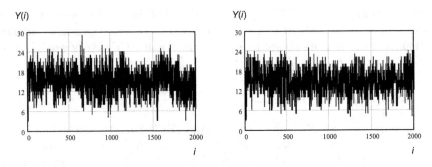

Fig. 2. Sequences of SNR observations for two experiments

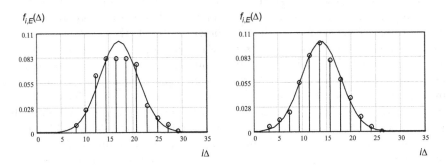

Fig. 3. Histograms of relative frequencies of SNR observations

characteristics. These are the histogram of relative frequencies of the SNR process and associated ACF. These two properties of the SNR process were found to produce the major impact on the performance of higher layers [1, 3]. In what follows, results for reference point 1 are demonstrated. Results for other reference points are qualitatively similar.

Sequences of SNR observations for two experiments are shown in Fig. 2. Respective histograms of relative frequencies of these SNR observations and their approximations by normal probability density functions (pdf) are shown in Fig. 3, where $f_{i,E}(\Delta)$, $i = 1, 2, \ldots$ is the relative frequency corresponding to the is histogram bin, m is the number of histogram bins, $\Delta = (\max_{\forall i} Y(i) - \min_{\forall i} Y(i))/m$ is the length of the histogram bin, $\max_{\forall i} Y(i)$ and $\min_{\forall i} Y(i))$ are the maximum and minimum values of the SNR, respectively. Approximations, shown in Fig. 3, allows us to assume that the SNR values are approximately normally distributed. The chi-square statistical test has shown that the statistical data belongs to the normal distribution with the level of significance set to 0.1.

The empirical normalized ACFs (NACF) of two SNR traces are shown in Fig. 4 using solid lines with circles. One may notice that the memory of the process is short and limited to several lags. In what follows, we propose to approximate such a behavior using a single geometrical term, e.g. $y(i) = K_Y(1)^i$, $i = 0, 1, \ldots$. The approximating functions are denoted in Fig. 4 by solid lines. The approximating functions exactly capture lag-1 autocorrelation coefficient of

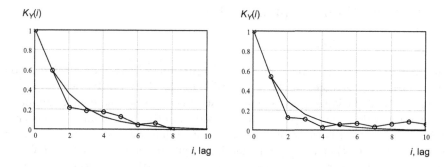

Fig. 4. NACFs of the SNR process and their approximation

the empirical processes and do not significantly overestimate or underestimate the autocorrelation coefficients for larger lags.

In what follows, we assume that when a mobile station is in stationary position, SNR observations compose realization of covariance stationary stochastic process. This assumption is supported by first- and second-order statistical characteristics shown in Fig. 3 and Fig. 4, respectively. Indeed, histograms of SNR observations were approximated using normal distributions with almost similar mean and variance. The lag-1 autocorrelation coefficient are also close to each other for both traces. Similar observations were made for other reference points.

4.2   Model for SNR Process

In order to model SNR traces we propose to use autoregressive process of order one AR(1). A process is said to be autoregressive of order one if it is generated using the following recursion

$$Y(n) = \phi_0 + \phi_1 Y(n-1) + \epsilon(n), \qquad n = 0, 1, \ldots, \tag{1}$$

where ϕ_0 and ϕ_1 are constants, $\{\epsilon(n), n = 0, 1, \ldots\}$ are independently and identically distributed random variables having the same normal distribution with zero mean and variance $\sigma^2[\epsilon]$.

If a process given by (1) is covariance stationary we have

$$E[Y] = \mu, \qquad \sigma^2[Y] = \gamma_0, \qquad Cov(Y_0, Y_i) = \gamma_i, \tag{2}$$

where μ, γ_i, $i = 0, 1, \ldots$, are some constants.

Mean, variance and covariance of AR(1) are given by

$$\mu = \frac{\phi_0}{1 - \phi_1}, \qquad \sigma^2[X] = \frac{\sigma^2[\epsilon]}{1 - \phi_1^2}, \qquad \gamma_i = \phi_1^i \gamma_0. \tag{3}$$

Parameters of AR(1) models can be found as follows

$$\phi_1 = K_Y(1), \qquad \phi_0 = \mu_Y(1 - \phi_1), \qquad \sigma^2[\epsilon] = \sigma^2[Y](1 - \phi_1^2), \tag{4}$$

where $K_Y(1)$, μ_Y and $\sigma^2[Y]$ are the lag-1 autocorrelation coefficient, mean and variance of SNR observations, respectively.

5   Change-Point Sequential Tests

5.1   The Methodology

In order to differentiate between rapid fluctuations of the SNR around a constant mean and changes in the mean value of the SNR process we propose to use the so-called change-point sequential statistical tests. There are a number of change-point detection algorithms developed to date. The common approach to deal with this task is to use control charts including Shewhart charts, cumulative sum (CUSUM) charts, or exponentially weighted moving average (EWMA) charts. These charts were originally developed in statistical process control (SPC) discipline where they are successfully used to monitor the quality of production.

The idea of control charts is to classify all causes of deviation from the target value into two groups. These are common causes of deviation and special causes of deviation. Deviation due to common causes is the effect of numerous causes affecting a given process. They are inherent part of a process. Special causes of deviation are not the part of the process, occur accidentally and affect the process significantly. Control charts signals the point at which special causes occur using two control limits. If observations are between them, process is 'in-control'. If some observations fall outside, the process is classified as 'out-of-control'.

For detecting changes in SNR statistics the following interpretation of causes of deviation is taken. We assume that common causes of deviation are those resulting from small-scale propagation characteristics. Special causes are those caused by movement of a user including large-scale changes of the distance between the transmitter and a receiver or shadowing of the signal by obstacles. Note that the change in a monitored parameter can be gradual or instantaneous. The whole procedure is as follows. Initially, a control chart is parameterized using an estimate of a parameter of the SNR process. When change in a parameter occurs, a new process is considered as in-control and the control chart has to be re-parameterized according to this process.

5.2   Change in the Mean Value

Assume that k observations $\{Y(n), n = 0, 1, \ldots, k - 1\}$ of a certain stochastic process have the same distribution F_0. In general, the change point statistical test refers to testing the null hypothesis, H_0, that a currently observed observation k has distribution F_0 against alternative hypothesis, H_1, that this observation has distribution F_1. Formally, it is written as

$$H_0 : F_{Y,k} = F_0, \qquad H_1 : F_{Y,k} = F_1. \tag{5}$$

where $F_{Y,k}$ is the distribution of observation k. The latter case represents a situation when a change occurs in a distribution and is also written as

$$H_1 : F_{Y,i} = \begin{cases} F_0 & i = 0, 1, \ldots, k - 1, \\ F_1 & i = k. \end{cases} \tag{6}$$

It is often assumed that distributions F_0 and F_1 are known except for some parameters of F_1. Control charts are used for detecting changes in these unknown parameters. In our case the form of the distribution is known in advance and the unknown parameter is the mean value. Then, the whole task is to detect a change in the mean resulting in following test

$$H_0 : E[Y] = \mu,$$

$$H_1 : E[Y] = \begin{cases} \mu_0 & i = 0, 1, \ldots, k-1, \\ \mu_1 & i = k. \end{cases} \qquad (7)$$

The major problem of change-point statistical tests is that they often require observations to be realizations of independently and identically distributed random variables. However, SNR observations are not necessary independent but can be correlated. Autocorrelation makes classic control charts less sensitive to changes in the mean. For detecting change in the mean of autocorrelated processes two approaches have been proposed. According to the first approach, control limits of charts are modified to take into account autocorrelation properties of observations. The idea of the second approach is to fit observations using a certain time-series model of autoregressive integrated moving average (ARIMA) type and subsequent control charting of residuals. The shift in the mean of observations is transferred to residuals that are to be charted. If the model fits empirical data well the residuals are uncorrelated and control charts for independent observations can be used.

Performance of change-point statistical tests for autocorrelated data has been compared in [6]. In was shown that residuals-based approach performs well when the autocorrelation is negative. When the autocorrelation is positive, modified control charts on initial observations perform better. This property has also been found in [7]. This is mainly due to the fact that changes in the mean of original observations is only partially transferred to residuals. The transfer of the change is also different for positive and negative autocorrelations [8]. Additionally, accuracy of residuals-based approach also depends on accuracy of fitting of the model to statistical data. Due to these reasons, we use the first approach.

5.3   EWMA Control Charts

Let $\{Y(n), n = 0, 1, \ldots\}$ be a sequence of SNR observations. The value of EWMA statistic at the time n, denoted by $L_Y(n)$, is given by

$$L_Y(n) = \gamma Y(n) + (1 - \gamma)L_Y(n-1), \qquad (8)$$

where parameter $\gamma \in (0, 1)$ is constant.

The first value of EWMA statistics, $L_Y(0)$, is usually set to the mean of $\{Y(n), n = 0, 1, \ldots\}$ or, if unknown, to the estimate of mean. As a result, for on-line real-time test there should always be a certain warm-up period involving estimation of the mean.

In (8) $L_Y(n)$ extends its memory not only to the previous value but weights values of previous observations according to constant coefficient γ. In (8) this previous information is completely included in $L_Y(n-1)$. To show it, let us rewrite $\{L_Y(n), n = 0, 1, \dots\}$ statistics recursively, starting from $L_Y(0) = Y(0)$

$$
\begin{aligned}
L_Y(0) &= Y(0), \\
L_Y(1) &= \gamma Y(1) + (1 - \gamma)Y(0), \\
L_Y(2) &= \gamma Y(2) + \gamma(1 - \gamma)Y(1) + (1 - \gamma)^2 Y(0), \\
&\dots
\end{aligned} \tag{9}
$$

Since for any constant n the following holds

$$
\gamma \sum_{i=0}^{n-1} (1 - \gamma)^i + (1 - \gamma)^n = 1, \tag{10}
$$

it is easy to see that (9) converges to

$$
L_Y(n) = \gamma \sum_{i=0}^{n-1} (1 - \gamma)^i Y(n - i) + (1 - \gamma)^n Y(0), \qquad n = 1, 2, \dots, n. \tag{11}
$$

The EWMA charts takes central part among other control charts. Although, according to (8), the most recent value always receives more weight in computation of $L_Y(n)$, the choice of λ determines the effect of previous observations of the process on the current value of EWMA statistics. Indeed, when $\lambda \to 1$ all weight is placed on the current observation, $L_Y(n) \to Y(n)$, and EWMA statistics degenerate to initial observations. As a result, EWMA control chart behaves like Shewhart one. Contrarily, when $\lambda \to 0$ the current observation gets only a little weight, but most weight is assigned to previous observations. In this case, EWMA control chart behaves similar to CUSUM one. Summarizing, EWMA charts give more flexibility at the expense of additional complexity in determining one more parameter λ.

Assume now that given observations $\{Y(n), n = 0, 1, \dots, N\}$ are taken from strictly stationary process whose all sections are independently and identically distributed random variables with the same distribution, mean $E[Y]$ and variance $\sigma^2[Y]$. In fact, (8) defines a new stochastic process as a function of initial observations and this process has different statistical characteristics compared to those of $\{Y(n), n = 0, 1, \}$. Given that $L_Y(0) = E[Y]$, the mean of the process is given by

$$
E[L_Y(n)] = E[Y](1 - (1 - \lambda)^n) + (1 - \lambda)^n E[Y], \tag{12}
$$

that converges to constant $E[L_Y] = E[Y] = \mu$ as $n \to \infty$.

The variance of $\{L_Y(n), n = 0, 1, \dots\}$ is given by

$$
\sigma^2[L_Y] = \sigma^2[Y] \left(\frac{\gamma}{2 - \gamma} \right) (1 - (1 - \gamma)^{2n}). \tag{13}
$$

Using (13) the control limits for EWMA charts are computed as follows

$$E[L_Y] \pm C(n) = E[L_Y] \pm k\sigma[Y]\sqrt{\left(\frac{\gamma}{2-\gamma}\right)(1-(1-\gamma)^{2n})}. \qquad (14)$$

where k is a design parameter whose values are tabulated in the literature.

According to (14) an out-of-control behavior is signaled when $L_Y(n)$ at some point in time is less than $(E[L_Y] - C(n))$ or greater than $(E[L_Y] + C(n))$. Note that in (14) upper and lower control limits are time-varying in nature. However, when $n \to \infty$ it is easy to see that

$$\lim_{n \to \infty} \left(\frac{\gamma}{2-\gamma}\right)(1-(1-\gamma)^{2n}) = \frac{\gamma}{2-\gamma} \qquad (15)$$

and constant control limits $E[L_Y] \pm k\sigma[Y]\sqrt{\frac{\gamma}{2-\gamma}}$ can be used instead.

Assume now that given SNR observations $\{Y(n), n = 0, 1, \ldots, N\}$ are taken from covariance stationary process with mean $E[Y]$ and variance $\sigma^2[Y]$ and can be well represented by AR(1) process. If $L_Y(0) = E[Y]$, observing (12) it is easy to see that $E[L_Y] = E[Y] = \mu$ when $n \to \infty$. The approximation of variance of $\{L_Y(n), n = 0, 1, \ldots\}$ for $n \to \infty$ is given by [6]

$$\sigma^2[L_Y] = \sigma^2[Y]\left(\frac{\gamma}{2-\gamma}\right)\left(\frac{1+\phi_1(1-\gamma)}{1-\phi_1(1-\gamma)}\right), \qquad (16)$$

where ϕ_1 is the parameter of AR(1) process.

The control limits are given by

$$E[L_Y] \pm C(n) = E[L_Y] \pm k\sigma[Y]\sqrt{\left(\frac{\gamma}{2-\gamma}\right)\left(\frac{1+\phi_1(1-\gamma)}{1-\phi_1(1-\gamma)}\right)} \qquad (17)$$

where k is a design parameter whose values are tabulated in the literature.

To parameterize the EWMA control chart a number of parameters have to be provided. Firstly, parameter γ determining the decline of the weights of past observations should be set. The values of k and γ determine the wideness of control belts for a given process with a certain $\sigma^2[Y]$ and ϕ_1. These two parameters affect behavior of the so-called average run length (ARL) curve that is usually used to determine efficiency of a certain change detection procedure. ARL is defined as the average number of observation up to the first out-of-control signal. The ARL is the function of both k and γ. Different parameters of k and γ for a given ARL, $\sigma^2[Y]$ and ϕ_1 are provided in [6, 9]. Finally, $E[Y]$ and $\sigma^2[Y]$ are not usually known in practice and must be estimated from empirical data. Therefore, estimates of $E[Y]$ and $\sigma^2[Y]$ should be used in (17).

6   Numerical Results

Let us consider two numerical examples. According to the course of the first experiment, the tester node was stationary at the reference point 1 for a long

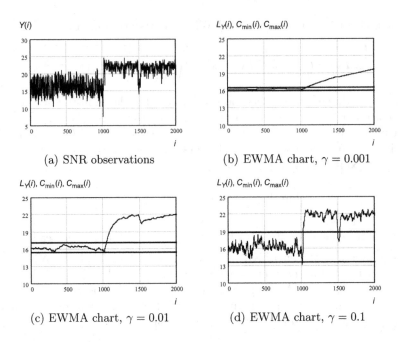

(a) SNR observations   (b) EWMA chart, $\gamma = 0.001$

(c) EWMA chart, $\gamma = 0.01$ (d) EWMA chart, $\gamma = 0.1$

Fig. 5. SNR observations and EWMA chart for reference points 1 and 2

time and then was moved to the reference point 2, where it was also stationary for a long time. The full time-series of SNR observations is shown in Fig. 5(a). The change in the mean of SNR observations occurs around 1000s observation. It can be easily observed from Fig. 5(a).

The results of EWMA change-point statistical test for different parameters of λ are shown in Fig. 5(b), Fig. 5(c) and Fig. 5(d). The warm-up period used to compute parameters of empirical observations was set to 50 SNR observations. It was found that this period is sufficient for most experiments. Note that for all λ the parameter k was set to 3. In general, usage of different values of λ requires different values of k to match a given ARL. It was found that usage of tabulated (theoretical [9]) data usually leads to many out-of-control signal even when the tester node is in stationary state. One of the reasons is that the monitored process may not be exactly covariance stationary and may occasionally contain some extreme observations. There observations are of local significance only and may not affect the future evolution of the monitored process. Since the test is real-time in nature, each out-of-control signal starts a new warm-up period. During this period new average value is estimated and the process cannot be monitored. From this point of view we should detect only those changes that occur 'for sure'. During experiments, it was found that value $k = 3$ provides a good choice for any value of γ in the range $\gamma \in (0.001, 0.1)$. One can observe from the Fig. 5 that the change in the average value of SNR observations is successfully detected for all values of k and γ.

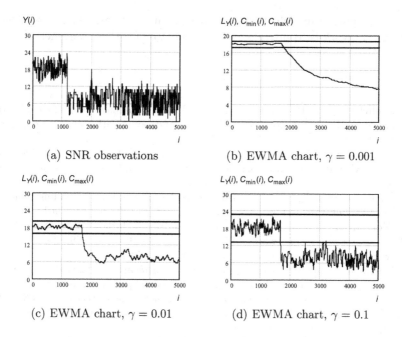

Fig. 6. SNR observations and EWMA chart for reference points 1 and 2

According to the course of the second experiment, the tester node was in the stationary position at the reference point 1 for a long period of time. Then, it was moved to the reference point 3 skipping the reference point 2. The node was then at the reference point 3 for a long period of time. The full time series of SNR observations is shown in Fig. 6(a). The change in the average value of SNR observations occurs around 1200s observation. It can be observed from Fig. 6(a).

The results of EWMA change-point statistical test for different parameters of λ are shown in Fig. 6(b), Fig. 6(c) and Fig. 6(d). For all λ the parameter k was set to 3. The warm-up period was constant and set to 50 observations. One can observe from the Fig. 6 that the change in the average value of SNR observations is successfully detected for all values of k and γ.

7   Conclusion

In this paper in order to discriminate the state of the wireless channel in terms of the covariance stationary SNR process we proposed to use EWMA change-point statistical test. In order to model SNR process when a mobile user is in stationary state we use AR(1) process. Then, EWMA test is applied to detect a point at which the mean value of the SNR process changes. We believe that the proposed approach can also be used for PDU error observations too.

The choice of the smoothing parameter and wideness of control charts is still an open issue. Our experiments have shown that theoretically-computed parameters lead to many out-of-control signals. This is due to a number of reasons including imperfect modeling, inaccurate estimation of parameters, etc. The aim of the future work is to provide on-line estimators for these parameters.

References

1. D. Moltchanov, Y. Koucheryavy, and J. Harju. Cross-layer modeling of wireless channels for IP layer performance evaluation of delay-sensitive applications. *Special Issue of Comp. Comm.*, In Press, 2005.
2. D. Moltchanov, Y. Koucheryavy, and J. Harju. Loss performance model for wireless channels with autocorrelated arrivals and losses. *Special Issue of Comp. Comm.*, In Press, 2005.
3. Y.-Y. Kim and S.-Q. Li. Capturing important statistics of a fading/shadowing channel for network performance analysis. *IEEE JSAC*, 17(5):888–901, May 1999.
4. A. Konrad, B. Zhao, A. Joseph, and R. Ludwig. Markov-based channel model algorithm for wireless networks. *Wireless Networks*, 9(3):189–199, 2003.
5. Network stumbler. Version 0.4.0, http://www.stumbler.net, 2005.
6. J. Wieringa. Control charts for monitoring the mean of AR(1) data. Available at: http://www.ub.rug.nl/eldoc/som/a/98a09/98a09.pdf, University of Groningen, Department of Econometrics, Faculty of Economic Sciences, Accessed on 06.07.2005.
7. T. Ryan. *Statistical methods for quality improvement.* John Wiley & Sons, New York, 1989.
8. D. Apley and J. Shi. The GLRT for statistical process control of autocorrelated processes. *IIE Transactions*, 31:1123–1134, 1999.
9. J. Wieringa. Statistical process control for serially correlated data, PhD Thesis. Available at: http://dissertations.ub.rug.nl/files/faculties/eco/1999/j.e.wieringa/, University of Groningen, Department of Econometrics, Faculty of Economic Sciences, Accessed on 18.10.2005.

Statistical QoS Assurances for High Speed Wireless Communication Systems

F. Ozan Akgül and M. Oğuz Sunay

Koç University, Department of Electrical & Electronics Engineering,
Rumeli Feneri Yolu Sarıyer, Istanbul 34450, Turkey
{fakgul, osunay}@ku.edu.tr
http://wireless.ku.edu.tr

Abstract. In this paper we propose the use of statistical QoS guarantees for transmission over the wireless channel. Here, instead of QoS assurances we propose to guarantee the percentage of time the QoS requirements are satisfied. We present an associated scheduling algorithm for the opportunistic multiple access system. We compare the proposed scheduler with popular schedulers from the literature. We observe that the statistical QoS guarantee is an attractive alternative to the assured QoS for the wireless platform since such strict QoS assurances decrease the wireless system performance significantly.

1 Introduction

With the ever increasing use of the Internet, there is a significant interest in making this technology available anywhere, anytime. To this end, research in wireless systems has lately focused on providing high speed packet data access. Recent advances in the design of wireless packet data systems have made it possible to achieve higher spectral efficiencies and thus higher system throughput. Such enabling technologies for high speed wireless data have also brought up possibilities for the provision of a multitude of services in addition to the traditional voice service. Streaming video, and audio as well as broadcast of multimedia content are a few such examples. As a result, wireless system designs of today need to explicitly take the quality-of-service (QoS) requirements of the services offered.

The term QoS may imply different service provisioning policies in several different contexts. It may be regarded as having a certain maximum delay requirement for packets, a certain minimum throughput level or a certain maximum data loss rate. In this paper we regard QoS as a certain minimum average data rate intended to be supplied to active users over a certain time window.

The current Internet provides only best effort type of service to all subscribers. Enhanced services to the Internet are being studied and a number of proposals are on the table. IETF's Differentiated Services (DiffServ) Working Group [1] propose offering QoS in terms of Assured Forwarding [2] and Expedited Forwarding [3] for the packet data transmission. Expedited Forwarding corresponds to a low loss, low latency, low jitter, assured bandwidth service whereas Assured

T. Braun et al. (Eds.): WWIC 2006, LNCS 3970, pp. 287–298, 2006.

Forwarding further classifies services into 4 classes and 3 degrees of drop precedence (high, medium, low). Each of these DiffServ mechanisms correspond to a Per Hop Behavior (PHB) Group [1]. The PHB Groups may be specified in terms of their observable traffic characteristics (e.g delay, throughput).

QoS assurances in the form of Expedited Forwarding or Assured Forwarding can become prohibitively costly in wireless systems. This is due to the time-varying and error-prone nature of the wireless channel. If QoS assurances are given to users, the wireless system design needs to ensure that even when all users' channels deteriorate simultaneously, the QoS requirements of these users are still satisfied. Physical layer resources need to be reserved accordingly, resulting in poor spectral efficiency. In fact, one can argue that, for practical purposes, it is very difficult to provide QoS guarantees in wireless systems, unless the QoS requirements are no more stringent than the current voice service.

An intermediate level for the definition of QoS is necessary then for wireless communications, between best effort and expensive and spectrally inefficient guaranteed service. In this paper, building on [4] we investigate a definition that is neither. Instead, we propose the use of statistical QoS guarantees. Specifically, we propose a wireless system where the QoS requirements are guaranteed to subscribers for a given percentage of time (PoT) . This definition allows flexibility to the physical layer resource allocation protocol so that the system profits from the channel fluctuations of the users rather than being penalized.

The definition of the PoT QoS assurance fits perfectly into the opportunistic multiple access scheme described in [5]. The opportunistic multiple access scheme allocates (schedules) all physical layer resources to only one user at a given pre-defined time slot. If the user observing the best channel conditions is scheduled for service at a given time, the scheme is shown to be optimal in terms of system throughput in frequency flat fading channels [5]. In opportunistic multiple access, adaptive coding and modulation need to be employed for each scheduled user so that the transmission is done at the highest possible data rate that is allowed by the current channel conditions [6]. The recently standardized 3G system, IS-856, is a packet data only system that utilizes opportunistic multiple access with adaptive coding and modulation [7].

At the heart of the opportunistic multiple system there is a scheduler that selects which user to service at a given time instance and its proper design is key in ensuring satisfactory system performance [8]. The scheduler allocates the system resources to different users in a time-multiplexed fashion. The choice of the scheduling algorithm affects the system throughput as well as the average delay experienced by users in between successive accesses to the system. The throughput-optimal scheduling rule is one where the user with the best channel conditions is scheduled for service for each time slot. In such a scenario, the larger the number of users in the system, the more likely it is to find a user experiencing a really good channel resulting in a better system throughput. This is referred to as multi-user diversity in the literature. The throughput optimal scheduling algorithm would be impractical as users closer to the base station would almost always observe better channel conditions than those further away and thus would grab the system resources continuously, starving the others for service. Then, ideally scheduling algorithms that provide fairness across subscribers while utilizing multi-user diversity as much as possible are desirable. The study of scheduling algorithms is an active research topic.

This paper aims to show that an opportunistic multiple access scheme such as IS-856, can provide PoT QoS assurances to its customers using an appropriately defined scheduling algorithm. Here, we present one example of such a scheduler, and show that it outperforms the traditional schedulers from the literature in providing statistical QoS assurances. The IS-856 system is described for a bandwidth of 1.25 MHz and provides peak data rates of over 2 Mbps. When the QoS requirements are stringent and a moderate number of subscribers are active in the system, this bandwidth may not be sufficient to properly operate the system. A multi-carrier extension of the IS-856 system is also studied in this paper that operates on a bandwidth of 5 MHz.

The rest of the paper is organized as follows: in Section II, we provide a brief overview of the IS-856 system and its multi-carrier extension. A brief overview of the traditional scheduling algorithms from the literature is given in this section as well. Building on these schedulers, we develop a statistical-QoS scheduler in Section III and provide a detailed, comparative performance analysis in Section IV. Finally, we conclude the paper with conclusions in Section V.

2   Overview of the IS-856 System

The wireless system under consideration in this paper is the recently standardized North American 3G system for packet data, IS-856 [7]. IS-856 offers spectrally efficient high data rate access by jointly utilizing the findings of [5] and [6] which state that the maximum spectral efficiency is achieved when one is able to adjust the transmission modulation, coding and power according to the changes of the channel characteristics and that it is best to provide all of the resources of the system to serve to only one user at a given time if the communication channel experiences frequency flat fading. Indeed, over a single-carrier of 1.25 MHz bandwidth (referred to as 1x), the IS-856 system divides the time into slots of length 1.67 ms and allocates all of its resources to a single user at a given time slot. A scheduler located at the base station decides which user to service at a given time slot. To aid the scheduling operation, all active users send channel quality feedback to the serving base station every 1.67 ms. Once a user is scheduled, based on the observed channel quality between the base station and this user the modulation and coding levels are adjusted to provide transmission at the maximum possible data rate while ensuring a given level of packet error rate (=1% in IS-856).

Adaptive coding and modulation allows for a total of 12 signaling schemes in IS-856 with 9 distinct data rates. Each signaling scheme has a corresponding physical layer packet size. In IS-856, the physical layer packet is defined as the block in which the information data is encoded. 4 physical layer packet sizes are defined. The notion of the physical layer packet is there to ensure that there is always a sufficient amount of data bits for the error control coding algorithm

Table 1. Available data rates in IS-856

Data Rate (kbps)	Slots	Packet Size (bits)	Code Rate	Modulation
38.4	16	1024	1/5	QPSK
76.8	8	1024	1/5	QPSK
153.6	4	1024	1/5	QPSK
307.2	2	1024	1/5	QPSK
614.4	1	1024	1/3	QPSK
307.2	4	2048	1/3	QPSK
614.4	2	2048	1/3	QPSK
1228.8	1	2048	1/3	QPSK
921.6	2	3072	1/3	8-PSK
1843.2	1	3072	1/3	8-PSK
1228.8	2	4096	1/3	16-QAM
2457.6	1	4096	1/3	16-QAM

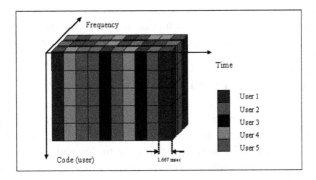

Fig. 1. Resource Allocation in Multi-Carrier Opportunistic Multiple Access

regardless of the transmission rate. Clearly, this results in physical layer packets sometimes spanning multiple slots depending on the data rate. The available data rates that can be served to the users in the IS-856 system are given in Table 1 along with the associated modulation and coding levels and the number of time slots necessary to transmit the physical layer packets.

A multi-carrier option for IS-856 is easily feasible where an integer multiple of neighboring carriers are used simultaneously by a base station. The simplest implementation of such a system would be to use exactly the same air interface as the 1x IS-856 for each of the carriers. In this case, for a system with n carriers, the scheduler can schedule up to n users in parallel and allocate all of the per-carrier resources to the scheduled user at a given time. It may be possible for a user to get scheduled for some or even all of the n carriers at the same time. Thus the peak data rate for the multi-carrier IS-856 is effectively $n \times 2.4576$ Mbps. The 3x IS-856 resource allocation is illustrated in Figure 1. In multi-carrier opportunistic multiple access, the scheduler may need to decide which user to schedule for each of the carriers by incorporating information from all of the carriers. Indeed, the active users need to send channel quality feedback for all of the carriers to the serving base station. Since scheduling of a given user for service in one of the carriers affect its QoS performance, the scheduler cannot perform resource allocation independently for each carrier.

Numerous schedulers have been studied in the literature for systems employing opportunistic multiple access, including the 1x IS-856, with the aim of offering various notions of fairness among users without deviating too much from the throughput optimal operating point. Next, we provide a brief overview of some of the scheduling algorithms from the literature.

2.1 Round Robin Rule

One well-known scheduling scheme is the Round Robin (RR) rule. In RR scheduling, the users are selected in cyclic order without any regard to their channel conditions unless they are in outage. If no user ever experiences outage, this scheduling has the highest level of fairness in terms of resource use time amongst users. However, the system performance suffers from low average throughput since multi-user diversity is not exploited.

2.2 Maximum Rate Rule

The maximum rate (MaxR) rule aims to maximize the overall system throughput without any delay or fairness constraints. This algorithm is theoretically the optimal algorithm for the total system capacity [5]. However it cannot be directly implemented in practice since it may cause user starvation. The rule schedules user s such that,

$$s = \arg \max_i \left(R_i(t) \right) \tag{1}$$

where $R_i(t)$ is the data rate user i can support at time t.

2.3 The Proportional Fair Rule

The proportional fair (PF) rule as described by [9] serves a user whose current channel condition relative to its own mean (averaged over a certain window) is the best. The rule schedules user s such that,

$$s = \arg \max_i \left(\frac{R_i(t)}{\overline{R_i(t)}} \right) \tag{2}$$

where $\overline{R_i(t)}$ is the average rate actually provided to user i over a window of size W_s. W_s is chosen as 1000 slots in this paper.

2.4 The Exponential Rule

The authors in [10] describe an exponential scheduling algorithm that takes into account the delays of the head of line (HOL) packets in the user queues as well as the current channel conditions of the users to find a compromise between fairness of the user observed latency and the overall system throughput. The rule schedules user s such that,

$$s = \arg \max_i \left(\frac{R_i(t)}{\overline{R_i(t)}} \right) \exp \left(\frac{L_i(t) - \overline{L}}{1 + \sqrt{\overline{L}}} \right) \tag{3}$$

where $L_i(t)$ is the latency of the HOL packet for user i at time t and $\overline{L}$ is defined as the observed latency averaged across all users.

In (3), a large latency observed by one of the users relative to the overall average latency results in a very large exponent, overriding the channel conditions and leading to the large latency user getting priority. On the other hand, for small latency differences, the exponential term is close to 1 and the policy is only ruled by the experienced user channel conditions relative to their own means.

2.5 Minimum Performance Rule

The authors in [11] describe a scheduling algorithm in which users are guaranteed a certain minimum throughput. The minimum throughput can be chosen differently for each user. The algorithm selects user s such that,

$$s = \arg \max_i \alpha_i(t) U_i(t) \tag{4}$$

where $\alpha_i(t)$ is a parameter with a minimum value of 1 (also the initial value for each user) that is updated every slot and $U_i(t)$ is the performance value of user i in time slot t. The performance value we are going to assume in this paper will be the throughput of a user normalized to the lowest throughput available in the system. For IS-856, the lowest throughput is 38.4 kbps so a user with a scheduled transmission rate of 614.4 kbps would, as the performance value, have 16.

The update of the parameter $\alpha_i(t)$ is made using a stochastic approximation [12] and includes the minimum performance guarantee. The update is as follows:

$$\alpha_i(t) = \max \left(\alpha_i(t-1) - a[\overline{R_i(t)} - C_i], 1 \right) \tag{5}$$

where $\overline{R_i(t)}$ is the average user data rate and C_i is the minimum guaranteed performance value for user i specified in this paper as the desired QoS value in terms of the average data rate.

3 Qos Aware Scheduling Algorithm for IS-856

As stated before, the goal of this paper is to develop a scheduling algorithm for wireless opportunistic multiple access systems such that QoS guarantees may be offered to users statistically. Furthermore, the appropriate scheduler should be fair to all its users in terms of these QoS assurances. The above described scheduling algorithms in their originally proposed forms do not have satisfactory QoS performances in terms of the percentage of time performance (PoTP).

A fair scheduling algorithm that aims for statistical QoS assurances should incorporate the QoS parameters directly into the decision process. We propose to use a modified version the exponential rule for this purpose. Our motivation for using the exponential rule is that instead of equalizing weighted delays of the queues, it is easily possible to equalize the average data rates of all the users with respect to the QoS requirements, provided that the QoS requirements (desired average data rates in this paper) for all of the users are the same. However, the proposed scheduling algorithms can also be extended for use in a wireless system that provides a multitude of services, each requiring different QoS values. The proposed Statistical QoS Aware Exponential scheduling algorithm can be described as follows:

1. For each of the carriers select user i that provides the largest argument

$$s_i = R_i(t) \exp\left(\frac{QoS - \overline{R_i(t)}}{1 + \sqrt{QoS}}\right) \tag{6}$$

   where QoS is the minimum average data rate requested by the service under consideration.
2. Check the current supported data rate of the selected user, $R_i(t)$.
3. If the current requested data rate for the selected user is equal to or greater than a certain threshold, $R_i(t) \geq T(t)$ service this user. The threshold values are a function of the number of active users in the system and is determined and stored a priori at the base station. Threshold values providing the best statistical QoS measures may be found via numerical optimization tools. Simulations may be run for all possible threshold values and the set providing the best performance may be chosen.
4. Otherwise select user j with the next highest argument, s_j, and proceed with step 2 until all the users are exhausted in the user array.
5. If none of the users satisfy the threshold requirement, select the user with the highest argument regardless of its requested data rate.

In (6), if the average data rate of a user falls below the QoS requirement by more than order $\sqrt{QoS}$ the exponential term dominates, overriding the $R_i(t)$ term thus favoring this user over users with better channel conditions. When the average data rate is close to the desired QoS, the exponential term is close to 1 and the algorithm behaves like the MaxR scheduler.

Without the steps 3-4, the proposed algorithm favors a user whose QoS level is below and furthest away from the desired QoS level over other users with better QoS levels. If, however, the scheduled user with the lowest QoS level also happens to have a low transmission data rate, $R_i(t)$, the scheduling operation will not provide a significant increase in the average data rate. In fact, the data rate may be so low that the QoS, even after the user is scheduled, may not get close to the minimum desired threshold. In this case, the system resources of time and transmission

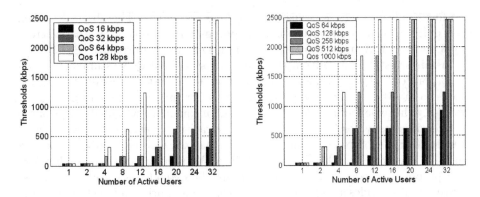

Fig. 2. Optimized threshold values for the 1x and 3x IS-856 System

power will be spent with no apparent benefit to the scheduled user. Furthermore, users that may actually benefit from utilizing these resources will not have access to them. The threshold operation is there to weed out such users from getting scheduled. This way, users in critical conditions with transmission data rates that are actually beneficial to them get priority over users in critical conditions that have no way of immediate recovery. The threshold levels are clearly functions of number of users as well as the specific QoS requirement. As the number of users increase, thresholds also increase. Similarly, an increase in the desired QoS level also results in an increase in the threshold level. Figure 2 presents the optimized threshold values for the 1x and 3x IS-856 system. The thresholds are computed using a simple optimization of the PoTP QoS via simulations. The details of the simulation set-up for this purpose is given in the next section.

4   Performance of the Statistical QoS Aware Scheduler

To assess the relative performance of the proposed statistical QoS aware scheduler and the scheduling rules from the literature described in the previous section, we have performed detailed simulations of the IS-856 system for both single carrier and multi-carrier options.

Table 2. System Parameters and Forward Link Budget

Carrier Frequency	2 GHz
Radiation Pattern	Omnidirectional
Path Loss Model (dB)	$30\log_{10} f_c + 49 + 40\log_{10} d$ $d(km), f_c(MHz)$
Log-normal Shadowing	4.3 dB variance
Short term fading	Rayleigh with Jakes spectrum
Total Forward Traffic Channel Tx Power	52.8 dBm

Table 3. Additional System Parameters for 3x

Carrier Frequencies	1.99875 GHz, 2 GHz, 2.00125 GHz
Correlation Between Carriers	$1/(1 + [\Delta f/B_c])$
	$\Delta f =$ Carrier Frequency Separation
	$B_c =$ Coherence Bandwidth

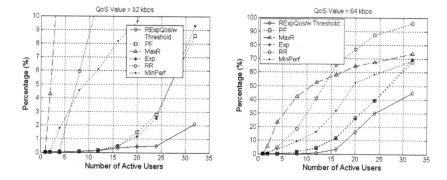

Fig. 3. PoT QoS is not satisfied for QoS $=$ 32 kbps and 64 kbps for 1X

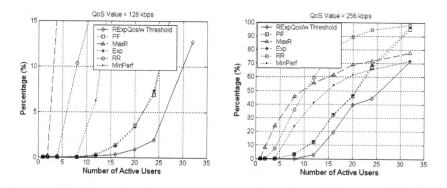

Fig. 4. PoT QoS is not satisfied for QoS $=$ 128 kbps and 256 kbps for 3X

We consider a 2-tier 19-cell environment. Here, the first tier has 6 and the second tier has 12 cells centered around the cell of interest. Each cell is considered to have a radius of 1 km in the layout. We assume that users are dropped uniformly over the center cell. For each user, the signal to interference plus noise (SINR) is calculated using the ITU pedestrian A channel model for each of the carriers [13]. The channel model includes path loss, Rayleigh fading and shadow fading effects. In modeling the pedestrian A channel we have assumed that the receiver can capture only 97% of what was transmitted. The link budget and the system parameters are summarized in Table 2.

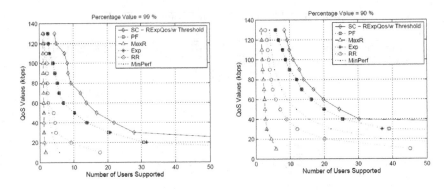

Fig. 5. PoT QoS is not satisfied for QoS = 32 kbps and 64 kbps for 1X

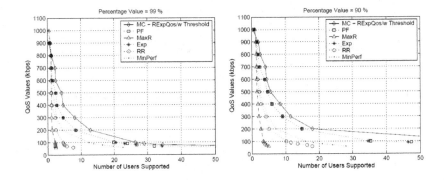

Fig. 6. PoT QoS is not satisfied for QoS = 128 kbps and 256 kbps for 3X

The multi-carrier system has the same propagation model of Table 2 for each carrier. However, if the sub-carriers are adjacent, inter-carrier correlation needs to be taken into account as well. The additional system parameters for the 3x multi-carrier system are given in Table 3.

The sampling rate for the simulations is 600 Hz which also corresponds to the channel quality feedback rate from all the users in IS-856. The simulations have been performed for 18000 slots corresponding to 30 seconds of real time.

For each time slot, the SINR value of each user is used to generate the channel quality feedback of the users and these values are used in the scheduling simulations to obtain PoT results.

Simulations have been performed to obtain the PoTP values for different scheduling algorithms based using the above described set-up. Figures 3 and 4 show the percentage of time the desired QoS is not satisfied as a function of the number of users for the proposed scheduling algorithm as well as the traditional algorithms from the literature for the single carrier and multi-carrier IS-856 system, respectively. Desired data rates of 32 kbps and 64 kbps are considered for the single carrier and 128 kbps and 256 kbps for the 3x multi-carrier system. From the graphs we can see that the proposed scheduling algorithm performs significantly better than the other scheduling algorithms for all of the QoS requirements. In fact, when the desired QoS level is relatively low, the difference between the proposed algorithm and the rest can be as high as 5-fold. For larger QoS levels and high number of users, the difference between the performances is reduced. This is because, the system operates near its full capacity in this case and even the best scheduler can not handle all of the active users at the same time.

Figures 5 and 6 illustrate results for the supported QoS levels at 99% and 90% operating levels as a function of number of users. In this illustration, it is once again clear that the proposed scheduler outperforms the others significantly. Once again, as the system capacity is neared, the gains somehow decrease, but gains are observed at all operating levels.

5   Conclusions

In this paper we have introduced the notion of statistical QoS assurances as a feasible alternative to assured QoS in wireless time-varying and error-prone channels. We have proposed a new scheduling algorithm for the IS-856 system that takes the statistical QoS requirements directly into account. Both single carrier and multi-carrier wireless systems are considered. The multi-carrier system naturally provides higher data rates and thus is capable of reasonable quality streaming video transmission over the wireless channel.

The proposed scheduling algorithm is shown to perform significantly better than previously developed scheduling algorithms from the literature. In fact, for the single carrier system, an average data rate of 60 kbps may be guaranteed 99% of the time for only 1 user using the maximum rate scheduler, 2 users using the round robin and minimum performance schedulers, 7 users using the exponential and proportional fair schedulers. The proposed scheduler on the other hand, provides this guarantee for 13 users, over 50% more users than the best performing scheduler from the literature. Similarly, for the 3x multi-carrier system, a data rate of 200 kbps may be guaranteed 99% of the time for only 1 user using the maximum rate scheduler, 2 users using the round robin, 4 users using the minimum performance scheduler, 8 users using the exponential and proportional fair schedulers. The proposed scheduler in this case provides the service for a total of 13 users, once again an over 50% increase over the best performing scheduler from the literature.

We conclude that the proposed statistical QoS assurance idea and the associated scheduling algorithm works very well for the wireless channel and is a perfect fit for the opportunistic multiple access scheme.

References

1. S. Blake, D. Black, M. Carlson, E. Davies, Z. Wang, W. Weiss, "RFC 2475: An Architecture for Differentiated Services", *IETF*, December 1998.
2. J. Heinanen, F. Baker, W. Weiss, W. Wroclawski, "Assured Forwarding PHB Group", *RFC 2597*, June 1999.

3. V. Jacobson, K. Nichols, K. Poduri, "An Expedited Forwarding PHB Group", *RFC 2598*, June 1999.
4. D. Clark, J. Wroclawski, "An Approach to Service Allocation in the Internet", *Internet Draft,* MIT LCS, July 1997.
5. R. Knopp, and P. Humblet, "Information Capacity and Power Control in Single Cell Multi-User Communications", *Proceedings of the IEEE ICC'95 Conference,* Seattle, WA, June 1995.
6. A. J. Goldsmith and P.P. Varaiya, "Capacity of Fading Channels with Channel Side Information," *IEEE Transactions on Information Theory,* vol. 43, no. 6, pp. 1986-1992, June 1997.
7. TIA/EIA/IS-856 "cdma2000 High Rate Packet Data Air Interface Specification", *3GPP2,* C.S0024, v4.0, Oct. 2002
8. M.O. Sunay and A. Ekşim, "Fair Scheduling for Spectrally Efficient Multi-Service Wireless Data Provisioning," *Wiley International Journal of Communication Systems,* vol 17, pp. 615-642, August 2004.
9. A. Jalali, R. Padovani, R. Pankaj, "Data Throughput of CDMA-HDR: A High Efficiency-High Data Rate Personal Communications System", *Proceedings of the IEEE VTC'00 Conference,* Tokyo, Japan, May 2000.
10. S. Shakkottai, A. Stolyar, "Scheduling Algorithms for a Mixture of Real-Time and Non-Real-Time Data in HDR", *Bell Laboratories Technical Report,* 2000.
11. X. Liu, E.K.P. Chong and N. Shroff, "Transmission Scheduling for Efficient Wireless Resource Utilization with Minimum-Performance Guarantees," *Proceedings of the INFOCOM Conference,* pp. 776-785, 2001.
12. X. Liu, E.K.P. Chong, and N. Shroff, "Opportunistic Transmission Scheduling with Resource-Sharing Constraints in Wireless Networks," *IEEE Journal on Selected Areas in Communications,* vol. 19, pp. 2053-2064, October 2001.
13. International Telecommunication Union, "Guidelines for Evaluation of Radio Transmission Technologies for IMT-2000," *Recommendation, ITU-R, M.1225,* 1997.
14. M. Gudmundson, "Correlation Model for Shadow Fading in Mobile Radio Systems," *Electronics Letters,* vol. 27, pp. 2145-2146, Nov. 1991.
15. G.L. Stuber, *Principles of Mobile Communications, 2nd Ed.,* Kluwer Academic Publishers, 2001.

Dynamic Indoor Localization Using Wireless Ethernet: The ARIADNE System

Yiming Ji[1], Saâd Biaz[1], Santosh Pandey[2], and Prathima Agrawal[2]

[1] Auburn University, Department of Computer Science and Software Engineering, USA
{jiyimin, sbiaz}@auburn.edu
[2] Auburn University, Department of Electrical and Computer Engineering, USA
{pandesg, pagrawal}@auburn.edu

Abstract. Location determination of mobile users within a building has attracted much attention lately due to its many applications in mobile networking including network intrusion detection problems. However, it is challenging due to the complexities of the indoor radio propagation characteristics exacerbated by the mobility of the user. A common practice is to mechanically generate a table showing the radio signal strength at different known locations in the building. A mobile user's location at an arbitrary point in the building is determined by measuring the signal strength at the location in question and determining the location by referring to the above table using a LMSE (least mean square error) criterion. Obviously, this is a very tedious and time consuming task. This paper proposes a novel and automated location determination method called ARIADNE. Using a two dimensional construction floor plan and only a single actual signal strength measurement, ARIADNE generates an estimated signal strength map comparable to those generated manually by actual measurements. Given the signal measurements for a mobile, a proposed clustering algorithm searches that signal strength map to determine the current mobile's location. The results from ARIADNE are comparable and may even be superior to those from existing localization schemes.

1 Introduction

Location determination of indoor mobile users is challenging because of the complexities of the indoor radio propagation characteristics. Prior to the widespread and popular deployment of RF 802.11 wireless networks, location systems were designed using a specific technology independently from data communication networks. Such location systems exploit infra-red (IR) (*Active Badge* [1]), ultrasound [2], magnetic field [3], or light (cameras) [4]. Such early location systems require specialized hardware used only for the location determination and incur in general a high deployment and maintenance cost. In the recent years, the popular success and widespread deployment of RF 802.11 wireless networks enticed many researchers to exploit existing RF 802.11 wireless network infrastructure to build location systems.

This RF based localization system works by first constructing a signal strength map where the signal strength at known and predetermined locations is manually measured by three or more reference sniffers. The sniffer could be an AP (access point) or a

T. Braun et al. (Eds.): WWIC 2006, LNCS 3970, pp. 299–310, 2006.
© Springer-Verlag Berlin Heidelberg 2006

computer with signal strength measurement capability, and the signal strength map is a database table of locations and the signal strength recorded by sniffers at these locations. In order to locate a mobile user, the signal strength of the mobile is measured and compared with the previous signal strength map for the "closest" location.

In this paper, we address the *dynamic* property of the indoor localization system, and propose a convenient and scalable location system dubbed **ARIADNE**. ARIADNE is a network-based location scheme that requires three (or more) sniffers to cover a floor plan. We refer to the three average signal strength measurements made by the three sniffers as one *signal strength measurement triplet*. ARIADNE consists of two modules: (1) the first *MAP GENERATION* module estimates a signal strength map **SS-MAP** when given as input a topview CAD floor plan and *ONE* signal strength measurement triplet $M(SA, SB, SC)(LR, t)$ for a mobile M located at some reference location LR in the building at some time t, and SA, SB, SC represent three sniffers; and (2) the second *SEARCH* module determines the location of a mobile M when given as input the estimated signal strength map *SS-MAP* and the current signal strength measurement triplet $M(SA, SB, SC)(L, Now)$ of mobile M at some location L.

Map generation and the location search were extensively tested and validated: simulation results illustrate that signal strength estimates fit well with actual measurements, with a *maximum* average difference around 1.4% of maximum Received Signal Strength Indicator (RSSI), and a *maximum* mean square error MSE around 0.75 . With the estimated signal strength map from *three* sniffers, the proposed localization scheme works comparable with most reported localization methods with average mean error around 2.5 meters for a typical office environment.

The remainder of the paper is organized as follows: Section 2 describes previous work done on location estimation over indoor 802.11 networks. Section 3 introduces ARIADNE system. Simulation and experimental comparison are presented in Section 4. Section 5 discusses the performance improvement and mobile user localization. And Section 6 concludes the paper and outlines future research.

2   Related Work

This section will separately survey related work for *map generation* and *location search*.

2.1   Map Generation

To construct a signal strength map *SS-MAP*, a brute force method is to carry out manual measurements of signal strength at short intervals within the building [5, 6, 7]. However, the manual measurement is time-consuming and it doesn't take into account the time-varying nature of the signal strength. In order to address the dynamic nature of the radio propagation, Krishnan *et al.* [8] suggests the deployment of *stationary emitters* to periodically monitor signal strength at specific locations on the site. However, the hardware cost and installation issues could make this method unpractical for large scale deployment.

Therefore, a more convenient method is to theoretically estimate the signal strength using appropriate indoor radio propagation model. When considering the *large-scale* attenuation model, most researchers model the radio propagation path loss as a function of the *attenuation exponent* n (Please, see Equation 1), which is two for free space but greater than two for an indoor environment.

$$P(d)[dB] = P(d_0)[dB] - 10 \times n \times log_{10}(\frac{d}{d_0})$$ (1)

where $P(d)$ is the power at distance d to the transmitter in meters; $P(d_0)$ is the power at a reference distance d_0, usually set to 1.0 meter. n is the attenuation exponent, which is often statistically determined to provide a best fit with measurement readings.

Much research has been carried out based on this model [5, 9, 10, 11], however, existing research requires extensive measurements in order to determine the building-specific attenuation exponent (i.e., n). Besides, most radio propagation models consider the path loss only along the *direct path* between the transmitter and the receiver. Therefore, these research is not convenient or scalable for the large deployment.

In contrast, ARIADNE requires only ONE signal strength measurement and a topview floor map to estimate the signal strength map. If the environment is highly dynamic, ARIADNE can be used to monitor a unique point of measurement and generate on demand an updated signal strength map. Simulated annealing (SA) algorithm is used to dynamically determine the attenuation parameters. Consequently, with realtime measurement, the signal-strength map table could dynamically be built.

2.2   Location Search

As pointed earlier, in order to locate a mobile user inside the building, a simple method is to search the *SS-MAP* for the signal strength of the mobile user. A general comparison metric is the least mean square error (LMSE). However, *LMSE* requires precise map table, or multiple candidate positions at different locations could be obtained.

In [12], Prasithsangaree *et al.* proposed a *closeness elimination scheme*, which is to first find more than three locations from the *SS-MAP* table with signal strength close to the measurement. From these, the three closest positions are selected and their position average is used to denote the estimated location for the mobile user. Similarly, Pandey *et el.* [13] used the second lowest MSE to assist the estimation. In [14], Youssef *et al. clustered* the positions in the *SS-MAP* where a set of locations sharing a common set of access points (called *cluster key*) are defined as one cluster. Therefore, the *SS-MAP* is sorted according to the cluster keys. To determine the mobile user's location, a small set of access points are used to determine a cluster for the most probable location.

In summary, to locate a mobile user, existing mechanisms assume the use of precise *SS-MAP* with which the *LMSE* technique is used to find a match. This research proposes a *clustering-based search method* based on the *LMSE*. This method is similar to Prasithsangaree *et al.*[12] with the difference that the final positions are not necessarily three. The proposed method is specially designed for imprecise *SS-MAP* tables, and is different from Youssef's clustering approach because this method does not *sort or cluster* reference positions according to *common* access points, instead, it selects and clusters a set of candidate positions. The largest cluster is chosen and its center is picked as the location estimate.

3   ARIADNE Indoor System

ARIADNE consists of two modules - namely map generation and search - that are developed in Section 3.1 and Section 3.2, respectively.

3.1   Map Generation Module

This section introduces the dynamic signal strength estimation method. We first propose a propagation model in next section.

Radio propagation model. The proposed radio propagation model is based on the *ray tracing* technology, which assumes the radio propagation is with a finite number of isotropic rays emitted from a transmitting antenna [15]. For an omni-directional antenna, each ray is assumed to transmit with the same amount of energy at the transmitter, and the energy of the rays will be attenuated, individually, at walls or floors due to reflections and transmissions. Due to the space constraints, the detailed ray technique is omitted here (a good reference can be found in [16]).

We assume the signal power at the receiver is the accumulated multipath power from all individual rays from the same transmitter [11]. For each ray, the attenuation path loss includes three components: i) The distance-dependent path loss, which is assumed as free space propagation loss; ii) The attenuation due to reflections, which is the product of the reflection coefficient and the total number of reflections from transmitter to the receiver; iii) The attenuation due to transmission, which is the product of the transmission coefficient and the total number of transmission walls. Consequently, the model is defined as:

$$P = \sum_{i=1}^{N_{r,j}} (P_0 - 20log_{10}(d_i) - \gamma \cdot N_{i,ref} - \alpha \cdot N_{i,trans}) \tag{2}$$

where P is the power (in dB) at receiver, $N_{r,j}$ is the total number of rays received at the receiver j; P_0 is the power (in dB) at a distance of 1 meter; d_i, $N_{i,ref}$, and $N_{i,trans}$ represent the total transmission distance, the total number of reflections and the total number of (wall) transmissions of the ith ray, respectively. γ is the reflection coefficient, and α is the transmission coefficient.

The site specific parameters (N_{ray}, d_i, $N_{i,ref}$, and $N_{i,trans}$) in Equation 2 can be obtained directly from ray tracing technique. The other three parameters (P_0, γ, and α), in other similar research, are usually derived from tedious measurements. ARIADNE does not require extensive on site measurements. Instead, simulated annealing (SA) technique is used to determine optimal values for the three parameters of the proposed model. *ONE* measurement only is required.

Parameters Estimation. Simulated Annealing (SA) is a method used to search for a minimum in a general system. The original Metropolis scheme [17] indicates that an initial state of a thermodynamic system is chosen at energy E and a desired temperature T. Holding at that temperature T, the initial configuration is perturbed and the change in energy dE is computed. Applying *Monte Carlo* sampling techniques, the physical annealing process is modelled successfully by computer simulation methods. From thermodynamics, the following formula:

$$\widehat{P(E)} = exp(-\frac{E}{kT})$$
(3)

expresses the annealing probability $\widehat{P(E)}$ of a change on energy E at temperature T, where k is Boltzmann's constant.

Given initial values of $x = [P_0 \ \gamma \ \alpha]^T$ at a temperature T, the power of each individual ray can be computed (Equation 2). Neglecting those rays with power below the threshold, and summing the powers of all others, yield the multipath power at the receiver. The least minimum squared error allows the comparison of the power estimates fitness with the measurements, and henceforth the adjustment of the parameters of x accordingly. To adjust the parameters, a random movement is generated by adding a deviate from the Cauchy distribution to each parameter of $x = [P_0 \ \gamma \ \alpha]^T$:

$$x_{i+1} = x_i + T \cdot tan(\widehat{P}), \ i = 1, 2, 3$$
(4)

The cooling schedule for the temperature T can use a simple method:

$$T_{i+1} = a \cdot T_i, \ a \in (0, 1)$$
(5)

Consequently, the Simulated annealing search algorithm can be detailed below: 1) Define initial values for $x = [P_0 \ \gamma \ \alpha]^T$; 2) Define the temperature, T_{max} for highest temperature and T_{min} for the cooling down value; 3) Calculate the annealing probability from Equation 3; 4) Update the displacement for the parameters using Equation 4; 5) Calculate the fitness between the estimates and the measurements using LMSE: if a better agreement is obtained, keep the displacement from the above step; else, keep the displacement with certain probability; 6) Update the temperature T by equation 5, and repeat steps 3, 4, and 5 until $T < T_{min}$ or specified minimum errors is achieved.

Simulated annealing method can effectively estimate parameter pair $x = [P_0 \ \gamma \ \alpha]^T$ with only ONE reference measurement.

3.2   Search Module: Clustering-Based Search Algorithm

To locate a mobile user, the current user's signal strength measurement triplet is searched from the signal strength map *SS-MAP* for a hit. Currently, most search algorithms are based on the *LMSE* and select a single location as the estimate. This method works if a *detailed* and *precise* SS-MAP for the building is available. As indicated in many papers [5, 9], the signal strength is observed to be very dynamic at different measurement time; and to collect a fine-grid signal strength map is time consuming for large scale building deployments. Consequently, *LMSE* method will not generate optimal estimates in most circumstances.

ARIADNE proposes a clustering-based search algorithm for the indoor localization of a mobile user based on the following findings: 1) ARIADNE dynamically constructs fine-grid signal strength map *SS-MAP* based on the radio propagation model and the

site specific geometry of the building; 2) The estimated *SS-MAP* is only a close fit to
the measurements; 3) Consequently, *LMSE* may result multiple possible locations in
the SS-MAP table, or the unique location corresponding to the LMSE is not necessarily
the right position; 4) If a set of candidate positions are to be grouped into several point
clusters. The largest cluster will generally have higher probability to contain the true
position for the mobile user.

The clustering-based search algorithm is a two-phase search algorithm. The first
phase is named as **data collection and cluster preparation phase**. In this phase, a
set of candidate locations with lower mean square error within the threshold are selected and preprocessed with the purpose to neglect isolated locations from the set.
The second phase is **clustering phase**, where the remaining candidate locations are
grouped into several clusters and the center of the largest cluster is chosen as the final
estimate.

To group the set of points in space, this research uses k-means algorithm. To determine the actual number of clusters (the k), we heuristically explore the selection process
through simulation by the Equation 6.

$$D_c = min(\sum_{i=1}^{N} \sum_{j=1}^{M} (x_{j,i} - \overline{x}_{i,ctr})^2)^{1/2}) \tag{6}$$

where D_c is the total distance of all locations to the respective cluster centers, a small
value represents better separation for the determined number of cluster. N is the predetermined number of clusters; M is the maximum number of position points in i^{th}
cluster; $x_{j,i}$ denotes the coordinates of jth position in i^{th} cluster; and $\overline{x}_{i,ctr}$ is the center coordinates of ith cluster.

The sensitivity of the selection to initial cluster centers is minimized by running the
clustering algorithm multiple times and an averaging result is used.

4   Simulation and Experiment

4.1   Experiment Setup

Figure 1 shows the floor plan ($45.72m \times 36.57m$) of the building used for this study.
Three sniffers A, B, and C are deployed inside the building. Through the AP, sniffers
connected with the global monitor, a central processing unit for localization.

In order to validate the proposed indoor radio propagation model, the signal strengths
were collected at 30 different locations, and they are marked in Figure 1 with faint dots
as marked from 1 to 30. In this experiment, the data collection and validation positions
are all in hallway because of the administration reasons, however, none of the validation
positions is *directly* connected with a sniffer without a wall partition. In the figure, the
'×' denotes grid positions in estimated *SS-MAP* table.

At each validation position, about 100 sample packets were emitted at an interval of
0.5 seconds and the signal strength of each packet is then measured at sniffers A, B, and
C. The same series of measurements at the 30 locations were repeated continuously for
a week. ARIADNE radio propagation model (see Section 3.1) is evaluated using the 30

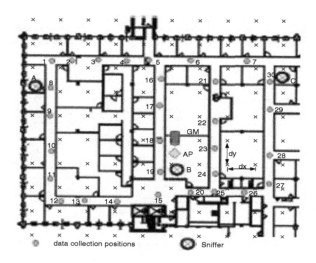

Fig. 1. Experimental floor plan

signal strength measurement triplets. Note that ONE of the 30 signal strength triplets is randomly selected to estimate site specific parameters in the ARIADNE radio propagation model and then to compute an estimated *SS-MAP* table for a specific set of grid positions. Given the estimated *SS-MAP* and the measured signal strength triplet $M(SA, SB, SC)(L, Now)$ for a mobile at some location L, different search localization algorithms were evaluated.

4.2 Radio Propagation Model Validation

The parameters $[P_0, \gamma, \alpha]$ of ARIADNE radio propagation model are estimated using ONE randomly selected signal strength measurement triplet. ARIADNE radio propagation model is then evaluated using the 30 signal strength measurement triplets from the same day.

For all experiments, the ARIADNE radio propagation model yields good estimates with the relative signal strength difference (between measurements and estimates) within $3\% \sim 5\%$ of the maximum RSSI. Figure 2 presents typical comparison results including three plots respectively for sniffers A, B, and C. For each plot, the x-axis represents the 30 positions from the data collection and the y-axis denotes the signal strength measured as received signal strength indicator. The points with symbol '⊖' are the signal strength measurements, and the points with symbol '×' are the estimates. It is clear that the proposed radio propagation model correctly estimates the signal strength.

We apply multiple reference measurement triplets in the radio propagation model, and to verify whether they would yield estimates that are closer to measurements. The answer is surprising: one reference measurement triplet will yield estimates as good as estimates from 2, 3, or 10 reference measurement triplets as shown in Figure 3.

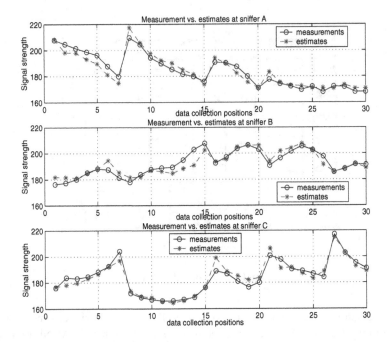

Fig. 2. Estimation results and comparison with measurements at data collection positions

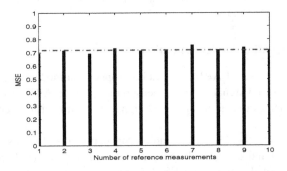

Fig. 3. MSE vs. number of reference measurements

In the Figure, the x-axis denotes the number of reference signal strength, and the y-axis represents the mean square error MSE of signal strength between measurements and estimates. For each run for x references, x references are *randomly* selected to be used to estimate the radio propagation model and construct the signal strength map.

Note however, for a building with *non-uniform* walls (i.e. different construction materials and thickness), or with *spatially different* (human) occupation, it is not appropriate to only select a single measurement at a reference position. In this situation, it is necessary to first identify all representative regions for the building such that each region is with homogeneous construction material and in uniform space. Thus a regional

Table 1. Localization performance of six experimental measurements

	Clustering		LMSE		2-N		3-N	
	err	std	err	std	err	std	err	std
Day1	2.8372	2.4304	2.7442	2.0349	3.7355	2.9256	3.5412	3.0458
Day2	2.5330	2.2388	3.5297	2.3543	4.5651	3.5070	4.1878	3.2926
Day3	2.7076	2.1568	3.7510	2.6856	4.1948	2.7037	4.0549	2.6667
Day4	2.9063	2.4727	2.9170	2.5019	2.7875	2.5861	2.6399	2.6080
Day5	3.0004	2.5388	3.6431	2.1429	4.3931	2.5808	3.9705	2.5022
Day6	3.1074	1.7975	3.0704	1.7990	3.5920	2.1638	3.5151	2.1886
Avg	2.8487	2.2725	3.2759	2.2531	3.8780	2.7445	3.6516	2.7173

SS-MAP can be constructed in advance, and the overall building based SS-MAP can then be stitched.

4.3 Localization Performance

ARIADNE radio propagation model constructs an estimated signal strength map *SS-MAP* on a grid of locations with resolution of $0.75m \times 1.5m$. Six different *SS-MAPs* for the 6 days were constructed to evaluate the localization performance of the three strategies.

To locate a mobile M "sniffed" as $M(SA, SB, SC)(L)$ at a location L, the signal strength map *SS-MAP* must be *searched* for a best match. This section evaluates the Least Minimum Squared Error, the multiple nearest neighbors (three closest neighbors *3-N* [12], and two closest neighbors *2-N* [13]), and the proposed clustering-based search techniques.

With the "sniffed" signal strength triplet as an input, the signal strength map *SS-MAP* is searched using *LMSE, multiple nearest neighbors,* or *clustering-based* techniques. Table 1 summarizes the error distance in meters between the real location and the estimated location. The error and standard deviation are reported for each search method continuously for the six days. The last row provides an overall average for all experiments. The *clustering-based* localization algorithm in general outperforms all other techniques. For a grid positions of $0.75 \times 1.5 \ meter$ apart, and for the floor plan in Figure 1 with only *three* sniffers, clustering-based method gives the position estimation with average error of 2.8487 meters. The estimation with *clustering-based* is respectively 14.99%, 36.13% and 28.18% closer than all other techniques.

5 Discussion

To improve the localization performance, the following problems have to be considered:

1. Optimal sniffer deployment: the deployment must be designed to first provide maximum overlapping signal coverage on the site, and it should also present best discrimination of signal strength for different locations in the building. During the research, it is found that deployment of the three sniffers is not optimal. Specially,

coverage insensitive areas do exist at corners in the studied floor of the building. To improve this, sniffers A and C may be placed a little closer to the center in y direction (Please, see Figure 1);

2. The deployment of additional sniffers: additional sniffers improves the localization performance, for example, Ladd et al. in [18] apply **14** sniffers in a floor plan of $65m \times 35m$, and achieve 1.5 meters accuracy with about 70% probability; Haeberlen et al in [6] use **35** sniffers in an area of 12,000 square meters and obtain 95% accuracy over 60% cells; and Bahl and Padmanabhan in [19] use **5** sniffers over a plan of $43.96m \times 21.84m$ and achieve the mean error around $2.65m \sim 5.93m$ with 90% probability. Therefore, if more sniffers are available, the performance of the ARIADNE system should be improved, and our latest experiment indicates that an estimation error within 2.0m is achievable if total **5** sniffers are deployed for a basement floor plan of $43.07m \times 19.16m$.

3. Dynamic SS-MAP update: The signal strength map *SS-MAP* table consists a grid of known locations in which the values of corresponding signal strength are stored. Generally, a higher resolution table is required in order to obtain better location estimation. Higher grid resolution induces more computation for the construction of the ray tracing from each point to a set of receivers (APs or sniffers). For example, the approximate time taken to run the ray tracing (in 3D) for 30 positions and 3 sniffers (for the building in this paper) is about 2 hours on a machine of x86 family processor at 1.4GHz with 256 MB physical memory. However, a building floor plan rarely changes. Therefore, ray tracing can be preprocessed and ray information can be stored in advance. The ray information can be used by ARIADNE to generate a dynamic signal strength map. Given the ray information, the construction of a *SS-MAP* table with 300 points and 3 sniffers takes less than two minutes. So, a dynamic signal strength map is possible as long as structure conditions in a building remain stable.

Consequently, it is *inappropriate* to compare the localization performance of various systems only based on the reported results, because the floor construction and the detailed experimental settings greatly affect the estimation precision of the indoor system.

6   Conclusion and Future Work

This paper introduced a new and automated signal strength estimation tool called ARIADNE. The radio propagation model derived in this paper enables the creation of he signal strength map for an entire building with minimal manual intervention. The scalable algorithm generates a signal strength map with high accuracy and thus can be easily deployed for generating these maps for indoor premises. The time varying nature of the propagation characteristics of the wireless channel poses problems to a signal strength table created manually. This is because, even though such a table is accurate at a given instant of time, it can be rendered useless at another instant. The map generation module presented in this paper enables the creation, on a demand basis, of a signal strength map automatically and almost instantaneously. The resulting map is comparable in accuracy to that of a signal strength map manually generated at that instant of time.

Moreover, on the search module, a clustering-based localization algorithm is developed to search the inaccurate signal strength map *SS-MAP*. The authors argue that the signal strength map, even measurement based, is discrete and is not accurate because of the measurement errors and time-variant property of the radio propagation channel. Consequently, search algorithms such as *LMSE* and *nearest neighbors*, are needed. However, they do not perform as well as the proposed clustering-based algorithm. Simulation results validate the algorithms and procedures used in ARIADNE.

All actual measurements in this paper are based on our previous work. Results from ARIADNE indicate that the performance of the indoor localization system relies on many site specific parameters including the building structure, the number of deployed sniffers and the sniffer deployment strategy. Future work will study these problems in more detail.

References

1. R. Want, A. Hopper, V. Falcao, and J. Gibbons. The Active badge Location Systems. *ACM Transactions on Information Systems*, 10(1):91–102, Jan. 1992.
2. N.B. Priyantha, A. Chakraborty, and H. Balakrishnan. The cricket location-support system. *Proceedings of MOBICOM'00*, Aug. 2000.
3. Ascension technology corporation, http://www.ascension-tech.com.
4. J. Krumm, S. Harris, B. Meyers, B. Brumitt, M. Hale, and S. Shafer. Multi-camera multi-person tracking for EasyLiving. In *Third IEEE International Workshop on Visual Surveillance*, Dublin, Ireland, July 2000.
5. P. Bahl and V. Padmanabhan. RADAR: An In-Building RF-Based User Location and Tracking System. *Proc. IEEE Infocom 200*, pages 775–784, 2000.
6. A. Haeberlen, E. Flannery, A. M. Ladd, A. Rudys, D. S. Wallach, and L. E. Kavraki. Practical Robust Localization over Large-Scale 802.11 Wireless Networks. In *MobiCom*, Sept 2004.
7. Ankur Agiwal, Parakram Khandpur, and Huzur Saran. Locator: location estimation system for wireless lans. In *Proceedings of the 2nd ACM international workshop on Wireless mobile applications and services on WLAN hotspots*, Oct. 2004.
8. P. Krishnan, A.S. Krishnakumar, Wenhua Ju, C. Mallows, and S. Ganu. A System for LEASE: System for Location Estimation Assisted by Stationary Emitters for Indoor Wireless Networks. In *Proceedings of IEEE Infocom 2004*, Hong Kong, March 2004.
9. Alex Hills, Jon Schlegel, and Ben Jenkins. Estimating Signal Strengths in the Design of an Indoor Wireless Network. *IEEE Trans. on Wireless Communications*, 3(1), Jan. 2004.
10. Supachai Phaiboon. An Empirically Based Path Loss Model for Indoor Wireless Channels in Laboratory Building. In *Proceedings of IEEE TENCON'02*, 2002.
11. M. Hassan-Ali and K. Pahlavan. A new statistical model for site-specific indoor radio propagation prediction based on geometric optics and geometric probability. *Wireless Communications, IEEE Transactions on*, 1:112–124, Jan. 2002.
12. P. Prasithsangaree, P. Krishnamurthy, and P.K. Chrysanthis. On indoor position location with wireless LANs. In *Personal, Indoor and Mobile Radio Communications, 2002. The 13th IEEE International Symposium on*, pages 720–724, Sept. 2002.
13. Santosh Pandey, B. Kim, F. Anjum, and P. Agrawal. Client assisted location data acquisition scheme for secure enterprise wireless networks. In *IEEE WCNC 2005*, 2005.
14. M.A. Youssef, A. Agrawala, and A. Udaya Shankar. WLAN location determination via clustering and probability distributions. *Pervasive Computing and Communications, 2003. (PerCom 2003). Proceedings of the First IEEE International Conference on*, March 2003.

15. H. Kim and H. Ling. Electromagnetic scattering from an inhomogeneous object by ray tracing. *IEEE Trans. Antennas Propagat.*, 40:517–525, May 1992.
16. A. Falsafi, K. Pahlavan, and G. Yang. Transmission Techniques for Radio LAN's - A Comparative Performance Evaluation Using Ray Tracing. *IEEE J. on Sel. Areas in Comm.*, 14(3):477–491, April 1996.
17. N. Metropolis, A.W. Rosenbluth, M. N. Rosenbluth, A.H. Teller, and E. Teller. Equations of state calculations by fast computing machines. *J. Chem. Phys.*, 21:1087–1092, 1958.
18. Andrew M. Ladd, Kostas E. Bekris, Algis Pl Rudys, Dan S. Wallach, and Lydia E. Kavraki. On the Feasibility of Using Wireless Ethernet for Indoor Localization. June 2004.
19. Paramvir Bahl, V.N. Padmanabhan, and A. Balachandran. Enhancements to the RADAR User Location and Tracking System. Technical report, Microsoft Research, WA 98052, Feb. 2000.

Simulation and Evaluation of Unsynchronized Power Saving Mechanisms in Wireless Ad Hoc Networks

Philipp Hurni[1], Torsten Braun[1], and Laura Marie Feeney[2]

[1] Institute of Computer Science and Applied Mathematics, University of Bern
{hurni, braun}@iam.unibe.ch
[2] Swedish Institute of Computer Science
lmfeeney@sics.se

Abstract. Power saving mechanisms in wireless ad hoc network nodes mainly switch off the transmission and reception hardware for a maximal amount of time and turn it on again within a given interval. Many approaches aim to synchronize the state changes of the nodes in the network through distributed beacon generation and introduce mechanisms where nodes synchronously wake up at designated points of time to exchange announcements about pending traffic. Synchronization however is difficult to achieve, in particular in ad hoc networks.

This paper describes the simulation, evaluation and refinement of a recently proposed power saving approach based on asynchronous wake-up patterns and wake-up announcements integrated with AODV. We show that significant improvements of the connectivity under low wake ratios can be achieved by carefully designed forwarding strategies of AODV route request messages.

1 Introduction

In wireless mobile ad-hoc and sensor networks, efficient power saving mechanisms can drastically increase network lifetime. However, reasonable connectivity properties are nevertheless necessary for wireless networks to operate properly. The major part of many power saving mechanisms consists in introducing central or distributed synchronization and periodic switching between a sleep state and a wake state. Such synchronization measures however always cause new overhead. Recent publications therefore proposed variants of unsynchronized power saving mechanisms.

One of the most important related work is the IEEE 802.11 [2] power saving mode, where all nodes ideally wake up at the same time, at the beginning of a beacon interval, and remain awake during the ATIM window (Asynchronous Traffic Indication Map) to exchange traffic announcements in case of pending traffic, and fall asleep again if there is none. Quorum based systems [3] divide a single hop network into intersecting groups of nodes which wake up in different wake intervals, thereby permitting to reach any node by relaying traffic announcements on intermediate nodes.

T. Braun et al. (Eds.): WWIC 2006, LNCS 3970, pp. 311–324, 2006.

The power saving mechanism specified in [1] avoids the overhead of time synchronization. It proposes to take advantage of intersections in asynchronous wake patterns by relaying messages on intermediate nodes.

Another approach aiming to bypass the overhead of permanent synchronization proposes an asynchronous sleep-wake cycle with two ATIM-windows to disseminate phase announcememts [4]. A transfer window is in between the two ATIM windows during which the node has to stay awake for at least 50% of the total wake cycle. This ensures that neighboring nodes are always able to forward pending traffic and phase announcements within one cycle.

This paper describes the integration of the basic concept of the power saving mechanism proposed in [1] into a multi-hop wireless ad hoc environment using AODV and the IEEE 802.11 medium access procedure. Section 2 describes the design of the routing and medium access layer and proposes modifications to these. In section 3, we outline and examine the results of different simulation scenarios and propose refinements of the mechanism [1]. The key results concern the optimization of the connectivity properties when applying carefully designed forwarding strategies to rebroadcast AODV route requests. For low wake ratios, we can significantly improve the connectivity by increasing the number of message rebroadcasts. Section 4 concludes the paper.

2   Power Saving in Multi-hop Wireless Ad Hoc Networks

2.1   Basic Power Saving Mechanism

The mechanism proposed in [1] defines two wake and two sleep periods during one basic cycle duration T, as depicted in Figure 1. Each of the wake periods shall have the same duration t. The nodes strictly alternate between a fixed wake period (A) and a random wake period (B). The fixed wake period (A) always starts at the same time, exactly at the beginning of the basic cycle. The start of the random wake period (B) is uniformly distributed between the end of the fixed wake period (A) and the start of the next one. All nodes are assumed to operate with the same basic cycle duration T, although remaining unsynchronized. All nodes shall switch between the wake and sleep states in their individual wake-up pattern. In addition, we assume all nodes to operate with the same wake ratio $W = 2t/T$. Due to low drifts in clocks, this should be achievable in practice. Small differences as they might occur due to clock drifts do not matter. The fixed wake period (A) enables a node aiming to contact any neighboring node, if

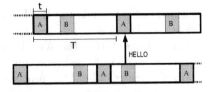

Fig. 1. Neighboring nodes with disjoint wake-up pattern announcing their wake state

its periodically occurring fixed wake period pattern is known. If however there is no intersection between the fixed wake periods of the sender and the neighbor, it may never learn about its presence. This motivates the choice for the random secondary wake period (B). It ensures that two nodes with disjoint wake-up pattern will sooner or later be awake at the same time and therefore be able to exchange announcements about their own wake period. By receiving these, the nodes will learn about the wake-up patterns of their neighbors, and thus be capable to reach any neighboring node during their fixed wake period (A).

2.2 Integration of the Ad Hoc on Demand Distance Vector Protocol (AODV)

AODV [7] is the most appropriate routing protocol considering the use with the power saving mechanism. The mechanism proposed in [1] is well integrable into on-demand routing. We modified the HELLO messages specified in [7] to contain a time entry indicating the time left until the beginning of the next fixed wake period (A). HELLO messages are broadcast within a HELLO interval during the next fixed or random wake period. If any neighboring node is awake, it will receive the wake-up announcement. With the time information contained in the HELLO message, it is able to calculate the relative time difference to its own fixed wake period (A). The node shall therefore update its routing table entry for the corresponding node with this time difference anytime it receives a HELLO message. Small clock drifts may only have little influence, because with every wake-up announcement received in a HELLO message, the table entries of the nodes can be updated and possible drifts can be corrected. Choosing a random interval duration for the HELLO interval guarantees that within a certain amount of time, any neighboring nodes will be detected. Even if their fixed wake periods (A) are disjoint, the mechanism specified in section 2.1 will ensure intersections with the random wake period (B), through which the nodes can learn about each other's presence by exchange of HELLO messages. Figure 1 shows such two neighboring nodes with non intersecting fixed wake patterns.

If a HELLO timer runs out during the sleep state of a node, the HELLO message is scheduled to be sent during the next wake period. The HELLO timer is furthermore restarted immediately. This ensures that the expected value of the count of HELLO packets sent remains independent of the wake ratio and is controllable solely through the parameter HELLOINTERVAL, which specifies the interval to choose a random time delay until scheduling the next HELLO message.

2.3 Medium Access Control (MAC) Layer Modifications

IEEE 802.11 [2] was chosen as the reference case for the integration of the power saving mechanism, as it is the most widely used standard for wireless communication. IEEE 802.11 proposes to access the medium immediately after the medium has been sensed idle for at least one DIFS, and to apply a random backoff procedure only if the medium had been sensed busy before. This immediate medium access guarantees minimal delays and better throughput under low medium utilization and low node densities. We adopted this MAC procedure to apply a random backoff in any case of medium access, as it led to fewer collisions and therefore proved to be more effective for the unacknowledged broadcast of route requests that is elementary for the success of the route establishment of AODV. The integration of the power saving mechanism proposed in [1] into a 802.11 environment leaves some design questions open, in particular concerning the behaviour of nodes in different states of the MAC layer protocol and the state changes of the power saving mechanism. The following assumptions were chosen:

- As unicast traffic is acknowledged, we decided to use DFWMAC (Distributed Foundation Wireless MAC) without RTS/CTS.
- If the wake state timer runs out while a node is receiving a frame, the node does not turn off immediately, but remains awake until the end of the transmission. In case of unicast traffic, the receiver stays awake until having sent the following ACK.
- If the wake state timer runs out while a node is waiting during the DIFS, the contention is aborted and the node turns to the sleep state.
- If the wake state timer runs out while a node is contending for medium access and is already counting down a random backoff interval, but has not yet accessed the medium, the node instantly switches to the sleep state. The node will restart contention by choosing a new random backoff value during the next wake state. The contention window will remain unchanged.
- If the wake state timer runs out while a node is transmitting, the node switches to the sleep state after having completed the transmission.

We decided to give unicast traffic a higher priority than broadcast traffic. If a node wakes up, and there are different types of messages in the queue to be sent, it sends the unicast (RREP or DATA) messages first. This should ensure predictable behaviour of unicast data traffic delays. Moreover, it is not necessary to handle HELLO broadcasts very quickly, and RREQ broadcasts yet have the advantage of redundancy through neighboring nodes.

3   Evaluation of Power Saving Mechanisms

3.1   Simulation Environment and Parameters

In the following sections, we perform several experiments to measure the ad hoc networks' properties. First, we examine the neighbourhood discovery process when no traffic is generated rather than the HELLO message transfers of the mechanism specified in section 2.2. We determine how long it takes for each node to learn about the presence and the wake-up patterns of their respective neighbors. Secondly, we study the performance of four algorithms concerning the forwarding of RREQ messages according to AODV route discovery. We discuss advantages and drawbacks of each approach in respect to connectivity optimization and power consumption.

For performance evaluation, we used the OMNeT++ Network Simulator [8, 9]. We made use of the Mobility Framework from TU Berlin [10], a framework to support simulations of wireless and mobile networks within OMNeT++. This framework incorporates a sophisticated transmission model which is based on calculation of SNR (Signal-to-Noise Ratio) and SNIR (Signal-to-Noise-and-Interference Ratio) values according to a restricted free space propagation model. This model takes transmitter power, distance, wavelength and path loss coefficient of signal dispersion into account. The following simulation parameters were kept fix throughout all simulation scenarios:

Nodes	200 (uniform distribution)
Area	1000m × 1000m
Bitrate	2 Mbps
Carrier Frequency	2 GHz
Transmitter Power	2 mW
SNR Threshold	3 dB
Path Loss Coefficient	2
Thermal Noise	-110 dBm
MAC Header	32 Byte
AODV Header	34 Byte
RREQ_RETRY_TIMER	800ms
HELLOINTERVAL	2s

Nodes are assumed to be stationary throughout all cases of the following sections. We adjusted the parameters such that the transmission range in case of one transmitter and no interferring other stations reaches 100m. In this case, the same station was considered not to interfer with a receiver farther than 200m (interference range). Furthermore, any station within the range of 200m (carrier sensing range) also considered the channel to be busy. In the following experiments, we basically varied the basic cycle duration T and the wake ratio W of the proposed power saving mechanism.

3.2   Neighborhood Detection

Basic Cycle Duration T	200ms

At the start of the simulation, we assume all nodes to be in one of the respective states (wake states A, B; sleep state). Furthermore, every node starts its HELLO timer in respect to the given interval length HELLOINTERVAL. The first HELLO message is sent after an offset t_H, which is a uniformly distributed random value in the interval [0, HELLOINTERVAL]. The random wake period (B) and the mechanism of choosing random time intervals between two HELLO messages ensures that every node should detect its neighbors within a certain amount of time. The following experiment deals with measuring how long it takes for the nodes to discover each other under the given parameters.

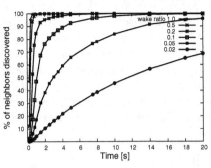

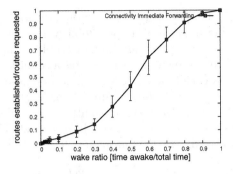

Fig. 2. Neighborhood detection

Fig. 3. Connectivity when forwarding immediately

To make sure that neighborhood detection succeeds quickly, we optimized the neighborhood detection process: if a node receives a HELLO message from a neighbor, for which it had no entry in its table before, it schedules a HELLO message at the start of the next fixed wake period of the sender node, waking up regardless of its actual state. In this case, there is a high probability that the receiving node is yet unknown to the sending node. With the wake-up time information in the HELLO message, the receiving node can announce its own wake-up pattern to the sending node and significantly speed up the neighborhood detection process.

With the given basic cycle duration T and $E(t_H) = 1s$, every node would broadcast a HELLO message every 5 cycles in average. Figure 2 depicts the results of the simulation when traffic only consists in periodic HELLO message transfer. The simulation results yield that approximately 80% of the neighbors are already detected within 2s for a wake ratio of 20%. For the very low wake ratio of 1%, 95% of the neighbors are discovered within 2 minutes. The evaluation of the neighborhood detection process yields, that nodes can discover most of their immediate neighbors within a few minutes.

3.3   AODV Route Establishment

Route Requests (RREQ)	60
Neighborhood Discovery Interval	2min
Basic Cycle Duration T	200ms

To evaluate the route establishment performance of the power saving mechanism proposed in [1], we triggered 60 AODV Route Requests (RREQ) after a neighborhood discovery interval of 2 minutes. Every second during one minute, a pair of nodes, sender and destination, was chosen randomly among the distributed nodes to trigger an AODV RREQ. This simulation scenario remained unchanged throughout this section. The reason not to choose a higher number of route requests lies in the route establishment mechanism of AODV, which allows to shorten route requests by letting intermediate nodes respond instead of destination nodes. The connectivity properties will therefore become slightly better with every route request triggered. We wanted this influence to remain small to measure the performance of the power saving mechanism, rather than pure AODV properties.

If after a given time interval there is no response to an outgoing RREQ, [7] proposes to retry the request again with a higher sequence number. The retry limit was set to 2 in all cases of this scenario, permitting 3 RREQ broadcasts in total for each route discovery process.

The selected node density is not necessarily sufficient to ensure that every random pair of nodes can reach each other. It is most likely that there are scattered clusters of nodes without any path to each other. Therefore, the route requests where sender nodes tried to reach unreachable destination nodes were not triggered and accounted in the evaluation. The further sections therefore take the number of routes that are actually possible under the given circumstances as a basis for the calculation of the success ratios.

Immediate Forwarding of Route Requests

If a sender node wants to establish a route to a destination, it sets up a RREQ packet, contends for medium access and broadcasts the packet. Every RREQ received is forwarded only once. Neither the sender node, nor any of the intermediate nodes make use of the time information contained in the RREQ message when rebroadcasting it. In contrast, the RREP packets, which are sent unicast, always make use of the announcement about the next fixed wake period. Their transmission is therefore scheduled for the beginning of the fixed wake period (A) of the receiving node.

We discovered that many RREQ messages broadcasted across the whole network were lost due to collisions with their copies. Since broadcasts are unacknowledged, every packet loss remains undetected for the originating node, and this proved to have a strong impact on the success of the RREQ-RREP query cycle. The problem of coherent RREQ discovery waves is studied in [11]. Imposing a jittering scheme on the retransmission of RREQ broadcasts significantly reduces the number of collisions. We chose every node to defer for a small random period between 0 and $3\times(RREQ\_length/bandwidth)$, which proved to deliver substantially lower collision rates.

Figure 3 depicts that this strategy works well with high wake ratios, but remains ineffective for low wake ratios. In theory, the probability for a RREQ to reach its destination is expected to decrease with increasing distance. The farther the destination is away, the more collisions may occur.

As we are dealing with a network of random topology, the length of the optimal route between two nodes was taken as a metric to measure the distance between sender and destination. Figure 4 displays the rates of successful RREQs. For each distance x, the value of y depicts the ratio between the number of successful RREQs to destinations with this distance and the totally sent RREQs. The ratio between the routes requested and the routes established decreases with increasing distance and decreasing wake ratio. It seems apparent, that the

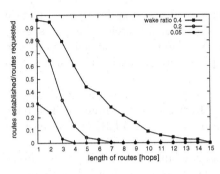

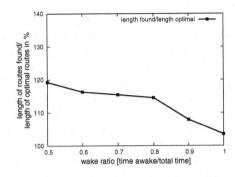

Fig. 4. Success ratio as function of the distance

Fig. 5. Path optimality as function of the wake ratio

influence of even small reductions of the wake ratio is vast using the immediate forwarding strategy.

Figure 5 illustrates the ratio between the length of successfully established routes and the actual distance measured as optimal path length from sender to destination node. The lower the wake ratio, the longer are the paths that are actually found, relative to the optimal distance. When operating with lower wake ratios, the paths to the destinations may still be found, but with significantly more hops than in the optimal case. The average path length for a wake ratio of 100% averages out to 9.75 hops, whereas the average optimal path length averages out to 9.05 hops. It is obvious that even with wake ratios of 100% there is still a difference between the optimal path length and the path length that was actually found. Because we are dealing with nonreliable broadcasts, the routing protocol can not guarantee optimality of the routes.

Forwarding at the Instant of Best Intersection
With the wake-up announcements contained in the HELLO messages, the nodes know when to reach their immediate neighbors. Given a fixed wake ratio W and a fixed basic cycle duration T, a node intending to broadcast a message can figure out the best instant to forward the message using previously received wake-up announcements. The best instant shall be found as follows:

Let A be the current node, S the source node, D the destination node, N_1, $N_2,\ldots,N_i$ the neighbors of A.

i) if A is S or an intermediate node and $D \notin \bigcup N_i \setminus N_j$, then the best instant is any instant when the largest subset of $\bigcup N_i \setminus N_j$ is awake, where N_j is the node from which A received the broadcast. In case A = S, N_j equals $\emptyset$.

ii) if A is S or any intermediate node and $D \in \bigcup N_i \setminus N_j$ then the best instant shall be any moment when D is awake.

Figure 7 depicts the concept to search the best instant to forward a RREQ. If there are more than one possible instants, one intersecting moment shall be

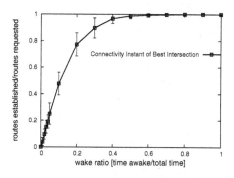

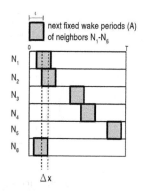

Fig. 6. Connectivity forwarding in the Instant of Best Intersection

Fig. 7. Announced fixed wake state periods in an intersection table

chosen at random. This shall prevent each retry attempt to fail because of identical choices of forwarding instants. In Figure 7, the node selects any instant in-between Δx, provided that neither N_1 nor N_2 nor N_6 happens to be the sender of the incoming RREQ. In such a case, the intersection between N_3 and N_4 would also be appropriate.

The node aiming to transmit shall schedule the RREQ for the designated moment, regardless of its own wake pattern. If the node is in a sleep state, it shall wake up at the designated instant, transmit the message, and then continue with the former wake pattern. The additional wake time is added up and accounted for within the evaluation.

Figure 6 depicts that the connectivity is vastly improved when choosing the moment to forward according to the algorithm specified above. Even with a wake ratio of 20%, approximately 75% of the routes could still be established.

Further investigations and evaluations of the message flow led to the conclusion that it was not the wake ratio, which caused some routes not to be established, but the topology and the design of the algorithm used to determine the best moment to forward a broadcast. Especially if there were bottlenecks in the network topology, certain indispensable nodes were never selected to receive a RREQ by its neighbors, which caused the mechanism to fail in every retry attempt.

Figure 8 confirms that the route establishment success ratio decreases with increasing distance. The improvement indeed lies in the utilization of the wake-up information announced in the previous messages.

Forwarding with Enhanced Broadcast

The insights gained during the evaluation of the approaches above implied the following mechanism to be tested out: If a node aiming to forward a route request would be permitted to forward the RREQ more than once, it could nearly reach full connectivity even for low wake ratios. The following algorithm was used to find the appropriate instants to forward route requests:

Let A be the current node aiming to forward a broadcast packet, S be the source node, D be the destination node, $N_1, N_2,\ldots,N_i$ are the neighbors of A,

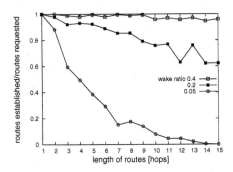

Fig. 8. Success ratio as function of the distance

and N_j the node from which A received the packet. Let R be the set of unreached neighbors and T the set of best instants. To figure out the min imal set of instants for A to rebroadcast the packet, proceed as follows:

$$R = \bigcup N_i \setminus N_j$$
$WHILE\ (R \neq \emptyset)\ do$
   find the best instant t_k to reach the largest subset $M \subseteq R$
   $T = T \cup \{t_k\}$
   $R = R \setminus M$
od

T then contains the minimal set of instants t_k for broadcasts to be sent to reach all neighbors. Yet it is still possible that some neighbors remain unnotified. Collisions can still occur and hinder RREQ broadcasts to be spread across the network. Furthermore, waking up at the minimal set of instants does not guarantee the intended broadcast to be successful, because the medium access is delayed due to the contention back-off mechanism of the MAC layer. If the node waking up has to wait for other stations to finish their transmissions until accessing the medium, the targeted nodes can already have turned to the sleep state again.

Figure 9 illustrates the effectiveness of this approach. The results however lead to the conclusion, that the more a route request is forwarded, the higher is the probability of reaching the destination. This approach leads to more message exchanges than the prior approaches. Nodes intending to send route requests must wake up several times and abandon their usual wake-up pattern. The additional wake-ups and message transmissions cause higher power consumption and wake time. The lower the wake ratio, the more additional wake-ups became necessary. We measured the additional overhead caused by the extra wake-ups. As the simulation scenario setup first lets the nodes discover their neighbors for 120 seconds and then only proceeds with a very low network load, the total of the additional overhead caused by the extra wake-ups did not carry much weight. We measured that a wake ratio fixed to 4% by setting the duration of the wake periods A and B turned out to be a net wake ratio of 4.087%. However, we discovered that the additional overhead clearly became bigger with decreasing

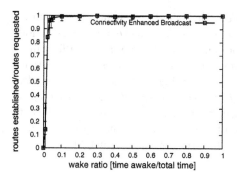

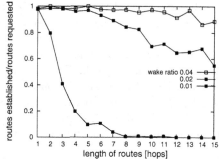

Fig. 9. Connectivity with Enhanced Broadcast

Fig. 10. Success ratios with Enhanced Broadcast

wake ratio. Probably, with higher network load, the additional wake time would increase as well.

One may object that transmission mode is the most expensive operation mode for wireless devices, and that the additional transmissions are costly. This concern is legitimate. Recent investigations [6, 5] on the of power consumption of wireless network devices showed that the power consumption of the transmit mode is indeed highest (182% of idle mode consumption) and that receiving is also expensive (121% of idle mode consumption). However, the sleep mode inherently has the lowest power consumption (6% of idle mode consumption). By maximizing the sleep time, the overall benefit of the approach studied in this section should still be positive.

Figure 10 displays the success ratios of the forwarding with *Enhanced Broadcast* approach in dependence of the distance, analogous to Figure 4 and 8. It shall be noticed that the connectivity properties reached with a wake ratio of only 10% are comparable to those of a wake ratio with 40% when using the prior forwarding approach. It shall be noticed, that the curve with the best connectivity function in Figure 10 was reached with a wake ratio of 10%, whereas in the approach using one single broadcast in the instant of best intersection a wake ratio of 40% were necessary to reach comparable connectivity. The fact that there is only one percent difference in wake time between the worst curve (1%) and the second worst curve (2%) of Figure 11 is astonishing. Furthermore, the network reaches a far better connectivity with 2% rather than 1%, whereas it does not perform that much better when doubling the wake time from 2% to 4%. It seems that the wake ratio can be decreased without major impact down to a certain limit, but further reduction leads to a sudden breakdown of the connectivity properties. This effect is commonly known as percolation and occurs in different aspects of ad hoc networks with random topology [14]. The critical values for the wake ratio using the simulation setup as described in 3.1 and the forwarding strategy of the *Enhanced Broadcast* are between 1% and 2%.

The comparison of the three approaches studied in this section suggest that the connectivity can be improved significantly by additional wake-ups and multiple rebroadcasts.

The approach of the *Enhanced Broadcast* has the fundamental disadvantage that it is not suitable for higher node densities. The more neighbors a node has, the more additional wake-ups will be scheduled and the more traffic will be generated, even if there is already a sufficient number of nodes awake to reach any node in the network. This may lead to much higher wake time and useless network load. In our simulation of the *Enhanced Broadcast*, the average count of RREQ forwarding operations increased from 2.24 for a wake ratio of 50% to 3.32 for 20% and to 4.38 for 5%. For even lower wake ratios, it approximated to 6 forwarding operations, which is is near the average count of neighbors.

Limited Enhanced Broadcast

It may not be suitable for high node densities that a node has to rebroadcast an incoming RREQ for almost every neighbor, but still it may be better to forward it more than once. We therefore define an upper limit for the number of forwards and thus limit the transmission overhead. Using the same scenario as before, we set the upper limit to 2 rebroadcasts. The results of the connectivity analysis are depicted in Figure 11. They provide evidence that a significant improvement of the approach using the *Instant of Best Intersection* is possible with a slight increase of the number of rebroadcasts.

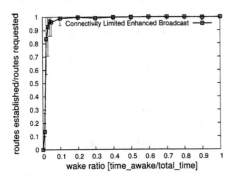

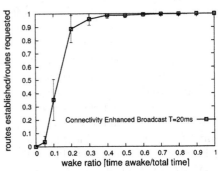

Fig. 11. Connectivity with Limited Enhanced Broadcast

Fig. 12. Connectivity with Enhanced Broadcast and T=20ms

3.4 Evaluation of Short Wake Periods

Basic Cycle Duration T	20ms

The results of the scenarios above may be interesting from the theoretical perspective, but in practice, an average delay of 100ms per hop is not suitable for many kinds of application services. Real time services (i.e. Voice-Over-IP) often require maximum end-to-end delays of 200ms. This motivated to analyze the *Enhanced Broadcast* approach of section 3.3 with a much shorter basic cycle duration of T=20ms. One may object that this is too short for todays wireless nodes, as there is a delay for the transition between the wake and sleep state, in particular the wake-up time of the radio hardware. In fact, todays newest ultra-low power wireless sensors such as developed in the WiseNET project [15] have a wake-up delay of only $800\mu s$. Using 2 wake periods and eventually some additional wake-ups in case of RREQ traffic should therefore still be possible in a total cycle duration of 20ms.

The ad-hoc mode of IEEE 802.11, which is synchronized using beacons from designated stations and ATIM (Ad Hoc Traffic Indication Map) messages to announce traffic, typically uses a beacon interval length of 100ms. The lower this interval duration, the less effective is the power saving mechanism, and collisions occur more likely. Less battery power can be saved then.

The scenario with T=20ms did not deliver reasonable results for wake ratios lower than 5%. Below this threshold, no traffic was possible anymore, because the wake periods A and B became too short. If the wake ratio is 4%, the wake period duration calculates as $(20ms * 4\%)/2 = 400\mu s$. If we assume a IEEE 802.11 slot time of $20\mu s$, the length of the initial wait period sums up to max. $190\mu s$. Hence, with very low wake ratios the duration wake periods beclome close to the time intervals that are necessary for the medium access layer to work properly.

4   Conclusions

In this paper we simulated and evaluated the power saving mechanism for a wireless ad hoc multi-hop scenario proposed in [1], integrated with AODV, and refined its forwarding strategies to make optimal use of the wake-up announcements. The results clearly state that unsynchronized power saving mechanisms can achieve sound connectivity properties even with low wake ratios, provided that a node can arbitrarily change its wake state without further loss of resources.

Potential for optimization lies in the number and the instant of the RREQ rebroadcasts of intermediate nodes participating in a route establishment. Future work should focus on the reliability of the forwarding operations, and mechanisms to limit the overhead and additional wake time of the wake-ups that are necessary to reach neighboring nodes in their announced wake state.

Decreasing the cycle duration furthermore leads to lower end-to-end delays at the cost of better connectivity and reliability at lower wake ratios, and is limited to boundary values that are be given by the medium access layer mechanisms and the properties of the radio hardware.

References

1. Torsten Braun, Laura Marie Feeney: *Power Saving in Wireless Ad hoc Networks without Synchronization*, 5th Scandinavian Workshop on Wireless Ad-hoc Networks, Stockholm, 2005
2. ANSI/IEEE Std 802.11 (ISO/IEC 8802-11), 1999 Edition (R2003)
3. Y.C Tseng, C.S. Hsu and T.Y. Hsieh: *Power Saving Protocols for IEEE 802.11-based Multihop Ad hoc Networks*, Proceedings of IEEE INFOCOM, New York, June 2003

4. Laura Marie Feeney: *A QoS aware Power Save Protocol For Wireless Ad Hoc Networks*, In Proceedings of the First Mediterranean Workshop on Ad Hoc Networks(Med-Hoc Net 2002), Sardenga, Italy, September 2002.

5. Laura Marie Feeney and Martin Nilsson: *Investigating the Energy Consumption of a Wireless Network Interface in an Ad Hoc Networking Environment*, IEEE INFOCOM, 2001

6. Jean-Pierre Ebert, Brian Burns, and Adam Wolisz: *A trace-based approach for determining the energy consumption of a WLAN network interface*, Proceedings of European Wireless, Florence, Italy, February 2002

7. Charles E. Perkins, Elizabeth M. Belding-Royer: *Ad hoc On-Demand Distance Vector (AODV) Routing*, IETF Internet draft RFC 3561, October 2003

8. OMNeT++ Network Simulation Framework (http://www.omnetpp.org)

9. Andràs Varga: *The OMNeT++ Discrete Event Simulation System*, Proceedings of the European Simulation Multiconference (ESM'2001) Prague, Czech Republic, June 2001

10. Mobility Framework for OMNeT++ (http://mobility-fw.sourceforge.net)

11. E. Osipov and Ch. Tschudin: *Improving the Path Optimality of Reactive Ad Hoc Routing Protocols Through De-Coherent RREQ waves*, Technical Report CS-2004-002, University of Basel, Switzerland

12. Jörg Rech, *Wireless LANs*, Heise Verlag, 2004

13. Jochen Schiller, *Mobile Communications*, Addison Wesley, 2003

14. O. Dousse, P. Thiran, and M. Hasler: *Connectivity in Ad-hoc and Hybrid Networks*, in Proceedings of the 21st Annual Joint Conference of the IEEE Computer and Communications Societies (INFOCOM'02), New York, June 2002.

15. C. C. Enz, A. El-Hoiydi, J.-D. Decotignie, T. Melly, and V. Peiris: *WiseNET: An Ultralow-Power Wireless Sensor Network Solution*, IEEE Computer Magazine, Volume 37, Issue 8, August 2004

Traffic Load and Lifetime Deviation Based Power-Aware Routing Protocol for Wireless Ad Hoc Networks

Dong-hyun Kim, Rhan Ha, and Hojung Cha

Dept. of Computer Engineering,
Hongik University, Seoul 121-791, Korea
{dhkim, rhanha}@cs.hongik.ac.kr
Dept. of Computer Science,
Yonsei University, Seoul 120-749, Korea
hjcha@cs.yonsei.ac.kr

Abstract. This paper proposes a new power-aware routing protocol, TDPR(Traffic load and lifetime Deviation based Power-aware Routing protocol), that does not only consider the residual battery capacity and transmission power, but also the traffic load of nodes and deviation among node lifetimes. It helps to extend the entire network's lifetime and to achieve load balancing. Simulation using ns-2 shows better the performance of the proposed routing protocol in terms of load balancing of the entire network, the consumed energy capacity of nodes, and paths reliability. TDPR has dead nodes 72% less than AODV, and 58% less than PSR. TDPR consumes residual energy capacity 29% less than AODV, 15% less than PSR. Error messages are sent maximum 38% less than PSR, and maximum 41% less than AODV.

1 Introduction

The ad hoc network is the set of mobile nodes that self-organize the network all alone. In ad hoc networks, nodes do not have any AP(access point) and infrastructure facility to communicate each other. Since the transmission range of each node is limited, in case that the distance between two nodes is larger than their transmission range, they have to use multi-hop routing protocols for data transmission and intermediate nodes may act as a router. As nodes in ad hoc networks have limited energy capacity, nodes whose residual energy are exhausted leave the network. Hence, it is necessary to improve the lifetime of wireless devices for reliable routing and high quality of service(QoS). The lifetime of node due to a limited energy capacity is an urgent factor for developing a routing protocol.

There are many routing protocols proposed in MANET[1, 2, 3]. When MANET was proposed, most routing protocols focused on low data transmission delay or control packet overhead. In the last few years, the research on the development of a routing protocol that provides a long-lived communication connection and the

T. Braun et al. (Eds.): WWIC 2006, LNCS 3970, pp. 325–336, 2006.
© Springer-Verlag Berlin Heidelberg 2006

high quality of service(QoS) have been a great interest for ad hoc networks. These routing protocols present methods to utilize limited energy capacity efficiently, so they are referred as power-aware routing protocol or energy-aware routing protocol. However, in existing routing protocols, only node battery residual energy capacity and transmission power are reflected on the route discovery process. In a power-aware routing protocol, it is essential that each node traffic load should be considered to estimate the lifetime of a path correctly. In addition, the deviation of node lifetimes should also be considered to compare candidate paths' reliability exactly.

The proposed power-aware routing protocol, TDPR(Traffic load and lifetime Deviation based Power-aware Routing protocol), considers all intermediate node lifetimes and the deviation among node lifetimes on active routes in the route discovery process simultaneously. The rest of the paper is organized as follows. In Section 2, existing power-aware routing protocols are described. Section 3 presents the proposed node lifetime prediction function and the behavior of TDPR. In section 4, simulation results show the enhanced performance of TDPR. Section 5 summarizes the paper and future work.

2   Related Work

AODV[4] and DSR[5] are on-demand routing protocols. An on-demand routing protocol issues a route discovery process when a source has data packets and does not have any path to the destination. AODV and DSR take the shortest hop path. However, in the shortest hop routing, some nodes may maintain too many paths relatively, it causes them to leave the network early.

In the last few years, the research on the development of a routing protocol that provides a long-lived communication connection and high quality of service(QoS) have been a great interest for ad hoc networks. The power-aware routing protocol proposed in [6] chooses the path whose the total transmission power is minimum. Although this method minimizes the energy consumption of nodes, it can not achieve load balancing of the entire network and the entire network can be partitioned. S. Singh et al.[7] proposes routing metrics for developing a new power-aware routing protocol and they focused on the trade-off between path energy consumption and load balancing of the entire network. Also, a new power-aware routing protocol based on the minimum residual battery capacity of intermediate nodes was proposed. In [8], a more flexible power-aware routing protocol is proposed and this routing protocol performs minimum transmission power routing(MTPR) when one or more candidate paths' all intermediate nodes have more residual battery capacity than the predefined threshold value. When the residual battery capacity of any intermediate node of candidate paths are lower than the predefined threshold value, the proposed routing protocol selects the best path based on minimum residual battery capacity. Similar to [8], a power-aware source routing(PSR) protocol considers both the residual battery capacity of intermediate nodes and the transmission power of nodes[9]. PSR computes the routing cost of each intermediate node by its cost function. Then, a destination node chooses the best path whose sum of cost is least. Other many routing protocols also compute node routing costs using its own cost function. The routing function proposed in [10] divides a node's residual energy capacity by its transmission power to get its lifetime. In [11], the transmission power of a node and residual energy capacity have different weighting values in the routing function and these weighting values can be changed according to the objectives. The energy consumption of a node is related to the distance between neighbor nodes. To reduce the distance between two neighboring nodes, the routing protocol proposed in [12] adjusts each node's broadcasting time based on the distance.

In existing routing protocols, only the residual battery capacity and transmission power of each node are reflected in the route discovery process. In a power-aware routing protocol, it is essential that the traffic load of each node should be considered to estimate the correct cost of a path. The deviation among node lifetimes should also be considered to compare candidate paths reliability exactly. In this paper, the lifetimes of all intermediate nodes and the deviation among lifetimes of nodes on active routes are considered in the route discovery process simultaneously. In the next section, the proposed lifetime prediction function and the behavior of TDPR are described in detail.

3 Traffic Load and Lifetime Deviation Based Power-Aware Routing Protocol (TDPR)

All nodes in ad hoc networks have limited transmission ranges. So, the path between a source and a destination consists of one or more intermediate nodes, and the cost of the path is dependent on the lifetimes of these intermediate nodes. TDPR includes the node lifetime prediction function, the route discovery process, and the route maintenance process. In this section, the node lifetime prediction function for the route discovery process is introduced, and then the route discovery process and the route maintenance process are described in detail.

3.1 Node Lifetime Prediction Function

The proposed node lifetime prediction function considers not only residual battery capacity and transmission power, but also traffic load. The calculated lifetimes of nodes are appended in a route request message, and these are used for estimating a path lifetime. TDPR defines the traffic load of a node as the total amount of the expected energy consumption by active paths of the node. In this paper, TDPR gets the transmission power of each route from the routing table. Traffic load is computed from the transmission power of each route and the residual battery capacity. TDPR calculates the expected lifetimes of nodes with the information from routing table at time t. The node lifetime prediction function is as follows.

$$l_i(t) = \frac{E_i(t)}{T_i(t)} \tag{1}$$

$$T_i(t) = \begin{cases} 1 & \text{if no transmission} \\ \sum_{k=1}^{N_i(t)} (r_{i,k}(t) \times \rho_{i,k}(t)) & \text{otherwise} \end{cases} \qquad (2)$$

$l_i(t)$: The expected lifetime of node i at time t (sec)
$E_i(t)$: The residual battery capacity of node i at time t (Joule)
$T_i(t)$: The traffic load of node i at time t (Joule/sec)
$N_i(t)$: The number of routing entries that passes through node i at time t
$r_{i,k}(t)$: The amount of data sent by node i per unit time
via the path k at time t (bit/sec)
$\rho_{i,k}(t)$: The transmission power of node i, when node
i send a packet via the path k at time t (Joule/bit)

The proposed node lifetime prediction function is based on the residual battery capacity of the node and traffic load of the node. In Equation (1), the current residual battery capacity of a node is divided by its own total traffic load to calculate its lifetime. The calculation of a node using Equations (1) and (2) is performed at all intermediate nodes except the source node and the destination node. A RREQ packet header keeps lifetimes of each intermediate node and the minimum lifetime value of them too. $T_i(t)$ is traffic load of the node i at time t. $r_{i,k}(t)$ is the amount of data sent by node i per unit time via the path k at time t before new path is established. In other words, it means each routing entry's data transfer rate. If the data transfer rates of all route entries in the network is same, $r_{i,k}(t)$ will be a constant. If there is no transmission in the node i at time t, $T_i(t)$ will be 1. As in Equation (1), when $T_i(t)$ is 1, it does not affect anything in Equation (1).

3.2   Route Discovery Process with Traffic Load

TDPR is a reactive routing protocol for ad hoc networks such as AODV[4] and DSR[5]. In reactive routing protocols, a source node does not have paths for all destination nodes. When the source node want to send data to any destination node, it searches the routing entry in its routing table for the destination node. If there is no path to the destination node, the route discovery process is issued with broadcasting route request message to its neighbors. Until the destination node receives the route request message, intermediate nodes re-broadcast this message to their neighbors. The destination node sends the route reply message in response to the route request message and the route reply message is sent through the reverted path of the route request message in a unicast way. After intermediate nodes received the route reply message, they add a new routing entry in its own routing table for the destination node and then send the route reply message to the upstream node. When the source node gets the route reply message, route discovery process is finished, and data packets are sent according to routing table. Because the ad hoc network assume that all nodes can move freely, the topology of the entire network can be changed dynamically. Proactive routing protocols that broadcast the change of the network's topology whenever some node moves cause very high overhead. Hence proactive routing protocols are not suitable for ad hoc networks. This section illustrates how TDPR can

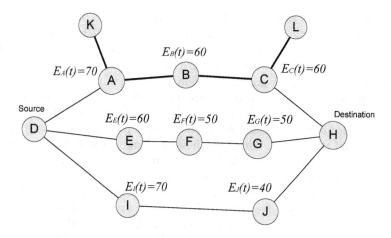

Fig. 1. The example of TDPR's route discovery process

establish a new path using the node lifetime prediction function in the previous section in detail.

The RREQ packet header includes the IP address of source node and destination node, the sequence numbers of two nodes, RREQ ID, hop count, lifetimes of intermediate nodes and the minimum lifetime. Intermediate nodes which receive the RREQ packet establish a reverted path to upstream node. Then the intermediate node calculates its own lifetime and appends it to the RREQ header. The RREQ is broadcasted again and broadcasting RREQ is performed until the RREQ arrives at the destination node. The destination node selects its next behavior according to whether it already received the same RREQ. When the destination node receives the first RREQ, it starts a RREP timer and stores the path lifetime temporarily. The path lifetime is the minimum lifetime value of intermediate nodes. In case that the destination node has already received same RREQs, TDPR compares two path lifetimes and the path is updated with the longer lifetime. When the RREP timer is expired, a RREP message is sent to the source node and it adds a new routing entry to the routing tables of intermediate nodes.

Fig. 1 shows the example of route discovery process between a source node and a destination node. The network consists of vertexes and edges. A vertex means a node and an edge means a link between two nodes. Links have two kind of lines in the graph. Thick line means that data packets are transmitted through this link now. Thin line shows that no connection is established and two nodes are just neighbors each other. In this example, data packets are transmitted from the node K to the node L and the nodes A, B and C are intermediate nodes. To explain this example easily, we assume the transmission power(ρ) of every node has same value and also the data transfer rate(r) of every node is same too. $E_i(t)$ means the residual battery capacity of node i at time t. In Fig. 1, Three paths are available between the source node D and the destination node H. The destination node H compares the minimum lifetimes of each path and chooses the best path whose minimum lifetime is maximum. Three RREQ packets from the source node have the expected lifetimes of all intermediate nodes. In Fig. 1, the lifetimes of node A, B, C, E, F, G, I and J are $70/(r \times \rho)$, $60/(r \times \rho)$, $60/(r \times \rho)$, 60, 50, 50, 70 and 40 respectively. The residual battery capacity of a node on the active path is divided by its own total traffic load to calculate its lifetime. When there is no transmission in the node at time t, $T_i(t)$ is 1 as described in previous section. If the destination node selects the best node based on the residual battery capacity of intermediate nodes, the path D-A-B-C-H will be selected. However, the nodes A, B, and C already maintain a path between the node K and the node L. Although they have large residual battery capacity, they will consume their own residual battery capacity too fast and will leave the network. It makes bad in terms of load balancing. It also causes the failure of existing path K-A-B-C-L. The minimum lifetime value of the path D-A-B-C-H, the path D-E-F-G-H, and the path D-I-J-H is $60/(r \times \rho)$, 50, and 40, respectively. If $r \times \rho$ is bigger than 6/5, $60/(r \times \rho)$ is smaller than 50 and the path D-E-F-G have to be selected instead of the path D-A-B-C-H. As seen this example, the traffic load of intermediate nodes have to be considered with the residual battery capacity in the route discovery process.

3.3   Route Discovery Process with Traffic Load and the Deviation Among Node Lifetimes

In previous section, the selection of a path is only based on lifetimes of intermediate nodes. In case that two paths have same minimum lifetime value, this paper proposes the route discovery algorithm based on the traffic load of nodes and the deviation among lifetimes. The behavior of this algorithm is the same as the section 3.2 until a RREQ packet is arrived at the destination node. However, when two or more RREQ packets are arrived at the destination node, the destination node does not choose the best path only based on paths' lifetimes. The destination node does not only store the minimum lifetime value, but also the average lifetime value of intermediate nodes and the deviation among lifetimes of them. The comparison between two paths consists of three phases. First, the path which has longer path lifetime takes precedence over the other one. If two path lifetimes are equal, and then TDPR compares the average lifetime value

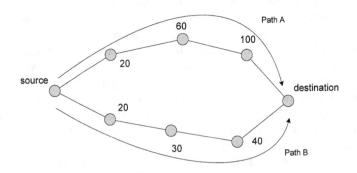

Fig. 2. Comparing two path at the destination node

of intermediate nodes of each path. Finally, if the average lifetime value of the intermediate nodes of each path are even same, the deviation among the lifetimes of the intermediate nodes of each path is considered. Fig. 2 shows that why these phases are needed. In Fig. 2, both two path lifetimes are 20. The deviation among lifetimes of the intermediate nodes of path B is less than that of path A. Intuitively, the path A, however, have to be selected for load balancing of the entire network. Namely, the comparison based on only the deviation among lifetimes of nodes leads to establishing an inappropriate path. Therefore, TDPR compares the average lifetime value of nodes first, and in case that the average lifetime value of nodes are same, the deviation among lifetimes of the intermediate nodes of two paths is considered as the third metric.

3.4   Route Maintenance Algorithm

As previously mentioned, nodes in ad hoc networks have limited energy capacity and random mobility. The movement of nodes makes the topology of the entire network change dynamically, which may break down the established paths. In the case that any node on the active path moves out of the transmission range of neighbors or exhausts its own residual battery capacity, an alternative path has to be established. In following two cases, nodes cannot route packets

1. When the distance between a node and its neighbor on active paths is larger than their transmission range
2. When a node's residual battery capacity is too low or its traffic load is too high

Each node on active paths sends HELLO message periodically to its one-hop neighbors. When it does not receive a reply message from its downstream node within the predefined interval, it sends a RERR message to the source node. Even though existing algorithms have proposed the local path repair mechanism, TDPR replaces the whole path for load balancing in terms of energy consumption.

4   Performance Evaluation

4.1   Experiment Environments and Metrics

We use the ns-2[14] simulator version 2.27 to confirm the improved performance of TDPR. Our experiment consists of four measurements and following metrics are used for the performance evaluation.

1. The variance of the number of dead nodes versus time
2. The variance of the average residual battery capacity of nodes versus time
3. The variance of the minimum residual battery capacity of nodes versus time
4. The number of error messages sent by nodes on active paths

We can get information about how well each routing protocol achieves load balancing of the network by the measurement of the number of dead nodes versus time. TDPR excludes nodes which have too much traffic load or too low residual battery capacity in the route discovery process. Such behavior is closely related to the network's lifetime. The network lifetime means the time taken to die as many as the predefined number of nodes. The second metric shows the amount of the energy consumption of nodes versus time. As each node consumes its own energy capacity mostly when it sends packets, and the number of packets sent by nodes is very related to its energy consumption. The final measurement on our experiment is the number of error messages sent by nodes on active paths. The number of error messages of each routing protocol shows its performance in terms of paths reliability and energy consumption. In other words, the more error message are sent, the more re-establishment of path are occurred and more residual battery capacity is consumed. We compare TDPR with AODV, well-known on-demand routing protocol for ad hoc networks, and PSR which considers the residual battery capacity and transmission power of intermediate nodes. We divide TDPR into TDPR-1 and TDPR-2 on our experiment. In route discovery process, TDPR-1 chooses the best path based on only path lifetimes. TDPR-2 compares path lifetimes, and then it considers the average lifetime value and the deviations among path lifetimes together when two paths have same lifetimes.

In our simulations, 20, 30, and 50 nodes move in 500m × 500m physical space for 6000 seconds and they have 10, 15, 25 connections for data communication, respectively. We assume that each node has the same data transfer rate and the transmission range of each node is 40 meters. The mobility of nodes is defined by random waypoint algorithm[5]. Random waypoint algorithm forces nodes to move around with predefined two parameters, maximum velocity and pause time. Each node moves to a random destination at random velocity. After nodes stay on the its own destination for predefined time and they move to the new destination. Our experiments are also performed under the different velocities. The maximum movement velocity of nodes is classified as the case of a person's velocity($2m/s = 7.2km/h$) and the case of a vehicle's velocity($16.6m/s \approx 60km/h$). We perform all experiments five times and take the average results. Due to space limitation, only the case for 20 nodes are included here; other 30, 50 nodes cases' simulation results are similar and their results can be found in [15].

4.2 Simulation Results

4.2.1 The Number of Dead Nodes in AODV, PSR, TDPR-1 and TDPR-2

When a node transmits data packets, it consumes its own residual battery capacity, and when it exhausts its own all residual battery capacity, it cannot operate any longer. In the Fig 3. when the number of nodes is 20, the number of dead nodes is small in general. However, in AODV and PSR, the number of dead nodes is bigger than TDPR. We can see the same trend when the velocity of nodes is 16.6m/s. The reason why TDPR has the number of dead nodes less than the others is that

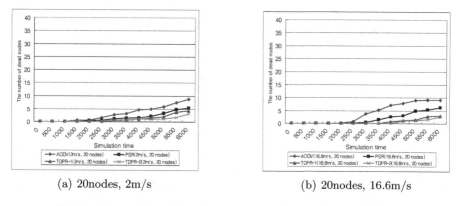

(a) 20nodes, 2m/s   (b) 20nodes, 16.6m/s

Fig. 3. The number of dead nodes when the number of nodes is 20

node lifetime prediction function calculates lifetimes of intermediate nodes based on their traffic load and the deviation among them. As TDPR-2 considers deviation among lifetimes of intermediate nodes, it outperforms TDPR-1. The establishment of many paths leads to a lot of packet transmission and a few nodes may have several paths simultaneously. TDPR disperses the traffic load of nodes and it has a good effect on load balancing of the network. TDPR has dead nodes 72% less than AODV, and 58% less than PSR.

4.2.2   Average Residual Energy Capacity of Nodes in AODV, PSR, TDPR-1 and TDPR-2

Fig. 4 shows the average energy capacity of nodes in AODV, PSR and TDPRs versus time. We can see AODV and PSR consume more energy capacity than TDPR. Because TDPR considers the traffic load of intermediate nodes in node lifetime prediction function and prevents the frequent failure of established paths. Most route discovery processes occur from 0 to 2500 seconds and a large amount of energy capacity is dissipated. In the latter half of simulations, several communications are finished and the amount of energy consumption rate is decreased. TDPR consumes energy capacity 29% less than AODV, 15% less than PSR.

4.2.3   The Minimum Energy Residual Capacity of Nodes in AODV, PSR, TDPR-1, and TDPR-2

This experiment shows the change of minimum residual energy capacity versus time. The minimum residual energy capacity shows how well each routing protocol achieves load balancing of the network. When this value is 0, the first node leaves the network. When the number of nodes is 20, as in Fig. 5 the first node in AODV leaves the network at 4000 seconds. However, in TDPR, the minimum residual energy capacity is not 0 when simulation time is 6000 seconds. Generally the minimum residual energy capacity is affected by the number of nodes rather than the velocity of nodes. Because the more the number of nodes is bigger, the more connections are established among nodes. TDPR evenly distributes entire traffic load, which makes the longest lifetime until the first node is dead.

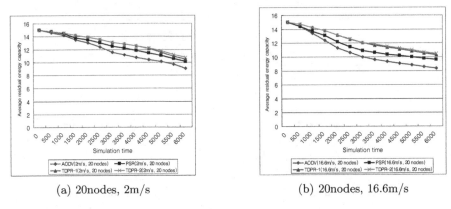

(a) 20nodes, 2m/s   (b) 20nodes, 16.6m/s

Fig. 4. The average energy capacity when the number of nodes is 20

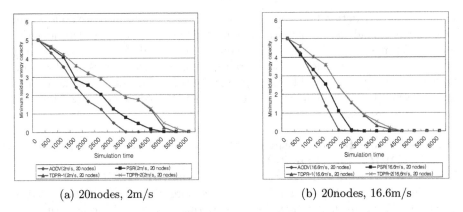

(a) 20nodes, 2m/s   (b) 20nodes, 16.6m/s

Fig. 5. The minimum energy capacity when the number of nodes is 20

4.2.4 The Number of Error Messages Sent by Nodes on Active Paths

In Fig. 6, we can observe the large number of error messages is sent when the number of nodes is large and the velocity is high. The more the number of nodes, the more paths break down. It cause the probability of path re-establishment high. When the velocity of nodes is high, intermediate nodes will be likely to move away from the transmission range of neighbor nodes and it also increases the probability of path re-establishment. TDPR constructs more reliable paths than the others in terms of energy consumption. In TDPR-2, error messages are sent maximum about 38% less than PSR, and maximum about 41% less than AODV.

4.3 Simulation Results Analysis

The experiment of the number of dead nodes shows how well each routing protocol achieves load balancing of the entire network. Since TDPR breaks up the network's traffic load, each node consumes similar amount of energy capacity. Frequent failure of established paths causes unnecessary energy consumption.

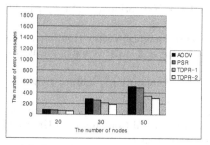
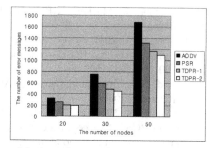
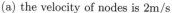

(a) the velocity of nodes is 2m/s   (b) the velocity of nodes is 16.6m/s

Fig. 6. The number of dead nodes in AODV, PSR, TDPR-1 and TDPR-2

TDPR chooses the best path between source and destination based on the traffic load and residual energy capacity of intermediate nodes. Consequently, it prevents the failure of established paths. Finally we can observe TDPR consumes the residual energy capacity of nodes less than other routing protocols. In comparison with other routing protocols in terms of the number of error messages, TDPR sends error messages less than the others, it also means TDPR prevents unnecessary and frequent path failure.

5 Conclusion

TDPR considers the traffic load of nodes and the deviation among lifetimes of intermediate nodes and it improves balancing the energy consumption of nodes and establishing reliable paths. The proposed node lifetime prediction function considers both the residual energy capacity and transmission power of intermediate nodes, which helps calculating exact node lifetimes. Route maintenance algorithm makes nodes re-establish a reliable path based on the computed lifetimes and mobility. The performance evaluation via comparison with existing routing protocols shows that TDPRs outperform existing routing protocols in terms of the entire network's load balancing, energy consumption and the number of error messages.

Acknowledgement

This work was supported in part by the National Research Laboratory (NRL) program of the Korea Science and Engineering Foundation (2005-01352), and the ITRC programs (HY-SDR Research Center, MMRC) of IITA, Korea.

References

1. Charles E. Perkins, "Ad Hoc Networking", Addison Wesley, 2000.
2. C.K. Toh, "Ad Hoc Mobile Wireless Networking", Prentice Hall, 2002

3. S. Corson, J. Macker, "RFC 2501:Mobile Ad hoc Networking(MANET)", IETF working group, Jan. 1999
4. C. Perkins and E. Royer, "Ad-Hoc On-Demand Distance Vector Routing", Proceedings of the 2nd IEEE workshop on mobile computing systems and applications, pp.90-100, Feb 1999
5. David B. Johnson and David A. Maltz, "Mobile Computing", Kluwer Academic Publishers, 1996
6. K. Scott, N. Bambos, "Routing and channel assignment for low power transmission in PCS", Proceedings of the 5th IEEE International Conference on Universal Personal Communications, pp.498-502, Vol.2, Oct. 1996
7. S. Singh, M. Woo and C.S. Raghavendra, "Power-aware routing in mobile ad hoc networks", Proceedings of the 4th annual ACM/IEEE international conference on mobile computing and networking, pp.181-190, Oct. 1998
8. C.K. Toh, "Maximum battery life routing to support ubiquitous mobile computing in wireless ad hoc networks", Proceedings of IEEE Communication Magazine, Vol.39, pp.138-147, Jun 2001
9. M. Maleki, K. Dantu, and M. Pedram, "Power-aware source routing protocol for mobile ad hoc networks", Proceedings of the IEEE international symposium on low power electronics and design, pp.72-75, Aug. 2002
10. M. Tarique, K.E. Tepe, M. Naserian, "Energy saving dynamic source routing for ad hoc wireless networks" Proceeings of the 3rd IEEE international symposium on Modeling and Optimization in Mobile, Ad Hoc, and Wireless Networks, pp.305-310, April 2005
11. K.-S. Kwak, K.-J. Kim, S.-J. Yoo, Power Efficient Reliable Routing Protocol for Mobile Ad-hoc Networks, Proceedings of The 47th IEEE Midwest Symposium on Circuits and Systems, Vol.2, pp.481-484, July 2004
12. S.-H. Lee, E. Choi, and D.-H. Cho, "Timer-based broadcasting for power-aware routing in power-controlled wireless ad hoc networks", Proceedings of IEEE Communications Letters, Vol.9, Issue 3, pp.222-224, Mar. 2005
13. M. Maleki, K. Dantu, and M. Pedram, "Lifetime prediction routing in mobile ad hoc networks", Proceedings of IEEE international conference on wireless communications and networking, Vol.2, pp.1185 - 1190, Mar. 2003
14. NS-2 simulator, http://www.isi.edu/nsnam/ns
15. D.H. Kim, Traffic load and lifetime deviation based power-aware routing protocol for wireless ad hoc networks, Master's Thesis 2005, Hongik University, 2005

An Energy-Efficient Location Error Handling Technique for Mobile Object Tracking in Wireless Sensor Networks

Sung-Min Lee[1], Hojung Cha[1], and Rhan Ha[2]

[1] Department of Computer Science, Yonsei University,
Seodaemum-gu, Shinchon-dong 134, Seoul 120-749, Korea
{sulee, hjcha}@cs.yonsei.ac.kr
[2] Department of Computer Engineering, Hongik University,
Mapo-gu, Sangsoo-Dong 72-1, Seoul 121-791, Korea
rhanha@cs.hongik.ac.kr

Abstract. The performance of an energy-efficient object tracking system depends on its accuracy in predicting the next destination of a mobile event. Unfortunately, a sophisticated prediction method cannot be operated in sensor nodes which have low computational power and storage. Moreover, precise prediction alone cannot be guaranteed to eliminate error in the future destination of the object in real circumstances. In this paper, we present a location error handling technique to prevent and handle this error efficiently. Real situations such as an unexpected change in the mobile event's direction, failure of event-detection and failure of transmitting an error message are considered when designing the error handling technique. This simple yet effective solution complements the weakness of the energy-efficient object tracking paradigm. From experiments on both real hardware and simulation, our method outperformed the existing work.

1 Introduction

A moving object tracking technique is one of the active research areas in wireless sensor networks due to characteristics of the technology, such as requiring low cost and offering satisfactory performance. Research on tracking techniques has been conducted within an extensive domain for the fundamental issues such as localization for concrete applications such as the military [1] and natural habitat monitoring systems [2]. Energy-efficient object tracking is an interesting research issue noticed in this domain because of the importance of power depletion problems in wireless sensor networks.

In the object tracking technique, a moving event appears on rare occasions; therefore, continuous activation of sensor nodes without the appearance of an event could waste energy. In order to resolve this problem, energy-efficient object tracking techniques have been developed. Each has a uniquely different method of predicting a moving event's future location, tracking mobile nodes and calculating the size of wake-up zone where the control message is disseminated. Even though they have some dissimilarities, they share the same basic operation which turns off the radio transmitter or lengthens system sleep time in the absence of an event. When an event occurs, on the other hand, all of the energy-efficient object tracking techniques should

T. Braun et al. (Eds.): WWIC 2006, LNCS 3970, pp. 337–348, 2006.
© Springer-Verlag Berlin Heidelberg 2006

provide a mechanism to predict the future location of the moving event for the preactivation of sleeping nodes. With precise and sophisticated prediction algorithms such as a prediction technique based on Pheromones, Bayesian and Extended Kalman Filter [3], prediction error can be minimized. However, the necessity of high-performance hardware to apply such a complicated algorithm violates some of the requirements of wireless sensor networks [4], such as low production cost and limited power and processing capabilities. In the real world, moreover, a number of unexpected directional changes of a mobile event can randomly occur at any time. In other words, prediction error cannot be completely avoided even if an accurate prediction method is applied. When an error occurs, the tracking process is no longer functional because the sensor nodes located near the moving event most likely turn off their sensors and radios to conserve energy. In this case the effort to both conserve energy and execute acceptable performance in object tracking systems terminates in utter failure. Thus the prediction error handling issue should be studied as much as prediction and other issues in energy-efficient tracking techniques.

Most existing work has neglected or considered as an insignificant problem the prediction error handling technique for the future location of a moving event. Therefore, we present a location error handling technique for energy-efficient tracking systems in wireless sensor networks. Two types of prediction error handling methods, error avoidance and error correction, are used under different circumstances. Error avoidance is a prevention technique, which detects possible error occurrence ahead of a moving event within the wake-up zone. To partially prevent prediction error, most energy-efficient tracking systems usually use a wake-up zone where the sensor nodes are awake and ready for a moving event. Thus, there is a chance that awakened nodes detect and report the moving event's different direction from the predicted direction. With this pre-detection and report of the possible prediction error, awakened nodes within the wake-up zone are able to recalculate the updated future location or disseminate wake-up control messages to sleeping nodes. Error correction is for the worst case scenario. There is no guarantee that deployed sensor nodes cover the entire sensor field. Moreover, failure of sensor nodes can occur at any time due to power depletion or a harsh natural environment, so an assumption of perfect coverage of the entire sensor field is unreasonable. This means that a moving event is able to slip away from the wake-up zone without pre-error detection. Thus, error correction is required in addition to error avoidance. An error is reported by a timer some time after the event slips away without pre-detection, and then some factors are used to recalculate the bigger wake-up zone. With these two error handling techniques, moving events can be tracked with high precision.

To evaluate our error handling technique, we use both implementation on real hardware and simulation. First, verification of our error handling algorithm is conducted with a simple test on real sensor nodes. Afterwards, it is simulated on the large-scale sensor field. From both evaluations we conclude that error avoidance and error correction methods reduce or revise location errors.

The remainder of this paper is organized as follows. Section 2 discusses previous research on energy-efficient tracking techniques and existing partial error handling techniques. Section 3 describes the background, assumptions and problem definition for the new error technique. Section 4 discusses the location error handling technique itself. The technique's performance is evaluated by both simulation and implementation in section 5. Finally, section 6 concludes this paper and depicts future research discussion.

2 Related Work

Energy-efficient object tracking systems are developed from Mobicast [5], which is a kind of multicast. This is not designed for tracking systems, but most energy-efficient tracking systems use the main concept of Mobicast. It activates sensor nodes only near an event, so its application with rare event occurrences in wireless sensor networks could conserve significant energy.

Research on topology maintenance and prolongation of network lifetime has been conducted based on the above energy-efficient concept. Peas [6] simply applies the energy-conserving technique to topology maintenance. IDSQ [7] selects a leader when a node detects an event, then the leader suppresses the other nodes to prevent multiple tracks of the same target.

The above techniques accomplish energy-efficient tracking. PECAS [8] is the advance version of Peas for tracking applications. It rotates the activated node to counteract load balancing problems, so it maintains network lifetime. DTM & OTC [9] are designed to reduce communication overhead and to increase accuracy of the prediction of mobile nodes' movement. DTM uses a moving tree to wake up sleeping nodes before a moving event arrives, but it uses a motion profile, which does not have sufficient accuracy for prediction of the mobile event's movement. Thus, OTC is proposed as a way to overcome DTM's prediction problem, but OTC also encounters problems with the large amount of communication overhead. This suggests that two separate protocols, which have complementary advantages, can be combined. PES [10] organizes the steps of the energy efficient tracking operation based on prediction-based strategies. It focuses "on time" when to wake up and sleep and also discusses a primitive error handling technique which disseminates wake-up control messages within a larger area than the previous one. Some research focuses on the prediction method. It presents a dual prediction technique [11] which more precisely predicts the future location of a mobile event. DPT [12] is one of the few literatures to consider the prediction error handling issue. It uses levels to distinguish the size of the wake-up zone. At the first level, it switches its radio range or sensor range to the maximum to manage error. If it fails, then the system operates at the second level method which simply wakes up sensor nodes within a fixed range r. If the above methods fail, then the size of the wake-up zone is increased as (2N-3)r where N denotes the number of levels. This algorithm is efficient only if there is no worst case due to possible redundancy of transmitting control messages at each level. ï

Most of the above literatures have adopted a primitive error handling technique with the assumption of no unexpected change of the moving event's direction, or have neglected the worst case scenario. There arises the importance of studying prediction error handling techniques in the energy-efficient object tracking paradigm.

3 Background and Problem Definition

In this section, the detailed concept of the energy-efficient object tracking technique is presented. In addition, some required assumptions and the problem definition for our error handling technique are discussed.

3.1 Energy-Efficient Object Tracking

This particular tracking technique's main metric is energy and its purpose is to conserve energy, as mentioned earlier. In order to achieve this goal, a tracking technique consisting of three stages was developed, which are initialization, surveillance and tracking; some literature uses only the last two stages.

The first stage is to organize clusters or a tree and exchange information with neighboring sensors. Most existing research assumes that fundamental operations such as time synchronization for ordering location data and localization of each node's geographic information are executed in this stage. This paper also assumes that those fundamental operations are done by some of the existing work. After the first stage, one of two stages is selected depending on the existence of an event. Without an event the system operates in the surveillance stage, in which nodes turn off their radios or sensors for a certain amount of time to save energy. When a node detects a moving event, the tracking stage is started, which is the most significant stage of three. Some literature classifies this stage as two: an unstable and a stable mode. The time when nodes are awakened by receiving control messages and predicting the next location is called the unstable mode. After the wake-up zone is created and preparation is done for the moving event, the system operates in stable mode. In the tracking stage, prediction and creation of the wake-up zone are the main issues. Unfortunately, applying a prediction technique is limited by hardware constraints. Thus, the wake-up zone has become a popular error handling solution for energy-efficient tracking techniques. The simple idea is that a wake-up message is propagated within a certain range centered on the predicted location; therefore, a slight change in the direction of the moving event does not cause an error. The size of wake-up zone is usually decided by given factors: the object's velocity, elapsed time, acceptable error rate, and so on. Of course, a certain amount of error can be reduced by incrementing the size of wake-up zone with a strict assumption that no sudden change of direction occurs. Our paper considers this possible and natural behavior of moving events. The problem of this wake-up zone and its analysis are discussed in the next sub-section. When the event moves out of the sensor field, the state of the system is switched from tracking to surveillance by a timer.

3.2 Problem Definition

As explained above, a limitation of using a primitive error handling technique, i.e., the wake-up zone, is unavoidable in the real environment. This section discusses a simple analysis of the possible location error. The analysis compares the ideal situation to the regular situation of using a primitive error handling technique.

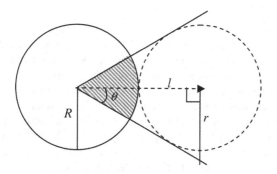

Fig. 1. Current and future wake-up zones

In Fig. 1, the solid and dotted circles represent the current wake-up zone and the future wake-up zone, respectively. Some of the literatures use overlapping wake-up zones in order to minimize prediction error, but they still cannot solve the prediction error. Thus, for the simple analysis, overlapping wake-up zones will be disregarded in this paper. If the moving event stays in the shaded fan shape until it crosses into the future wake-up zone, sensor nodes will detect the event. However, if the event moves out of the shaded area, its destination will probably differ from the prediction. This analysis can be expressed as below.

$$2\left(\pi R^2 \times \left(\frac{\arctan\left(\frac{r}{l}\right)}{360°}\right)\right) < \pi R^2 \text{ , where } \theta < 90° \tag{1}$$

Equation 1 compares the area of the circle that represents ideal accuracy to the fan shape that represents the accuracy of the primitive error handling technique. The area of the fan shape increases while the radius r of the future wake-up zone increases to reduce the error. However, the fan shape's maximum area cannot be equal to half of the circle's area. This means that the primitive error handling technique assures less than 50% accuracy. This analysis neglects energy usage, but incrementing the size of future wake-up zone would result in unacceptable energy waste. Without an improved error handling technique, therefore, the energy-efficient tracking technique cannot achieve its main objectives: accurate tracking and energy conservation.

4   Energy-Efficient Location Error Handling Technique

Presenting the location error handling technique consists of two parts: error avoidance and error correction. Error avoidance is designed to prevent the occurrence of errors. Error correction is for the worst case when the moving event somehow manages to slip away undetected.

4.1 Error Avoidance

The purpose of error avoidance is to detect location error in advance and correct or prevent the error. It is possible because the process for predicting a moving event should be finished with time to spare to transmit the control message to the predicted location and to broadcast wake-up messages within the future wake-up zone. In other words, a certain amount of time is required to transmit data through a number of nodes and to handle possible retransmission operations. In addition, the time should be long enough to broadcast a wake-up message within the future wake-up zone, so its nodes are prepared to sense the event. This spare time is a key factor for determining the size of the wake-up zone. For example, we can set the system as follows. Prediction should be finished before the moving event crosses the middle of the current wake-up zone. In this case, the system can monitor the event for some time, providing a chance to detect possible errors in advance.

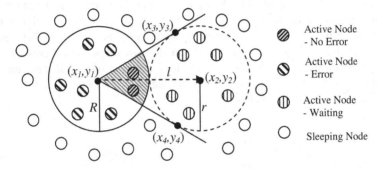

Fig. 2. Overview of the error handling technique

First, the error detection technique is required for avoidance. As shown in Fig. 2, sensor nodes can be classified into four types: active nodes with no error, active nodes with error, active nodes at the future location and sleeping nodes. The decision for sleeping nodes and active nodes at the future location is not an issue. The problem is how to distinguish active nodes with error from those without error. If the predicted location (x_2, y_2), the radius of the future wake-up zone r and the last prediction point or the location of the cluster header (x_1, y_1) are known, it is possible to find two tangent lines to the dotted circle, which is the future wake-up zone. Therefore, the nodes between the two tangent lines within the current wake-up zone, called the error-free zone (shaded area in Fig. 2), are error-free nodes. This process can be completed by comparing the gradients of the tangent lines and a line from a detecting node to the predicted point. Therefore, if those error-free nodes detect the event, the system does nothing. On the other hand, if nodes outside the error-free zone detect the event, it is an error, so the nodes must report or handle the situation. This whole process of designating a node's role is shown by the equations below.

$$(x_1 - x_2)(x' - x_2) + (y_1 - y_2)(y' - y_2) = r^2 \qquad (2)$$

The above equation is easily constructed from the equation of the dotted circle in Fig. 2. x', y' represent x_3, y_3 or x_4, y_4. This equation can be simplified as below.

$$(x_1 - x_2)m + (y_1 - y_2)n = r^2, \quad m^2 + n^2 = r^2 \tag{3}$$

Let m be $(x' - x_2)$ and n be $(y' - y_2)$ to obtain Equation 3. After substitution using the two equations shown above, we can solve for n or m to find the points of tangency to the future wake-up zone. Equation 4 generates n and then is substituted for m in Equation 3.

$$n = \frac{r^2(y_1 - y_2) \pm \sqrt{r^4(y_1 - y_2) - \{(y_1 - y_2)^2 + (x_1 - x_2)^2\} \times \{r^4 - r^2(x_1 - x_2)^2\}}}{(y_1 - y_2)^2 + (x_1 - x_2)^2} \tag{4}$$

Thus, m can be calculated, and then the two pairs of answers, which are the coordinates of the two points of tangency, are finally obtained. After obtaining (x_3, y_3) and (x_4, y_4), this coordination data is disseminated to nodes within the current wake-up zone. When the nodes receive it, they start to construct equations of the two tangent lines. Afterwards, four values are generated by substituting the node's own coordinates (x_m, y_m) and the predicted point (x_2, y_2) into two equations as shown in Equation 5. With these four values, each node is able to decide whether it belongs to the error-free zone or not. Only if the sign of $f(x_m, y_m)$ equals that of $f(x_2, y_2)$ and the sign of $g(x_m, y_m)$ equals that of $g(x_2, y_2)$, is the node in the error-free zone. After the decision is made, each node starts to monitor the mobile event's location.

$$f(x, y) = (y - y_1)(x_3 - x_1) - (y_3 - y_1)(x - x_1)$$
$$g(x, y) = (y - y_1)(x_4 - x_1) - (y_4 - y_1)(x - x_1) \tag{5}$$

Two circumstances are possible when a node detects a possible location error. First, the error is detected within a short time, so enough time remains to recalculate and update the moving event's future location. In this case, the error detected node can recalculate the prediction point and to disseminate wake-up control messages to nodes within the updated wake-up zone. The second circumstance is when the remaining time is too short to perform all the necessary operations; this usually occurs when a node located near the border of the wake-up zone detects the error. Therefore, avoidance requires two different error handling techniques. When enough time remains, the node simply performs the necessary operations to wake up the sleeping nodes with prediction. Nevertheless, if a node near the border detects the error, sleeping nodes most likely cannot be awakened before the moving event enters the new wake-up zone. Thus, the border node creates a new wake-up zone whose central point is its own location in order to buy time when an error is detected. After the initial process, the steps of the regular error avoidance technique are executed. A decision whether it is a border node or not can be made by checking its neighbor list. If more than 50% of neighbor nodes do not belong to the wake-up zone in the neighbor list, the node should be in border node.

4.2 Error Correction

If nodes are deployed proportionally and node failure is neglected, using error avoidance alone should be enough to handle location errors. However, random deployment with a limited power supply in harsh environments creates a need for the worst-case solution, called error correction. Nothing guarantees that the moving event will contact an activated node before it escapes from the wake-up zone. Sensor nodes may fail due to power depletion or natural disaster even if the hypothesis is made that nodes are proportionally deployed. Of course, this hypothesis is too strong an assumption for real-world applications. Even if the event contacts an activated node, reporting the message for error may not be successfully transmitted due to jamming. Therefore, error correction is required to cope with location error problems.

First, error detection is not possible in the worst case, so a timer is required to be aware of the error occurrence. When the node at the predicted location receives the control message, it starts the timer, which expires after a certain amount of time. The amount of time can be approximated by multiplying the speed of the moving object by its distance between the cluster head to the predicted position. If the event is not detected before the timer expires, an error message is transmitted to the departure node. The departure node is the last witness to the moving event, most likely the cluster head, so a larger wake-up zone has to be created from this node. The last operation of error correction is in creating the wake-up zone. It must be big enough to catch the moving event, but it will waste energy if it is too big. If the zone is too small, repeated re-broadcasting causes even more energy waste. Therefore, a simple yet intelligent technique for creating a reasonably sized wake-up zone is required. The usual solution for the worst case is to use the moving event's maximum speed. However, an object rarely runs at top speed all the time, nor can it accelerate to its maximum speed instantaneously. Considering acceleration when creating the wake-up zone should minimize its size while guaranteeing that the missing event is captured. The range of the optimized wake-up zone is adapted from our previous work [13], and calculated by the equation below.

$$r_{optimal} = \frac{((v_{max})^2 - (v_{latest})^2)}{2a} \tag{6}$$

The acceleration a can be calculated by knowing the latest speed v_{latest}, the maximum speed v_{max}, and the elapsed time t. The event's maximum speed is a given value, and the other speed can be obtained from historical data. When we know the elapsed time to accelerate from the latest speed to the maximum speed, we can generate a zone that has optimal radius $r_{optimal}$ and that is smaller than the zone based on the maximum speed for finding the missing event.

5 Evaluation

Evaluation was conducted by both implementation and simulation. In order to verify our algorithm, we used a small number of real sensor nodes, which were MoteIV's tmote SKY [14]. For extensive experiments with a large-scale sensor field, a TOSSIM

[15] simulator was used. To verify our algorithm, 13 sensor nodes were used. Each node was equipped with photo, temperature and humidity sensors, a CC2420 radio controller and an 802.15.4 MAC. The event was defined as light, so photosensors were used. The specific description of the topology is shown in Fig. 3.

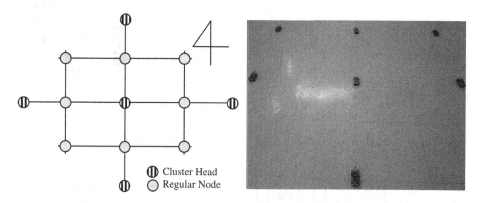

Fig. 3. Topology of the sensor field

The moving event, light, moves from the southern cluster head to the middle one, and, at this point, the middle head has already calculated and transmitted the error-free range data. The northern cluster head is the predicted destination. When the event is detected by a western, eastern or southern regular node, that node detects the error and sends control messages to the western, eastern and southern cluster heads, respectively. In this experiment, all three of the moving event's unexpected and different directional changes were detected by error nodes, which updated the new destination point. Therefore, the event could be traced under any circumstance.

After the simple verification of our algorithm, an extensive evaluation was conducted by simulation. The topology was 40m × 40m with 100 nodes and the grid structure. Other steps and the environment were similar to the above experiment. This simulation focused on the performance of our location error handling technique.

As shown in Fig. 4(a), the tracking system with error avoidance outperformed the tracking system without it. The error ratio is the number of sensor nodes that missed the event/the number of nodes that were supposed to detect the event. When the number of unexpected directional changes increased, the error ratio of the tracking system without our method increased exponentially. A larger predicted wake-up zone might reduce this error ratio, but it did not have a significant effect. The system with the error avoidance method maintained an error ratio close to zero. However, there was a sudden and slight increment in the error ratio even though error avoidance was applied. This phenomenon occurred because of unavoidable errors such as node failure and data transmission failure. In this experiment, lossybuilder provided by TOSSIM, which randomly creates data transmission failures, simulates the real wireless environment. The Fig. 4(b) shows the total time that data are absent. Because of prediction error, the nodes cannot wake up and sense the event, so a user will not receive any data during this time.

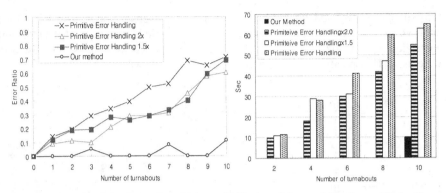

(a) Number of change of directions v. Error Ratio   (b) Number of change of directions v. Missing Time

Fig. 4. Comparison of error ratio while increasing the number of directional changes

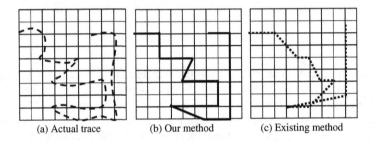

(a) Actual trace   (b) Our method   (c) Existing method

Fig. 5. Trace of a moving object with ten directional changes

A trace of a moving object with ten directional changes was evaluated as shown in Fig. 5. It describes that the tracking data generated with our error handling technique are more precise than with the regular technique. Unfortunately, the trace generated from our method was not identical to the real trace due to the occurrence of unavoidable errors as mentioned earlier. Nevertheless, our method minimized the failure.

The last evaluation was conducted on overhead, which is the number of control messages, of our error correction method compared to the existing method. The existing method only uses the maximum speed for creating the wake-up zone. In this simulation, the event's maximum speed was 4m/s, and the distance between the nodes was 4m. The event's recent speeds were set as 1m/s, 2m/s, 3m/s and 4m/s. Finally, the elapsed time was set as three seconds. The results of the experiment are shown in Fig. 6. The first graph compares the radius of the wake-up zones generated by our method and by the existing method while increasing the recent speed of the event. The second graph, which shows transmission overhead, is closely related to the first one. Our method intelligently finds the optimal size of the wake-up zone, so it reduces transmission overhead and conserves energy.

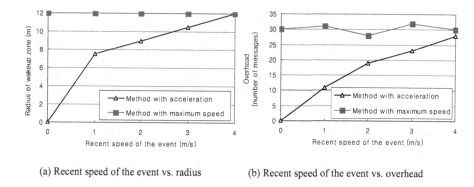

(a) Recent speed of the event vs. radius   (b) Recent speed of the event vs. overhead

Fig. 6. Comparison of the size of radius and transmission overhead

6 Conclusions

The proposed energy-efficient location error handling technique enhances the capability of energy efficient tracking systems in wireless sensor networks. The error avoidance method effectively prevents possible location errors using a simple algorithm. In addition, unavoidable errors can be handled by error correction with low transmission overhead. Without our technique, energy-efficient and precise object tracking cannot be achieved in the real-world environment where unexpected changes of direction and node failures can occur. Moreover, our algorithm is simple enough to run on a machine with low computational ability, limited resources and an unreachable power source.

Future work will consider the variant speeds of moving events, because speed can also cause location errors. Our work handles this problem by error correction in this paper. Nevertheless, it may be a way to detect errors in advance to optimize the energy-efficient object tracking systems.

Acknowledgements

This work was supported by the National Research Laboratory (NRL) program of the Korea Science and Engineering Foundation (2005-01352) and the ITRC programs (MMRC, HY-SDR) of IITA, Korea.

References

1. Nemeroff, J., Garcia, L., Hampel, D., DiPierro, S.: Application of Sensor Network Communications. Military Communications Conference. (2001).
2. Szewczyk, R., Osterweil, E., Polastre, J., Hamilton, M., Mainwaring, A., Estrin, D.: Habitat Monitoring with Sensor Networks. Communications of the ACM, vol. 47. (2004) 34-40.
3. Brooks, R., Griffin, C., Friedlander, D. S.: Self-Organized Distributed Sensor Network Entity Tracking. International Journal of High Performance Computer Applications, vol. 16. (2002) 207-220.

4. Akylidiz, I. F., Su, W., Sankarasubaramaniam, Y., Cayrici, E.: A Survey on Sensor Networks. IEEE Communication Magazine, vol. 40. (2002) 102-114.
5. Tan, C. L., Pink, S.: Mobicast: A Multicast Scheme for Wireless Networks. ACM Mobile Networks and Applications. (2000) 259-271.
6. Ye, F., Zhong, G., Lu, S., Zhang, L.: Peas: A Robust Energy Conserving Protocol for Long-lived Sensor Networks. The 23rd International Conference on Distributed Computing Systems. (2003) 169-177.
7. Chu, M., Haussecker, H., Zhao, F.: Scalable Information-Driven Sensor Querying and Routing for Ad Hoc Heterogeneous Sensor Networks. International Journal of High Performance Computing Applications, vol. 16. (2002) 90-110.
8. Gui, C., Mohapatra, P.: Power Conservation and Quality of Surveillance in Target Tracking Sensor Networks. 10th annual international conference on Mobile computing and networking. (2004) 129-143.
9. Bhattacharya, S., Xing, G., Lu, C., Roman, G., Chipara, O., Harris, B.: Dynamic Wake-up and Topology Maintenance Protocols with Spatiotemporal Guarantees. Information Processing in Sensor Networks. (2005) 28-34.
10. Xu, Y., Winter, J.: Prediction-Based Strategies for Energy Saving in Object Tracking Sensor Networks. IEEE International Conference on Mobile Data Management. (2004) 154-163.
11. Xu, Y., Winter, J.: Dual Prediction-Based Reporting for Object Tracking Sensor Networks. International Conference on Mobile and Ubiquitous Systems. (2004) 434-439.
12. Yang, H., Sikdar, B.: A Protocol for Tracking Mobile Targets Using Sensor Networks. IEEE International Workshop on Sensor Networks Protocols and Applications. (2003).
13. Sung-Min, L., Hojung, C.: A Locating Mechanism for Multiple Nodes in Wireless Sensor Networks. 11th IEEE International Conference on Embedded and Real-Time Computing Systems and Applications. (2005) 273-276.
14. MoteIV. Tmote-sky-datasheet.
http://www.moteiv.com/products/docs/tmote-sky-datasheet.pdf
15. Levis, P., Lee, N., Welch, M., Culler, D.: TOSSIM: Accurate and Scalable Simulation of Entire TinyOS Applications. ACM SenSys (2003) 126-137.

Author Index

Lecture Notes in Computer Science

For information about Vols. 1–3865

please contact your bookseller or Springer

Vol. 3914: A. Garcia, R. Choren, C. Lucena, P. Giorgini, T. Holvoet, A. Romanovsky (Eds.), Software Engineering for Multi-Agent Systems IV. XIV, 255 pages. 2006.

Vol. 3910: S.A. Brueckner, G.D.M. Serugendo, D. Hales, F. Zambonelli (Eds.), Engineering Self-Organising Systems. XII, 245 pages. 2006. (Sublibrary LNAI).

Vol. 3909: A. Apostolico, C. Guerra, S. Istrail, P. Pevzner, M. Waterman (Eds.), Research in Computational Molecular Biology. XVII, 612 pages. 2006. (Sublibrary LNBI).

Vol. 3908: A. Bui, M. Bui, T. Böhme, H. Unger (Eds.), Innovative Internet Community Systems. VIII, 207 pages. 2006.

Vol. 3907: F. Rothlauf, J. Branke, S. Cagnoni, E. Costa, C. Cotta, R. Drechsler, E. Lutton, P. Machado, J.H. Moore, J. Romero, G.D. Smith, G. Squillero, H. Takagi (Eds.), Applications of Evolutionary Computing. XXIV, 813 pages. 2006.

Vol. 3906: J. Gottlieb, G.R. Raidl (Eds.), Evolutionary Computation in Combinatorial Optimization. XI, 293 pages. 2006.

Vol. 3905: P. Collet, M. Tomassini, M. Ebner, S. Gustafson, A. Ekárt (Eds.), Genetic Programming. XI, 361 pages. 2006.

Vol. 3904: M. Baldoni, U. Endriss, A. Omicini, P. Torroni (Eds.), Declarative Agent Languages and Technologies III. XII, 245 pages. 2006. (Sublibrary LNAI).

Vol. 3903: K. Chen, R. Deng, X. Lai, J. Zhou (Eds.), Information Security Practice and Experience. XIV, 392 pages. 2006.

Vol. 3901: P.M. Hill (Ed.), Logic Based Program Synthesis and Transformation. X, 179 pages. 2006.

Vol. 3900: F. Toni, P. Torroni (Eds.), Computational Logic in Multi-Agent Systems. XVII, 427 pages. 2006. (Sublibrary LNAI).

Vol. 3899: S. Frintrop, VOCUS: A Visual Attention System for Object Detection and Goal-Directed Search. XIV, 216 pages. 2006. (Sublibrary LNAI).

Vol. 3898: K. Tuyls, P.J. 't Hoen, K. Verbeeck, S. Sen (Eds.), Learning and Adaption in Multi-Agent Systems. X, 217 pages. 2006. (Sublibrary LNAI).

Vol. 3897: B. Preneel, S. Tavares (Eds.), Selected Areas in Cryptography. XI, 371 pages. 2006.

Vol. 3896: Y. Ioannidis, M.H. Scholl, J.W. Schmidt, F. Matthes, M. Hatzopoulos, K. Boehm, A. Kemper, T. Grust, C. Boehm (Eds.), Advances in Database Technology - EDBT 2006. XIV, 1208 pages. 2006.

Vol. 3895: O. Goldreich, A.L. Rosenberg, A.L. Selman (Eds.), Theoretical Computer Science. XII, 399 pages. 2006.

Vol. 3894: W. Grass, B. Sick, K. Waldschmidt (Eds.), Architecture of Computing Systems - ARCS 2006. XII, 496 pages. 2006.

Vol. 3893: L. Atzori, D.D. Giusto, R. Leonardi, F. Pereira (Eds.), Visual Content Processing and Representation. IX, 224 pages. 2006.

Vol. 3891: J.S. Sichman, L. Antunes (Eds.), Multi-Agent-Based Simulation VI. X, 191 pages. 2006. (Sublibrary LNAI).

Vol. 3890: S.G. Thompson, R. Ghanea-Hercock (Eds.), Defence Applications of Multi-Agent Systems. XII, 141 pages. 2006. (Sublibrary LNAI).

Vol. 3889: J. Rosca, D. Erdogmus, J.C. Príncipe, S. Haykin (Eds.), Independent Component Analysis and Blind Signal Separation. XXI, 980 pages. 2006.

Vol. 3888: D. Draheim, G. Weber (Eds.), Trends in Enterprise Application Architecture. IX, 145 pages. 2006.

Vol. 3887: J.R. Correa, A. Hevia, M. Kiwi (Eds.), LATIN 2006: Theoretical Informatics. XVI, 814 pages. 2006.

Vol. 3886: E.G. Bremer, J. Hakenberg, E.-H.(S.) Han, D. Berrar, W. Dubitzky (Eds.), Knowledge Discovery in Life Science Literature. XIV, 147 pages. 2006. (Sublibrary LNBI).

Vol. 3885: V. Torra, Y. Narukawa, A. Valls, J. Domingo-Ferrer (Eds.), Modeling Decisions for Artificial Intelligence. XII, 374 pages. 2006. (Sublibrary LNAI).

Vol. 3884: B. Durand, W. Thomas (Eds.), STACS 2006. XIV, 714 pages. 2006.

Vol. 3882: M.L. Lee, K.-L. Tan, V. Wuwongse (Eds.), Database Systems for Advanced Applications. XIX, 923 pages. 2006.

Vol. 3881: S. Gibet, N. Courty, J.-F. Kamp (Eds.), Gesture in Human-Computer Interaction and Simulation. XIII, 344 pages. 2006. (Sublibrary LNAI).

Vol. 3880: A. Rashid, M. Aksit (Eds.), Transactions on Aspect-Oriented Software Development I. IX, 335 pages. 2006.

Vol. 3879: T. Erlebach, G. Persinao (Eds.), Approximation and Online Algorithms. X, 349 pages. 2006.

Vol. 3878: A. Gelbukh (Ed.), Computational Linguistics and Intelligent Text Processing. XVII, 589 pages. 2006.

Vol. 3877: M. Detyniecki, J.M. Jose, A. Nürnberger, C. J. '. van Rijsbergen (Eds.), Adaptive Multimedia Retrieval: User, Context, and Feedback. XI, 279 pages. 2006.

Vol. 3876: S. Halevi, T. Rabin (Eds.), Theory of Cryptography. XI, 617 pages. 2006.

Vol. 3875: S. Ur, E. Bin, Y. Wolfsthal (Eds.), Hardware and Software, Verification and Testing. X, 265 pages. 2006.

Vol. 3874: R. Missaoui, J. Schmidt (Eds.), Formal Concept Analysis. X, 309 pages. 2006. (Sublibrary LNAI).

Vol. 3873: L. Maicher, J. Park (Eds.), Charting the Topic Maps Research and Applications Landscape. VIII, 281 pages. 2006. (Sublibrary LNAI).

Vol. 3872: H. Bunke, A. L. Spitz (Eds.), Document Analysis Systems VII. XIII, 630 pages. 2006.

Vol. 3871: E.-G. Talbi, P. Liardet, P. Collet, E. Lutton, M. Schoenauer (Eds.), Artificial Evolution. XI, 310 pages. 2006.

Vol. 3870: S. Spaccapietra, P. Atzeni, W.W. Chu, T. Catarci, K.P. Sycara (Eds.), Journal on Data Semantics V. XIII, 237 pages. 2006.

Vol. 3869: S. Renals, S. Bengio (Eds.), Machine Learning for Multimodal Interaction. XIII, 490 pages. 2006.

Vol. 3868: K. Römer, H. Karl, F. Mattern (Eds.), Wireless Sensor Networks. XI, 342 pages. 2006.

Vol. 3866: T. Dimitrakos, F. Martinelli, P.Y.A. Ryan, S. Schneider (Eds.), Formal Aspects in Security and Trust. X, 259 pages. 2006.